The Rise of the Research University

The Rise of the Research University

A SOURCEBOOK

Edited by Louis Menand,
Paul Reitter, and Chad Wellmon

The University of Chicago Press CHICAGO & LONDON

The University of Chicago Press, Chicago 60637
The University of Chicago Press, Ltd., London

Printed in the United States of America

26 25 24 23 22 21 20 19 18 17 1 2 3 4 5

ISBN-13: 978-0-226-41468-3 (cloth)
ISBN-13: 978-0-226-41471-3 (paper)
ISBN-13: 978-0-226-41485-0 (e-book)
DOI: 10.7208/chicago/9780226414850.001.0001

Library of Congress Cataloging-in-Publication Data
Names: Menand, Louis, editor. | Reitter, Paul, editor. | Wellmon, Chad, 1976– editor.
Title: The rise of the research university : a sourcebook / edited by Louis Menand, Paul Reitter, and Chad Wellmon.
Description: Chicago ; London : The University of Chicago Press, 2017. | Some texts translated from German originals. | Includes bibliographical references and index
Identifiers: LCCN 2016025377 | ISBN 9780226414683 (cloth : alk. paper) | ISBN 9780226414713 (pbk. : alk. paper) | ISBN 9780226414850 (e-book)
Subjects: LCSH: Universities and colleges—History—19th century—Sources. | Universities and colleges—United States—History—19th century—Sources. | Universities and colleges—Germany—History—19th century—Sources. | Education, Higher—Germany—Philosophy. | Education, Higher—Unites States—Philosophy. | Education, Higher—United States—German influences. | Education, Higher—Aims and objectives.
Classification: LCC LA181 .R57 2017 | DDC 378.009034 —dc23 LC record available at https://lccn.loc.gov/2016025377

♾ This paper meets the requirements of ANSI/NISO Z39.48–1992 (Permanence of Paper).

To Bob Holub, consummate citizen of the research university

CONTENTS

PART 6 General Education

General Introduction

The modern research university is under intense scrutiny. Some critics argue that with student debt at unsustainable levels, it is ripe for "disruption" by new digital technologies and the Internet. Some state legislatures seem eager to remake public research universities as institutions whose sole focus is teaching—the teaching, that is, of preprofessional and vocational fields. And within the academy, the professorial critique of the university has become a distinct genre.

Within the context of this debate, there has been much talk about the mission of research universities in the United States and their indebtedness to a model that developed in nineteenth-century Germany. Calls for new modes of organization as well as attempts to defend core structures are often tied to historical claims. What the research university should be is oftentimes framed in terms of arguments about what it once was. Thus, the present debate is the poorer for the fact that these arguments seldom engage with the history of the research university, and particularly with the issue of its German heritage, in a meaningful way. A more deliberate consideration of these complex origins and institutional influences will address many of today's concerns and prove some of them misplaced. This book provides resources to facilitate just such engagement.

The nineteenth-century German university, both real and imagined, was especially important for the first American research universities. The key reformers of American higher education in the second half of the nineteenth century—Daniel Coit Gilman at Johns Hopkins, Charles William Eliot at Harvard, William Rainey Harper at Chicago, and Henry Tappan at Michigan, among others—either studied in Germany or cited the German university as a model. When Johns Hopkins opened in 1876, nearly the entire faculty had studied in Germany.

The early textual formulations of the research university remain important for understanding how the institution has evolved since its inception. Yet access to many crucial sources is hard to come by. Most of the classic German writings on the university either have not been translated at all or were rendered into English long ago and not very well. Some of the most consequential English-language writings on the early American research university are surprisingly difficult to track down.

Our hope is that *The Rise of the Research University* will redress this situation. It provides a set of seminal writings on the university and attempts to make them more accessible by framing them historically. All of the translations are new, and some stand as the first English translation of a key source.

By focusing on the German origins of the modern research university, we are not suggesting that a particular *German* plan for higher education was ever fully implemented, either in Germany or in the United States. It is true that the concepts to which many German and American universities appeal today—the unity of teaching and research, academic freedom, the open-ended character of research—echo some of their earliest formulations in the work of writers such as Wilhelm von Humboldt, Johann G. Fichte, Friedrich Schleiermacher, and Friedrich W. J. Schelling. But the evolution of the university was hardly a smooth and continuous process, determined only by the ideas of the most insightful reformers, and our volume is not an attempt to present a complete narrative in sources. Its historical frame stretches from late eighteenth-century German debates on the future of higher education to late nineteenth- and early twentieth-century American statements about the form and purpose of higher education. The book concludes with a series of texts related to the general education debates in and around American universities in the first decades of the twentieth century.

No work is more central to this history than Wilhelm von Humboldt's fragmentary text "On the Internal Structure of the University in Berlin and Its Relationship to Other Organizations" (1810), and yet it was not published until the late nineteenth century, too late for any direct appeal to Humboldt on either side of the Atlantic. In other words, the ur-text of the modern research university, often invoked but only occasionally cited, was not published until 1896, over eighty years after the University of Berlin was founded, when a German scholar named Bruno Gebhardt, who was writing a biography of Humboldt as statesman, discovered the fragmentary work in an archive and included it as an appendix in his own book. The manuscript breaks off almost in midsentence. Almost immediately, however, this short document was held up by some German academics as the original, founding text of the modern university, and as espousing the underlying principles of the modern research university: the integration of teaching and research, academic freedom, and the unending nature of academic inquiry.

Humboldt was not the first to formulate these ideas, but he was the first to tie them so closely to a particular institution. Although this text came to represent *the* German model of higher education, many critics, especially over the last decade, have suggested that there was neither one *German* nor one *Humboldtian* model for the university. These criticisms—see, for example, the recent volume *Mythos Humboldt* for an overview of this debate—provide a necessary corrective to the more canonical, almost hagiographical texts from early twentieth-century German scholars such as Max Lenz or Eduard Spranger. They tend to overlook the fact, however, that the value of origin stories lies less in their correspondence to actual origins than in the history of the ends to which such stories are put.

Humboldt still offers perhaps the most perspicuous distillation of the underlying logic and ethic of the modern research university. First, the university exists for the sake of knowledge (*Wissenschaft*). In the university, "the teacher is not there for the students' sake, rather they are all there for scholarship and knowledge's sake." Second, the academic freedom of the university must be safeguarded from external influences. Or as Humboldt puts it, "the state must understand that intellectual work will go on infinitely better without it." Third, the nature of scholarly inquiry, or what Humboldt called research, is inexhaustible. These basic principles became the guiding assumptions of the institutions that we now call research universities.

What is less often observed in Humboldt's arguments, especially in English-language discussions, is the complicated relationship of the research university to the state. For Humboldt, writing as a Prussian bureaucrat charged with planning a new institution of higher learning in Berlin, the university should never be fully autonomous. The endless pursuit of knowledge by scholars, argued Humboldt directly to King Friedrich Wilhelm III in 1809, could only be guaranteed by the state. And if the state wanted useful knowledge, it would do best to allow scholars their academic freedom, that is, to leave them alone. For Humboldt, universities should be of use to the state and the broader public, but never immediately so. Scholars need time and space to pursue knowledge that might one day be of use beyond the university. As loud and as popular as the calls for a focus on vocational training and applied research have been, at times, over the past 150 years, it remains difficult to identify what is distinctive about research universities without bringing up the features to which Humboldt gave such effective expression. Indeed, one of the better recent attempts at a definition of the modern university, *What Universities Are For* (2012) by the Cambridge scholar Stefan Collini, reads at crucial moments like a paraphrase of Humboldt's writings.

In *Schools and Universities on the Continent* (1868), the British school inspector Matthew Arnold attested to the extent to which the ideas of Humboldt and company had already traveled beyond Prussia: "Such is the system of the German universities. *Lehrfreiheit* and *Lernfreiheit*, liberty for the teacher and the learner; and *Wissenschaft*, science, knowledge systematically pursued and prized in and for itself, are the fundamental ideas of that system. It is in science that we need to borrow from the German universities. The French have no liberty, and the English universities have no science; the German universities have both." The international reception of these concepts became increasingly central to the University of Berlin's own self-understanding as well. Observing the centennial celebration of the university in 1910, Nicholas Murray Butler, president of Columbia University, wrote that the purpose of the entire event was "to acclaim the place of *Wissenschaft*" in an age of scientific specialization. The university was the metaphor for the unity of knowledge, a unity that was undergirded by neither a divine natural order nor a political one.

In the United States, James Morgan Hart, a German-trained philologist and future president of the MLA, had lionized the German university in *German Universities* (1874). His portrait of the German research university was perhaps an appeal to a myth—what many German scholars now dismiss as the *Humboldt Mythos*—but it nonetheless pointed to a model of an independent, internally coherent university, whose "researcher" embodied a different set of norms and practices than those of the genteel, liberal arts "professor" of the American college. Whether they were institutionalized or circulated in monographs or centennial addresses, the concepts first given shape in early nineteenth-century Germany became norms that guided the architects of the modern research university.

The continued presence of these norms in the American tradition is perhaps most evident in the university presidential address, whose basic genre convention seems to demand an appeal to some or all of these purportedly Humboldtian elements, especially the claim that the university exists neither for the sake of the church nor for the sake of the state but for the sake of knowledge itself. Humboldt's language embedded academic professionalization—the higher standards of entry and the division of intellectual labor according to specialization—in a set of ethical ideals that, over the course of the nineteenth century, came to be embodied by the individual scholar and his particular virtues: industriousness, self-discipline, openness to debate and devotion to something that exceeded the self—science (*Wissenschaft*). For generations of American scholars, Humboldt's vision represented the reconciliation of modern, scientific research with the more traditional, collegiate emphasis on moral formation.

If, as we have suggested, the real Humboldtian legacy lies in an articulation of a broad cultural ethos, any attempt to understand the influence of the German university model in the United States is necessarily an exercise in cultural translation. It involves complex cultural transfers and borrowings through which German university ideals, themselves anything but monolithic, were taken up, altered and adapted in unique ways by different American institutions. The primary influence we enable readers to track extends well beyond particular institutional changes and into questions about the ends of scholarly inquiry and education.

Speaking at the University of Chicago's convocation in October 2009, President Robert J. Zimmer situates Chicago squarely in the German tradition:

> In 1810, 600 years after the establishment of the universities in Bologna, Paris, Oxford, and Cambridge, . . . the University of Berlin was founded under the leadership of Wilhelm von Humboldt. He was deeply influenced by some of the ferment in thinking about universities in Germany at the time, in particular by the thinking of the philosopher and theologian Friedrich Schleiermacher. In Humboldt's university, the spirit of the modern university was born, in what came to be known as the German model. This entailed three major ideas: first, that the goal of education was to teach students to think, not simply to master a craft; second, that research would play a role of central importance and teaching students how to think would be accomplished through the integration of research and teaching; and third, that the university should be independent, and not be in direct service to the state. . . . As we can imagine, the effort to create and instill a new system met with considerable opposition from faculty invested in other approaches, particularly those with no emphasis on research and independent thought. But the model was powerful in its results and became not only the dominant model in Germany, but slowly spread its influence through Europe over the 19th and early part of the 20th centuries.

One of the basic assumptions of this book is that the purported crisis of the contemporary university—the increasingly acute demand that it justify itself in an age of shrinking budgets and rising tuition rates—is in part a failure to reckon with this complex history beyond vague appeals to American traditions of moral education and the ever-presence of a German university model.

When the University of Berlin was founded in 1810, there was a perceived crisis of the university, and in no small part it had to do with the sense that the existing system of higher education needed to be reshaped in the face of a new age of (free-flowing) information. If contemporary universities are struggling to deal with a digital revolution and its effects on the university's monopoly on knowledge production, then late eighteenth-century German universities were, as Fichte put it, struggling to find a purpose amid the late eighteenth-century proliferation of print. The sense of crisis had to do, as well, with the question of academic freedom; with the relationship of teaching and research; with the obligations of the university to the state; and with related issues of class and prestige. Early on, as now, moreover, the cry of crisis could resonate even as the obvious accomplishments mounted. At the same time as the university system in Germany was becoming a model for other countries and thus also a national point of pride, some critics—for example, the philosopher Friedrich Nietzsche—were convinced that the system was in steep decline. Then as now, debates about universities were really debates about the state of the broader culture.

These German models and ideals were, as Roy S. Turner puts it, adopted and adapted to more particularly American needs over the second half of the nineteenth century. The American research university, as Laurence Veysey argued, assumed its basic form in the half century between 1870 and 1920. In terms of internal organization—disciplinary and departmental divisions, conceptions of research, the relationship between undergraduate and graduate education—the American research university is still the university that many of us either inhabit or assume to be the norm.

For the most part, the research university movement in the United States was led by Americans who had studied in Germany and embraced, as even a critic of the affection for German universities like Yale president Noah Porter put it, "the desire for research and culture." The influence of these Americans was especially strong at newly established universities like Johns Hopkins, Chicago, and Clark, all of which were founded on a commitment to research—that is, to the production of new knowledge and not merely the defense and transmission of established knowledge or the moral formation of undergraduates. But American research universities developed in a different cultural and national context than their German predecessors. Proponents of American research universities consistently, for example, cast them as civic goods and appealed to distinctly American traditions of democracy and political thought.

Initially these reform efforts unfolded primarily at private, East Coast institutions such as Harvard, where Charles Eliot, as president from 1869 to 1909, fundamentally altered American higher education. Eliot's reforms are exemplary because of both their content and the extent to which they demonstrated the process of cultural transfer through which German educational ideals found their way into American universities. On the one hand, Eliot embraced the logic of research as central to the university's mission. Just as he professionalized schools of medicine and law by instituting higher standards of admission (principally by requiring a bachelor's degree for admission), he also professionalized graduate education by raising the standards of entry into academia. In particular, as he competed for faculty with Johns Hopkins, he made scholarly reputation—published scholarly work and study in Europe above all—the central academic currency at Harvard. He helped systematize scholarly standards. At the same time, he worried that the research mission might be injurious to undergraduate education. His solution was to sharply differentiate the two by making a liberal arts education a separate preparation and prerequisite for a professionalizing graduate education.

By 1890, public universities began to remake themselves more explicitly in the research university model. They expanded their graduate programs and added law, business, and medical schools. And in a significant departure from the German model, they also began to turn toward private foundations, like the Carnegie and Rockefeller Foundations, to support research. In many instances they also began a gradual blurring of the distinction between college and graduate education that Eliot had institutionalized at Harvard and, in the long tail of the Morrill Act, focused on training students in more explicitly practical knowledge.

These early debates and transformations laid the groundwork for the increased federal funding (post 1945) and rapid expansion of university education (post 1960) that produced what Clark Kerr termed the "multiversity"—the university as a complex of various, often-competing communities engaged in myriad activities with a range of extra-university interests. And it is these kinds of tensions and questions that we will seek to highlight, because, in our estimation, these questions, hopes, and doubts about what the university once was or might one day be are still driving our contemporary debate about the university.

In selecting our texts, we have followed two basic criteria. 1) Historical significance: Each text affords insight into how the modern university developed over time. Some texts are representative of historical debates about curricular issues, the nature of academic work, or the place of the university in the broader culture and society, while others are exemplary of how particular institutions (Göttingen, Berlin, Harvard, Johns Hopkins) dealt with important historical challenges and positioned themselves in terms of a larger university tradition. 2) Contemporary relevance: Each text is relevant not only to a specific historical context but to contemporary issues in higher education. These texts address questions that are basic to the modern university: the relationship between the state and the university, the proper ends of academic research, the place of the university in the broader culture, the ever-present anxiety that the university is irrelevant, or the challenge that new media (print then, digital now) pose to the university.

The book is divided into five sections: "German Research Universities," "Americans Abroad and Returning," "American Adaptation," "Undergraduate Education in the University," and "Aftermath." The first section, "German Research Universities," contains two texts on the University of Göttingen, which was established in 1734, well before the University of Berlin. In terms of its organization, funding models, and library, Göttingen, as the historian William Clark has recently emphasized in his book *Academic Charisma and the Origins of the Research University*, may well have been the first proto-research university. These two texts will give a sense of some of the basic concepts that Humboldt and his colleagues were working with when they proposed a university in Berlin. This section also collects some of the most central texts from the decade preceding the founding of the University of Berlin. They represent the main arguments in a debate that lasted from 1795 to 1810 on whether an institution of higher learning should be established in Berlin, and they form a canon of thinking about the modern university to which many commentators regularly appeal but which few have read with care.

The second section, "Americans Abroad and Returning," focuses on the experiences of Americans while studying abroad in Germany. These texts give firsthand accounts of what elements of the German university impressed American scholars the most.

The third section, "American Adaptations," collects some of the most seminal texts surrounding the emergence of the modern American research university. Central to them all are questions concerning the ends of academic research, the place of the university in the broader culture, and the nature of academic freedom—all concerns that guided debates about the early nineteenth-century German university as well. But in contrast to the earlier German texts, most of these American statements, such as Andrew D. White's 1889 lecture or William Rainey Harper's "The University and Democracy," offer still classic and compelling visions for the essential role of higher education in a democracy.

The fourth section, "Undergraduate Education in the University," demonstrates that the changes in American higher education were not limited to private institutions. Each of these texts situates the debates about different university models into a larger debate about the role of higher education in the United States. This section also includes one key but highly representative instance of late nineteenth-century discontents with the German university system, Nietzsche's "On the Future of Our Educational Institutions" (1872).

The fifth section, "Diversity and Inclusion: Female University Students," contains documents that, in a way very different from Nietzsche's text, address what was for many commentators one of the crucial challenges facing the German university in the late nineteenth century: How was it to retain its identity amid rapid expansion and the inclusion of new kinds of students, especially women?

The sixth section is a collection of primary texts related to the history of general education programs and how the American research university has historically struggled to accommodate them. They are chosen as reflections on liberal education specifically in its relation to the modern research university.

NOTE ON TRANSLATION

Two of the most central terms in the German texts, *Wissenschaft* and *Bildung*, are also two of the most difficult to translate. Depending on the specific context, we generally translate *Wissenschaft* as "knowledge," but we also translate it as "science," "systematic knowledge," or "scholarship." Broadly speaking, it refers in these late eighteenth-century and early nineteenth-century German texts to any systematic way of knowing or the pursuit of such knowledge. In Friedrich Nietzsche's lectures, we also translate *Wissenschaft* as "academic" or "specialized" knowledge. The second key term is *Bildung* (from *bilden*, to form), which we often translate as "formation" but also as "education" in particular or "shaping" in general. *Bildung* was, and would remain, a key term in German culture, and it is worth noting that it had strong connotations of autonomy. That is, *Bildung* often connoted formation or development through a process of *self*-cultivation and *self*-education. To cite just one example, not long before Humboldt weighed in on reform in higher education, the philosopher J. G. Herder (influentially) defined the goal of *Bildung* as self-authorship—becoming the author of one's own self. The translations of the German-language texts in this volume are all new and were made by Paul Reitter and Chad Wellmon, unless otherwise noted.

* Part 1 *

German Research Universities

CHAPTER 1

Report to King Friedrich Wilhelm II of Germany*

Friedrich Gedike

INTRODUCTION TO GEDIKE'S REPORT

In 1789 a Prussian minister named Friedrich Gedike submitted his report on German universities to King Friedrich Wilhelm II. The fifty-nine folio pages were the product of an academic scouting trip that Gedike had undertaken earlier that year to assess, as he put it, "the condition of foreign [i.e., non-Prussian] universities" and to gather gossip on Prussia's own universities. Gedike, a member of the council responsible, among other things, for making all academic appointments, visited fourteen universities, where he interviewed faculty members and students and generally tried to unearth why some universities enjoyed fame and prestige, whereas others suffered ignominy and disregard. He paid close attention to faculty members and was especially interested in how they had been hired and how much they were paid. Gedike was identifying prospective professors whom Prussian universities might poach. Between his interviews and informal discussions with faculty members and students, he visited university libraries and buildings, and wrote detailed reports on those as well. Gedike's university travelogue, replete with academic anecdotes and statistics, was a reconnaissance report on the state of German universities, written with a singular purpose—to help Prussia increase the prestige and quality of its own universities.

But one university stood out—the University of Göttingen. Established in 1734 by George II, king of England and elector of Hanover, and funded

* Excerpt translated from Richard Fester, ed., *"Der Universitäts-Bereiser" Friedrich Gedike und sein [1789] Bericht an Friedrich Wilhelm II*, Archiv für Kulturgeschichte, sup. 1 (Berlin: Duncker, 1905).

primarily by noble-dominated estates in the region, the university may well have been the first modern research university. It introduced a series of mostly unprecedented reforms: state oversight of faculty appointments, higher salaries and teaching fees for professors, the expansion of the philosophy faculty, and a stringent commitment to nonsectarianism. As a matter of university policy and in hopes of avoiding theological divisions, Göttingen's state overseers tried to avoid hiring doctrinaire and contentious faculty members, especially when it came to theology professors. It also built the first research library, assembling it in close consultation with its faculty members.

Göttingen had been designed and run as a financial and personnel resource for the state. One Göttingen graduate compared his alma mater to a royal factory: "You, Mr. Curator, are the factory director; the teachers at the university are workers; the young people studying and their parents . . . are the customers; the sciences taught are the wares. Your King is the master and owner of his [scholarly] factory." The university and its resources—faculty, students, scholarship—were goods to be managed and exploited by the state.

As Gedike's report makes clear, however, the university's most valuable resource was its fame and reputation. It was also its most fragile resource. Göttingen's ability to attract wealthy foreign students and their fees, not to mention the money they spent on alcohol, depended primarily on the renown of its faculty members. And, unlike the academic currency of the contemporary academy, a professor's reputation was not based primarily on what or how much he published, but rather on the regard in which his local colleagues and students held him. A professor's ability to keep an audience of students engaged was more important than his ability to write.

FROM THE REPORT: GÖTTINGEN

This university, sustained by royal munificence from its founding, is more well-known and better regarded than any other university in Germany. Its organization and condition have been thoroughly described in several books, especially in Pütter's academic history of Göttingen.[1]

Nowhere else have I found as much fondness for their university on the part of professors as here. They seem to take it as a foregone conclusion that their university is the best in Germany. They often speak of other universities with disdain or pity. It's as if they are all intoxicated with pride in the university's merits—partly real, partly alleged, and partly imagined. Several professors confidently assured me that even the most famous scholars, were they to leave Göttingen for another university, would lose a considerable amount not only of their celebrity but also of their usefulness (as, for example, happened to Selchow[2] and Baldinger,[3] former Göttingen professors who are now on the faculty at Marburg). If, on the other hand, an unknown scholar were to become a professor at Göttingen, he would secure a great reputation and value, simply upon his appointment. The professors here assured me that from the glory that for them always surrounds the university, a few rays are always cast upon every individual.

It is hard to keep from smiling when hearing some of these Göttingen scholars speak in such enthusiastic tones, as though no erudition, no light, were to be found outside the charmed circle of Göttingen's walls. That said, in Göttingen itself this university pride has some very positive effects. It creates a certain esprit de corps that I have found nowhere else in this form and to this extent. Every professor not only thinks of the university's reputation as his own but conversely sees his own and his colleagues' honors as rightly the university's as well. For this reason, one hardly finds here the kind of factionalization, envy, backbiting, and need to diminish one another's accomplishments that so often cause bitterness and rancor among the members of the faculty at other universities. Or at least, they are less apparent here. Professors discuss their colleagues' shortcomings here far more mercifully than is normally the case at other universities; they are inclined to praise or excuse whatever conceivably can be praised or excused. Professional jealously is not absent here either, but it is expressed in a way that is not as raw, base, or contemptuous as at other universities.

As a result, however, it is more difficult here than elsewhere to elicit from the professors reliable accounts of all those things one would wish to know about. They are all extremely eloquent about the advantages of their university, but in equal measure silent and secretive about its deficiencies. It seems to me that it would indeed be desirable for this esprit de corps animating the Göttingen professors and making the honor of the university the focus of all their desires and endeavors to be the rule in our Prussian universities as well. That said, this very esprit de corps also prompted me to prefer to gather information about some situations and circumstances from knowledgeable, sensible students, rather than from professors, because I was afraid that the latter's anxious care for the university's reputation would lead them to provide me with partial accounts.

[. . .]

Among the various incentives that the Hanover government can grant professors, one that particularly stands out is a distinction of a civic character [Civil-Character]. In the theology department, one or more professors regularly receive the title of consistorial councilor [Konsistorialraths]. In the other three faculties, the title of court counselor is very common (there are five from the law faculty, five from medicine, and ten from philosophy with this title). Furthermore, three professors (Böhmer, Pütter, and Michaelis)[4] have the title of privy justice councilor [Geheimen Justizrathes]. The professors seem to attach great importance to this incentive, which is quite common at most other universities and very unusual only at Saxon universities. A professor's seniority typically plays an important role in the decision to grant such a title, but oftentimes, as is presently the case here, older professors are passed over for a younger one. These titles have no influence on academic rank, but this much is certain: the Hanover government often avoids having to pay salary increases through this far less expensive incentive.

It is hard to obtain reliable information about professors' salaries in Göttingen. Almost all the professors are very secretive about it, and for the most part each one knows only his own salary, not his colleagues'. In particular, the raises that one or the other professor receives over time remain for the most part unknown. This is because the university's finances are handled not in Göttingen but in Hanover. This secrecy has its positive consequences: it prevents storms of jealousy as well as feelings of superiority.

[. . .]

A hardworking and popular professor can earn a great deal from his courses. Compared to other universities, there are disproportionately fewer courses given for free. The honoraria are higher here than at most other universities. No course costs less than 5 thalers; many cost 10 or more. Beyond these public courses there are the private courses [collegia privatissima], so called even though forty or fifty students attend them and pay 3 to 4 louis each. Some professors earn 4,000 to 5,000 thaler a year or more, although here as elsewhere there are professors who live in poverty due to their unpopularity.

[. . .]

It has always been a fundamental principle in Göttingen that the philosophy faculty, more than the others, requires particularly excellent and famous professors. And indeed, since the university's founding, the philosophy faculty has always particularly distinguished itself through the merits and fame of its members. That continues to be the case.

The most senior member of the philosophy faculty is currently Privy Justice Councilor Michaelis, professor of Oriental languages. Age has dulled his mind considerably; in particular, his memory is noticeably weak. It was therefore recently deemed necessary to hire another excellent Orientalist alongside Michaelis while Michaelis was still alive, so that the famous and successful Oriental literature program at Göttingen would not be allowed to decline. Privy Councilor Eichhorn[5] was selected and hired. Since then, old Michaelis's popularity has diminished still further; it is fair to say that he has more or less been retired. [. . .]

Privy Councilor Heyne[6] is well known as one of the most preeminent and important lynchpins of the university's renown. He has thus to this day enjoyed more of the Hanover government's confidence than any other professor. He has been consulted for advice before anyone else, and his recommendations are always carefully considered, especially concerning vacancies, etc. He has up to now been effectively the chancellor of the university, without the actual title, for since Mosheim's[7] death Göttingen has not had an actual chancellor. Heyne's tireless work to bring honor to the university is recognized by all. Thanks to him, humanistic studies have risen to extraordinary heights at Gottingen. Not a single other university has pursued these studies with the same assiduousness. No other university has trained so many erudite and elegant philologists in recent times. Even the wealthiest and most prominent students attend his courses. [. . .] The three higher faculties unanimously recognize the great influence that Heyne's lectures have in making his students' education more rigorous and scholarly. The utility of his courses for theologians is particularly noticeable. And all the while, this excellent man's lectures are nothing less than magnificent and magnetic. They are indeed fruitful enough, rich in both new ideas and the application of old ideas, to make up for any dryness and unpleasantness they might have had.

[. . .]

Two course catalogues are printed twice a year in Göttingen:

1. A Latin one, in which lectures are listed in order of the professors' seniority. This catalogue includes only the professors, not the other lecturers [Privat-docenten].
2. A German one, systematically organized according to particular sciences. This catalogue lists all the lecturers as well as the professors. However, this is done mostly for appearance's sake, because lecturers seldom attract an appreciable number of students to a course of their own. Most lecturers spend their time giving private instruction, and in the so-called private courses.

Göttingen has more public institutes than any other university, both those associated with the university in general as well as those under various individual faculties. Let me here describe them briefly.

General Institutions

1. Standing above all others is the library. Perhaps no other public library has ever achieved as much as Göttingen's. The entire university owes a great deal of its fame to it. And if Göttingen has produced a greater number of actual scholars than any other university in recent times, this is less an achievement of its professors than a result of this excellent library and the unparalleled ease with which one can use it. Many professors owe their fame as authors entirely to the library, which provided them with whatever they could wish for to assist their academic work. Many young scholars have educated themselves here simply by using the library. The example of Göttingen seems to truly prove that nothing is more conducive to a university's public recognition, flourishing, and fame than a great library arranged according to a well-considered plan. The Hanoverian government has spent large sums of money on this institution. Even now they continue to spend around 3,000 thalers a year on the library, often more. For there is no fixed sum of money permanently allocated to the library; instead, the government budgets money according to its current circumstances and constraints, sometimes more, sometimes less.

   The library is currently estimated to contain around thirty thousand volumes. The decision about which books to acquire is not left to the discretion of the librarian, as is the case at most other universities; instead, every professor writes down the books in his particular subject he would like the library to acquire, and then the head librarian, Privy Councilor Heyne, acquires them. One benefit of this process is that, unlike the case at many other universities, no single field is given preferential treatment while others are neglected. All have their collections expanded and completed according to the same criteria. In addition, nowhere is the library made as easy for teachers and students to use as here. Instead of being open only twice a week, as is normal at other universities, the library here is open daily. There are at least some librarians present all day, to help locate requested books, etc. The library maintains a file for every professor and lecturer, to keep the slips of paper with which he has requested books for himself or, by signing his name, for his students. All of these details concerning the organization of the library are managed with great precision. [. . .]
2. The museum was established sixteen years ago. It originated with the purchase of Professor Büttner's[8] natural history collection and has since been expanded both by sizable bequests and through further purchases. It

contains many rare and exquisite pieces from all the realms of nature and is, especially given its short history, already well regarded.

3. The Society of Sciences. Not all professors are members, since the society limits membership to the fields of physics, mathematics, and history. The society is meant to meet once a month. Its funds come from the income from scholarly periodicals published under its direction. Anyone who lectures is paid an honorarium of 20 thalers.

[. . .]

Institutions in Particular Faculties

In the philosophy faculty:

a. The philology seminar, which, under the supervision of Privy Councilor Heyne, is an extremely useful institution. Many capable humanists, now famous in their positions as university or secondary school teachers both within and outside Hanover, emerged from this seminar. So too have a number of students intending primarily to study theology or law been excellently prepared here. The actual seminar lessons are very practical. Seminar students are taught both oral interpretation and to write Latin essays from across whole field of humanistic studies, which are then evaluated by the director or defended in an oral examination.

[. . .]

I had the opportunity to attend a dissertation defense in the medical faculty. The public disputation here is treated as an empty formality, unlike in Saxon universities, where it is considered an actual test of the graduating student's ability. Here, respondent and opponent prepare for this scholarly shadowboxing match together, with arguments and answers regularly set down on paper beforehand. The opponents extraordinarii, typical at many other universities, who normally ask the first question and give the respondent his first opportunity to prove his skill, have here been entirely done away with. The respondent here need never fear being stumped.

[. . .]

When it comes to filling vacant positions, Göttingen does not always proceed according to uniform principles. Oftentimes, candidates are recruited from other universities. Tübingen in particular seems to have served as a feeder for Göttingen for quite some time. It is also not uncommon to judge a professor by more than merely his literary reputation and his books: someone is sent to travel to his home university to listen to him lecture and provide a report.

[...]

There were 819 students enrolled in the summer semester, including:

1. 235 theology students
2. 392 law students
3. 108 medical students
4. 84 studying simply philosophy, mathematics, or philology

The highest enrollment to date was 947, in 1781. There have always been considerably more law students than theology students; the number of students not enrolled in one of the higher faculties has increased almost every year. No other university has so many students outside the practical, preprofessional departments. Incidentally, the exact number of students can be ascertained here more easily than at other universities because of something useful called a housing registrar. Every semester, this department records the address of every student currently in Göttingen and lists them alphabetically, so that every student can be easily tracked down if need be.

The University of Göttingen enjoys a universal reputation for better-behaved students than at other universities. This is certainly true, in some respects, and quite understandable, because here, due to the large cost increases, there are far fewer poor students than at other universities. In fact, no other university has so many sons of rich, prominent, and noble families, from whom one can expect as a rule a better upbringing and behavior. The majority sets the tone at every university, but here the majority of students are wealthy, as one might expect from the fact that the law students outnumber the theology students. Crass outbursts of bad upbringing, blatant eruptions of loud and crude behavior, such as predominate at other universities, are here naturally seen far more rarely.

Here, immorality is more often found under the veil of refinement. Whether the morals as a whole are better here is another question. Crude excesses may be rarer here than elsewhere, but debauched and profligate young men are not lacking, whose less noticeable unruliness makes them just as unfortunate and useless for the world as the crass licentiousness at other universities. Perhaps the more elegant, less obvious irregularities are the more dangerous, for just this reason. Here the student does not frequent beer halls but gets drunk on wine in his room that much more often. I have heard directly from a number of students that this finer sort of overindulgence is very much in fashion. They also assure me that gambling is common. Many students even have mistresses.

All the problems to which excessive luxury lead prevail here as much as anywhere else. It is easy and normal to incur debts; the proximity of Kassel is extremely tempting. Coarse excesses are found here as well. Even during the few days I spent here, a group of several drunk students first attacked a young woman in the street, then followed her into her own house and mistreated her so horribly that her life was in danger.

[. . .]

One thing that especially contributes to the local students' dignified way of life is that a student here has greater access to professors than elsewhere. Every professor sets aside every Sunday afternoon after the sermon to talk to any student who cares to visit him.

[. . .]

CHAPTER 2

On the Importance of Protestant Universities in Germany*

Johann David Michaelis

INTRODUCTION TO MICHAELIS'S *ON THE IMPORTANCE OF PROTESTANT UNIVERSITIES IN GERMANY*

At the beginning of the eighteenth century, there were thirty universities spread across the German territories, more than anywhere else in Europe. This relatively large number was due in large part to the aftermath of the Thirty Years War and the Treaty of Westphalia (1648), which resulted in a Germany made up of numerous, small confessional territories. With so many abutting interests, competition for prestige, resources, and money was intense. And over the course of the eighteenth century, territories increasingly embraced universities as emblems of distinction and sources of revenue. By the middle of the century, however, this competition had resulted in a sharp divide. While a small few universities flourished, most languished with low enrollments and perpetually precarious finances. The abundance of universities, argued a growing group of critics, had proven to be the biggest obstacle to university reform in Protestant Germany. With the exceptions of Halle and Göttingen, most German universities had enrollments of between one hundred and two hundred students. These paltry figures were exacerbated by a grossly uneven distribution of state funds. In the early 1700s, for example, the Prussian crown allotted the University of Halle a budget three times the size of its closest competitor's.

One of the first professorial critiques of the modern university, Johann David Michaelis's *On the Importance of Protestant Universities in Germany*, published in four volumes between 1768 and 1776, argued that the primary

* Excerpt translated from Johann David Michaelis, *Raisonnement über die protestantischen Universitäten in Deutschland*, 4 vols. (Frankfurt am Main, 1768–76).

purpose of universities was to serve the interests of the state. But, as Michaelis, a biblical scholar and professor at the University of Göttingen, noted, if the primary purpose of universities was to bring a state glory and money, then the current surfeit of universities risked undercutting their fiscal benefits.

In early eighteenth-century Germany, universities were not necessarily the center of intellectual life; nor were they the primary creators of new knowledge. Many intellectuals and thinkers did not even have university positions. Some, most notably Leibniz, held positions in the newly established academies of science, such as Berlin's Royal Academy of Sciences, founded in 1700. These institutions and not universities were the institutional centers of new forms of learning in history, the natural sciences, and mathematics. "The improvement of the sciences and the pursuit of new discoveries," observed Michaelis, "is actually not the duty of a university; these are the activities of individual geniuses or, if a public institution is preferred, a society of the sciences." A "flourishing" university, he continued, might not have created new knowledge, but it always filled the coffers of the state. Universities were objects of mercantilist policies designed to attract wealthy foreign students, out-of-staters as it were, and their money, which they would spend on fees and pump into the local economy. (Göttingen made a point of ensuring that its students had ample nonacademic spending opportunities—taverns, for example, were plentiful.) Universities were to expose students to just enough scholarly knowledge to qualify them to serve in some state office.

Over the course of the eighteenth century, an entire science, cameralism (*Cameral-Wissenschaft*), developed around how best to administer the revenue and expenditures of the local sovereign. And universities were gradually incorporated into these economic calculations. Over time, the more traditional confessional orientation of the university was superseded by a fiscal and political one. The University of Halle was an early example of these shifts. Founded in 1694 by the absolutist and reformed (Calvinist) Hohenzollern dynasty, the university was granted full legal privileges and made directly subject to the crown. This unique legal maneuver granted the university and faculty members relative independence from Halle's local civil authorities, who were resolutely Lutheran and notoriously hostile to reformed ideas.

When the University of Göttingen was founded in 1734 under the reign of George II, king of England and elector of Hanover, it expanded upon Halle's attempts to provide a political check to sectarian universities. Under the attentive and direct leadership of Gerlach Adolph von Münchhausen, a Hanover minister who served as university rector for forty years, the state withheld the traditional corporate privileges of faculties to appoint their own members and curtailed the right of the theological faculty to censure faculty members whose writings or teaching it deemed heretical. For Michaelis, such innovations made Göttingen the preeminent model of a modern, nonsectarian university, but not simply in the religious sense of the term. The gradual alignment of university and state interests undercut other orthodoxies as well, namely, those of the traditional university's guildlike character. Here Michaelis was referring to the well-established ways of universities: sons and sons-in-law inheriting professorships, the "inquisition-like" authority of faculties to quell dissenting views, the preferential hiring of a university's own students. A sectarian university was one that jealously upheld not only its confessional orthodoxy but its institutional orthodoxy as well. With the University of Göttingen as his model, Michaelis described the modern rational university as an institution that had finally freed itself from its ecclesial and corporate identity, but only by becoming a central part of an emergent state bureaucracy.

THE EXCERPTS

Preface

The universities in Protestant Germany have certain advantages over richly endowed foreign universities, because of their low cost, but also certain disadvantages. Their deficiencies arise, in part, from the fact that there are too many of them. Some of them are comparatively well organized, others poorly so. Having had occasion to make remarks about this situation, and to hear from those who are part of university life, I decided, finally, to offer these remarks to the public. Something useful for the improvement of universities can perhaps be gleaned from them, or, at least, they might be of use to individual professors and students.

The first draft of these observations was written during the last war. I wanted to wait a few years before I had it printed, because the peace would surely transform some of our universities. And indeed it did. Some universities increased in size, while others decreased. In general, however, it seems that the number of enrolled students, previously somewhat excessive, has declined.

[. . .]

Part One: On the Advantages to a State of Having Universities

§1

For some time now, German princes and their ministers seem to have accepted the idea that universities provide certain benefits to a state. Were this not the case, there would hardly be so many government-funded schools of higher education, and so many new ones being established that Germany now suffers from too many universities rather than too few. It would be hard to argue that these great men were motivated to incur great expenses, which their ancestors left to neighboring states, simply out of a love for scholarship, especially since it has no effect on the sciences and arts whether the schools in which they are taught can be found inside or outside the borders of a given small- to medium-sized country. The proliferation of universities has been no real boon for the arts and sciences, rather more of a liability.

The time is also long since past when a new university had to be established to maintain and spread the Protestant religion. Halle is likely the last university founded with religious aims in mind. In part, it was Spener's[1] spiritual intentions, as well as those of his friends, that played a role here; they were working to foster a devout Christianity. Also playing a role was a political goal of the royal court, which wanted to educate relatively nonsectarian Lutheran preachers, who would neither chafe against any state authority allied with the reformed tradition nor treat as their enemies citizens with convictions different from their own. Since then, however, no universities have been established for the sake of religion, nor have any universities too old to be of use any longer been maintained simply out of affection. Perhaps the occasional founder, the local sovereign himself or his minister in some cases, has been inspired by the pursuit of glory, of immortality, through the praise of scholars. But universities were not founded and maintained for the sake of these fragrant ornamentations alone; the founders will have hoped, rightly or wrongly, for some concrete benefit.

It would, of course, be redundant to discuss these matters if the use of universities were not so often misjudged, in two ways. On the one hand, universities are seen exclusively in terms of their cameralist function, and far more important contributions are overlooked; on the other hand, this cameralist thinking often overestimates what it takes to be the value of universities, which require great expenditures and frequently yield too little revenue.

§2

First, I want to clarify my thoughts on the cameralist uses of a university. By this, I simply mean primarily that a university attracts money into a state or keeps within a state money that would have otherwise gone to other states. Both amount to the same thing: the prevention of loss is just as important as gain.

With a flourishing university, this gain is considerable. If my calculations are correct, at various universities that do not give lavish grants to attract the poor students, the median sum a student spends amounts to 300 thaler per year. Assuming they have five hundred students, a modest number, universities bring in 150,000 thaler in spending for the state every year. If the number of students could be doubled to a thousand, by appointing the best professors and introducing an attractive lifestyle, the state could bring in three tons of gold a year.

I know that some will object that my calculation of 300 thalers per student on average is too high, given that there are many poor students and few wealthy ones. Recall, however, that I spoke of universities that were flourishing. As I will note below, my calculation would look quite different for universities that are not flourishing. These universities must make do with poor students and scholarship students [Convictoristen]. I admit just as readily that when a university attracts the needy from all around with a large number of grants or stipends [beneficien], my calculations are inaccurate. I may well be wrong about Halle, for example, because a large portion of poor students go to school there through the financial support of the orphanage. I have confirmed these calculations, which in any case I myself call provisional, for other universities by checking their actual income statements; on occasion, their income can be seen to be even higher than my calculation, although I consider this state of affairs dangerous for the universities themselves.

[...]

§12

I have said enough about the uses of universities from a financial point of view, and about what they have in common with a factory or a glassworks designed to use up any excess wood. We should not blame or disparage a lord of great means for founding or maintaining a university with these intentions. However, universities do bring other and perhaps greater, or at least nobler, benefits to a state, ones that are in danger of being overlooked.

The first major contribution of a well-organized university is the flourishing of the sciences and arts in a country. I assume it is widely known that this is not unrelated to political flourishing. I am not aware of a single field in science, art, or scholarship that statesmanship would not want enlightened and perfected, in order to increase or ensure the well-being of the country. Even theology, which seems only to concern individual lives, is no exception. Where theology remains in a state of barbarity and ignorance, priests would inevitably deceive citizens and even rulers; theology would not spread reasonable and useful morals, but instead concern itself with innumerable useless, incomprehensible, or even fallacious claims. And if a few eager teachers prop up such a religion and infect others with their enthusiasm, a conflict over nothing could convulse the state. [. . .] Even if, given the magnitude of human depravity, [good theology] can only produce a few good Christians, the rational morality of the pulpit will still form many good citizens, and instruct the obedient ones in their duties better than laws could. Theology also promotes scholarship in general, and thus the taste and level of knowledge in the people, because of its connection with philosophy, ancient languages, history—in short, with a range of fields relevant to researching the Bible. When a truly trained theologian studies the doctrines and difficult passages in the Bible, he comes across a hundred obscure things in other disciplines that he can shed light on, even in natural history and geography.

[. . .]

§13

But, one might object, isn't it really irrelevant how a country acquires knowledge? It makes no difference whether it is learned in foreign or domestic universities.

I do not agree. If the state wants to ensure that the arts and sciences flourish, it must have its home university staffed with the best professors. The state cannot pursue this goal in foreign schools; it must simply accept those who graduate from there as they are, without any opportunity to make up for shortcomings in their education, even when important elements of scholarship have been poorly taught, or not at all.

Very few of our German universities are designed as we might wish. Even if one does happen to find a good university among all the average and bad ones, then the young men from other parts of the country may not choose it. They might be drawn in greater numbers to the average universities instead. If, however, the state has a good domestic university, parents will voluntarily prefer to send their sons there. It can be shown by several examples that scholarship has prospered and expanded more in countries that have had a truly scholarly domestic university for at least twenty years.

I must also mention that students at a domestic university work harder and try to live more virtuously than those who are studying abroad, because of the social supervision they are under. I know all too well how little the supervision of a teacher alone can accomplish, how little such supervision is even possible. [. . .] But this much is clear: as a rule, young people, unless they are completely savage, restrain themselves when their parents are only ten or twenty miles away. When they are in their fatherland and the local families know them, their own families will find out much more about them than if they were left to themselves among strangers in a completely foreign land thirty or forty miles from home.

[...]

§14

In addition to what I have just stated, I should add that some countries, in order to flourish, need expertise in some sciences that may be of less interest to the neighboring countries, and that perhaps are not so commonly taught at foreign universities. These sciences can be established at the domestic university.

[...]

CHAPTER 3

What Is Universal History and Why Study It? An Inaugural Academic Lecture*

Friedrich Schiller

INTRODUCTION TO SCHILLER'S LECTURE

Friedrich Schiller held his inaugural address as "extraordinary" (i.e., his income depended on student lecture fees) professor of history at the University of Jena in the spring of 1789. Thus it was with world-historical change in the offing that the celebrated author of *The Robbers* and *Don Carlos* thought to explore the concept of universal history. Accordingly, there was no shortage of anticipation and excitement. Well over half the nearly eight hundred students enrolled at Jena turned out for Schiller's lecture, which had to be moved to the largest auditorium at the university.

The students who had come hoping for bold strokes from a man associated with the German literary movement traditionally known as "Storm and Stress" weren't disappointed. They cheered as Schiller called for nothing less than a Copernican turn in the writing of "world history." This, he maintains, should be constructed not from its beginnings forward but rather from the present backward, with the criterion for inclusion being that events must have exerted an essential and traceable influence on the current "shape of the world." Pursuing such an intellectual goal would of course require certain capacities and attitudes, and Schiller's boldest stroke of all may lie in how—and where—he

* Excerpt translated from Friedrich Schiller, "Was heißt und zu welchem Ende studiert man Universalgeschichte?" in *Friedrich Schiller Historische Schriften und Erzählungen I*, ed. Otto Dann, vol. 6 of *Friedrich Schiller Werke und Briefe* (Frankfurt am Main: Deutscher Klassiker Verlag, 2000).

introduces the mindset necessary for the study of universal history. After just a few preliminary remarks, Schiller sets about evoking this mindset by way of describing the opposite, undesirable type—the Goofus of scholarship—whom he presents as the norm at German academic institutions. Upon joining the university, Schiller immediately called for a housecleaning.

The figure for whom Schiller sees no place in the university is the careerist scholar—the *Brotgelehrte*. The German term, which Schiller's address helped popularize and whose meaning it continues to anchor, suggests a scholar or academically trained professional who plies his trade to pay the bills. *Brot* means "bread," and a literal translation would be "bread scholar." But Schiller makes it clear that the scholars he has in mind are not simply motivated by money. They are after fame and institutional prestige as well. They are not driven by the ideals internal to the university that Schiller, anticipating Wilhelm von Humboldt's and Friedrich Schleiermacher's writings, puts at the center of university study and academic striving: the free cultivation of the highest mental faculties, the endless nature of research, the unity of all knowledge, and the importance of open collaboration. Indeed, careerist scholars stand in the way of the "philosophical mind," the countertype who embodies those ideals.

The image of the university that emerges from Schiller's lecture is, then, not a particularly flattering one. In his portrait, German universities are blighted. Petty, proprietorial, careerist professors and administrators, who dislike actual research and thus experience every innovation as a threat, try to keep academic specializations as compartmentalized as possible, so as to avoid having to branch out into new areas. Obsessed with getting the maximum credit for their efforts, these men are, moreover, hostile to the spirit of collaboration that Schiller prized. Yet the tone of Schiller's lecture is hardly grim. After all, the vision of world history that he offers is a sanguine one, a secular vision of progress that doesn't look away from the darker side of history but rather treats it as often advancing, dialectically, greater rationality and happiness. But the contempt that Schiller, who had spent years living in straitened circumstances, felt toward careerist scholars is palpable, and the critique he carries out using the figure may well be the most iconic moment in his inaugural address. For with his *Brotgelehrte*, Schiller gave forceful expression to what was, in his day, a widespread source of frustration: the problem of unimaginative professors clinging to the old guild system and the comforts it afforded, despite the intellectual ferment of the era, as well as the fact that most German universities were sclerotic institutions badly in need of reform. Indeed, much more than Schiller's reflections on what universal history is, his discussion of how not to be a professor breathes through later writings on university culture, including Humboldt's, Schleiermacher's, Fichte's, and Nietzsche's.

Schiller may have helped make Jena a center of philosophical reception on the university, but the historians were not impressed. Because he was unable to lecture in Latin, they regarded him as unqualified to be part of their guild, and they pushed him out. Lecturing in philosophy proved to be an unsatisfactory solution. Interest in the subject at Jena was great, but it was also highly concentrated. Students wanted to learn the basics of Kant's system, and the professor at Jena who obliged them attracted huge numbers of them, along with their lecture fees. Since lecture fees were Schiller's sole income from the university, his academic career became a financial liability, one he could scarcely afford. In something of a sad irony, considerations of *Brot* played no small part in Schiller's decision to leave the university just a few years after giving his address on universal history.

SCHILLER'S LECTURE

Gentlemen, I am pleased and honored to have the opportunity to explore with you a field that has provided the contemplative observer with so many objects of study, the active man of the world with such excellent role models, the philosopher with such important insights, and every last one of us with such rich sources of the noblest pleasures—the broad field of general history. The very sight of so many fine young men gathered around me, drawn by your noble thirst for knowledge, possessing a genius that will have powerful effects on the coming age already beginning to flower in your midst, transforms my duty into a pleasure. Yet it also makes me feel the full extent of the demands this important duty places upon me. The greater the gift I have to give you—and what can one man give another greater than truth?—the more I will necessarily worry about its value diminishing in my hands. The greater the vitality and purity with which your minds take things in, in this, the happiest phase of your intellectual life, and the quicker your youthful emotions are to ignite with enthusiasm, the more urgent my responsibility not to let this enthusiasm, rightly inspired only by truth, be wasted unworthily on deception and illusion.

The realm of history is fertile and wide-ranging, encompassing the whole moral world in its domain. History accompanies us through all the circumstances of our lives, through all the shifting shapes of opinion, through our foolishness and our wisdom, our declines and ennoblements. Above all, history must offer an account of everything we have *given to* and *taken from* ourselves. There is no one among us to whom history does not have something important to say. All the different paths we take to our future callings intersect with history somewhere, but there is one calling you all share, the one you brought along with you into the world—the task of forming and educating yourselves as human beings. It is precisely to this human being that history speaks.

Gentlemen, before I define more precisely the expectations you should have for the object of all this hard work you must do, and before I begin to lay out its connection to the specific goal of your various studies, it will not be superfluous to ensure that we agree about *the purpose of your studies* as such. A preliminary clarification of this question, which strikes me as fitting and worthy enough to serve as the starting point of our academic relationship, will put me in a position to draw your attention to the most worthwhile aspect of world history.

The course of study that the careerist scholar lays out for himself is quite different from that which a philosophical mind lays out for himself. The careerist scholar, who sees his efforts solely as a way to put food on the table and satisfy the prerequisites of an official position, thereby gaining the advantages that go with it, sets his mental powers in motion only in order to better his material lot and satisfy a petty desire for fame. Such a person, embarking on his academic career, has no higher priority than separating out, as painstakingly he can, the academic fields he sees as a way of earning his bread from all the rest, which give the mind pleasure. He sees any time he spends on the latter as time taken away from his future career, and he would never forgive himself for this theft. He puts all his efforts into meeting the demands that the future lord of his destiny will make of him, and believes that he has done his all if he can put himself beyond this higher power's possible criticisms. Once he has passed his courses and reached the goal he desires, he will dismiss those who have guided him—why bother about them anymore? His greatest concern will now be to display the treasure trove stockpiled in his memory and make sure that its value doesn't sink. Every expansion in his area of professional competence makes him nervous, because it means he will have to do more work, or else makes work he has already done useless; any truly significant advance terrifies him, because it blasts apart the old learning he so laboriously acquired in school and puts him at risk of losing all the work he has done in his life up to that point. Who has ever let out a greater howl and cry about reformers than the pack of careerist scholars? Who does more to impede the progress of useful revolutions in the realm of the knowledge than they do? Every light a fortunate genius casts, in whatever field, reveals their lack of substance. They fight bitterly, with cunning and desperation, because in defending the school system they are simultaneously fighting for their very existence. There is thus no more implacable enemy, no more small-minded bureaucrat, no one more willing to excommunicate his foes, than a careerist scholar. The less rewarding his knowledge is *in its own right*, the greater his demands for compensation from others, and he judges intellectual laborers and manual laborers by *one and the same* standard: *amount of effort.* Thus no one can be heard to complain more about ingratitude than the careerist scholar: he seeks his reward not in the form of richness of thought but in recognition from others, honorary professorships, material benefits. When these things elude him, who is more miserable than the careerist scholar? He has lived in vain, stayed up nights and worked hard for nothing—the truth he has sought is meaningless if it is not transformed into gold he can pocket, praise from the newspapers, favors from princes.

It is an unfortunate man who works with the noblest of all tools—science and art—yet wants and achieves nothing greater than the day laborer with the most common tools! Who roams the kingdom of the most perfect freedom bearing with him the soul of a slave! Even more unfortunate, though, is the young man of genius whose naturally beautiful path is diverted by harmful teachings and models onto this sad wrong course, who lets himself be talked into gathering knowledge with a wretched fixation on his future profession. His professional scholarly field will soon disgust him as a piecemeal patchwork; desires will awaken within him that he cannot satisfy; his genius will rebel against his destiny. Everything he does will seem to him like a fragment. He will see no purpose in his work, and yet he will not be able to bear the absence of that purpose. The arduous labors and insignificance of his professional activities will crush him, because he cannot oppose to them with the cheerful spirits that accompany only keen insight and the prospect of completion. He will feel cut off, torn away from the context of things, because he has failed to connect his efforts to the great totality of the world. The moment the shimmer of a better culture reveals the failings of legal theory to the legal scholar, the whole thing is ruined for him, instead of this inspiring him to create the theory anew, filling in from his own inner fullness the gaps that he has discovered. The doctor rejects his profession the moment an important failure exposes the unreliability of his principles. The theologian loses respect for his the moment his belief in the infallibility of his doctrines begins to waver.

How different the actions of a philosophical mind! As meticulously as the careerist scholar tries to draw a clear borderline between his field of knowledge and all the rest, the philosophical mind tries to expand his domain and reestablish its connections with the others—*reestablish*, I say, because it was only the abstractions of the intellect that created the boundaries separating the fields in the first place. Where the careerist scholar divides, the philosophical mind unites. He has learned early on that in the intellectual realm, as in the material world, everything is interrelated, and his bustling drive for harmony refuses to be content with fragments. All his efforts aim at the perfection of his knowledge: nobly impatient, he cannot rest until all his ideas have been integrated into a harmonious whole, until he stands at the center of his art, his science, and can survey his domain from there with a satisfied gaze. New discoveries in his sphere of activity, which devastate the careerist scholar, delight the philosophical mind. Perhaps they will fill in a gap that disfigures the developing totality of his ideas, or provide the last missing brick in his intellectual edifice—the one that will complete it. If, however, it should wreck his edifice—if a new set of ideas, a new natural phenomenon, a newly discovered law of physics were to send the whole structure of his knowledge crashing down—he has *always loved the truth more than his system*, and he would gladly replace the old inadequate system with a newer and more beautiful one. Yes, if no blow from the outside topples his intellectual edifice, he himself will be the first to disassemble it, compelled by his eternal drive for improvement, so that he can put it back together as a more satisfying and perfect structure. By continually creating new and more beautiful forms of thought, the philosophical mind proceeds toward ever higher levels of excellence, while the careerist scholar, trapped in an eternal intellectual standstill, watches over and defends the barren sameness of his school learning.

No one can evaluate the accomplishments of others more justly than the philosophical mind. Discerning and inventive enough to make use of any scholarly activity, he is also fair enough to give credit to the person responsible for even the smallest contribution. All minds work *for* him; all work *against* the careerist academic. The former understands how to make everything that happens around him, everything that is thought, his own, for there is a deeply collective ownership of all intellectual property among thinking people: what one person acquires in the realm of truth, everyone has acquired. The careerist scholar, though, fences himself off from all these neighbors, to whom, jealous as he is, he begrudges even the light and the sunshine; he anxiously monitors the dilapidated barriers that afford him only poor protection against the triumphant truth. The careerist scholar, in order to do anything, needs to borrow stimulus and encouragement from others; for the philosophical mind, the object of study and his own efforts are stimulating enough, and bring their own rewards. How much more enthusiastically he sets to work! How much more intensely eager he is, how much longer-lasting his strength and ability to work, for with him, work only rejuvenates him for more work. Even what is small becomes great in his creative hands, because he always has his eye on the greatness that the small is in the service of, while the careerist scholar sees only the small even in what is great. What distinguishes the philosophical mind isn't *what* he studies but *how* he handles what he studies. Whatever his field, in whichever domain he is working, he is at the center of the whole, and however far the object of his study takes him from his brothers, he remains tied to them and *close* to them through their harmoniously operating intellect. He encounters his brothers in the place where all bright minds find each other.

Shall I continue this depiction any further, gentlemen, or may I presume that you have already decided which of the two portraits that I've presented is the better one to take as a model? Whether to recommend you for or exempt you from the study of universal history depends on the choice you have made between the two. I have something to say only to the *second* group; in trying to make itself useful to the *first*, scholarship strays too far from its higher ultimate purpose, and sacrifices too much for far too little.

If we are now in agreement about the viewpoint from which the value of a scholarly pursuit should be judged, I can proceed to the concept of universal history itself, the topic of today's lecture.

The discoveries our European explorers have made in foreign seas and on remote coasts are spectacles as edifying as they are entertaining. They show us peoples scattered around the globe at the most various stages of cultural development, like children of different ages standing around an adult and reminding him, by example, what he himself once was and where he started from. A wise hand seems to have saved these primitive peoples for us until the time when we, in our own culture, had progressed far enough to be able to put this discovery to use and reconstruct the lost beginnings of our own race from this mirror. How shameful and sad, though, is the image of our childhood that these peoples give us! And this despite our not even seeing them in the earliest stage. Human beings were even more abject at the beginning. To be sure, we already encounter them as ethnic groups, as political units—but people had to make an extraordinary effort to raise themselves to the level of a political society.

What do the descriptions of the voyagers tell us about these savages? Some found them unfamiliar with the most indispensable technologies—iron, the plow, in some cases even fire. Some of the savages still fought wild animals for food and lodging. Many had barely raised their language from animal sounds into a system of comprehensible signs. Here, they did not even have the simple bond of *marriage*; there, they had no concept of *property*; and in yet another place, feeble minds could not even retain an experience repeated daily—one saw savages blithely giving up the spot where they had slept today because it didn't occur to them that they would sleep again tomorrow. War, on the other hand, was common to all, and the prize of victory was not seldom the flesh of the defeated. Other peoples, who were acquainted with greater comforts and had reached a more advanced stage of civilization, presented a horrifying picture of slavery and despotism. Here an African despot was seen to trade away his subjects for a sip of brandy; there they were slaughtered on his grave so that they could serve him in the underworld. There they kneel in simple-minded piety before a ludicrous fetish, and here before a gruesome monster—people portray themselves in their gods. However deeply slavery, stupidity, and superstition in one place oppressed man, he is made just as miserable elsewhere through the opposite extreme of limitless freedom. Always armed for attack and defense, startled by every sound, the savage strains his sensitive ear to listen into the desert. Everything new is his enemy; and woe to the stranger a storm blows onto his shores! No welcoming hearth will burn for him, no sweet hospitality refresh him. But even where people have raised themselves up from hostile isolation to community, from necessity to comfort, and from fear to joy—even there, how bizarre and monstrous they are to our eyes! Their crude tastes seek pleasure through anesthetization, beauty through distortion, fame through excess. Even their virtues horrify us, and what they call happiness can only excite our disgust or pity.

We were the same way. Caesar and Tacitus found us in much the same shape eighteen hundred years ago.

What are we now? Let me linger for a moment on the age in which we live—the present state of the world we inhabit.

Human industriousness has built up the world, and our perseverance and skill have conquered its recalcitrant soil. Here we have won land from the sea, there brought water to arid land. We have brought together zones and seasons, toughened the delicate plants of the Orient so that they might endure our rougher skies. As we have carried Europe to the West Indies and the South Sea, we have given Asia new life in Europe. A sunny sky now laughs over Germany's forests, which the strong hand of humanity tore open for the sun to shine into, and Asian vines are reflected in the waves of the Rhine. Populous cities, which work and pleasure fill with vibrant life, rise up along its shores. We find a man there, among a million other men, in peaceful possession of what he has acquired—at most, a neighbor might rob him of some sleep. Having lost equality by entering into society, he has gained it back through wise laws. He has fled from the blind compulsion of accident and poverty to the gentler rule of contracts, and given up the freedom of the beast of prey to salvage the nobler freedom of humanity. His cares are now shared, his tasks parceled out, to the benefit of all. Dictatorial necessity no longer forces him to his ploughshare; enemies no longer compel him to leave his plough and take to the battlefield, to defend his home and fatherland. Now the farmer's arms fill humanity's silos while the soldier's weapons defend his territory. The law watches over his property, and the invaluable right to determine his own duty remains with *him*.

How many artistic creations! How many wonders of industry, how much light has been shed on all fields of knowledge! Ever since humankind stopped squandering its powers in the sad pursuit of self-defense, and instead resolved to make peace with necessity, which we will never be able to overcome completely, thereby winning the precious privilege of using our abilities freely and following the call of our genius. How much bustling activity everywhere, since our ever more varied desires gave new wings to the spirit of invention and opened up new spaces for our industriousness! The barriers that states and nations once erected in hostile egotism have now been broken; a cosmopolitan bond now joins together all thinking people, and the whole light of our century can now illuminate the mind of a new Galileo, a new Erasmus.

As the laws descended to meet human weakness, we have also risen to meet the laws. They have made humans softer, just as they once made them more savage; barbaric crimes have gradually followed barbaric legal punishments into the past. That the laws have become more moral—even if people in general have not—is a large step toward a more noble condition. Where compulsory obligations fall away, ethics take over. Now the rules of decency and honor restrain those who are neither scared of punishment nor reined in by conscience.

It is true that some barbaric remnants of previous ages have made their way into ours as well—the products of chance and violence, which should not be perpetuated in the age of reason. But what shape has human reason conferred upon even this barbaric legacy of antiquity and the Middle Ages! How harmless, or even useful, reason has often made what it has not yet dared do away with! Germany built its system of political and religious freedom on the rough terrain of the fiefdoms and their anarchy. The shadow of a Roman emperor, persisting on this side of the Apennines, does infinitely more good now than the terrifying original did in ancient Rome, for it holds a useful state system together through *concord*, while the earlier one crushed the most active human powers into a slavish *homogeneity*. Even our religion, so badly distorted by the unfaithful hands that have passed it down: Who can fail to see in it the ennobling influence of higher philosophy? Our Leibnizes and Lockes were as much concerned with the *doctrine* and *morality* of Christianity as Raphael's and Correggio's paintbrushes with sacred history.

Finally, our states: With what ardent artistry they are intertwined! And how much more durably joined through the salutary pressure of necessity than through the solemn treaties of the past! An eternal readiness for war keeps the peace, and the self-love of a state is what induces it to watch over the well-being of the others. The European confederacy of states seems transformed into a large family—members of a single household may sometimes make enemies of each other, but hopefully will no longer tear each other apart.

What antithetical pictures! Who would look at the refined European of the eighteenth century and divine simply a more advanced brother of the contemporary Native North American or the ancient Celt? All these accomplishments, artistic impulses, and experiences, all these creations of reason, have been cultivated and developed in humanity in the space of a few millennia; all these wonders of art, these giant works of industry, have been called forth from us. What brought the former to life? What lured the latter out? Which conditions did humanity traverse to rise from *that* extreme to *this*, the asocial caveman to the brilliant thinker and educated man of the world? World history holds the answer.

If a given population in a given place presents such immense dissimilarities when observed at different time periods, the differences are no less striking between members of a given race living at the same time in different countries. What a multiplicity of customs, laws, morals! What rapid shifts between darkness and light, anarchy and order, happiness and misery we see when observing mankind merely in the small part of the world called Europe! On the Thames, they are free and owe their freedom solely to themselves; here they are invincible in their Alpine fortress; there they are unconquered amid redirected rivers and marshlands. On the Vistula, strife has brought powerlessness and misery; beyond the Pyrenees, they are made miserable and powerless by peace. Wealthy and blessed in Amsterdam, though without a harvest; poor and unfortunate in the paradise unused along the Ebro. Here two far-flung peoples, separated by a great ocean, are neighbors through common needs, industry in art, and political alliances; there the people living *along a single* river are irreparably divided over their different liturgies! What was it that carried Spain's might across the Atlantic into the heart of America, and not even across the Tagus and Guadiana Rivers? What sustained so many thrones in Italy and Germany and caused all but one to disappear in France? Universal history answers these questions.

Even the fact that *we personally* find ourselves here together right now, with this national culture, this language, these moral codes, these advantages as citizens, this degree of freedom of conscience, is arguably the result of *all* past global events. At the very least, world history as a *whole* is necessary to explain this single moment. For us to be here as Christians, this religion had to proceed forth from Judaism, its way made possible by countless revolutions, and had to find the Roman state *exactly* as it found it in order to spread across the world in its rapid, victorious march and eventually ascend to the Caesars' throne. Our crude ancestors in the forests of Thuringia had to succumb to the superiority of the Franks to adopt their faith. The cleric had to be seduced and abetted by his growing riches, the ignorance of the people, and the weakness of their rulers to abuse his high standing and turn his quiet *force of conscience* into a worldly sword. The papacy, in the form of such figures as Gregory and Innocent, had to unload all of its horrors upon humanity for the resulting ascendance of moral corruption and egregious scandal of spiritual despotism to give a fearless Augustinian friar the impetus to call for rebellion and rip half of Europe away from the Roman hierarchy—and to make it possible for us to gather here as Protestant Christians. The weapons of our King Charles V had to force a religious truce; a Gustavus Adolphus had to avenge the breaking of this truce, establishing a new and lasting peace for the centuries to come. Cities had to emerge in Italy and Germany and open their doors to industry, shatter the chains of serfdom, wrestle the judge's scepter out of the hands of ignorant tyrants, and earn respect through the military power of a Hanseatic League, in order for manufacturing and trade to bloom and for the surplus to call forth the arts of joy, for nations to honor the useful farmer, and for the *middle class*, the creator of our whole culture, to ripen as an enduring boon for humanity. Germany's emperors had to render themselves powerless in their centuries-long battles with popes, their own vassals, and their jealous neighbors—and Europe had to send its dangerous population overflow into Asian graves, the stubborn nobility had to bleed out its furious spirit in a murderous honor code, crusades to Rome, and holy pilgrimages—for the chaotic disorder to resolve itself and the warring powers of the state to come to rest in a blessed balance, the prize of which is our current leisure. The long-extinguished spark of learning had to flare up anew, under its most violent persecutors, and an al-Mamum had to compensate the sciences for the theft that an Omar had committed, for our minds to fight their way out of the captivity of ignorance in which intellectual and material compulsion had kept them. The unbearable misery of barbarism had to drive our ancestors from the bloody *judgments of God* to the benches of human judges; devastating epidemics had to summon a medicine that had gone astray back to the observation of nature; the idleness of the monks had to prepare the way for something that would replace the evils of their activity, while secular work in the cloisters had to preserve the shattered remains of the Augustan epoch until the time of the printing press. The downtrodden spirit of the Nordic barbarians had to pull itself up using Greek and Roman models, and scholarship allied with the muses, if it was to find a way to the heart and be worthy of the name of Education, of a shaper of human culture. But would Greece have given birth to a Thucydides, a Plato, an Aristotle—would Rome to a Horace, a Cicero, a Virgil, a Livy—if these two states hadn't forced their way up to the political preeminence whose heights they in fact reached? If, in short, their *entire* history had not played out as it did? How many inventions, discoveries, and political and religious revolutions had to *come together* for these new, still fragile seeds of science and art to grow and spread! How many wars had to be fought, how many treaties signed, violated, and signed again, to finally bring Europe to its foundations of peace, which are all that allow states and citizens alike to attend to themselves and concentrate their powers on a rational end!

Even in living the most ordinary bourgeois life, we cannot avoid being in debt to the previous centuries: the most various phases of humanity lead to our culture, just as the most remote parts of the world contribute to our luxuries. The clothes we wear, the spices in our food and the price we pay for them, many of our most powerful medicines and just as many instruments of our ruin—do they not presuppose a Columbus who discovered America, a Vasco da Gama who sailed around the southern tip of Africa?

Thus a long chain of events leads from the present moment back to the beginning of the human race, linking them together like cause and effect. Only an infinite intellect can command a *full* and *complete* view of this chain; human beings are more narrowly constrained. First, countless of these occurrences either had no human witnesses or observers, or were not preserved in writing. This category includes everything that preceded the human race as well as what occurred before written language was invented. The source of all history is tradition, and the vehicle of tradition is language. The whole period *before language*, formative as it was for the *world*, is lost to *world history*. Second, even after language had been invented and it thus became possible to describe and communicate what had happened, this communication initially proceeded along the uncertain and variable path of *oral tradition.* An event was passed down from one mouth to another, through a long succession of peoples, and because it passed through a medium that changed and was changed, it necessarily underwent these transformations too. Living tradition and oral legends are thus very unreliable sources for history. As a result, all events *before the advent of writing* are as good as lost to world history.

Third, writing is not indestructible either. Time and accident have destroyed countless monuments and records of antiquity; only a few ruins survived from ancient times into the eras of book printing, while the great majority of them, along with the information they would have given us, are lost to world history. Fourth and finally, of the few remains that time has spared, most have been deformed and made unrecognizable through the *passion*, the *misunderstanding*, and even the *genius* of those who described them. The earliest historical testimony awakens our mistrust, which in fact stays with us even to chronicles of the present day. If it is hard to arrive at the truth from the contradictory statements of witnesses reporting on something that took place today, among those with whom we live, in the city we inhabit, then what courage must we bring to nations and eras whose foreignness of customs make them even more remote than the millennia that separate us from them? The few events that remain after all these losses constitute the material of history in its broadest sense. So then *what*, and *how much*, from this material belongs to universal history?

The universal historian selects from the sum total of these events those with an essential, irrefutable, and easily traceable influence on the *present* shape of the world and the condition of the generation alive today. It is thus the relationship between a historical moment and the *present* state of the world that we must pay attention to when collecting material for world history. That is to say, world history proceeds from a principle pointing precisely backward, to the beginning of the world. The actual sequence of events descends from the origin of things to their newest system; the universal historian goes upstream from the world's most recent state back toward its origins. Once he has climbed in his thoughts from the current year and century to the next most recent one, and has noted, from among the events presented, the ones that offer insight into those that followed—once he has made this journey, step by step, all the way back to the beginning, not of the world, for no signposts lead there, but of monuments and records—he must then turn back around on the path he has forged and descend, swiftly and unobstructed, along the trail of facts he has identified, from the beginnings of monuments and records back to the modern age. This is the world history we have, and which is to be presented to you.

Because world history is dependent on the wealth and poverty of sources, there will necessarily be as many gaps in world history as there are empty spaces in what tradition has preserved for us. As uniform, inexorable, and well defined as the process is by which transformations in the world develop from each other, the links between these changes in history are marked to the same degree by interruptions and accident. We see here a remarkable disparity between the course of the *world* and the course of *world history.* We might compare the former with a continuously flowing river, while in world history a wave is illuminated only here and there. Furthermore, since it often happens that we see the connection between a remote world event and the circumstances of the present sooner than we do that event's relationship to what preceded or happened simultaneously with it, events linked most closely to the present age will unavoidably appear as *isolated events* in their own context. For example, one such event would be the origin of Christianity and especially of Christian morality. The Christian religion has played such a multifaceted role in shaping the world that its emergence has become the most important fact of world history. But neither in the time when it first appeared, nor among the people in whom it arose, is there a satisfying explanation of its emergence (because of a lack of sources).

Our world history might thus never be anything but an aggregation of fragments, and never deserve to be called a science. At this point, however, the philosophical intellect comes to its aid; by artfully providing the links between these fragments, it raises the aggregation into a system, a rationally coherent totality. The plausibility of its efforts lies in the uniformity and unchanging unity of both natural laws and human nature. This unity is why, when similar external circumstances come together, events from the most ancient times can be repeated in the present; this unity is why we can use the events of modern times, lying within our field of observation, to draw conclusions about and shed light back on events that are lost in times without history. In history, as elsewhere, the method of drawing conclusions based on analogies is a powerful aid. But it must be justified by an important goal, and must be applied with as much caution as judgment.

A philosophical mind cannot be occupied with world history for long before feeling a new urge, one that irresistibly pushes him to bring things together, drives him to assimilate everything around him to his own rational nature and elevate every phenomenon he comes across to the highest form he knows: a *thought.* The more often, and the more successfully, he repeats his attempts to link the past with the present, the more inclined he will be to take what it sees as the interplay of *cause* and *effect* and link the two in a relation of *means* and *end.* One phenomenon after another starts to free itself from blind approximation, from lawless freedom, and take its proper place within a coherent totality (which, of course, exists only in his ideas). Before long, it is hard for him to convince himself that this sequence of phenomena, which has gained so much regularity and purposefulness in his mind, lacks those qualities in reality—hard to relinquish back to the blind rule of necessity what had begun to take on such a pleasing form under the borrowed light of the intellect. He therefore takes this harmony from himself and plants it in external soil—in the order of things. That is, he introduces a rational purpose into the course of world events, and a teleological principle into *world history*. With this principle in hand, he wanders once again through world history, holding the principle up to examine every phenomenon that the great theater offers. He sees this principle *confirmed* by a thousand corroborating facts, and *contradicted* by just as many others. But as long as important links are still missing from the sequence of world transformations, as long as fate keeps the decisive information about so many events hidden from us, he will declare the question *undecided*, and the view that wins the day will be the one that offers more satisfaction to the intellect and more contentment to the heart.

I do not need to remind you that world history in this deepest, teleological sense can be written only from the perspective of the most recent times. Applying this great standard prematurely will likely tempt a historian to do violence to events, thereby delaying this fortunate era for world history more and more in trying to speed its arrival. But it is never too early to turn our attention to this luminous and yet so badly neglected side of world history, through which world history is linked with the highest object of all human striving. Merely contemplating this goal, even if it remains a mere possibility, cannot but spur on, and sweetly reward, the hard work of the researcher. Even the smallest effort will matter to him if he sees himself as being on the path—or even just leading a later follower along the path—to solving the problem of the order of the world, and encountering the highest spirit in its most splendid manifestation.

Treated in this manner, gentlemen, the study of world history will be a task as attractive as it is useful. It will illuminate your intellect, spark beneficent enthusiasm in your heart. It will wean your mind from the common petty perspective on moral matters, and by unfolding the great portrait of ages and peoples before your eyes, it will correct the hasty determinations of the moment and the narrow judgments stemming from self-interest. By accustoming us to an account of the whole past, and to projecting conclusions far into the future, world history blurs the borders of birth and death that clamp so tightly on either side of a human life. It thus, by a kind of optical illusion, extends our short existence into infinite space and unobtrusively merges the individual into the species as a whole.

The individual person changes, and leaves the scene; his opinions change and leave with him; only history remains on the stage, sovereign, an immortal citizen of all nations and times. Like Homer's Zeus, it looks down with the same bright gaze upon the bloody work of war and the peaceful tribes innocently drawing nourishment from the milk of their flocks. However lawless human freedom seems to be in steering the course of the world, history calmly looks upon the baffling game, and its far-reaching gaze can discover, even from a distance, where this lawlessly roaming freedom is led by the tether of necessity. It hastens to reveal to humanity what it keeps a secret from the punishing conscience of a Gregory or a Cromwell: that "while the selfish individual can aim for what is low, he always unconsciously promotes what is higher."

No false luster will blind history, no prejudice of the age will lead it astray, for history knows the ultimate fate of all things. Everything that *ceases to be* has, from the perspective of history, lasted only a short time. History keeps the olive wreath of merit fresh and blasts the obelisk erected by vanity. By analyzing the delicate mechanisms through which nature's quiet hand, since the world's beginning, has purposefully developed mankind's powers, and by showing precisely what has been gained for nature's great plan in every epoch, history retrieves the true standard for happiness and accomplishment, which the prevailing delusion of every century has falsified differently. It cures us of an exaggerated admiration of antiquity and of the childish longing for times past, and by making us notice what we have ourselves, it keeps us from wanting to return to the celebrated Golden Age of Alexander or Augustus.

Without knowing it, without intending it, every past age has labored to bring about our *human* century. All the treasures that industry and genius, reason and experience, have gathered up over the long life of the world are ours. It is only when you study history that *you* will learn to value these assets that habit and uncontested possession make us so ungrateful for. Precious, costly assets, stained with the blood of the best and brightest, that were won only through the hard work of so many generations! And who among you, wedding a bright mind to a sensitive heart, can think of this exalted debt we owe without the quiet urge stirring within him to pay to *future* generations what he can never hope to repay to the past? A noble longing must inspire us to contribute whatever *we* can to the rich inheritance of truth, morality, and freedom that prior ages have passed down to us, and that must be passed farther along, richly increased, to the ages to come—a longing to anchor our fleeting existence to this immortal chain that winds through all the generations of mankind. However different the callings that awaits you in bourgeois society might be, every one of you can contribute something! Every gain forges a path to immortality, to true immortality, I mean, where the deed lives and hastens onward even if the name of the doer is left behind.

CHAPTER 4

Occasional Thoughts on German Universities in the German Sense*

Friedrich Schleiermacher

INTRODUCTION TO SCHLEIERMACHER'S ESSAY

In 1808 Friedrich Schleiermacher, a Protestant theologian and philosopher and a central figure in hermeneutics, entered the debate about a possible institution of higher learning in Berlin, adding one of the most lucid and, as it turned out, influential contributions. Published anonymously, Schleiermacher's essay appeared just as the support for a new university in Berlin had begun to wane.

Many of the initial reform proposals saw no place for an actual university in any historical sense of the term; instead, many of them sketched out a reorganization of already existing institutions, collections, vocational schools, and academies. In one proposal, Friedrich Gedike (see chapter 1) argued that the antiquated practices of universities—academic titles and degrees, disputations, faculty hierarchies—should be dispensed with and replaced by a loosely organized group of institutions that focused on practical as opposed to theoretical education.

Although Schleiermacher rejected certain elements of a more traditional scholastic university model, one more clearly distinguished from the state, he joined figures such as Schelling and Fichte in arguing for the continued importance of universities as distinct social institutions. Situated between schools, which introduced students to the "whole of knowledge," and academies,

* Excerpt translated from Friedrich Schleiermacher, "Gelegentliche Gedanken über Universitäten in deutschem Sinn, Nebst einem Anhang über eine neue zu errichtende," in *Friedrich Daniel Ernst Schleiermacher: Kritische Gesamtausgabe*, vol. 1, ed. Dirk Schmidt (Berlin: Walter de Gruyter, 1998).

which simply advanced knowledge, universities cultivated students into a scholarly life. They were transitional institutions that transformed young secondary school students into scholars, who would then go out into the world as civil servants or professionals with a lifelong commitment to the authority of real, systematic knowledge. The university was not just an instrument of the state; it was a community dedicated to knowledge and the cultivation of those who sought and preserved it. Central to this process was the development of a distinct individual character. In Schleiermacher's vision of the university community, students were active participants who engaged not only one another but their teachers as well. Hence, the seminar, in which professors worked intimately with students, played just as important a role in his vision as did the lecture, which, in his view, should also be a site where new ideas were developed.

For Schleiermacher, the university could not remain cloistered from the broader world. He outlined a middle ground between an Enlightenment university, beholden to the immediate needs of the state, and true knowledge and the sciences, whose progress national boundaries and languages could never contain. The state inevitably fragmented knowledge through its constant demands for immediate solutions and usable facts. It couldn't help but undercut the unity of knowledge. In order to ensure the advancement and integrity of knowledge, however, the university required guarantees that only the state could afford—freedom from censorship, freedom for professors to teach what they wanted to, and the freedom to govern the university's internal organization through the granting of degrees and honors. And, following Kant, Schiller, and Fichte, Schleiermacher held up the philosophy faculty, the equivalent to a modern-day college of arts and sciences, as the center of a university's real authority. It was there that the pursuit of knowledge was protected from the immediate demands of the state and the professions.

OCCASIONAL THOUGHTS ON GERMAN UNIVERSITIES IN THE GERMAN SENSE

Preface

A short preface for a short work. The title alone should, I hope, warn away readers who, owing to some sort of misunderstanding, are looking for a systematic, exhaustive treatment of the subject. If such were in fact my intention, it would be false modesty to present this work merely as something occasional, just as it would be presumption and empty boasting to put on systematic airs for something written as, and meant to be read as, merely a series of occasional works. Our topic warrants a rigorous and thorough treatment, to be sure; moreover, the author is no stranger to the area of scholarship the topic belongs to, and he hopes that many of the thoughts articulated here will find a place there as well. But the present work makes no claim to be fully developed and rigorously presented systematic knowledge. The author has put forth his views without that level of completion—casually, as lightly as possible, and in comprehensible words. May they be taken to heart in an age when, amid the destruction of so much of what is old, some new seeds are sprouting as well.

Whoever has the task of helping found or rebuild institutions of higher knowledge must do everything he can to make sure he has understood what he is to advise about, as well as the true relationships among its individual parts. For quite some time, opposing views about our topic have been advanced, each one doubtless true to some extent and worth taking to heart. But if each view is one-sided, whether by inclination or due to other circumstances, then the resulting idea of the whole will necessarily be uneven, rigid, and eccentric. For individual parts and relationships can never encompass the thing itself, or even properly take their own measure. Moreover, it often happens, unfortunately, that personal inclinations, special ties, or even outside requirements exert an influence on the considerations of those charged with taking action.

Thus the voice of someone with the leisure to observe the object in question from all sides, and in the various shapes it has taken among us over the years, should be welcome. For even where something new must be built, it is of the greatest importance to know what was essential in its past forms, what was inessential, and what was perhaps even erroneous or the product of misunderstanding and therefore to be rejected, as some things always are in any branch of human activity.

Such reflections are best addressed to a broad public. They are not meant merely for the few people who create, reorganize, and make decisions in this area, but rather for everyone with a vital stake in the matter. The author would therefore like to invite this broad public to look on as he examines the subject, and to reach an understanding of the subject either like the author's, or better than the author's, but in any case deeper than the one they had before.

1. *On the Relation of the Learned Academy to the State*

It is an idea almost universally held, we may assume, that people should have not just all kinds of basic practical knowledge but systematic and scientific knowledge as well. An intuition of systematic knowledge, a desire for it, stirs in us all. Even those who carry out their business almost entirely along traditional lines feel obliged to invoke their forebears, which would make no sense if they didn't have a dim sense that these forebears, in performing the same actions, had not merely the justification of tradition but a higher rationale as well. Likewise, those who make advances in human affairs, even if they do so purely instinctively, invoke the idea that others should explain and justify their actions intelligibly. All this points to systematic knowledge.

Surely the belief is equally universal that systematic knowledge is not an individual affair—not in the least. One person alone cannot bring it to completion or possess it entirely; it can only be a communal project, in which everyone makes a contribution of his own, everyone's aims depend on everyone else's, and we can claim a piece as our own only to a partial extent, by tearing it out of its context. In the area of knowledge, everything is so interdependent and so interconnected that we might well say: the more something is presented in isolation, the more incomprehensible and confused it will seem. Strictly speaking, every individual part can be fully understood only in relation to all the rest, and thus learning about each is dependent on learning about all the others. This necessary inner unity of all scholarship can be felt everywhere that there are strivings of this kind. All efforts toward achieving systematic knowledge exert a centripetal pull on the others and tend to flow together into one; there can hardly be any area of human activity that rivals the pursuit of knowledge in creating such widespread community and in having been, from its very beginnings, so continuous a tradition.

Naturally, in this as in other domains, human efforts are compartmentalized and divided in various ways, even sometimes forcibly and arbitrarily kept apart. The simultaneous scientific pursuits of different peoples often have very little to do with each other, at least on the surface; periods of time can seem even more isolated from each other. Only someone who sees the bigger picture can bring together all that seems divided in these advancing efforts; the governing force of an inner unity will not escape him.

In this context, it can only be an empty illusion whenever a true scholar appears to live his life cut off from others in his lonely studies and endeavors. Indeed, the first law of any attempt at knowledge must be: communication. And by making it impossible for anyone to bring forth new knowledge for himself alone, without language, nature has proclaimed this law quite clearly. Therefore, all the necessary connections, the most various means of communication, and a community of all engaged in the common effort will arise on their own, purely to satisfy the thirst for whatever knowledge has come to light.

And it would be a mistake to believe that all such institutions of knowledge have to be the work of the state, however much that may seem to the case now.

No one can demonstrate why the state in particular has to bring together in this way knowledge that was originally dispersed. The only places where all educational institutions must necessarily be rooted in the state are where a small minority of the educated rules over a still entirely crude and undeveloped people in whom the drive for knowledge has not yet been awakened. We need only consider how the basic elements of learning and of a community of knowledge are formed in the lap of the family. As for the larger institutional structures, it remains in general an open question whether they were established by the state or the church, or emerged independently. The consequence of all this seems to be that, if we want to be true to the nature of knowledge, we should see the educational institutions as primary, arising from free inclinations, out of an inner urge.

Naturally, however, the more these institutions develop, the more they require resources, tools of various kinds, and authorization for those involved, including the authorization to interact with other entities in legally binding ways. All this can only be provided by the state, of course; and thus we request of the state that it recognize, tolerate, and protect as moral agents all those who have, as we would put it, entered into an alliance for the sake of systematic knowledge. This demand should be least onerous among the German peoples and territories, for a wide range of free associations for all sorts of purposes have arisen and persist here. Moreover, we have seen that the state not only tolerates these associations as long as they remain above suspicion (it must be proven that they have acted subversively against the state before the state can prosecute them) but also accords them various privileges, as is only appropriate for social agents who are, after all, greater than individuals.

As often happens with other groups when the state is convinced of their usefulness, though, the state has tended gradually to annex scholarly and scientific associations, to incorporate them into itself, with the result that one can no longer determine whether they came about freely on their own or were instituted by the ruling power. This is the case however much we might doubt that, given the connectedness of all the strivings after systematic knowledge in the same cultural moment, institutions that arise within a certain state would be willing to cut themselves off so entirely from institutions elsewhere and, in effect, become part of that state, something that is actually foreign to them. At least, we could doubt that institutions would be willing to do this if we had not so often seen them doing it in actual fact. Neither, of course, is there any lack of equally conspicuous resistance to this too-close connection on the part of scholarly and scientific institutions. The true and natural state of affairs here seems to be as follows.

All scholarly and scientific activities taking place in a given language have a natural affinity with one another; they fit together more closely with each other than with anything else, and thus form, to some extent, a self-contained whole within the even larger whole. For anything systematic produced and presented in one language partakes of the special nature of that language; as long as it is not a matter of experiences and experiments that are necessarily the same everywhere, such as in mathematics and the experimental natural sciences, what arises in one language cannot be translated exactly into a different language, and so, on account of its connection with the language, it forms a unified whole. For scholars and scientists, however, it remains a necessary task to overcome the separation between these different spheres, break through the barriers of language, and connect through comparison that which seems to be separated by language—a task that is arguably the highest goal of the systematic engagement with language. Unfortunately, this task is clearly the highest one that the community of knowledge has been unable to accomplish, which means that the linguistic divide remains all the more impossible to avoid. Scholarly and scientific connections on all matters, arising out of the free thirst for knowledge, tend to be formed within the territory in which a given language is spoken. This is the closest bond, to which all others are merely secondary.

But the state also recognizes that knowledge, and even particular sciences, are important and useful. However large or small the state may be, however just or unjust its efforts to gain and retain independence, it can exist as such only through an accretion of knowledge that is, as much as possible, a totality—at least to the point where some trace, some awareness, of every branch of knowledge can be found there, the results of lively minds, persistent inquiry, and determined receptivity, even if only some branches of knowledge attain any measure of completeness. A noble and upstanding life is no more possible for a state than for the individual if its necessarily limited abilities in the realm of knowledge are not linked to a higher meaning. Similarly, the body of knowledge itself must naturally and necessarily be grounded in systematic inquiry, for the state no less than for the individual, and only through systematic inquiry can it truly be perpetuated or brought to fruition. The state thus tries to forge vital connections by every means possible. It takes over the institutions that it would have had to create if they had not existed already. And since the academy, too, needs the state, to protect and support it, both parties will try to strike agreements and ultimately unite with each other.

The state, however, works only in its own interests; seen in a historical light, too, it has always been thoroughly selfish. Accordingly, it will not want the support it gives to higher learning to benefit anyone or anything outside its borders. If these borders coincide with the territory that speaks a given language, then the scholarly and scientific association in the state will not try to extend beyond those borders, and the unification between the state and its scientific institutions will proceed, faster or slower depending on whether both sides truly believe that they need each other and can help each other or lack insight into the fact. If, however, the state occupies only part of a given language's territory, then it and its scholarly and scientific institution will have different interests. Scholars want to use the state and its support to work effectively toward their goals within the larger language area; they do not want to recognize the more circumscribed borders of the state as their own. If they are forced to provide services to the state in exchange for its support, they see these services as merely secondary. Governments, in contrast, are all the more jealous of each other the more they have in common, and fear that scholarly and scientific associations extending beyond their borders might promote an indifference toward the state itself, or even a preference for how things are set up in other countries, and will have other disadvantageous influences on the minds of its subjects. Thus they do all they can to keep close ties among scholars restricted to within their own borders. Conversely, if several languages are spoken within a single state, that state will urge all the scholars in its territory to come together and form a whole. This whole, however, would in fact consist of multiple parties divided by language; each side would try to minimize the favors shown to the leaders of the other or others, and a sincere brotherhood would be found only among the speakers of a single language. A great monarch [Napoleon] himself claimed recently that it is unnatural for a state to try to expand beyond its linguistic borders, which makes one wonder what sort of urgent necessity could have prevailed in the end over such a clear insight.

Whether it is equally unnatural for a territory in which one language is spoken to be divided into so many little states, as Germany is—that is an open question. It seems advisable, however, for these states at least to have close links with each other, and foolish for them to each want their own separate scholarly and scientific apparatus. For these individual apparatuses can be shaped into a whole only in a superficial and forced way, and trying to make them full-fledged and independent is all the more ridiculous the smaller the state is. The nature of things is such that they can only be parts of a larger association, and the more they try to isolate themselves the more they rob themselves of the beneficial influence of the rest, and thus of their sustenance and health. Indeed, there is perhaps nothing more bizarre, nothing farther removed from what the public good demands, than for a German state to shut itself off with its scholarly and educational institutions. On the contrary, scholarship and the sciences exemplify the confederation in which such states should stand. And if in fact the natural course of things is for states to become ever more unified, like their language, then what could prepare the way more easily, surely, and naturally than the creation of a community as diverse, loyal, and selfless as possible in the realm of systematic knowledge, thereby bringing to light the inner unity of what is superficially separated? The realm of systematic knowledge is an intermediary with an equally close reciprocal relationship to the state as to language. And how else should we clearly and dispassionately decide how long these divisions are to last, and how far they should extend, if not through an education in systematic scholarship and science that is as widespread as possible? For education entails deliberation, not misled by special interests and gradually eradicating petty passions and prejudices.

Few governments in our own fatherland have avoided these missteps, however. Rather than each state promoting what it can, and every government and its citizens enjoying and using, happily and proudly, the resources to be found throughout the German fatherland, two policies entirely opposing this aim have gradually gained the upper hand. First, governments have competed to try to make the institutions of higher learning under their respective control the centers of all scholarly and scientific interchange in Germany, by luring away all excellent scholars from far and wide, even if that leaves other states lacking. If this were at bottom a true ambition to achieve everything one can, well-intentioned toward the smaller states with smaller budgets and meant to support their institutions and help reward their talented men, then it would be largely unobjectionable. But in fact every state's aim has been primarily to eliminate its dependence on every other one by satisfying its scholarly and scientific needs. This is just empty posturing, since true independence in this regard comes only when each state contributes as generously as its size allows to maintain and promote the public good. Instead, each state wanted to use intellectual predominance, as well as dominance of other kinds, to gain power and respect beyond its borders. While admittedly the most peaceful and attractive method of conquest, using sums of money as bait for scholars can easily endanger the pursuit of systematic knowledge. And if these conquests are disproportionate to the natural importance of a state, or are brought about in underhanded ways, the whole enterprise becomes ludicrous or even harmful.

The second policy that has become increasingly common is that of the scholarly embargo: governments limiting or prohibiting the exchange of knowledge with foreign states and preventing their citizens from taking part as they wish in the scholarly pursuits of neighboring states. When this occurs where the church controls the state, as was largely the case in Catholic Germany until recently, it constitutes sad proof of a dark age. When it is a medium-sized state surrounded by larger ones that erects these barriers, feeling that it must exert itself however it can to assert its independence from them as long as possible, then what is regrettable is that one can err so badly when one's intentions are so good. For the intellectual narrowness that necessarily results from such isolation will never secure or enhance independence. When, finally, it is a powerful state with real conquests of its own that, dissatisfied with its achievements in the scholarly and scientific sphere, imposes these barriers until it can catch up there, too, this is clearly an act of illiberal arrogance, a low and money-grubbing stinginess that makes the intent behind such conquests appear in an unfavorable light. More than anything else, it makes the educated people of that nation hate their government.

There is another, even more essential point in the administration of scholarly and scientific institutions about which the state's view tends to be entirely opposed to that of scholars. The state wants to annex these institutions, whereas scholars are more closely allied with each other in the pursuit of systematic knowledge. Concord would prevail between the two sides if the state would take to heart the deepest meaning of a wise old man's admonitions: perhaps not his first guideline—that men of knowledge should rule—but at least his second, that rulers should be men of knowledge. Statesmen, even those who do the most to promote education, seem both to themselves and to others more like artists than like scholars in their running of the state. With happy intuitions, feeling out what is right, they create unconsciously, skillfully shaping unformed matter in accord with a primal image residing somewhere within them, just as every artist does. This is clear to see, and sincerely to be praised—but they are not ruling as men of knowledge. Even so, this artistic sensibility will be most cultivated and truest among those who understand how to view facts and experiences systematically, or at least how to use systematic ideas about them. Like anyone who works creatively, the statesman must draw, directly or indirectly, upon the treasure of systematic knowledge for his art, while also in turn enriching that treasure house through his works.

Real improvements in every branch of government administration can be introduced and flourish all the more readily when rulers and, as much as possible, their subjects, too, have properly comprehended not only the true idea of the state in general but also the nature of their particular state, and where, with their consciousness of these ideas, they also know how to apply examples from the whole of world history. In short, good governance of every sort requires true knowledge. These points should be acknowledged all the more readily since experience shows what happens whenever these insights are neglected. Either tumultuous and anarchic conditions arise, as in what was Poland and in various other countries where there is practical understanding but little systematic knowledge, or a caste system arises, a sad empiricism clinging rigidly and desperately to tradition and obviously out of step with branches of knowledge that are managed differently and thus advancing. Yet precisely these facts often go unrecognized, and the state is more likely to fear and hate than welcome any influence from systematic scholarship and science upon its governance.

Naturally, then, the state only cares about the immediate use of knowledge. It tries to promote general familiarity with facts, phenomena, and achievements of all kinds, and when it annexes academic institutions, it tries to steer them in that direction. However, for those who come together freely in the service of scholarship and science, what matters most is something very different from the mere accumulation of knowledge. What unites them is their awareness of the necessary unity of all knowledge, the laws and conditions of its genesis, and the forms and structures by which every perception, every thought, actually becomes a real part of our systematic knowledge. And what these scholars try to awaken in others, and spread, is first and foremost this awareness—the sole means by which truth and certainty can be preserved, indeed in all forms of knowledge and their dissemination.

Thus they strive wherever they can to give even modest amounts of knowledge a systematic character. Where only the most paltry information about an object is known, they try to draw it into the realm of systematic knowledge, find the unity in it that will make all its multifariousness comprehensible, and strain to see the whole in each individual part (and, conversely, each part within the whole). Similarly, they lead each person they intend to educate, however modest his preparation may be, straight to this main point of unity and form in systematic knowledge; they train him to see systematically; and only after he has found his footing do they let him go deeper into the particulars, because he needs to know things truly, in the strict sense—otherwise, all this piling up of isolated facts is just unsteady stumbling, with a value that is merely provisional and only suited to more practical uses. The state, on the other hand, all too often fails to see the value of these efforts. The purer the speculations are—for this is how we should always refer to scholarly and scientific pursuits that are primarily concerned with the unity and common form of all knowledge—the purer these speculations, the more the state will try to limit them, and the more it will try to use all its influence, both positive encouragements and negative restrictions, to promote knowledge that can be measured, the mass of concrete discoveries, and characterize such knowledge as the sole genuine fruit of any search for truth, regardless of whether or not it bears the stamp of systematic knowledge.

Now universities and academies must necessarily resist this orientation, and their nobler members will always work to achieve as much independence from the state as possible, both by minimizing their institution's subjection to the power and directives of the state and by increasing their own influence over the state. They will try to promote a more worthy and systematic manner of thinking in the state, wherever they can; where this is impossible, they will at least work toward gaining credibility and standing for themselves. But the more that academics become involved with and co-opted by the state, so that political considerations outweigh systematic thought and occlude it in their minds, the more readily they will bow to the state's interventions. And the more closely the two sides are linked like this, the more one group within the larger national group of scholars and scientists will be isolated from the others who hold more firmly to their core principles, and that smaller group will devolve into a collective merely serving the state. Above all, where a powerful and imposing state has already united an entire linguistic territory, it will tend to have the upper hand over systematic knowledge. And among the circumstances most favorable for the other side [i.e., the cause of scholarship and science], not the least of them is when the state grants systematic knowledge greater freedom, even if it thereby aims at nothing more than a feather in its own cap.

We will often need to refer back to what has been put forth here in only an abbreviated manner so far, for without keeping in mind the most important aspects of the interplay between the state and the pursuit of systematic knowledge, we can neither understand the destiny (in an external sense) of the academy nor, when there is a specific problem to be solved, find the right path appropriate to the relationship between state and scholarship. Least of all could we understand why the state tends to treat universities in the way that we can see it does, and why the universities so vigorously push for independence from the state, regarding it as best when the state intervenes the least in their administration. First, however, we must examine what place universities occupy among educational and scholarly institutions, and what their primary activity should be.

2. *Schools, Universities, and Academies*

"Academies" here means learned societies of all kinds, as well as the associations they should all be a part of and, in principle, surely are a part of. By "schools," though, we mean only those that can at least be considered as arising directly from the need for and thirst for knowledge—in other words, only the academic schools, whose directors have necessarily been fully educated in the pursuit of systematic knowledge, and where what is taught fits directly into that domain.

Schools, universities, and academies, then, are the three main forms that all associations pursuing the sciences take today. They can be found all over modern Europe, but it is fair to see Germany as the center of modern education, because while there are excellent examples of some of these forms, especially schools and academies, in other countries, nowhere but among us are there such pure instances of all three. In fact, we might well say that the whole system is at root German, and conforms to other institutions likewise German in origin. The schools are like a master with his apprentices, universities a master with his journeymen, and academies masters among themselves. For most people, however, filled with deep contempt for any sort of guild system, this explanation merely tries to clarify one thing by comparing it to something more obscure, if indeed it does not disparage institutions of learning by equating them with those infamous systems (though the guilds actually contain much that is excellent). Better to consider each of these institutions separately—school, university, and academy—and examine the meaning of each one and how they all fit together. For without having understood all three, we will hardly be able to agree about the nature and proper organization of the one that is our object of study.

Systematic knowledge, as it exists among all educated peoples as their collective achievement and common possession, is meant to form the individual into knowledge, while the individual in turn should also help advance his part of science. These are the two goals of all the collective activity in this realm. Clearly the first of these goals is predominant in schools, and the second in academies. The tasks in schools are like gymnastic exercises that develop strength, and it is only right that the German language calls such a school by the foreign name "gymnasium." The gymnasiums accept the young man of a higher nature and conspicuous gifts, which suggest that he might be well suited to scholarship or science, or at least able to process a mass of information effectively, and then test him in every way to see if this is actually the case. There are two criteria, though, that reveal whether someone is suited for higher education: he must have a particular talent that draws him to a single field of study and keeps him there, and he must also have a general sense for the unity and pervasive interconnectedness of all knowledge—a systematically philosophical spirit. Both must coincide in anyone who is to become something outstanding. Without such a spirit, even the most striking talent will be unoriginal, suited for nothing better than being a diligent assistant to others possessing the systematic principle. And without a particular talent, the systematic spirit—the spirit of true scholarship and science—will spin its wheels in a very small circle, exhausting itself in strange elaborations, repetitions, and reconsiderations of the same highly general themes, for it has not truly mastered any material.

Even where both capacities are present, in some people the talent predominates, in others the general systematic spirit. Both capacities, though, unless they are present to a truly extraordinary degree, require a deliberately applied stimulus: it takes artful treatment—sometimes more, sometimes less—to awaken them and bring them to light. And thus schools must work on both. On the one hand, they must present the whole content of knowledge in a fundamental way and in meaningful outlines, so that any slumbering talent will have a chance to feel the attraction of its proper object. On the other hand, they must emphasize and teach especially thoroughly that in which the systematic form, with its unity and its connectedness, can first be readily perceived, and which is, for that reason, the universal aid of all other knowledge. This is the true reason why schools, justifiably, have grammar and mathematics as their main subjects—I would go so far as to say that these are the only subjects that can be taught there with a modicum of systematicity. At the same time, however, schools have to methodically train students in all their intellectual capacities, so that these capacities can be distinguished and their different functions identified; students should be strengthened to the point where every one can easily and completely conquer a given topic.

The goal of schools is to achieve all these things at once, by the simplest and surest means. Of course, no school will be able to accomplish every part of this goal to the same degree of perfection, even with the best organization and leadership; some schools will excel in certain areas, others in different ones. But as a result it is all the more important to keep the overall goal in sight, so that while the school pursues the virtuosity that is its own, it avoids any damaging one-sidedness. All the more desirable, as well, is a school leadership that is not overly specialized, so that each such institution can be made to provide whatever support it can for scholarship as a whole.

In academies, on the other hand, the masters of scholarship and science come together, and if they cannot all be members of the academy in the same way, they can at least all be represented; there can be a vital connection between the members and everyone else worthy of the name of scholar or scientist, such that the works produced in academies can rightly be considered the collective efforts of them all. Every scholar and scientist must strive to be a part of this community, because the personal talent each one has developed amounts to nothing in the pursuit of systematic knowledge without the supplement of others' talents. They all form a whole; the members of this community feel as one, because of the living sense of and enthusiasm for knowledge itself, and through their insight into the necessary relatedness of all knowledge.

This is precisely why they divide up once more into different departments: each branch of knowledge needs an even more closely knit community to study it thoroughly and effectively. The more delicate the branches into which it multiplies, and the livelier the unity of the whole remains, without losing itself in empty forms, the more perfect the organization of the whole will become—so long as participation in the progress of the whole and enthusiasm for one's own particular field reciprocally inspire each other in every scholar, and thus it is easy to maintain the closest connections among the different areas of knowledge under the wing of the academy.

How many academies of this kind does Germany need? One at the most, or two (one in the north and one in the south) with the closest possible connections between them. And they should have offshoots all over—anywhere that scholars in various fields naturally come together, and in any place particularly well suited for a particular scholarly or scientific field. By the nature of things, such a comprehensive association is what everything is working toward. But until it exists in reality, we can only regard our scattered scholarly societies as fragments, and only through the liveliest exchange with each other have they been able to maintain their existence while awaiting that ideal end point, which perhaps lies not far in the future.

The activities of schools and academies correspond to the view of these institutions presented above. With their public exams, schools put on an exhibition that is entirely gymnastic, so to speak: able to reveal nothing but the extent to which the intellectual muscles necessary for knowledge have been trained. Belletristic productions, however, are not appropriate for these exams, because nothing should be publicly presented that does not promote systematic knowledge. The same is true of the school directors' programs and invitations—either they do not deserve to be made public at all, or they are not appropriate for their primary audience. It is therefore an excellent sign in many ways when a school simply dispenses with such documents. Every academy, on the other hand, is expected to produce works—not major books encompassing a whole field, to say nothing of revolutionary books, but rather collections of articles that shed light on particular, previously unstudied objects, present original discoveries, and publicize or test new methods. For this is how, through many small contributions, systematic knowledge is advanced once it has achieved a certain measure of size and stability—and that is the purpose of the academies. The more substance and coherence their works display, the more merit is ascribed to those works. In the same spirit, the academies sometimes publish problems that remain to be solved, in part to find help elsewhere in cases where not enough experiments can be performed or the necessary investigations cannot be pursued on-site (it is therefore only right that the academies' own members be excluded from their prize competitions), and in part as a way to discover which nonmembers are seriously and successfully working on a given scholarly topic, so that the academy can bring these sometimes worthy additions into its ranks.

What, then, is the university, situated as it is between school and academy? It might seem as though these latter two can carry out all educational and intellectual functions between them, and that the university is therefore superfluous. Certain men among us have in fact come to this conclusion, but hardly in an authentically German spirit, for this view is predominant among a different people [i.e., the French], who, in pursuing a policy of consolidation, have more and more lost everything that resembles a university and been left with nothing except schools and academies in countless number and the most diverse forms. What one overlooks in such consolidation is a very essential point.

Schools are concerned only with information as such: they may, in a preparatory way, seek to awaken insight into the nature of knowledge itself, the systematic spirit, and the ability to make discoveries and unique combinations—but none of these things are actually taught in the schools. Academies, though, necessarily presuppose all these things in their members, and they promote systematic knowledge solely through the common ground that all their members share and are conscious of sharing (their whole mode of organization suggests this, even if the academies never have any reason to state it directly). This can occur only in a coherent way. How empty the works of the academy would be if they dealt in sheer empiricism and had no faith in any principles of systematic knowledge! How empty the very idea of a collective pursuit of all scholarship and science would be if these principles did not cohere with each other into a whole! And how pitiful the execution would be if the members disagreed about all these principles. Clearly, every member of the academy must first have come to understand the philosophical principles of his field, both in his own mind and in agreement with all the other members; each must approach his field in a philosophical spirit, and it is precisely this spirit, similar in all members, that is wedded to every individual's unique talent to make him a true member of the association. Is this spirit supposed to come to people in their sleep? Is the scholarly or scientific life supposed to emerge out of nothing, unlike every other begotten form of life? This form of life alone, even in its first tender shoots, requires no care or cultivation?

Here, then, lies the essence of the university. It is charged precisely with this begetting, this cultivation. It thus forms the transition between the time when a young man is first prepared for systematic knowledge, by his own studying and by acquiring a knowledge base, and the time when, in the prime of his intellectual life, he expands the field or adds on a beautiful new wing to the edifice of knowledge through his own research. Above all, then, the university's role is to start a process, and to monitor its initial development. But this is nothing less than a completely new intellectual phase of life. To awaken the idea of systematic knowledge, of science in the noble youth, already equipped with knowledge of various kinds; to help lead him to mastery over whatever particular field he will devote himself to, so that it becomes second nature for him to view everything from the perspective of systematic inquiry, see individual things not in isolation but rather in their intellectual interconnection and place them in a larger context, always with reference to the unity of all knowledge; to ensure that he learns to remember the laws of systematic knowledge in all his thinking and thereby develops the capacity to do independent research, make discoveries, and present his findings systematically—this is the task of the university. The name "university" itself suggests this, for here it is not a question of collecting several kinds of knowledge, however diverse and worthwhile, but rather presenting the totality of knowledge in such a way that the principles and blueprint of all knowledge are brought to light. This is what makes it possible for a student to work his way into any area of knowledge.

Here we have the explanation for the fact that students spend less time in the university than in school. Learning everything would, of course, take more time, but learning how to learn takes less. Also, what is brought to life at the university is but one moment, one act: the idea of knowing—the highest consciousness of reason as a guiding principle in humankind—is awakened within him.

All of the special features that distinguish the university from the schools on the one hand and academies on the other hand can be traced back to this general fact. In schools, instruction follows the path of least resistance from one particular thing to another, with little attention to whether the students are always attaining the whole. In universities, on the other hand, encyclopedic knowledge in a given field and a general overview of its scope and context are emphasized above all else, as the most important thing and the foundation of any instruction the students receive. The main works one reads at university are textbooks: anthologies or compendiums whose goal is not to exhaust a given topic, or even enrich our knowledge of it, but rather to provide a broad perspective and a systematic presentation. Thus neither the easiest textbook, nor the hardest, nor the most unusual will be chosen over the others; the best is the one that most emphasizes the idea of the whole, makes it easiest to grasp, and presents its scope and inner connections most clearly.

Later, in the academy, what matters in every more concrete field is to treat each individual thing perfectly correctly and precisely; pure philosophy, speculation, and engaging with the unity and connectedness of all knowledge and the nature of knowledge itself, are thoroughly deemphasized. These matters, however, are in no way inconsequential for the more concrete sciences, much less unimportant or worthless. For whatever approach one takes, all particular knowledge is in fact based on that general perspective; it is impossible to produce science without the speculative spirit, and the two go together so closely that anyone who has failed to develop a well-defined philosophical way of thinking will never independently produce anything scientific that is solid and respectable. Consciously or not, and even as he makes discoveries guided by a marvelous instinct, such a scholar will always remain dependent on a speculative direction of reason that is perhaps clarified only by other people. Furthermore, in every scientific work the author's philosophical mode of thinking is expressed through his language, method, and presentation. This is why philosophy recedes to the background: if systematic knowledge is to be pursued collectively, as is the case in academies, everything purely philosophical must first be established so correctly that there will be little more to say about it. To be sure, this prerequisite does not seem to have been fully attained among us German scholars and scientists yet, and it would perhaps not be too much to grant if we admitted that such complete agreement and resolution in matters of philosophy can never actually be fully achieved among a people that truly takes such matters seriously; one can only come ever closer to full agreement. And yet any academy makes this prerequisite necessary, at least insofar as it is natural for it to view whatever agreement has been reached as primary, and any that has not as secondary. The academy can have a speculative branch only in the sense that, assuming there is only one mode of philosophical thinking within a given people, it presents the unity of what has been expressed differently at different times, illuminates the oppositions that exist in the present, and exposes that which pretends to be philosophical but is really just a polemic against philosophy—in short, promotes progress and greater agreement within the nation through historical and critical studies in this field. To produce something new and pathbreaking in the field of actual philosophy seems not to be the academy's role. It is, on the other hand, widely recognized that philosophical instruction is the basis for everything that takes place at the university. And because these highest views are to be communicated, and indeed differentiated as much as possible and distinguished from everything similar that exists alongside them, it is at and between universities that philosophical debates and arguments have their place; it is above all at universities that philosophical schools are formed.

The university therefore has an entirely particular aim and purpose, fundamentally different from the aims of both schools and academies. Only superficially—which is not to say arbitrarily, but rather in the sense that every inner nature necessarily has an exterior form—only superficially is the university necessarily somewhat similar to the other two institutions. Otherwise, there would be fantastic leaps in the scholarly and scientific lives of individual people. The spirit of systematic knowledge as the highest principle, the immediate unity of all knowledge, cannot be presented as existing all by itself in pure transcendental philosophy, like a ghost, as some have unfortunately tried to do, thereby conjuring up phantoms and unearthly beings. Nothing could be emptier than a philosophy that strips itself so bare and waits for real knowledge, as something lower, to be given or received from somewhere else entirely. And nothing could be more fruitless for systematic knowledge than for young people in their best years to spend time on a philosophy that provides no definite direction for future scholarly life in all fields, but rather serves, at best, to tidy up the mind, something that has already been claimed for mathematics.

Rather, philosophy—this systematic spirit—can and must be presented and grasped only in its living influence on all knowledge, only through real science as the body to its soul. This is why universities also teach information that is not taught in schools—partly higher, and in any case different. To that extent, additional learning takes place, and the university is a continuation of school. It is likewise a pre-academy: The systematic spirit, awakened by the philosophical instruction and reinforced and clarified by the student's reexamining from a higher perspective what had already been learned, must, by nature, immediately test and train its powers by trying to penetrate more deeply into individual topics from this grounded center—researching, connecting, and producing something new, and thereby confirming the insight into nature and the connectedness of all knowledge that has been achieved. This is the significance of scholarly seminars, medical clinics, and the like at universities, all of which are completely along the lines of the academies. We can see from the above why both other terms are relevant to universities, which are often called "schools of higher education" and "academies." It is senseless to claim that universities should not have seminars or places to do practical work because those are the sole purview of academies.

What has just been presented seems to be, essentially, the relationship of each of these three institutions to their common goal, as seen from examining their main features. In fact, when they are set up well and fit together properly, nothing seems to be missing—their common goal must necessarily be reached. All the more ruinous is it, therefore, when these institutions misunderstand their tasks and the boundaries between them. It is destructive for schools to overreach and play with philosophical instruction, pretending that the fundamental differences between schools and universities are only apparent. For there is no surer way to spoil young people for universities, and for the scholarly life in general, than by leading them to see even the highest knowledge—which can only be spirit and life, with only a minimal external form—as merely the sum of individual propositions and facts, which one can acquire and possess like any other piece of school learning. It is likewise destructive when universities lend credibility to such pretentions and actually do become "advanced schools," by trying prematurely to be academies—by trying to be greenhouses, as it were, for mature scholars, making them delve deeper and deeper into the details of scholarship, and thereby neglecting the actual responsibility of the university: to awaken the systematic spirit and give it a particular direction. It is destructive, finally, when academies, carried away by the spirit of partisanship, enter into speculative polemics, and no less so when, cocooned in their not all that well-founded concrete knowledge, they arrogantly look down on these battles, which only seem passionate because of the participants' enthusiasm; when they are unconcerned whether those they take into their ranks for the enrichment of knowledge have made it through these speculative trials or not.

What makes all these misunderstandings so prevalent? Certainly, for the most part, the lack of inner unity in everything that passes among us for systematic knowledge. Anyone who has spent time in even one of these types of scholarly association will likely have had the experience that, misled by prejudices, forgetting what the other institutions once meant to him, he regards them as nothing and his own institution as everything. We find this prejudice everywhere. What is more widespread than academy scholars looking down on the schoolteacher as an unfortunate man stuck under a heavy burden, unavoidably mired in pedantic details simply in order to do his job, and eternally excluded from the highest pleasures of systematic knowledge, trapped as he is in its antechamber? Or dismissing university professors as schoolteachers with an inflated opinion of themselves, who at the same time function in a service capacity, destined to propagate scholarship or science as it is handed down to them and humbly follow the path of the academicians as though walking in the footsteps of immortals? Schoolteachers, for their part, disparage academicians as lazy, because they do comparatively little to attract new manpower to scholarship and science, and complain about university professors as presumptuous ingrates who tend to ruin the better part of what they themselves have accomplished. University professors, in turn, belittle schoolteachers as people who cling to the letter, largely blind to the spirit, of their own scholarship or science, and consider academies as charitable institutions for overambitious, unjustly famous scholars or ones who have burned out.

How wrong and perverse this all is! Any capable leader of an intellectually rigorous school must have an overview of the whole, as a counterweight to the duties he must constantly perform—and also so that he can lead the way in those duties. Thanks to this overview, he as it were personifies the academy: he must possess the same scholarly deliberation, the same pure spirit of observation, as one who advances systematic knowledge, and in fact the task of cultivating the youth whom he guides is probably more difficult than any single experiment. The academician, balancing and evaluating every result in lonely meditation and using every hint and clue to advance new discoveries, and the university professor, remaining in the same circle and spending his time with young people thirsty for knowledge, trying to do whatever he can to excite them—admittedly, these are two very different pursuits. But only someone who has never connected the two can look down on one pursuit from the perspective of the other as something debased. And no truly outstanding scholar can be in that position. For even the most reclusive, industrious researcher will necessarily feel, in his happiest moments—those of discovery, which always lead to a new and livelier view of the whole—a desire to communicate, excitedly and excitingly, and to pour out his knowledge into young minds. And no distinguished university teacher can be worthy of his position without having encountered experiments and assignments that make palpable to him the great value of an association in which each person gets help and support from everyone else as he follows his scholarly path. But in order to permanently sustain this well-founded reciprocal esteem among all parties, a closer community of public educational institutions needs to be created. The best schoolteachers, university professors, and academy members must stand together: this would foster a truly communal spirit for their whole enterprise, spreading out from them to encompass scholars of every type.

Hasn't this already been taking place? one might ask. Doesn't the state unite scholars at all these different levels in the administrative councils through which it manages public education? It does, but it brings them together as civil servants, along with other professionals, in forums that are characteristic of the state but foreign to the scholars; their oversight is intended to be primarily in the interests of the state. The circumstances of educational institutions look quite different when viewed from this perspective, and the more an educator's civil servant role comes to predominate (something that happens quite naturally), the easier it is for him to show this different face to the scholarly community in which he is active, evaluating and treating everything according to its direct impact on the state—certainly not a good thing in terms of intellectual improvement, as experience shows. It is in keeping with the whole course of modern European culture for governments to encourage scholarship and set up institutions to promote and expand it. They do the same with the arts and vocational skills of all kinds. However, here as everywhere, there comes a time when this custodianship must end. Shouldn't this gradually begin to happen in Germany? And wouldn't it be advisable, now or not far in the future and at least in the Protestant parts of Germany, for the state to leave science to fend for itself, give scholars qua scholars full responsibility for managing their internal affairs, and keep control over nothing but finances, police oversight, and monitoring the direct influence of these institutions on the civil service?

The academies, which governments always believe can have only an indirect effect on their own aims, have always been freer than schools and universities, and have enjoyed this greater freedom. Schools and universities, on the other hand, suffer at the hands of the state. The state sees them as institutions pursuing knowledge not for its own sake but for the state's, misunderstands and hinders their natural efforts to shape themselves according to the laws that systematic knowledge promotes, and fears that schools and universities would focus entirely on an unproductive teaching and learning far removed from life and any practical applications if given a greater measure of autonomy—that a pure thirst for knowledge would completely undermine the desire for action, and no one would want to engage in any civic activities. These ideas seem to have long been the main reason why the state manages these institutions too much, and in its own fashion; the longer these conditions last, the more schools and universities suffer.

Indeed, we cannot deny that, if the occasional proclamations of some of our leading philosophers were to be believed, they would all prefer to discourage their students from taking up any nonscholarly activity—and they certainly know how to attract and enthrall young people. But why should we believe what they say, and why ascribe such a lasting influence to a passing fascination? Such things have always been said, and yet young men have always streamed from the schools of the wise into the halls of justice and administrative offices, to help with the challenges of governance. Observing and doing, even if in conflict with each other, always work hand in hand; nature itself defines the relations between those who devote themselves solely to knowledge and the rest, and always correctly and with smooth regularity. Compare the great mass of people who go through schools and universities to the small number who end up filling a nation's academies; consider, too, how many of the latter are also highly regarded civil servants. You will then put your fears to rest forever, and have to admit that the state has advantages enough over science and scholarship, through the many concrete benefits it alone can offer and the power with which political talent can emerge wherever it is found. But if, through misguided worries and the resulting regulations, the state fosters such misunderstandings among scholars concerned with spreading systematic knowledge, then the schools will have no real basis; in universities, the main point will be lost under a mountain of trivialities; academies will become all the more contemptible the longer and the more they work only on directly practical matters; and in the long run the state will rob itself of the most essential advantages that the sciences and scholarship provide, those which ensure the continuation of science. Less and less will the state be able to conceive of and carry out great things, or to uncover, with sharp insights, the roots and the interconnectedness of all its mistakes.

CHAPTER 5

A Plan, Deduced from First Principles, for an Institution of Higher Learning to Be Established in Berlin, Connected to and Subordinate to an Academy of Sciences*

J. G. Fichte

INTRODUCTION TO FICHTE'S PLAN

In the final decades of the eighteenth century, German universities came under widespread criticism from academics and nonacademics alike. The contemporary university, argued some, was little more than an antiquated guild designed to protect the limited interests and incestuous structure of a scholarly class either oblivious or indifferent to the interests of the world beyond the study or the lecture hall. Others suggested that the proliferation of print threatened to render the university irrelevant. In one of the most popular German novels of the eighteenth century, Christian Salzmann's *Carl von Carlsberg; or, On Human Misery* (6 vols., 1783–88), Deacon Rollow, a spiritual adviser of sorts to the young protagonist Carl, claims that universities had been established when the "world lacked books and when a man who could read and write was the exception. In our day, however, universities are pitiful. They are like the

* Excerpt translated by Damion Searls from J. G. Fichte, *Deduzierter Plan einer zu Berlin zu errichtenden höhern Lehranstalt, die in gehöriger Verbindung mit einer Akademie der Wissenschaft stehe*, in *J. G. Fichte Gesamtausgabe der Bayerischen Akademie der Wissenschaften*, II, 11, ed. Reinhard Lauth, Hans Gliwitzky, Peter K. Schneider, and Erich Fuchs (Stuttgart–Bad Cannstatt: Friedrich Frommann, 1998).

fortresses built to withstand the bombs and cannons of the Crusades." What was the purpose of the university in an age of readily accessible information?

But novelists and intellectuals were not the only ones concerned about the future of German universities. Prussian bureaucrats were as well, and beginning in the 1780s they initiated a series of reforms, studies, and plans to modernize what they oftentimes referred to as bastions of privilege and anachronistic thinking. Most of these reforms sought to better align universities with the interests of a growing public and, above all, with those of the state.

In 1802 Karl F. von Beyme, the head of the Prussian Civil Cabinet and key adviser to King Friedrich Wilhelm III, invited several Prussian officials and a number of intellectuals to consider not just the general university question but more particularly whether there should be an "institution of higher education" in Berlin. Long the seat of Prussian power, Berlin had several academies and scientific institutions of various kinds but no university. Beyme's omission of "university" was intentional. His call for proposals was meant to distinguish any future institution of learning from the guildlike medieval relic that he considered the university to be.

Long after Beyme's initial request, in 1807, J. G. Fichte, a philosopher who had taught at the University of Jena, secretly sent him a detailed plan for a university in Berlin. In a letter that accompanied the manuscript, Fichte claimed that he had personally copied the text. In the event that his plan were to be acted upon, he didn't want the new institution to be seen as the result of one person but rather, as he wrote, "the pure effusion of the general will." The German people needed a new university, and Fichte, whose attempts at reform as professor in Jena had led to violent confrontations with students, had a plan.

Although Fichte entitled his piece a "deduced" plan, the actual text begins not with abstract philosophical principles but rather with a discussion of the university and the history of how knowledge was communicated. The first universities, wrote Fichte, emerged in the twelfth and thirteenth centuries before the "scholarly edifice of the modern world" had taken shape—that is, when there were few books. Oral lectures, in which masters read aloud to students from a manuscript, were the central means of communication and instruction. Until the widespread adoption of print technologies in the fifteenth century, the university was a means of compensating for the lack of books.

In the centuries since the development of modern printing technologies, however, books had become ever more prevalent. Now, at the beginning of the nineteenth century, claimed Fichte, there was an "excess" of books. And yet professors continued to read books aloud to their students as though nothing had changed in the six-hundred-year history of the university. Universities had allowed themselves to become institutions for the "repetition of . . . content that was already in a book." By not transforming themselves, universities risked becoming redundant.

For Fichte, such a transformation required that universities be embraced not just as another, competing communications technology but rather as a distinct community. A university safeguarded a particular form of life, in which scholars and teachers were bound together through a devotion to knowledge and scholarship, to what Fichte and his colleagues called *Wissenschaft*.

On the other hand, Fichte was attentive to practical exigencies. Having been poor during his own student years, he stressed the importance of providing students in need with material support, and wrote at some length about the difficulty of doing intellectual labor on an empty stomach. In order for the university to be truly meritocratic, it would have to take steps to level the playing field.

Fichte's proposal also included detailed plans for oral examinations, essays, and informal discussions—pedagogical exercises designed to train students in the practice of scholarly knowledge under the caring and demanding guidance of a master teacher. He even outlined the material conditions he considered necessary for a university to flourish: students would wear uniforms; they would be provided with housing and even pocket money; they would not be subject to civil courts but only to faculty oversight. All of these would be external signs of the students' unique devotion to the university and, conversely, the university's commitment to ensuring that students could pursue knowledge without distractions. The university, however, would then send its young scholars out into the world, where, as Fichte imagined it, they would be the guardians of social progress.

As the first rector of the new University of Berlin, against the protests of Schleiermacher, Fichte had the opportunity to try to implement his plan. This did not go as well as he had hoped, and he gave up the position within a year.

A PLAN, DEDUCED FROM FIRST PRINCIPLES, FOR AN INSTITUTION OF HIGHER LEARNING TO BE ESTABLISHED IN BERLIN, CONNECTED TO AND SUBORDINATE TO AN ACADEMY OF SCIENCES

Section One: The Concept of an Institution of Higher Learning Corresponding to the Needs of Our Time

§1

When universities first came into being, the scholarly edifice of the modern world was to a large extent not yet built. There were not many *books*, and the *few* that existed were rare and hard to find. Anyone with something new to impart rarely attempted to do so by following the difficult path of authorship. *Spoken transmission* was the most generally useful means for constructing, maintaining, and adding onto the edifice of scholarship and science, and universities took the place of books, rare or nonexistent as they were.

§ 2

After the art of printing was discovered and books became so common, and after the spread of the book trade made it much easier to communicate in writing than by spoken lectures—now that there has ceased to be any branch of scholarship or science not covered, indeed inundated, by an abundance of books—it has still been thought necessary for universities to place this entire universe of books before the world *again*, and have professors *recite* the very same thing that already lies *printed* before everyone's eyes. Since the same material is thus presented in two different forms, lazy students seize the opportunity to neglect both: they skip the *spoken* instruction, since they can perfectly well just read the same thing in a book later, while disregarding the instruction to be found in *books*, since they can simply *hear* it in class. The result, a few exceptions aside, is that no one ever learns anything at all, except whatever happens to stick to them as it floats by along one of these two channels. Certainly nothing is learned as a whole, only as these isolated scraps. Recently, the mass of half-educated people that this approach produces has come to hold academic knowledge in deep contempt—after all, it is only something to be acquired to whatever extent one wants and in the easiest possible way.

Now in fact, the more preferable of these two means of instruction is studying books on one's own, since we can freely direct our attention toward a book. We can *reread* any part of the book we first read while distracted; we can reflect on whatever we fail to understand right away, until we reach full understanding; we can read for as long as we feel strong enough, and break off when we run out of energy. The professor at the podium, on the other hand, generally says his piece for his hour without paying any attention to whether anyone is following him, breaks off when his hour is up, and starts up again in the next class and not a moment sooner. The student's position—unable to intervene in the flow of the teacher's speech in any way, or stop it when he needs a pause—generally produces in the young man a painful passivity, an abdication of responsibility, that destroys any impulse to act he might have, and robs him of his ability to make use of the second means of instruction, books, with any self-generated attention either. Continuing to use these *emergency measures* long after the emergency has disappeared—even aside from the public and private expense of this system, and the barbarization of morals that results from it—degrades our capacity to use the *true and better measures* at our disposal.

§3

To be fair, and to avoid being superficial, we must add, however, that modern universities do, to a greater or lesser extent, incorporate another, nobler component of teaching besides merely *repeating* the already existing contents of a book. This is the principle that the teacher should *improve* on the already existing content. There have been independent spirits, in one area of knowledge or another, who were not satisfied with the contents of well-known books until they, as it were, held what was satisfying in those books in their hand, and were able to set that material down again in a new and better book of their own. These independent spirits gave preliminary spoken testimony in the classroom of their struggle for greater perfection, either to use this interaction with others to gain greater inner clarity for the book they planned to write, or, in case they turned out to lack the necessary intellectual power or died in the attempt, in order to leave behind successors and surrogates who could produce the planned book, or maybe an even better one from the same premises.

Still, even taking this component of teaching into account, we must recognize a few undeniable facts about it. It has always played a far smaller role in every university than the kind of book-lecturing described above. No administration has been able to ensure its presence, or even know with any certainty whether it is present at all. And if by good fortune it ever does come into existence somewhere or another, this kind of teaching only rarely operates with a clear recognition of its own efforts and the rules it must follow.

§4

It is superfluous from the start, and harmful in its consequences, to repeat the same thing that can already be found presented far better in another form. The practice should not exist at all. If universities can do nothing else, they should be abolished immediately, and anyone who requires instruction can simply be pointed toward the appropriate books to study. Nor is the nobler kind of teaching mentioned above enough to save these institutions, since there is no specific case (at any existing university) of this nobler component giving an account of itself, nor proving its own existence, nor being in any position to guarantee its continuation—and even if these things were true, the worst part of the university, the mere repetition of book knowledge, would need to be discarded anyway. Just as everything that claims the right to exist must *be* and must *achieve* something that *nothing* besides it could be and do, thereby justifying its continuation in its current form and its undying perpetuation, so too must the university—or, as we provisionally like to say in the classical sense of the word, the *academy*. If it cannot so justify itself, it must perish.

§5

What the academy's higher prerequisite for continued existence might be—and, if the academy should exist at all, what it *must* be—follows directly from the relationship of science and scholarship to actual life.

The point of studying is not, after all, to enable someone to spend his whole life spouting off what he had learned for an exam years before. The point is for him to be able to *apply* what he has learned to the situations and predicaments that come up in life, and thus transform what he has learned into *action*: not merely repeat it but make something else from it and with it. In other words, here as elsewhere, the ultimate goal is not knowledge but the art of using knowledge.

Now, this art of applying academic knowledge in real life presupposes other things, which are foreign to the university: familiarity with life, and practiced judgment in evaluating the situations in which knowledge is to be applied. Our discussion must omit these matters for now. But the following question does belong here: How can scholarship be made into a free and infinitely adaptable possession, a tool we can readily apply to life (even if, naturally, other approaches to understanding life are necessary as well)?

Clearly, scholarship can become such a thing only if we grasp it from the start with a clear and free consciousness. Let me be clear. There is much that takes shape in our minds, or enters into our minds, through a blind mechanism that we ourselves do not perceive. What arises in this way is not permeated with clear and free consciousness; nor do we possess it securely, able to summon it up at any time. Rather, it comes and goes, returns or vanishes, according to the laws of the same hidden mechanism by which it first appeared. On the other hand, what we come to grasp while conscious *that* we are learning it, and conscious *of the rules* by which we are learning it, will thereby become a signature part of our personality and our life, something we are able to develop freely.

This free activity of comprehension is called reason. In the mechanical type of learning discussed above, reason does not come into play at all—only blind nature prevails. When, however, the activity of reason—the specific ways it operates in comprehending something—is *raised into clear consciousness*, the learning process will give rise to an art of judiciously putting reason to use. Artfully developing our consciousness of the act of learning any given thing, despite the distraction it entails from actually learning that thing, results in, over and above what we learn, the formation and development of the *capacity* to learn. I said "despite the distraction it entails from actually learning that thing"; in fact, this effort lets us learn that thing much more fully, since you know things fundamentally and permanently when you also know how you came to know them. By not only learning the given, more or less arbitrary thing, but by learning the art of learning at the same time, and practicing this art upon that given thing—this is how a person develops the *ability* to easily and confidently learn everything else, at will, unto eternity; this is how *artists* of learning are formed. Everything learned or learnable at last becomes a secure possession, with which you can do what you please. The first and necessary condition for the practical art of using scholarship in real life is thereby met. An institution that thoughtfully and systematically develops the consciousness here described, and trains students in the art intended to result from that consciousness, might truly be described as *a school in the art of putting scholarly reason to use.*

Now and then in contemporary universities, more or less by chance, brilliant men may turn up who train students in a given field in the way described above. That said, we have utterly failed even to clearly envision and propose this idea, much less actually put it into practice, in any regular, reliable, and unerringly systematic general way. As a result, the perpetuation and promotion of truly scholarly and scientific education in humankind have been left to good luck and sheer chance. There is only one way to reclaim it and bring it into the domain of clear consciousness: by laying out the concept currently under discussion. What must now be done is implement this concept, bringing the academic system in line with what it should be *sub specie aeternitatis.* And the academy, whose very existence is under attack, would do well to take on this task, since what the academy has hitherto been no longer has any right to exist.

§6

But the academy's claim that it has sole and exclusive responsibility for this task will no doubt be contested by another institution, namely, the secondary academic schools. These, perhaps only now for the first time becoming aware of their true nature, will point out that up until the era of trivializing modern pedagogy, they were better at being *schools in the art of putting scholarly reason to use* than any university. Therefore, the academy must first and foremost redraw the proper boundary between itself and these lower academic schools.

The way to rectify this border to both parties' satisfaction is doubtless along the following lines. The lower school should train students in the art of using the general instrument of communication, language, as well as introduce the general scaffolding and framework of the given content from the edifice of science and scholarship, without critique; the higher academic schools, in contrast, should have as their exclusive domain the art of critique: separating the true from the false, separating the useful from the useless, and subordinating the less important to the more important. Thus the lower school would teach the use of scholarly reason as a mere capacity for comprehension or memorization, while the academy would teach the use of scholarly reason as a faculty of judgment.

§7

The only way to cultivate the art of something is to have the learner do work of his own, following a specific plan of the teacher's and under the teacher's supervision; the learner must methodically practice, step by step, from its first beginnings to total mastery, without skipping any stages, the art in which he will someday become a master. Here, the art to be practiced is the art of putting scholarly reason to use. The teacher merely supplies the material and prompts the student to action; it is the learner himself who must work on the material. The teacher must, however, remain in a position to see whether and how the learner is working on the material, to assess the level of skill he has reached, and to judge accordingly what kind of new material he should be given.

Not only the teacher but also the student must constantly communicate and express himself, turning their reciprocal educational relationship into a continual conversation where every word of the teacher's answers a student's question posed by what has come just before, and presents a new question for the learner to answer in the utterance to follow. The teacher will thus not be addressing an individual he does not know at all, but rather will be speaking to someone who reveals himself to him more and more, to the point of total transparency. The teacher needs to perceive the student's immediate needs, slowing down and expressing himself differently if the student fails to grasp the point, while moving on without delay whenever the student has grasped it. This process transforms academic instruction from a lecture that simply flows along in its channel, just like what already exists in a book, into a dialogue, and a true academy is created—an Academy in the Socratic sense, in whose memory we use the word "academy" in the first place.

§ 8

The teacher, as we have said earlier, must direct his efforts at a specific, known individual whom he keeps always in mind. Now, in cases where, as is only natural, the teacher's audience is not in fact a single person but multiple people, these individuals must merge together into a spiritual and intellectual whole, forming a single organic student body, because the teacher's addressee must remain singular and specific. The students must therefore constantly communicate among themselves as well, continuing their academic interchange, each presenting to all the rest whatever knowledge he has, from the perspective by which he, as an individual, understands it—some of the quickness of the more agile minds rubbing off on the more ponderous ones, and some of the latter's calm gravity onto the former.

§ 9

To clarify my basic concept here with some additional points:

The material that the master gives to those apprenticing in his art will consist in part of his own lectures, in part of printed books that the learner is assigned to study in an artful, well-structured way. The master assigns books because, ultimately, gleaning information from books is a main component of the academic art, and students must be introduced to this art, too. But he also does it simply because the great majority of the scientific and scholarly material at the kind of academy we are describing will necessarily be learned from the books that are to be found there.

The ways in which masters give *themselves* to their students, as it were, are as follows:

Exams, not in the spirit of testing knowledge, but in the spirit of art. In this latter spirit, any question that seeks to makes the test-taker regurgitate what he has heard or read is ill chosen and counterproductive. Instead, the question must presuppose what has been learned, and require an answer that applies this premise to draw some sort of further conclusion.

Konversatoria, in which the student asks questions, and the master asks counterquestions, creating an expressly Socratic dialogue within the invisibly continuing dialogue that constitutes the whole of academic life.

Through the written elaboration of assignments for students to solve, again always in the spirit of art, expecting the student not to repeat what he has learned but to do something else with that knowledge, make something else from it. The purpose, in other words, is to see whether and to what extent the student has made this knowledge his own, a tool for various uses. The obvious person to come up with such assignments is the master, of course, but the advanced student should also be challenged to invent assignments and put them forward for himself or others to complete. This task is good practice in the art of presenting scholarly material in writing, and so the master should evaluate the organization, specificity, and clarity of the presentation as well as the content.[1]

§ 10: On the Students in Such Institutions

The three external prerequisites for creating and sustaining such students are as follows:

1. *Thorough preparation in the lower academic school for the higher school.* We have already seen above (§6) what the lower schools must be expected to accomplish in terms of creating a mind suited to systematic scholarship. Now, if the higher schools are to proceed securely on this basis, the lower schools must have accomplished their task not merely by chance and luck but rather by following a fixed plan, so that it is always clear what has succeeded and what has not. Any improvement in the institutions of higher learning necessarily presupposes an improvement in the lower, while any fundamental improvement in the latter will likewise only be possible by improving the former, since that is where the lower-school teachers will learn the art of teaching, which currently is largely lost. This reciprocity alone shows that we will not be able to resolve everything at one stroke but only approach our goal gradually, in stages.

   To clarify my basic idea here, I would like to add the following. A young man destined for a scholarly life must first of all learn the vocabulary and grammar of the universal language of the academic world, Latin, as the only tool with which he can understand others and make himself understood in turn. This is obvious. However, a positive knowledge of the language, indispensable as it is, is simply an extra benefit to the practice of studying Latin, as becomes clear when we consider the following. (1) Learning the language of another world—one that organizes qualities into word-concepts in an entirely different way—is the best way to transcend the mechanism by which a student's native tongue holds him fast, as though it could never be different, and to introduce him to the free and easy play of concept formation. (2) Interpreting a text teaches the student, on the easiest and most readily available material, how to turn his attention at will, now here and now there, in the service of a goal that he brings to that material, and how not to leave off from his work until that goal has been achieved. It will thus be necessary, in the interest of this relationship between the *lower* and *higher* arts of putting scholarly reason to use, that language instruction in the schools pursue both aims: teaching the historical language, and at the same time forming the student's ability to reason confidently in that language on all topics, and well enough to write clearly. At every stage of instruction, the student must learn to understand, perfectly and completely, what he is supposed to understand, and also learn *how* to know *whether* he has understood it and can prove his understanding. In no way, however, should this be a question of luck and groping around in the dark, as has so often been the case up until now, since often the teacher himself has no true idea of what understanding means, and no sense of the kinds of question that a student would have to answer to show that, say, he has understood a given passage of an author's work.

As for the basic framework of the content of a given scholarly domain—the second piece of necessary preparation that the lower school is responsible for [see §6 ¶2]—let me be clear here as well. Some have argued, in order to sidestep the demands of an artful formation of the mind as laid out in the present essay, that such thorough, deliberate training of a student's intellectual abilities may have been possible in classical antiquity, because the drastically limited extent of the positive knowledge they had to learn left them enough time for such training, but that today our time is taken up entirely with the immense quantity of material that needs to be learned, leaving no time for anything else. As though it were not precisely *because* we have so much more to do with this capacity that a sophisticated training in it is all the more necessary! Given how great a task of learning lies before us, we have to pay all the more attention to our proficiency and agility in learning. Indeed, the only time we fear the immensity of the scientific and scholarly material before us is when we perceive it without an organizing spirit, and without a deliberately trained and thoughtfully practiced art of memory, which is largely enabled by precisely that organizing spirit. Without these capacities, one is plunging blindly into chaos, rushing into the labyrinth without any guiding thread, and losing time with every wandering step, so that the few who are able to swim back to the surface and avoid drowning in this immense ocean look back at the path they have followed and are terrified by the work it took and the luck that brought them this far. Recognizing the gaps in their knowledge that still exist, they believe that what would have helped them was merely more *time*—for they are strangers to the organizing art with which no step is taken in vain, which infinitely multiplies time, and which expands the short span of a human life into an eternity. Once even the lowest school stops considering one boy's good memory a lucky stroke of fate and another boy's more sluggish memory an unavoidable accident of nature, but instead learns how to artfully develop and educate both memory as such and its particular capabilities as appropriate for particular branches of knowledge; once it deposits in this memory thus developed an image of the whole substance of a particular scientific or scholarly topic, compressed and abbreviated but nonetheless clear and vivid, and engraves that image firmly and ineradicably in the student's mind (for example, in the case of history: a general picture of human transformations via the main events in the histories of the ruling peoples, along with geography to give a general picture of the setting where these transformations took place); when the school then calls forth and reinforces these images day after day, and extends them, gradually but proportionately among all their parts, in accord with clear rules about the necessary sequence of *perspectives*, so that no one part grows too large at the expense of the others—once schools do this, the fear of immensity will vanish completely, and the minds thus educated will easily and confidently connect everything they encounter to these basic images that have merged with their own personalities, each in its proper place, not scattered across a trackless ocean but as though filling up the well-trodden rooms of their paternal home with treasures that they can retrieve from where they themselves have put them, whenever the need arises.

The preparation that the student needs to have received from his lower school, the proof he needs to give of his proficiency before he is accepted to a higher school, and the full extent to which the lower schools need to be improved can be summed up in the following two concrete requirements. First, the candidate must learn how to understand completely any passage of text (appropriate to his abilities) presented to him, and must be able to demonstrate within a given time limit that he understands it rightly by showing that it cannot be understood any other way. Second, he must be able to demonstrate that he possesses, and can manipulate and apply at will, a general picture of the substance of all of knowledge, elevated and enriched to the level of the standpoint at which the higher school will begin its instruction.

2. *Devoting his whole life to his scholarly purpose, and thus living entirely separated and isolated from other ways of life.* The son of a middle-class family pursuing a middle-class profession may attend a good secondary civic

school for several hours a day, where some of the same things are taught as in an academic school, but that school is not where his true, real life is lived; he is not, as it were, at home there. His true life is his family life and helping his parents in the family business. School is secondary, a mere means to the real end of further success in the family's middle-class profession. For the scholar, however, scholarship must be not a means to an end but an end in itself. In any case, as a fully formed scholar applying his education in his future life, he will someday live a life rooted solely in the ideal; he will view, shape, and organize reality solely from that standpoint, in no way admitting that the ideal must defer to reality. It is never too early for him to start this life in his proper element and reject its opposite.

It has often been pointed out that a few talented teachers in universities in smaller cities can quite easily produce a general academic tone and spirit among the students, something rarely if ever achieved in bigger cities. I would argue that this is a consequence of students in the first case dealing only with each other and the material they are being taught, whereas in the second case they constantly trickle away into the general mass of middle-class society and are distracted by everything it has to offer. Studying never becomes these students' real life—they never come to feel that there is nothing else they could possibly spend their time doing. Instead, it becomes at best a professional obligation. The common objection to universities in large cities—that students have to travel a long way between lecture halls—is thus not the deepest criticism; in fact, it is negligible compared to the greater evil of dissipating the community of students into the general mass of the bourgeoisie pursuing their businesses or enjoying their crude pleasures. When learning is practiced in this way, as a sideline, little or nothing is actually learned; even aside from that, the whole world is thereby made commercial, and the view of reality that can see beyond mere reality—the only way for humanity to find a cure for all the evils that ail it—is utterly extinguished. Now more than ever, in an age such as ours already at risk of almost universal commercialization, this is a real danger.

3. *Refuge from all external cares by means of support to cover current expenses and a guarantee of appropriate support in future.* Countless minor cares and practical concerns are not appropriate for the life of a student; worrying about one's next meal oppresses the spirit; moonlighting for bread dissipates one's abilities and casts scholarly work as itself a way of earning a living; the slights of the well-to-do because of one's poverty, or the humility one imposes upon oneself to avoid these slights, debase one's character—all these facts are more or less universally acknowledged to be

true, even if they are not always sufficiently taken into account. But let us take a deeper view of the same facts.

It will soon be crystal clear that in a state, and especially among the more high-ranking servants of that state, a certain way of thinking must necessarily take firm root: we must not want to serve society in order to live, but rather live in order to serve society. In this way of thinking, no compassion, no regard for one's own or anyone else's enjoyment of life, will move us to do, suggest, or (where it is possible to prevent) allow anything that is not completely justified on other grounds. But this way of thinking can take root only in a spirit ennobled by the scholarly life. And a powerful preparation for this ennobling, and for independence from such low considerations, comes when future scholars, including, of course, those who will occupy state offices, are acclimated from early youth to see the needs of life not as reasons for a particular action but as things that will take care of themselves. This takes place when support is guaranteed irrespective of the scholar's efforts at any given time—his strivings should, in any case, result solely from his love for the subject.

§ 11: The Nature of, and Necessary Preparation for, Teachers in Such Institutions

First and foremost, of course, since no one can teach what he does not know, the teacher must possess systematic knowledge, and possess it as a free artist able to apply it to any given purpose and reshape it into every possible form, as described above. But even this virtuosity must not simply guide him as it were mechanically, and must not reside in him as an inborn natural talent or gift: here, too, if he is to be able to observe, evaluate, and guide any and every student in this art, he must have penetrated down to its core with clear consciousness, attaining insight into this ability both in general and in the particular forms it takes in various individuals.

But even this clear consciousness and comprehension of the art of knowledge as an organic whole is not enough, because it, too, like all mere comprehension, can be dead—developed only to the point where it takes the form of a historical record in a book. To truly practice his profession, he requires more: the ability to summon up at any time the rule to be applied, and the art of seeing how to apply it anywhere. This is the high degree of clarity and freedom he must attain as an artist of scholarship. Underlying this ability is the art of creating an artist of scholarship, whose first prerequisite is a systematic knowledge of the art of systematic knowledge, which presupposes in turn that he himself possesses this art. This combination and its implications define the true nature of a teacher at a gymnasium dedicated to teaching the art of putting scholarly reason to use.

The art of scholarship rises to such heights only through a love of art.

It is also through this love that the true art of educating artists is continually revived, motivated in each particular case, and directed rightly. Such love, like all love, is of divine origin and genius-like nature, self-created and freely self-perpetuating; from it, certainly and as it were mathematically, follows all the rest of advanced academic education, whereas it itself, the art of educating these artists, cannot be expected from everyone; nor does it condescend to remain if genius in his free flight wings his way elsewhere.

This love nonetheless invisibly propagates itself, and mysteriously excites anyone in its vicinity. Nothing affords greater pleasure than feeling a free and purposefully active spirit, and feeling the growth of this freedom. And so, from this training and the material itself, the life of the learner—the life richest in joy and love—is born.

This love of art is *respectful* of others, and such respect, directed first at the teacher as its primary focus, extends out from the individual to the community of others practicing the same art with him. Each is thereby drawn to the other, and what thus arises is what I called for in §8, although there I postponed the explanation of how it might be possible: mutual communication among all students and the fusion of the individual into a learning organic whole, the kind that can be formed only by these learning individuals.

(This is a communal life of the mind and spirit, in the service of, *at first*, a more rapid, fruitful, and various intellectual development, and *later*, in bourgeois life, the creation of a cohort of businessmen. No longer will the practical man of business see the truly educated man as an odd and disturbing character; nor will the truly educated man in turn see the businessman, usually rightly, as a dullard and practical-minded dud. Rather, they will have long since come to understand each other deeply, in this shared common life, and learned mutual respect. They will be able to proceed in all their deliberations from a common basis, well known to all and controversial to none.)

§ 12

If this art of forming an artist of academic inquiry ever does happen to break through into clear consciousness and flourish in real life to any extent, the question of whether it is to progress and grow to fuller completeness must not be left to blind chance. Rather, this art must find a fixed setting—ideally at the already existing gymnasiums—where it can be thoughtfully maintained with fixed rules and shaped into greater perfection. The gymnasium thereby justifies its continued existence, the way everything truly worthwhile can and should.

As said above, this is the highest level of the scholarly art, demanding the greatest love and the highest preparation and intellectual ability. Clearly, therefore, it cannot be expected from everyone in the way it is required among the few who practice it. But it must be offered to all—the attempt must be made with all—to ensure that this rare talent never goes unused, lost because it was never discovered.

To this end, the student—without, of course, skipping any steps, and only after achieving adequate proficiency in the lower levels of his art—should be made to practice all the duties of a teacher mentioned above, under the same supervision and evaluation from the actual teacher that everyone else at his level has. The teacher had to walk this path alone, helped by no one, groping around in the dark, but the student now traveling the same path under the practiced teacher's guidance, shown and mastering all his tricks and strategies, will doubtless advance much further in the art of clear and skillful teaching than his teacher, and will someday leave behind in turn a still more clear and skillful generation.

(It follows from these considerations that the best such greenhouse for nursing artists of knowledge through all the various stages of mastery of their art would be what one might call a professor-seminar. Let us give it this name. We have had exercises in rhetoric to develop the art of addressing the public; we have had schoolteacher seminars to develop the art of giving lectures in the lower schools; but as far as I know, no one has ever thought to give special training, or exams, in the art of giving an academic lecture—instead, it has been taken as self-evident that a man can say what he knows. This is striking proof that, insofar as any clear consciousness has penetrated into this realm at all, the university is expected to do nothing more than place a second, verbal book-learning alongside the already printed book-learning. With this, our argument returns to its starting point, proof that it has come full circle.)

§ 13: Corollary

The idea outlined up to this point, seen itself as part of the unified whole of systematic knowledge, gives the art of education, or pedagogy, the crowning peak it has hitherto lacked. Another man in our time[2] has found the roots of this pedagogy, which have likewise been lacking until now. The crown makes possible the highest and final school of the academic art; the roots make possible universal general education in popular elementary schools—"popular" meaning not for the mob but for the nation. The trunk of pedagogy, as it were, in the middle, is the academic secondary school.

But the crown rests firmly on the trunk, and the trunk draws its sap of life from the roots; they all live as one, and are assured of continuing in, through, and resting on one another. The same is true of the upper and lower academic secondary schools and the popular lower schools. We have traced out our argument, as best we can in the current circumstances, from our particular and isolated focus—the university—only as far as the secondary schools, with which the universities are most closely in contact, and without whose help we would be unable even to begin appropriately. Similarly, from that starting point, general education will follow its own path as best it can, without our help and without following our lead since we are only pursuing our own destiny. But let us carry on, each striving bravely toward his own goal: someday we will come together and each enter fully into the other's domain, for every part, true only in itself, is part of a greater, eternal whole, which is revealed only with the fusing together of the individual parts. And where we join, poor humankind, now totally helpless, will find succor and salvation—for this salvation depends upon one thing and one thing alone: education being entirely liberated from the hands of blind chance and coming under the shining eye of a deliberate art.[3]

Let this insight—and the consciousness of finding ourselves in a great moment that, if squandered unused, will not easily return again—prompt a sacred gravity and serious attention to our proposals here.

CHAPTER 6

Lectures on the Method of Academic Study*

F. W. J. Schelling

INTRODUCTION TO SCHELLING'S LECTURES

By the first decade of the nineteenth century, German universities were facing not only widespread criticism from writers but also the very real possibility of extinction. Over the course of the eighteenth century, enrollments had declined from 4,400 in 1720 to just under 3,000 in 1800. And this during a period when the population of the German territories almost doubled. These declines were exacerbated by the uneven enrollment patterns across Germany's thirty-nine universities. While institutions in Halle and Göttingen flourished, most other German universities languished, each enrolling on average fewer than a hundred students. By the end of the Napoleonic Wars in Germany, half of all German universities had either closed or had been consolidated with other, larger universities.

But even before Napoleon marched through Berlin in 1806, German critics had long decried declining enrollments, outdated pedagogies, and the slow pace of reform. Although the higher university faculties—the traditional term for law, medicine, and theology—struggled to maintain enrollments, none struggled more than the lower faculty, the traditional term for the philosophy or arts faculty. Philosophy faculties prepared students for study in one of the higher faculties. They were a propaedeutic for students and professors, who sought the higher pay and prestige of a position in one of the higher faculties.

* Excerpt translated from Friedrich J. Schelling, *Vorlesung über die Methode des akademischen Studiums*, in F. W. J. Schelling, *Werke: Auswahl in drei Bänden*, vol. 2 (Leipzig: Fritz Eckardt Verlag, 1907).

Over the course of the eighteenth century, university students began to forgo the philosophy faculty entirely and enroll directly into one of the higher faculties, widely considered more practical and professionally oriented. These enrollment patterns only reinforced the claims of critics that universities should give way to more specialized professional schools.

One of the first German thinkers to confront anxieties about the decline of universities and posit a new vision for their future was F. W. J. Schelling. Along with Fichte and Hegel, Schelling was one of the three towering thinkers of German idealism, a philosophical tradition that took shape in the 1790s and sought to rethink basic concepts such as nature, freedom, and art in the wake of Immanuel Kant's critical philosophy. Like many of his philosophical contemporaries, Schelling was also a university professor with an abiding interest in the past and future of higher education. And like Kant, he was one of the first professional philosophers—that is, he spent his life teaching and writing philosophy as a university professor.

In 1798 Schelling landed his first professorship at the University of Jena, a small university in a small town but home to many of Germany's literary and philosophical giants. Between 1794 and 1810, Friedrich and August Wilhelm Schlegel, Novalis, Friedrich Schleiermacher, Goethe, Schiller, and Alexander and Wilhelm von Humboldt all spent time there. Jena was a hotbed of post-Kantian philosophy and the center of an effort to reimagine the Enlightenment university. Over the course of the 1790s, several Jena professors offered what they referred to as isagogic (from *isagogius*, meaning introductory) lecture courses. Instead of introducing students to the study of the Bible, however, as was traditionally the case, they introduced students to the university—its methods of study and, as Schelling put it, the culture of *Wissenschaft*, or scholarly knowledge.

In his lectures published in 1803 as *The Method of University Study*, Schelling infused his vision for a new type of university with his own philosophical system, which emphasized the underlying unity of knowledge and action, as well as the transformative potential of scholarly knowledge. He juxtaposed a university beholden to the "utility gospel" of the Enlightenment to a future one organized around a community of scholars seeking the unity of all knowledge. The "false and superficial" culture of the Enlightenment, he warned his students and readers, had turned knowledge into an instrument of the state. And a renewed university, with its philosophy faculty and the cultivation of scholarly practices and virtues at its core, was the only institution that could counter these trends.

THE LECTURES

Lecture One: The Absolute Concept of Science

It may not be redundant to explain briefly what prompts me to deliver these lectures. It would doubtless be redundant to linger at length over a general argument that lectures such as this, on the method of university study for the young student, are not only useful but necessary, and beneficial for the rejuvenation and improvement of systematic knowledge itself.

At the start of his university career, the young student enters the world of systematic scholarship and the sciences. The more sense and drive for the whole he has, the less this world can seem to him as anything but a chaos in which nothing can be distinguished, a vast ocean upon which he has been launched without compass or guiding star. Exceptions to this experience—young students whose paths are marked early on by a steady light—are few, and need not be considered here.

The typical consequences are something like this. Better-organized minds dedicate themselves to all possible areas of study in a random, disorganized way, wander around aimlessly without ever penetrating to the core of any particular one (which is the beginning of a well-rounded and continuing education), and at best realize toward the end of their university career how fruitless their efforts have been, how futile their work, and how much they have neglected what was actually essential. Others, made of lesser material, resign themselves early on, surrender to what is simple and undemanding, and at most try to acquire, through mechanical hard work and memorization, whatever from their particular field they think will be necessary for their future lives.

The confusion in which the better student finds himself—concerning not only the method of study but the objects of study as well—often leads him to trust unworthy advisers, who fill him with their own debased ideas about, or even hatred of, systematic knowledge.

It is therefore necessary that universities offer public, general instruction on the purpose and method of university study, both as a whole and with reference to its particular subjects.

There is an additional consideration. In systematic knowledge and art, too, the particular has value only insofar as it can incorporate the universal and absolute. As experience shows, however, it happens all too often that in a particular activity the general pursuit of a universal education is forgotten. In the quest to become a prominent lawyer or doctor, the much higher vocation of the scholar—the mind ennobled by systematic knowledge—is forgotten. One might argue that the study of the more universal sciences [both humanistic and otherwise] is a sufficient antidote to this one-sided education. In general, I am not inclined to deny this; in fact, I would assert it myself. Geometry and mathematics cleanse the mind for a pure rational knowledge that does not need material. Philosophy, which apprehends the whole of the human and touches upon all aspects of his nature, is even better suited to free the mind from the limitations of a one-sided education and raise it into the realm of the universal and absolute. The only problem is, either there is no relationship at all between the more universal science and the particular branch of knowledge to which the individual dedicates himself, or systematic knowledge in its universality cannot lower itself to disclose this relationship, or lower itself far enough. As a result, whoever is unable to recognize this relationship himself feels forsaken by the guidance of the absolute science, at least in respect to particular sciences. He prefers to isolate himself from the living whole intentionally, rather than waste his energy on a futile pursuit of a unity with the whole.

Knowledge of the organic whole of all sciences must therefore precede a particular education focused on a single specialty. Whoever devotes himself to a particular science must first be familiar with the place it occupies in this whole, the particular spirit that enlivens it, and the type of training through which it is connected to the harmonious structure of the whole—in other words, must know how to relate this particular science to himself so as to think not as a slave but as a free man, in the spirit of the whole.

You will see from what has just been said that a doctrine of the method of academic studies can only grow out of real and true knowledge of the living relationships among all the sciences. Without such knowledge, instruction is necessarily dead, mindless, one-sided, and intrinsically limited. Perhaps, though, the demand for such knowledge has never been more urgent than in our present age, when all knowledge and art, even what seems to be most remote in its own realm, appears to be pushing so forcefully toward unity. Every tremor emanating from the center, or from near the center, is transmitted faster and as it were more directly out into all the parts. A new, more universal organ for perception, one for almost all objects, is taking shape.

An age such as ours cannot pass without the birth of a new world that will bury in nothingness those who do not take an active part in it. The preservation and cultivation of something so noble can ideally only be entrusted to the fresh and unspoiled powers of this youthful world. No one is excluded from participating in this process, since there is an element of this universal process of rebirth in any part one might play. In order to participate successfully, a person must, gripped by the spirit of the whole, conceive of his particular science as being a part of the organic whole; must recognize in advance its vocation in the new world being created. Either through himself or through others, he must reach a point where he is not yet fossilized in obsolete forms of thought, where the higher sparks within him have not yet been extinguished by the exercise of his own mental dullness or the effects on him of others'.—In other words, this must happen in his youth; given our current institutions, at the beginning of his university studies.

But how should students obtain such knowledge? Whom should they trust? First and foremost, a student should trust himself and the better genius that guides him with a sure hand. Everyone has an inner friend, whose inspirations are purest in youth; only frivolity scares him off, while an inclination to pursue common goals finally drives him into complete silence. Then, he should trust those who can most clearly be seen to have been brought by their particular science to the highest and most general view of the whole of knowledge. Those who do not themselves possess a general idea of systematic knowledge are surely the least able to awaken it in others; whoever devotes his diligent hard work—laudable as it is, let me add—to a subordinate and limited science is not in a position to rise to an overview of an organic whole. This view in the most general sense may be found only in the systematic study of all knowledge, philosophy, and hence we expect it primarily from philosophers, whose particular field is also the absolutely universal field whose efforts are intrinsically directed toward the totality of knowledge.

These are the observations, gentlemen, that have prompted these lectures, whose intention should by now be clear. As for whether I am able to live up to my idea of what these lectures should be, and thus my intentions in giving them, by adequately giving a preliminary answer to this question, I can only rely on the trust you have always placed in me. I will try to prove myself worthy of it.

Now let me dispense with any further introductory remarks and proceed directly to the central point. Everything else depends on it; without it, we cannot take a single step toward completing our task. This is the idea of a knowledge that is in itself absolute—a knowledge that is simply one, and in which all knowledge is unified. It is a primordial knowledge that splits into different branches and spreads out into the whole immeasurable tree of knowledge only at different stages of the ideal world as it unfolds over time. This, as the knowledge of all knowledge, must be what most perfectly fulfills the requirements and contains the premises that every form of science and scholarship requires and assumes in its own way; it does so absolutely, not just in this or that particular case. Whether this premise is expressed as a correspondence with the object, a pure dissolution of the particular into the universal, or in any other way, it is unthinkable, either in general or in any particular case, without the higher premise that the truly ideal is alone and without any further mediation the truly real. There is no other reality beyond it.

We cannot actually prove this essential unity, even in philosophy, because it is in fact the access point to all systematic knowledge. All that can be proven is that there is no particular science whatsoever without it, and consequently, that anything that claims to be a science must aim at this identity—the complete resolution of the real into the ideal, and conversely, the possibility of completely transposing the ideal into reality.

This premise of identity unconsciously underlies everything that the various sciences trumpet about the universal laws of things or of nature in general in the course of their various pursuits of knowledge. The aim of the sciences is to resolve what is concrete and opaque in particular appearances into pure evidence, into the transparency of universal rational knowledge. This premise is granted as applicable in the more limited spheres of knowledge and in particular cases, even if, universally and absolutely, as expressed in philosophy, it is neither understood nor accepted.

The geometer more or less consciously bases his science on the absolute reality of the purely ideal, for instance when he proves that in every possible triangle the sum of the three angles is 180°—not by directly using actual, specific triangles, nor by comparing them, but rather from their archetypal image. He knows this directly from knowledge itself: the purely ideal and, for that reason, also the simply real. But if we try to limit the question of the possibility of knowledge merely to finite knowledge, then even this type of empirical truth can never be arrived at through any relationship to what is called an object. For how is it possible to arrive at this knowledge other than through knowledge? Thus it would be inconceivable for the ideal in itself, which according to temporal knowledge appears only in finite form, not to be itself the reality and substance of things.

Even this first premise of all sciences, however—the essential unity of the unconditioned ideal and the unconditioned real—is possible only because these two things are the *same*. This identity, though, is the idea of the absolute. That is to say: with respect to the absolute, the *idea* is also *what is*. Thus the *absolute* is the highest premise of knowledge; it is primary knowledge itself.

All other knowledge is in the absolute, and is itself absolute, through this first knowledge. For even though in the beginning originary knowledge in its perfect absoluteness resides only in this first knowledge, as the absolute-ideal, we then picture it as the essence of all things and the eternal concept. Our knowledge in its totality is defined as a likeness of this eternal knowledge.

Clearly, I am not speaking of particular sciences insofar as they are detached from this totality and thus separated from their true originary image. It is only knowledge in its entirety that can be the perfect reflection of that paradigmatic knowledge. Still, all individual instances of knowledge and all particular sciences are understood to be organic parts of this whole. All knowledge, therefore, that is not directly or indirectly (through however many intermediaries) related to originary knowledge lacks reality and meaning.

The capacity to see how everything, even individual instances of knowledge, connects with the originary and the unitary depends on whether one works in a particular science with spirit, and with that inspiration from a higher source that we call scientific genius. Every thought not conceived in this spirit of unity and universality is intrinsically empty and worthless. Whatever cannot be harmoniously included in this living, striving whole is dead matter that, in accord with organic laws, will sooner or later be expelled. In the realm of systematic knowledge, too, there are of course plenty of sterile worker bees who, since reproduction is denied to them, duplicate their own spiritlessness in multiple copies through inorganic extrusions.

Having formulated this idea of the destiny of all knowledge, I have nothing more to add about the dignity of systematic knowledge as such. In what follows, I will derive solely from this idea any standard that I will present for the cultivation or reception of systematic knowledge in itself.

Writers of the history of philosophy say that Pythagoras was the first to transform *sophia*, or wisdom, which had been the name for his particular science current until then, into *philosophia*, the love of wisdom. He did this, they say, on the grounds that no one except God is wise. However much historical truth this account may or may not have, the change itself and the reason given are signs of recognition that all knowledge is a striving toward communion with the divine being, toward participation in the originary knowledge whose image is the visible universe and whose birthplace is the head of the eternal power. According to this view, all knowledge is one, and every kind of knowledge enters into the organic whole as a mere component part. All individual sciences and all kinds of knowledge are parts of the one philosophy, namely, the striving to partake in this originary knowledge.

Now, everything that grows directly from the roots of the absolute is itself absolute. It does not have an external purpose; it is its own purpose. In its universality, however, knowledge is the one, likewise absolute, appearance of the one universe; Being or Nature is the other. In the realm of the real, finitude rules; in the realm of the ideal, infinity rules. The former is what it is by necessity;

the latter should be what it is through freedom. The human being, the rational creature as such, is placed into the world to supplement its becoming: what is lacking in the totality of God's revelation should unfold from him and from his activity. Nature contains the whole of the divine being, but only in the real; the rational creature, the human, should express the image of this same divine nature as it is in itself, namely as ideal.

There is a common objection to this claim of the unconditioned nature of scholarship and science, one that I will here express in terms higher than those we usually see it in. Namely: knowledge is only a part of that representation of the absolute understood as infinite. It is only a means, whose end is action.

Action! Action! is the call that rings out from all sides. But it resounds the loudest from those who would prefer not to proceed with knowledge.

Such a call to action has much to recommend it. Everyone, we think, can act, because action requires only free will. Knowledge, on the other hand, especially philosophical knowledge, is not for everyone. Even with the best will, one cannot attain it without other qualifications.

But let us ask the following, in response to the previous objection: What kind of action is it for which knowledge is a means, and what kind of knowledge is it for which action is the end?

What can we see as the basis for even the possibility of such an antithesis?

Even if only philosophy can shed a full light from all sides on the propositions I will suggest here, that does not prevent them from being comprehensible for the present purposes. Whoever has even generally grasped the idea of the absolute will also recognize that only one basis for this alleged antithesis can be thought within it: if oppositions can be conceived as deriving from it at all, then they must derive from this one reason.

The nature of the absolute is this: the absolutely ideal is also real. In this definition lie two possibilities: first, that the ideal absolute unfolds its essence in specific real forms; second, that form dissolves into essence again, in eternally the same way, so that essence and form completely permeate each other, because the form of the essence can only be an absolute form. The one and only action of originary knowledge must be one of these two possibilities. Since this knowledge is intrinsically indivisible, however—since it is utterly and completely both reality and ideality—there must be an expression of this indivisible duality in every act of absolute knowledge. That which appears in the whole as the real, and that which appears in it as the ideal, are one and the same. For instance, just as in nature (the image of the divine transformation of ideality into reality), reality is also changed back into ideality and perfected through the light of reason, so too must we also find, in that which is conceived in the whole as the ideal, both a real and an ideal aspect, in which the former is the ideality in reality, while the latter, as ideal, reveals the opposite kind of unity. The first type of phenomenon is knowledge, to the extent that subjectivity appears in it as objectivity; the second type of phenomenon is action, to the extent that in it the particular is thought to be taken up into the universal.

Grasping this relationship, even in these abstract terms, is enough to let us show that the antithesis of knowledge and action within the single identity of originary knowledge is a contradiction only for a merely finite understanding. For it is self-evident that, if this original knowledge is the infinite conforming to the finite in ideal terms, action is likewise how the finite conforms to the infinite. Each of these expresses the same absolute unity of originary knowledge, either in the idea or in being-in-itself.

Temporal knowledge, like temporal action, posits in a merely conditional, sequential way what is posited unconditionally and simultaneously in the Idea. Therefore, knowledge and action appear necessarily separated in the former, while they are equally absolute and thus necessarily one in the latter. Likewise, in God, the Idea of all ideas, absolute wisdom is at the same time unconditional power as a direct result of the fact that it is absolute. The idea does not precede action as an intention that determines it; accordingly, such action is at the same time absolute necessity.

It is the same with these oppositions as with all others: they are oppositions only insofar as each component part is grasped not absolutely but merely with finite understanding. The basis of the antithesis above is thus merely an imperfect conception of knowledge and of action. This conception must be elevated for knowledge to be conceived of as a means to action. Knowledge cannot have such a relationship to truly absolute action, because such action, being absolute, is not determined by any knowledge. This same unity, in knowledge, also develops in action into an absolute, self-contained world. I am not speaking here of concrete phenomena of action, just as I am not speaking of concrete phenomena of knowledge. Each stands and falls with the other, for each has reality only in opposition to the other.

Those who make knowledge a means and action an end have no other conception of knowledge besides what they have derived from their own daily affairs, in which knowledge must indeed conform to being a means in the service of action. Philosophy should teach them to do their duty in life; this is why they need philosophy. They live in accord with duty not out of free necessity but out of obedience to a concept that a particular science hands them. In general, a science should tell them how to farm their field, improve their trade, or make their spoiled wine drinkable again. Geometry, they think, is a beautiful science, not because it is the purest evidence for, the most objective expression of, reason itself, but rather because it teaches them how to measure fields and build houses, and makes merchant shipping possible; true, geometry also serves the waging of war, and this lowers its value, because after all war is directly opposed to universal human love. Since philosophy is not even good for any of these former practical purposes, and is at best good for the latter, namely, waging war against shallow minds and the apostles of utility in science, philosophy is thus fundamentally worthless.

Those who cannot grasp the meaning of the absolute unity of knowledge and action raise such vulgar objections as: if knowledge were one with action, action would always follow from knowledge; but it is perfectly possible to know what is right and fail to do it; and so on. They are right to say that action does not follow from knowledge, and in so doing they even refute the claim that knowledge is a means to action. But they are wrong to expect such a result. They do not understand the relationships between absolutes—how each one in particular can be unconditioned in itself—and they make knowledge dependent in its relation to the end, action, as much as they make action dependent in its relation to the means, knowledge.

Knowledge and action can never be in true harmony other than through equal absoluteness. Just as there is no true knowledge that is not directly or indirectly the expression of originary knowledge, so too can there be no true action that does not express, through however many intermediaries, originary action and the divine being within it. The freedom one seeks, or believes one finds, in empirical action is just as little true freedom and, thus, just as much an illusion as the truth one finds in empirical knowledge. There is no true freedom other than through absolute necessity—freedom has to be integrated with necessity. And there is the same relationship between this freedom and this necessity as between absolute knowledge and absolute action. It is thus freedom, i.e., action itself, that creates necessity, just as conversely only a truly absolute knowledge possesses both absolute necessity and absolute freedom.

Lecture Two: The Intellectual and Moral Vocation of the University

The concept of university study has, on the one hand, pointed us back to the higher concept of an already existing unity of knowledge, which we tried to grasp in its highest ideal form, that is, as originary knowledge. On the other hand, it leads us onward to the specific conditions under which particular sciences are taught and communicated in our universities.

It may well seem more worthy of a philosopher to sketch out a picture of the whole of the sciences and of the way we first come to know that picture in and of itself, irrespective of the forms of merely contemporary institutions. Except I believe I can prove in what follows that precisely these forms arose of necessity in the modern age. Or at least that the external conditions for the reciprocal interpenetration of the distinct elements of their development will remain, until this interpenetration refines the cloudy mixture of these elements into more beautiful compounds.

The previous lecture established why knowledge, as it appears to us, exists in time. Just as the unity of the ideal and the real reflected in the finite is expressed in space as a closed totality, as Nature, so too does this unity, viewed in the infinite, appear in the universal form of endless time. But time does not exclude the infinite; in fact, systematic knowledge, even if it is a product of time in its apparent form, still aims to establish an eternity within time. The true, like the beautiful and the just, is eternal by nature. It is in the flow of time, but it has no relation to time. The unity of knowledge is temporal only insofar as it is expressed by the individual. Knowledge as such, however, is just as little a matter of individuality as action as such. Just as true action is that which could be performed in the name of the whole human race, so too is true knowledge that in which it is not the individual who knows, but Reason that knows. The fact that the unity of knowledge is a matter of the species, which is eternal, expresses the fact that it is independent of time.

It is therefore necessary for the unity of knowledge, like life and existence, to be communicated from individual to individual, generation to generation. Tradition is the expression of its eternal life. This is not the place to argue that all the science and art of today's humanity has been passed down—the arguments are readily available. It is inconceivable that the human being, as he now appears, could have raised himself up on his own from instincts to consciousness, from animality to rationality. There must therefore have been a different human race preceding the present one, which ancient legends have fixed in images of the gods and humanity's first benefactors. The hypothesis of an originary people gives a rough explanation for the traces of a high culture in a world before ours, a culture whose corrupt remains we discover after the first separation of peoples, as well as for the agreement between the myths and legends of various ancient peoples, if we do not want to attribute anything to a common world-spirit innate to all of humankind. But it cannot explain the *first* beginning. Like every empirical hypothesis, it simply pushes the explanation farther back in time.

Be that as it may, we know that actions, forms of life, practices, and symbols were the first means of communicating higher ideas to future generations. The dogmas of the earliest religions, for example, were embodied only in the instructions of religious practice. The states, laws, and individual institutions that were established to maintain the predominance of the divine principle in humanity—to help in its battle against the ungodly—were likewise inherently just so many expressions of speculative ideas. The invention of writing at first merely gave the tradition greater security; it reduced the danger of forgetting the meaning of the symbols. The idea of setting down in the spiritual material of language an expression of form and art that itself had lasting value could emerge only later.

During the golden age of humanity, just as morality itself was not for the individual but was instead the spirit of the whole out of which it flowed and into which it flowed back, so too did science live in the light and ether of public life and a general social structure. And later times, just as they thoroughly repressed the real and made life more inward, did the same with science. The modern world, which exists in both the past and the present, is a divided world—in everything, but especially with respect to science. Every particular science now demands that this later age must proceed from historical knowledge; it thereby expresses a belief that we have a lost world of the greatest and most splendid forms of science and art behind us, separated from us by an insurmountable gulf, a mass of barbarism. The only bond that connects the modern world with this lost world is external: historical tradition. There is no internal connection, no organically progressing development from one world to the other.

In the first rebirth of the sciences in our part of the world [i.e., in the Renaissance], the drive to renewal could not calmly or exclusively concern the productions of science itself, but could only aim at understanding, admiring, and explaining the wonders of the past. Alongside the original objects of knowledge, in other words, past knowledge about them was added as a new object of knowledge. Thus, because a penetrating exploration of what exists demands a self-aware spirit, the ideas of scholar, artist, and philosopher became synonymous. Even those who had not contributed any of their own thoughts to what already existed were recognized as scholars. If the Greeks, as an Egyptian priest once said to Solon, were eternally young, the modern world was, in contrast, already old and experienced even in its youth.

The study of the sciences in their historical development, like that of the arts, has become a kind of religion. The philosopher sees in their respective histories the still-undiscovered intentions of the world spirit, so to speak. The most profound science, the most rigorous genius has squandered itself in such knowledge.

To the movements of the external world correspond, according to necessary laws, the quieter but not therefore any less profound metamorphoses of the human mind. To believe that intellectual transformations, the revolutions of the sciences, the ideas that they produce, the works themselves in which a particular scholarly, scientific, or artistic mind has expressed itself are without necessity, do not happen according to law, but are merely accidental—that is the highest barbarism. Antiquity is and shall be eternally sacred. It is an act of piety to make a pilgrimage to the remains of classical antiquity, to the world of the past, the same way it is in religion when the devout innocent seeks out the purported relics of a saint. Diligently, Goethe writes:

> Diligently the pilgrim marches. Will he find the saint?
> Hear and behold the man who performed these miracles?
> No, time has carried him off; you will find preserved
> Mere remains, a few of his bones, his skull.
> Such pilgrims are we all, seeking Antiquity;
> We pay homage, faithful and happy, to mere scattered bones.

To make the past itself into an object of scholarship or science, however, is something altogether different from putting knowledge of the past in the place of knowledge itself. Historical knowledge in this latter sense forecloses access to the original, primary image; it no longer asks whether something accords with true knowledge, but only whether it corresponds with some derivative knowledge, a mere imperfect copy. Aristotle, in his writings on natural science and natural history, was concerned with nature itself; in later times, the memory of such an approach was so thoroughly lost that Aristotle himself took the place of the primary image and his authority was invoked against the clear claims of nature as made by Descartes, Kepler, and others. As a result of this same kind of historical education, many so-called scholars today feel that no idea has meaning and reality until it has passed through other heads and become historical, a thing of the past.

It was more or less in this spirit of historical knowledge that our universities were established, perhaps not so much during the first rebirth of literature as later. Their entire academic organization can be completely derived from this separation of knowledge from its originary image through historical scholarship. Initially, the enormous quantity of what had to be learned, simply in order to possess what there was to know, was what made people split up knowledge into so many different branches, as distinct as possible, and thereby unravel the living, organic structure of the whole into the tiniest possible strands. Since every isolated part of knowledge, i.e., each particular science insofar as the universal spirit has been drained away from it, can only be a vehicle of absolute knowledge, the necessary consequence of this dismemberment of knowledge was that *knowledge itself* was basically lost through its methods and institutions of education. While a busy crowd held the various means to be the end of knowledge itself, and tried to make them serve as an end, that which is singular and absolute in its unity withdrew completely into the highest parts of knowledge. Only on occasion did it appear in its full, unrestrained life.

The question in this regard is as follows: Given these historical constraints and the present form of our universities, what can we ask of them, so that a unity may once again emerge from this thorough fragmentation of knowledge into the particular?

I will not be able to answer this question without also discussing the necessary requirements for those who permanently constitute a university—its teachers. Here, with *you*, I will not shy away from speaking with complete candor on the topic. The young man's entrance into university life is also his first entrance into maturity and his first emancipation from blind faith. It is here that he is supposed to first learn, and then practice, how to make judgments for himself. No teacher worthy of his calling will want to be respected except on the basis of his intellectual superiority, his level of scholarly or scientific learning, and his zeal to share the latter more generally. Only an ignorant, incompetent teacher would aim for respect based on other factors. The following observation can only reinforce my resolution to speak unreservedly on this topic: whether the claims that students make of the university and its teachers are fulfilled depends in part on what those claims are, and once the scientific spirit is awakened within the students, it has an advantageous effect on the whole, by scaring off the incapable through the higher demands made on them, and by inspiring those capable of fulfilling the call to embrace this sphere of activity.

It is no objection to the demand that we treat all the sciences in the spirit of a universal and absolute knowledge, a demand that derives from the idea of the subject itself, to ask where the teachers capable of achieving this are supposed to come from. Universities, after all, are the places where teachers acquire their first education. If they were given intellectual freedom and not limited by considerations that had nothing to do with science, they would naturally become teachers on their own, teachers who could meet these demands and be able to educate others in turn.

One might also ask whether it is right to make demands of the university in the name of systematic knowledge at all, given that, as is generally known and accepted, universities are instruments of the state and must be whatever the state designs them to be. If the state wants scholarship and science always to observe a certain moderation and restraint, and focus exclusively on the ordinary and the practical, then how can we expect from teachers a progressive inclination or a desire to develop their particular science according to ideas?

Of course, we commonly assume, and must assume, that the state does want its universities to be actual institutions of scholarship and science. Everything we are arguing about universities is valid only under this assumption. No one denies that the state has the right to dissolve universities completely, or turn them into business, professional, or other such training schools. But it cannot want these scientific institutions without also wanting the life of ideas and the freest possible circulation of scholarly and scientific ideas, the lack of which is usually due to the pettiest concerns, most often intended solely to reassure incompetent teachers. Genius is rebuffed, talent crippled.

The usual view of universities is that "they should educate those who serve the state to be perfect instruments of its intentions." These instruments, though, should without question be formed through systematic knowledge. If this is the goal of education, then one must want systematic knowledge as well. But scholarship and the sciences cease to be systematic knowledge as soon as they are reduced to being a *mere* means and not fostered for their own sake. Systematic knowledge for its own sake will definitely not be fostered, however, if, for instance, ideas are rejected when they are useless in everyday life, have no practical application, or play no role in our experience of the world. This may well be the case, especially with respect to experience as it currently exists, or rather, as it is taken to be nowadays because of the neglect of all ideas. In such a context, this understanding cannot correspond to ideas. True, actual experience must first be defined through ideas. Experience is certainly good and valuable, if it is *genuine* experience, but what constitutes genuine experience and what is thereby actually experienced—those are the big questions. Newtonian optics, for example, is supposedly based completely in experiences and perception, and yet, in both its basic conception and its further corollaries, it is obviously false, as soon as one possesses first and foremost the *idea* of light. Similarly, the supposed experience of doctors may in some points contradict a true theory deriving from ideas. However, when the doctor himself first constructs the symptoms of a disease and then passes them off as the spontaneous effects of nature, this is not a pure experience. Instead, if the doctor had treated the sickness from the first in accordance with the proper medical views, that is, those derived from ideas, then these symptoms would never have appeared to him—he would never count them among his experience at all, or at least would see in them no contradiction to the true theory. What Kant says about practical ideas goes for theoretical ideas as well: there is nothing more harmful and undignified than the appeal to experience, which would not even exist at all were it defined from the start with better notions and not with crude concepts. This concludes my digression.

External completeness in no way produces a true, organic, total life in all the parts of knowledge, but such an organic whole is what universities should produce, as their name itself suggests. This requires the life-principle of the communal spirit that comes from absolute science, of which the individual sciences should be the instruments or the objectively real aspects. I cannot elaborate on this view here, but clearly I am not proposing an application of philosophy, which has been incrementally attempted in nearly every field, even those that treat the basest objects. Agriculture, obstetrics, bandaging—all have essentially tried to make themselves "philosophical." There is nothing sillier, and more ridiculous to philosophers themselves, than the efforts of lawyers and doctors to clothe their field of knowledge in philosophical garb while they remain ignorant of the basic principles of philosophy. It is like trying to measure a sphere, cylinder, or other solid without even knowing Euclid's first proposition.

What I mean to address is the formlessness in most of the objective sciences. They have not an inkling for art or even the logical rules of thinking, and cannot rise above the particular and lift themselves out of this stupor with any amount of thought. Nor are they capable of imagining that they also have to represent that which is not simply physical, the universal, in their particular material.

Only the universal as such is the source of ideas, and ideas are the lifeblood of systematic knowledge. Anyone who knows his particular field only as particular, and can neither recognize the universal in it nor make it a form of universal-scientific culture, is unworthy of being a teacher and guardian of the sciences. He can make himself useful in many ways: as a physicist who makes lightning rods, as an astronomer who makes calendars, as a doctor who uses galvanism to treat illnesses, or in whatever other way he wants. But the calling of the teacher demands more than the talents of craft. "Staking out the fields of the sciences," Lichtenberg[1] says, "may be very useful for partitioning them among *farmers*, but *philosophers*, who always have the context of the whole in view, are warned at every step by their reason, which strives toward unity, to pay no attention to these stakes in the ground, which were often driven merely for the sake of comfort and restriction." Doubtless it was not his particular skill in his science, but rather his ability to penetrate it with the ideas of a mind trained to universality, that made Lichtenberg the most intelligent physicist of his time and the most superb teacher in his field.

Here I must touch on a notion that is common among those who are required to treat their particular field in the spirit of the whole, namely, that they are being asked to treat it *merely* as a means to an end. Just the opposite is true. The demand is that they practice their particular science in the spirit of the whole, and in so doing consider it as an end in itself and as independent and absolute. It is intrinsically impossible to conceive of anything as a part of a true totality if it is simply a means. Every state is perfected by each individual member, a means to the whole, being also at the same time an end in itself. Precisely because the particular is inherently absolute, it is also in the absolute and is an integral part of the absolute, and vice versa.

The more a scholar conceives of his particular area of study as an end in itself, even treating it as the center of all knowledge, the midpoint he would like to expand to an all-encompassing totality that reflects the whole universe, the more he will strive to express ideas and universals in that area of study. In contrast, the less he is able to conceive of his area of study in a universal sense, the more he will think of it merely as a means, consciously or not, because that which is not an end in itself can only be a means. And any self-respecting person will quite rightly find this intolerable. Such narrow-mindedness is usually associated with a base disposition and the lack of any *true* interest in systematic knowledge, except as a means for very real, concrete, external purposes.

I know full well that many people, especially those who conceive of science only in terms of utility, see the university merely as an institution for the transmission of knowledge, as a kind of club whose only goal is to teach every young man what has been accomplished in the sciences up to his day. In this view, it can only be considered an accident if the teacher does more than communicate what already exists and enriches the sciences through discoveries of his own. But even granting that universities aim for nothing more, and should aim for nothing more, it is still acknowledged as necessary for them to transmit this knowledge with spirit. Otherwise, there is no way to understand the need for live university lectures—the young student could simply be directed to the comprehensive textbooks written especially for him, or the thick compendia available in all fields. A spirited passing down of tradition, however, certainly requires that the teacher be in a position to comprehend the discoveries of others from past and present, and do so properly, sharply, and in all their interrelations. Many of these discoveries are of the sort whose innermost spirit can only be grasped by a similar genius, through actual rediscovery. Someone who merely passes along knowledge will thus, in many instances in a range of sciences, pass it along entirely wrongly. Where, for example, is the historical account of ancient philosophy, or of a single ancient or even modern philosopher, that could be confidently judged to be successful, true, and adequate to its object?

In general, however, whoever lives in his particular science as though in a foreign land, whoever does not personally possess it, has not acquired a sure and living organ for it, is unable to even begin to produce it anew from within himself at any moment—he is an unworthy teacher, and even in trying to transmit the thoughts of the past or the present merely historically, he goes beyond his own limitations and undertakes something he can never achieve. Without question, the spirited transmission of knowledge is bound up with judgment; but if even a comprehensive and proper grasp of others' discoveries is impossible without the capacity to produce one's own ideas, then is not judgment still more impossible? So many people in Germany pass judgment of whom it is fair to say that if you stood them on their heads, not a single thought would fall out. But that proves nothing. Such judgments certainly do not serve systematic knowledge.

The necessary consequence of someone's inability to construct the whole of his particular science from out of himself and to represent it based on vital inner intuition is the mere historical exposition of it. These are all too well known in philosophy: "When we direct our attention to ourselves, we become aware of different manifestations of what we call the soul. These various effects have been referred back to different faculties. These faculties have been called, in different terminologies, sensation, understanding, imagination, etc."

Nothing is more soulless, more soul-killing, than such a presentation. Moreover, it is the particular vocation of the university lecture to trace the emergence of things. Herein lies the true advantage of live instruction: the teacher does not provide results, like a writer, but rather, in all higher sciences at least, he shows how these results can be reached and in each particular case allows the whole of science to emerge before his students' eyes. Now, how can someone unable to reconstruct his particular science on his own present it, not as something given, but as something to discover?

To be an effective and successful teacher, someone must do more than merely pass along knowledge without any independent intellectual activity of his own. It is obviously just as important to have studied as much as possible in the field he wants to teach. In any art, even the most common craft, a person must first give proof that he has completed his apprenticeship before he can practice as a master. When we consider how easy it is for some people to acquire a professorship at certain universities, though, we would say that no other calling is easier than that of a teacher. And as a rule, it would be wrong to take a drive to produce one's own work as a good reason for rapid promotion to a professorship, because it is precisely those who are in a position to produce most quickly who can least afford to teach.

So far, we have explored how universities could be constituted simply in order to fulfill the intentions with which they were established. It appears, however, that because of the one-sidedness of the idea that originally informed them, they have further to go. According to this original idea, they are institutions established simply for *knowledge.*

Since we do not grant the validity of any oppositions, e.g., that between knowledge and action, it is universally necessary in any relationship where something is opposed to something else that as the former approaches absoluteness, the opposition itself is lifted. So if universities, as the greenhouses of scholarship and science, have not yet begun to be universal institutions of culture, this is simply because of the crudeness of knowledge. It is necessary here also to touch on the constitution of universities insofar as it has an essential influence on their ethical purpose.

If bourgeois society presents a clear disharmony between the ideal and reality, that is because, for the time being, it is pursuing completely different ends than those that derive from the ideal, and because the means have become so powerful that they undermine the very purpose for which they were invented. Universities, because they are nothing but associations for the sciences, need nothing (other than what the state voluntarily and self-interestedly provides for their external needs) to support their real existence besides what derives from the Idea itself. Here, wisdom and prudence are one: we have only to do what the idea of an association for science prescribes anyway in order to perfect the constitution of a university.

As long as bourgeois society continues to pursue empirical ends to the detriment of the absolute, it will have only an apparent and forced identity, not a true inner identity. Universities have only an absolute purpose: they can have none other. In order for the state to achieve its aims it needs distinctions, not arising from class differences but rather from internal ones, arising from the separation and confrontation of individual talents, the suppression of the range of personalities and the direction of their powers in various, very different directions to make them better instruments of the state. In a scholarly or scientific association, all members have, by the nature of the thing, a single purpose; in universities, the only thing that *should* count is scholarship and science, and there *should be* no other distinction except those of talent and education. People who are there merely to act in some other way—by wasting their money, wasting their time on mindless pleasures, in a word being the same kinds of privileged idler as can be found in middle-class society (and typically it is such people who are responsible for most of the crudeness at universities)—such people should not be tolerated. Anyone who cannot prove his industriousness and deliberate commitment to science should be expelled.

Where systematic knowledge alone rules and all minds are possessed by it alone, nothing else can lead astray the urges of the young—so noble and glorious, and preferring in any case to be directed toward ideas. Where crudeness has been the rule in universities, and if it once again gains the upper hand, this is primarily the fault of teachers, or those responsible for supervising the spirit that teachers disseminate. If teachers were to disseminate nothing but the true spirit and had no concern for anything but knowledge and its advancement, and if outbreaks of rowdiness among unworthy teachers who disgrace their calling were not tolerated by a community that is itself base, then the students unable to distinguish themselves except by their crudeness would leave on their own.

The realm of the sciences is not a democracy, even less an oligarchy. It is an aristocracy, in the noblest sense of the word. The best should rule. Those who lack any ability, whom nothing recommends but convenience—these pushy windbags who dishonor the scientific estate with their petty little efforts should be kept entirely inactive. No one unaided can avoid the disdain he deserves because of his ignorance and mental impotence; in fact, since such qualities usually go with ridiculousness and genuine villainy, such people are a joke to the young. They merely wear out much too early the natural feeling of disgust in these inexperienced minds.

Talent needs no special protection as long as its opposite is not promoted. The power of ideas itself will have the highest and most decisive effect.

This is the only policy needed to make all institutions of systematic knowledge flourish, to give them the greatest possible dignity within and prestige without. In order to make universities in particular models of organization, nothing is required other than what one categorically cannot avoid wanting anyway (without falling into contradiction). And because, as stated, I refuse to admit any gulf between knowledge and action, I cannot allow it in reference to universities in these circumstances.

The education that produces rational thinking—by which, of course, I mean not a merely superficial habituation but a process of cultivation that involves the very essence of a human being—is the only genuine scientific one, and thus the only one for rational action. Purposes that lie beyond this absolute sphere of scientific training are excluded from universities by definition.

Whoever has progressed from his particular science through a complete education to absolute knowledge is automatically raised into the realm of clarity and rationality. The most dangerous thing for a person is for obscure concepts to dominate. Curtailing them already gains a great deal; everything is gained when he has pushed through to absolute consciousness, when he walks completely in light.

Systematic knowledge leads the mind directly toward a lasting formation of the self, the worldview that leads directly to self-identity and thus a genuinely blessed life. Life and experience provide this education gradually, and not without much loss of time and strength. Whoever dedicates himself to science can anticipate this life-experience and recognize in himself from the start what is ultimately the result of the most thoroughly cultivated and richly experienced life.

CHAPTER 7

On Germany's Educational System*

Wilhelm von Humboldt

INTRODUCTION TO HUMBOLDT'S TEXTS

In 1808 the German statesman, bureaucrat, and scholar Wilhelm von Humboldt was recalled from his post in Rome as Prussian ambassador and appointed head of the newly established Section for Culture and Public Education, which had been charged with modernizing the Prussian educational system. Although in office for less than two years, Humboldt transformed a fledgling educational reform effort into a vision that would have a lasting effect on the modern research university. In a flurry of memoranda, letters, and bureaucratic maneuvering, he consolidated over a half century's worth of educational and scholarly reforms in Germany, such as those introduced by his alma mater, the University of Göttingen, into a clear and, as it would turn out, highly portable argument for the necessity of the university in a modern age characterized by increasing state demands and increasingly accessible forms of information. And he did so against pointed arguments that the very idea of a university was a medieval relic. The university's guildlike character belonged to another, now lost time when the dominant power was the church, not the state. In response to these doubts as to whether an institution of higher learning should be established in Berlin, Humboldt and his contemporaries imagined the university anew. In a modernity defined by professional specialization, social fragmentation, and the collapse of epistemic

* Excerpts translated from Wilhelm von Humboldt, "Über die innere und äussere Organisation der höheren wissenschaftlichen Anstalten in Berlin" and "Antrag auf Errichtung der Universität Berlin, 12–14 Mai 1809," in *Wilhelm von Humboldts Gesammelte Schriften,* vol. 10, ed. Königlich Preussischen Akademie der Wissenschaften (Berlin: B. Behr, 1903).

authority, the university, they argued, was the only institution that could both produce and translate knowledge for the good of scholarship and society.

Humboldt and his Prussian colleagues, the theologian and philologist Friedrich Schleiermacher foremost among them, framed their arguments for a uniquely German university in Berlin, in part, in opposition to Napoleon's educational reforms in France. After his rise to power in the 1790's, Napoleon had transformed French universities into specialized academies designed to produce efficient bureaucrats for the state. After Napoleon's military victories in the German territories and the resulting suspension of instruction at Halle, Prussia's flagship university, there was a new receptiveness to investing in an institution that seemed distinctively German and promised to foster innovative thinking. In 1807, when a delegation of professors from shuttered Halle visited Friedrich Wilhelm III and enjoined him to support a new university, he is supposed to have said: "The state must replace through intellectual powers what it has lost in the way of physical ones."

But if some of the impetus for reform was new, the ideas behind Humboldt's proposals for a new university were not. They were a compelling synthesis of an ongoing debate about the purpose of universities and their relationship to the state. Humboldt's historical accomplishment was to craft an argument for the social value of an institution dedicated to the creation and transmission of a particular kind of knowledge, one that met certain standards of authority and moral worth, while also serving the needs of society. The university, he contended, should consider but not be subordinate to the needs of the state or the church.

If there is a single text that has come to be associated with the *German* research university, it is Humboldt's "On the Internal Structure of the University in Berlin and its Relationship to Other Organizations," written most likely in 1809. And this is particularly ironic, since this ur-text—alluded to and cited by university presidents worldwide in almost ritual fashion—was not published until 1896. The original manuscript was also a fragment; the text breaks off in almost midsentence.

Over eighty years after the University of Berlin was founded, a German scholar named Bruno Gebhardt, who was writing a biography of Humboldt as a statesman, discovered the manuscript and published it as an appendix to his own book. Almost immediately, this short, syntactically complex fragmentary text was embraced by German academics and intellectuals as the founding text of the modern university, espousing the underlying principles of *the* modern research university: the integration of teaching and research, academic freedom, and the infinite, unending nature of academic inquiry.

In the text itself, a memorandum proposing an organizational structure not just for a new university but for related institutions as well, Humboldt offers a concise vision for a modern German educational system, its goals, its structure, and the place of the university within it. This vision is built around the claim that the university should not be an institution unto itself; instead, it should be the center of a unified system of education and knowledge creation in which all institutions of knowledge—from elementary and secondary schools to libraries, museums, and academies—function as a whole. The modern research university, as Humboldt envisioned it both in his memorandum and in his more official "Request for the Establishment of the University of Berlin," would be at the center of a modern culture of knowledge.

For Humboldt, the particularity of the modern university lay in the fact that it embodied a unique form of life, one defined by a devotion to scholarly knowledge, or what Humboldt, following Schelling, Fichte, and Schleiermacher, referred to as *Wissenschaft.* The task of the university, he argued, was to connect the moral, subjective development of individuals with the objective forms of knowledge. The university institutionalized not just an epistemic order but an ethical one as well. As a form of life, scholarly knowledge was characterized by a devotion to research (*Forschung*). Although the logic of research had been deployed in fits and starts in Göttingen, it was Humboldt who branded it most forcefully as a particular type of learning and knowledge production. He cast it as the underlying ethic of the university. On this account knowledge was not something to be gathered up and displayed in tomes of erudition but something to be infinitely pursued. Research referred to a distinct orientation. It was to be the pursuit, not the attainment, of knowledge.

From this articulation of a new university ethos, a number of other imperatives followed, imperatives that would be repeated from Berlin to Baltimore. The first imperative was the *unity of teaching and research.* The teacher, argued Humboldt, was not at the university for the student, just as the student was no longer there for the teacher; instead, they were both at the university for the sake of knowledge. The student-teacher relationship is refigured as one in which the student researches and the professor guides that research. Good teaching depended on good research—the stock convention common to every tenure portfolio and university press release. As Jacob Grimm would observe a half century later, in German the words "to learn" (*lernen*) and "to teach" (*lehren*) were formed directly from one another.

A second imperative that followed from Humboldt's proposal was the necessity of *academic freedom.* Although most American discussions of the concept cite Dewey and his AAUP address of 1915, Humboldt's text condenses a heated early nineteenth-century German debate on academic freedom into a nuanced call for scholars to pursue *Wissenschaft* for its own sake. The call for academic freedom, however, was not a call for the absolute autonomy of scholarship and the university. On Humboldt's account, the university was to mediate the competing demands of the ceaseless and unencumbered pursuit of knowledge with the more practical interests of society as represented and organized by the state.

ON THE INTERNAL STRUCTURE OF THE UNIVERSITY IN BERLIN AND ITS RELATIONSHIP TO OTHER ORGANIZATIONS

Higher academic institutions are the pinnacle of a nation's moral culture. This notion follows from the calling of such institutions: to pursue knowledge in the broadest and deepest sense of the word and devote themselves to the use of knowledge not as material arranged according to particular external purposes, but rather as the autonomous, self-arranging material of intellectual and ethical formation.

The essence of higher academic institutions is twofold. Internally, these institutions join objective knowledge with the process of forming the subject. Externally, they connect the endpoint of secondary education with the starting point of self-guided education—or, rather, lead from one to the other. But the primary standpoint must be that of knowledge alone. For insofar as knowledge is allowed to exist as pure knowledge, people (though, of course, not everyone) will be able to see what it is in itself and as a whole.

Since higher academic institutions can realize their purpose only when they operate as much as possible in accordance with the pure idea of knowledge, their leading principles are solitude and freedom. And yet the intellectual labor of humankind also needs collaboration in order to flourish. Nor is it enough simply for one person to compensate for what another person lacks—the productive activity of each is essential in exciting and encouraging the other, and the universal, original vitality that resides in and shines forth from each individual only in isolated, or derivative, form becomes visible to all. Therefore, the internal organization of our higher academic institutions must foster and sustain a free, uninterrupted, self-revitalizing, open-ended collaboration.

Another characteristic of these higher academic institutions lies in the fact that they treat the problem of knowledge as one that has not yet been fully solved. While the lower institutions, such as secondary schools, are concerned only with limited forms of knowledge, higher institutions are always involved in research. This completely changes the relationship between teacher and pupil in the higher institutions. Here, the teacher is not there for the students' sake; rather, they are all there for scholarship and knowledge's sake. The teacher's work depends on students and cannot succeed without them; if students did not gather around him on their own, he would have to seek them out in order to reach his goal by linking his students' strengths with his own. The teacher is better trained, but for that reason also more likely to be narrow in his views and have less energy; the students may be less experienced, but they are more open, intrepidly probing in all directions.

Thus, what we call our higher academic institutions are—when uncoupled from their concrete existence in a given state—nothing other than the intellectual life of humanity. They are the intellectual life to which our inner strivings for knowledge lead when we have the external leisure that allows us to pursue those strivings. One person might be inclined to ruminate and gather facts on his own, another to work together with members of his cohort, a third to bring together a circle of younger men. The state, too, must remain faithful to this ideal if it is to eventually fashion research that is indeterminate and can seem somewhat random into a more fixed and manageable form. The state must see to it that (1) scholarly inquiry is kept as strong and vital as possible; and, so as not to weaken it, the state must (2) preserve a pure and clear distinction between the higher academic institutions and the secondary schools (not just the theoretically oriented ones, but also, and especially, the various practical ones).

The state must always remain aware that it cannot and will not acquire on its own the scientific and scholarly knowledge it wants; in fact, that it is never anything but an impediment as soon as it meddles directly in the production of knowledge. The production of knowledge would go infinitely better without such involvement, and the relationship between the state and higher academic institutions should really be as follows:

- In a society such as ours, there must be external structures and means for anything to have a widespread effectiveness. It is the state's duty to provide these things for the pursuit of knowledge.
- The state harms scholarship not only by fulfilling this obligation inadequately, but by virtue of the very fact that something foreign to scholarship is providing the external structures and means at all. This has the infelicitous effect of pulling what is intellectual and higher toward a more material and base reality.

- Thus the state must keep its focus, above all, on the essence of scholarship. Only then will the state be able to make up for the damage and obstruction it will have naturally, although unintentionally, caused.

This account represents, to be sure, merely another perspective on the fundamental relationship between the state and our higher academic institutions. The advantages of this approach will become clear only through its results. After all, if the state adopts this perspective, it will intervene more and more cautiously; moreover, when it comes to the practical activity of the state, no flawed theoretical perspective goes unpunished, whatever people might say to the contrary. For no state action is merely mechanical.

That said, when it comes to the internal organization of our higher academic institutions, everything clearly depends on upholding the principle that knowledge has never been, nor ever will be, fully discovered in final form. It must be seen as something to be endlessly pursued.

As soon as one stops actually pursuing knowledge, or if one imagines that it can be strung together by comprehensively collecting facts rather than being drawn forth from the depths of the mind, the whole endeavor is utterly and irrevocably lost. Lost to science, since if this dynamic persists, knowledge itself will vanish, leaving its language behind like an empty shell, and lost to the state as well. For what matters to the state, just as to humanity, is not merely knowing and talking but character and action, and only the kind of knowledge that comes from within and can be cultivated within transforms character.

To ensure that we do not go down this wrong path, we need only take care to engage—continually and with all due energy—in the following three intellectual pursuits.

- First, derive everything from first principles, the way scientific explanations of nature will ascend within the best intellect from mechanical to dynamic, then organic, and finally psychological explanations.
- Second, everything must be developed toward an ideal.
- Third, the principle and the ideal should always be connected in a single idea.

Needless to say, it is far from clear how to promote such an agenda, and surely none would say that Germans were most in need of encouragement in this direction. The German national intellectual character inherently possesses these tendencies. We need only protect them, so that neither brute force nor the opposing tendencies that are naturally to be found here as well can overpower them.

We must banish all one-sidedness from our higher academic institutions, but naturally there will be many people in those institutions who do not understand this effort, and some who are even opposed to it. Only a few pursue it forcefully and completely—and indeed, the effort need not be widespread to have broad and enduring effects, but what must prevail is respect for this effort, among those who can feel it, and awe and timidity among those who would destroy it.

It is through philosophy and art that such striving for openness is expressed most often and in the clearest form. But it is also in those realms that it degenerates easily, and moreover, not much can be expected from philosophy and art as long as their spirit cannot be fully carried over into other branches of knowledge and types of inquiry, or, in the case of philosophy, as long as it is carried over only through a logical or mathematical formalism.

But if one central principle—the pursuit of knowledge for its own sake—finally gains the upper hand in our higher academic institutions, there will be no need to worry about any particular details. Such institutions will be both unified and complete, qualities that seek and presuppose each other in a naturally reciprocal relationship. This is in fact the secret of a good scientific and scholarly method.

We have now covered everything necessary about the internal structure of these institutions.

As to their external relations with others—first and foremost, their relationship to the state and the state's active role in them—the state's basic concern is twofold. First, it has to accumulate a wealth of intellectual power, both in quality and breadth of faculty, which it achieves through its choice of personnel. Second, it has to ensure that these men have the freedom they need to be effective. Not only does the state threaten this freedom, but so do the institutions themselves, especially soon after being founded, when they adopt a certain stance and try to keep other perspectives from emerging. The state must work to prevent the disadvantages that arise from such one-sidedness.

Still, the primary issue is the first one: selecting the men who are to pursue this work. A successful selection procedure, and correctives to prevent poor choices, can be established only once the entire institution has been divided up into individual parts. At that point, selection is only a matter of establishing a few organizational rules, simple enough but with greater reach and influence over the process than most general rules. These, too, depend on the various individual parts of the university.

Finally, it is necessary to take stock of the additional resources that these institutions have at their disposal. Here the main thing to keep in mind is that the goal is not to pile up lifeless collections—indeed, such collections can easily dull and degrade the mind. This is why the wealthiest academies and universities have by no means always been the ones where the sciences and scholarship have been pursued most deeply and fruitfully.

These points about the state's active role in advanced academic institutions also bear upon the relationship between the higher institutions and secondary schools, and the relationship between academic life and practical life. The state should treat its universities neither as gymnasiums nor as places for vocational training. Similarly, it should not use its academies as groups of specialists there to do the state's technical or scientific work. In general, the state should demand nothing purely self-interested from either the university or the academy (isolated exceptions to this general rule will be discussed below). Rather, it should harbor the inner conviction that when these institutions achieve their own goals, they will also achieve the state's goals, and from a much higher point of view as well—one that synthesizes more knowledge and can bring entirely different forces and mechanisms to bear than the state could on its own.

On the other hand, it is primarily the state's obligation to organize its secondary schools so that they effectively feed into the higher academic institutions. This requires first and foremost a proper understanding of the relationship between secondary schools and universities. The conviction must be put into practice that secondary schools are not supposed to anticipate university instruction; nor are universities supposed to be simply higher grades of school, providing mere complementary classes of the same type. Rather, the passage from secondary school to university is a defining stage in the life of a young man. If schools succeed, they produce young men who can be physically, morally, and intellectually entrusted with freedom and autonomy. Without any external coercion, they will not devolve into idleness or a merely practical life, but instead will bear within their hearts a longing to rise up to the level of systematic knowledge, which until that point will have been only pointed out from afar.

The path that secondary schools must take to achieve this goal is simple and sure. They must aim to harmoniously develop *all* the abilities of their pupils; they must conserve the boys' strength by limiting the number of subjects but let them exert that strength in all directions as much as possible; they must sow all kinds of facts in the minds of their pupils in such a way that understanding, knowledge, and intellectual creativity are attractive not only due to external circumstances but due to their inner precision, harmony, and beauty. The best way to achieve these goals and prepare the mind for pure scholarship is through mathematics, which should be used from the beginning in the training of mental faculties.

A mind trained in this way will grasp science and scholarship on its own, while others with the same diligence and talent but different training will be overwhelmed by practical demands, either at once or before the completion of their education. This will render them uneducable, or else, without the higher drive for knowledge, they will be distracted and lost among the scattered facts they acquire.

On the Different Kinds of Higher Academic Institutions and the Necessity of Divisions among Them

Ordinarily, the term "higher academic institution" covers universities, academies of the sciences, and academies of the arts. It is easy enough to derive these institutions from a single idea, even though they emerged from contingent, historical circumstances. And yet, in all of the efforts, popular since Kant, to provide such a justification, there has been something amiss. Indeed, the entire endeavor is in some ways useless.

Another set of questions, in contrast, is truly important: Is it worth the effort to establish and maintain academies alongside universities at all? If so, what should be their goals, individually and working together, so that each institution can do what it alone is capable of?

If it is claimed that the only tasks of the university are instruction and the dissemination of knowledge, whereas the academy is supposed to actually advance knowledge, this is clearly unjust to the university. Knowledge has obviously been advanced by university teachers just as much as, or in Germany more than, it has been by members of academies. University teachers have made progress in their particular fields precisely because of their teaching activities—because giving a public lecture before an audience, many of whom are thinking along with the lecturer, inspires the man who is used to having once been a listener himself. It is certainly at least as inspiring as the lonely leisure of the writer's life, or the looser connections among academy members. Scholarship clearly makes quicker and livelier strides at a university, where its problems are constantly tossed back and forth in a large group of strong, vigorous young minds. Knowledge as such cannot truly be presented in a lecture without it being grasped anew every time, and it is inconceivable that such a practice would not lead, relatively often, to new discoveries. Furthermore, university teaching is not such arduous labor that it should be seen as interrupting the quiet space needed for study and research. On the contrary, teaching fosters it. Finally, even if it were better to rarely lecture, to study and research in solitude, there are just as many people who do so at any large university as in the academies.

Surely the advancement of knowledge could thus be entrusted solely to universities, provided they were organized for this purpose, and it would then be in keeping with the same aim to dispense with the academies.

Furthermore, the goal of creating groups in which academy members can come together (social associations that are, incidentally, not exactly common among university professors) is hardly enough to justify establishing such costly institutions. Even in the academies, collaboration is only loosely encouraged; in addition, such collaboration works best in sciences that are based on observation and experimentation, in which the rapid exchange of particular facts is useful. And in these fields, as a rule, private groups and professional societies emerge without difficulty or state intervention.

Upon further examination, what becomes clear is that academies have flourished primarily abroad, in countries that lack German universities or even are unaware of their advantages. In Germany itself, academies have flourished in places without universities and in times when universities lacked a liberal and open spirit. No academy has truly stood out in recent times, and academies in general have played little or no role in the rise of German scholarship, science, and art.

To keep both types of institution vibrant, it is necessary to integrate them so that while each maintains its own distinct activities, individual scholars do not always have to belong exclusively to one or the other. This integration will enable each institution to exist on its own while also being put to a new and more appropriate use.

The differences between them are a function far less of their unique activities than of their particular forms and their different relationships to the state. (Indeed, university teachers can achieve everything an academy is supposed to achieve without establishing an academy at all, as in Göttingen, where they formed a learned society of their own that is very different from an actual academy.) The university is closer to practical life and the needs of the state, because it carries out a practical task: educating the young. The academy's sole concern, on the other hand, is scientific knowledge in its own terms. University teachers have only a general connection to each other in matters concerning the inner structure of the disciplines and their relationships to one another. Regarding their own work, they communicate with each other as much as they are inclined to; otherwise each follows his own path. The academy, in contrast, is a group organization in which every member must submit his work to the judgment of all the others.

Thus we must uphold the idea of the academy as the last and highest sanctuary of scholarship: the organization most independent of the state. It may turn out that such an organization will act too narrowly or be overly insular, and that the best results might not be achieved even under the best external conditions. And yet, I say, the risk must be taken, because the idea is beautiful and beneficial and there may well eventually be a moment when it is fully and worthily realized.

Competition and antagonism will arise between the university and the academy, as well as a reciprocal relationship in which any worrisome excess or period of decline in one will likely be balanced by the other.

The main cause for tensions between the academy and the university will involve the choice of who is to join both of these organizations. This is because every member of the academy should have the right to hold lectures without a habilitation,[1] even without being a faculty member of the university. Of course, there will be a number of scholars who are both university faculty and academy members, but there will be others who belong to only one institution.

The right to appoint professors must be reserved exclusively for the state. It is certainly not a good arrangement to allow the faculty to have more influence on such matters than a fair and prudent board of overseers would afford. For conflict and friction are necessary and beneficial in the university, and the conflicts that emerge among university faculty in their work can change their perspectives, even without their realizing it. Furthermore, the composition of universities is too closely tied with the immediate interests of the state.

The selection of academy members, however, must be left to the academy itself, requiring only the approval of the king (which, to be sure, is not likely to be withheld). This is because academy members form a group in which unity is much more important, and the academy's purely academic purpose is of less interest to the state as such than the university's.

From this arise the correctives to the process of selecting members of these advanced academic institutions, mentioned above. Since the state and the academy have a more or less equal influence on the process, the spirit in which they act will soon become evident. Public opinion will judge them objectively and immediately if they go astray. However, since it is highly unlikely that both correctives would fail at the same time and in the same way, all selections will be protected, to at least some degree, from being compromised, and the institution will be, as a whole, well protected against imbalances in specialization. Instead, the abilities of those joining the academy will be very diverse, since in addition to both classes of members (i.e., those named by the state and those elected by the academy), there will also be the private instructors [Privatdozenten], who at least at first will be sustained by nothing but the applause of their audiences.

Beyond its regular academic work, the academy can also distinguish itself through another activity unique to it: the studies and experiments that it systematically carries out. Some of these studies the academy will design and carry out itself, while others will be assigned to it, and the university will have a large influence over this latter group. A new reciprocal relationship between academy and university will arise as a result.

In addition to the academy and the university, there are other higher academic institutions, many of which have fallen into state of torpor or decay. These must remain separate from the other two, and under the state's direct supervision; both the academy and the university must be able not only to use—provided certain modifications are made—but also to direct these institutions. However, they should be able to exercise the latter of these rights only by submitting their memoranda and proposals for improving these institutions via the state.

By having institutions such as anatomical and comparative anatomical theaters at the university, the academy will gain access to resources that no other academy has, because up to now these institutions have only been seen from the perspective of medicine, not from a broader, scientific perspective.

In short, the academy, the university, and these auxiliary institutions are *both* three separate institutions *and* integrated parts of a single whole. All, however—the last two more than the first one—remain under the direction and supervision of the state.

The academy and the university are both self-sufficient, linked only insofar as (1) they have common members, (2) the university grants all academy members the right to give lectures, and (3) the academy carries out studies and experiments as suggested by the university. Both of them use and oversee the auxiliary institutions, but oversee them, in practical matters, only via the mediation of the state.

Academies

[The original manuscript breaks off here.]

REQUEST FOR THE ESTABLISHMENT OF THE UNIVERSITY OF BERLIN, MAY 12–14, 1809

It may seem off-putting, just now, to venture to lay out a plan whose execution seems to require happier and more peaceful times. Except Your Royal Majesty has shown, in multiple and prominent ways, that even amid the pressure of disquieting circumstances you have not lost sight of the importance of national education and culture. This disposition of yours, as rare as it is sublime, has instilled in me the courage to make the following request.

Your Royal Majesty has deigned to approve the organization of a new university in Berlin, through an imperial cabinet order of September 4, 1807. Since then this plan has been pursued with various hirings and newly established institutes. But in order for it to be truly carried out, a second, decisive step must be taken, and there are two reasons why I feel it is necessary to do so now.

It is far from the case that the level of trust all of Germany once placed in the influence of Prussia over true Enlightenment and higher intellectual achievements has fallen because of recent unfortunate events—it has, on the contrary, risen. It is clear to see that in all of Your Royal Majesty's new state institutions a sensibility predominates in which these most important of all assets also serve the highest purpose of any unification of states. Observers have marveled at the willingness with which, even in times of such great hardship, academic institutions have been supported and even considerably improved. Your Majesty's states can and will continue, therefore, to maintain their leading position in Germany in this respect and thus exercise a decisive influence on Germany's intellectual and moral direction.

The idea of establishing a university in Berlin has contributed significantly to this trust. Schools and gymnasiums are of great use to the territory in which they are found, but only universities can ensure the same influence beyond its borders as well—and on the culture of the whole nation that speaks the same language. If Your Majesty can again formally confirm the approval for this organization as well and guarantee its realization, you would ensure anew that everything in Germany that engages with culture and enlightenment is connected most firmly to you. You would also stir a new warmth and enthusiasm for the renewed thriving of your states, and at a time when one part of Germany is devastated by war and another is governed by foreign rulers in a foreign language, you would establish a sanctuary for German scholarship and science that hardly anyone dares hope for.

This confluence of circumstances has also led more extraordinarily talented men than usual to want to join new associations, and this is the second reason to establish a university now.

I do not think I need to address again Your Majesty's earlier decision with respect to the comparative advantages and disadvantages of establishing a university in Berlin. However useful domestic universities such as Königsberg and Frankfurt already are and will surely become in the future, they still can never, even with great expenditures, achieve a meaningful influence abroad.

The choice of a new location presents still further challenges. Thus only one option remains: a university must be established in Berlin, or else we have to forgo the prospect of a magnificent university that attracts foreigners as well.

Furthermore, two particular factors speak for Berlin.

Berlin already has many large scientific institutes and suitable scholars, and in fact an actual medical university. But any division of the faculties is detrimental to nonsystematic education, which is the only kind we have known to date here in Germany.

Even the name "university," if I may say so, will not require me to offer an excuse to Your Majesty. It is meant simply to signify that no field of knowledge is excluded, and that the teaching institution will also grant academic titles. Everything else about the university that is antiquated or detrimental will, of course, be avoided. But the establishment of a higher teaching institution that is not a university, however attractive the idea might be by virtue of being new and to some extent easier to realize, would be misguided, because not even the idea behind such an institute can be clearly defined. A purely practical institution would be even more dangerous, because in teaching, theory and practice can never be so separate. No institution, however one conceives of it, can be introduced alongside the existing three kinds that are determined by the nature of the matter—scientific institutes and schools, universities, and academies—except arbitrarily.

[. . .]

I therefore venture to propose most respectfully to Your Majesty:

1. that through an official decree you establish a university in Berlin and assign it to the Section for Public Education, effective immediately;
2. that you secure a substantial annual income for the new university, 60,000 thalers per year, through an official royal grant of as many demesnes as necessary, conferring them so that the revenues begin to accrue from the day of the grant and are set aside for the benefit of the university until they are used, with the stipulation that these estates are the permanent property of the university and, if they ever cease to be, that they remain a property dedicated to the maintenance and improvement of the education system;
3. that you permit the Section for Public Education to present Your Majesty with the following plan: incorporate into or join with the university, as appropriate in each case, the Academy of Sciences and the Academy of Arts (which must still, of course, retain their independence); the Academy of Architecture, which should be incorporated into the latter; all of

the medical institutes, so that their main purpose will be only fostered, not hindered; and all the other scholarly, scientific, and technical institutes and collections (botanical garden, veterinary school, library, astronomical observatory, etc.). In addition, instruct these institutions to set up this organizational framework, which can only be advantageous to each one of them, according to the measures set forth in this plan;

4. instruct the lord high chancellor and finance minister to consult with the Ministry of the Interior and the Section for Public Education about how to introduce the conferral of the necessary estates, in whatever way is most in accord with the state constitution and to the university's benefit;
5. finally, allocate the 7,000 thalers of the former Silesian Jesuit Fund—5,000 of which currently belongs to the city of Halle and 2,000 of which was recently set aside by Your Majesty for educational improvements—entirely to the University of Frankfurt from this point on.

Should Your Majesty wish to take the opportunity to put the Academy of Sciences and Academy of Arts on surer footing at this time—institutions that will otherwise be an ever-recurring burden to the royal treasury, but whose complete discontinuance would lead to many unfortunate consequences—the appropriate method for doing so would be to expand the conferral of state demesnes, so that the annual revenue increases by 40,000 thalers. When Your Majesty considers that each of these academies has received to date more than 20,000 thalers from the royal treasury, an expense that would now disappear, this sum of 40,000 thalers will not seem so large.

Should Your Majesty be inclined to approve this request, I would like to most humbly request that, in the decrees you enact to institute these measures, you declare in general terms that this sum is meant for both academies, but that it is in the end reserved to Your Most Sovereign Self to decide in advance how it is distributed and used for the reorganization of both academies that are to go along with it. For it is ultimately necessary to reorganize both of these institutions, if they are to continue to truly and seriously serve the causes of science, scholarship, and art.

Konigsberg, May 14, 1809
To: His Royal Majesty

* Part 2 *

Americans Abroad and Returning

CHAPTER 8

Letters to Thomas Jefferson and Edward Everett

George Ticknor and George Bancroft

INTRODUCTION TO TICKNOR'S AND BANCROFT'S LETTERS

When George Ticknor graduated from Dartmouth in 1807, he was sixteen and frustrated. He felt that the years he had spent at college were pleasant but intellectually uninspiring. He had learned far more, he believed, under the guidance of his parents. Having amassed considerable wealth in business, Ticknor's father was in a position to support his son's scholarly ambitions, and Ticknor spent the years after Dartmouth studying the classics with private tutors in Boston, his hometown. Scholarship was clearly his vocation; Ticknor pursued, but quickly abandoned, the plan of going into law. The question that remained as he entered his early twenties was this: Given the extraordinary standards to which he held himself, as well as his extraordinary love of the main apparatus of learning, books, how and where should he foster his scholarly development? At the time, Ticknor lacked acquaintances who had studied at a German university. But he had read the famous account of German letters by the French writer Madame de Staël, as well as a sketch of the University of Göttingen by a different French author, and, most important of all, he had read a description of the university's library, whose holdings were ten times greater than Harvard's. The allure proved irresistible. Ticknor resolved to go to Göttingen.

Before leaving, he sought letters of introduction from a number of influential figures, among them Thomas Jefferson, with whom he shared a passion for collecting books. Jefferson asked Ticknor to purchase editions for him during his time in Europe, and this often gave Ticknor occasion to write to Jefferson, who later tried, unsuccessfully, to recruit Ticknor for the faculty of the newly established University of Virginia. Thus many of Ticknor's missives from Göttingen are addressed to Jefferson, and they tend to move between updates on procuring the best editions of classical works and observations about the intellectual situation at and beyond the university.

Ticknor had his share of low moments in Göttingen. He once remarked that his time there was "the darkest" of his life. And like quite a few other Americans who studied in Germany during the nineteenth century, he didn't come away with a particularly high opinion of German students, with whom he seems not to have had much productive interaction. But more often his tone is enthusiastic. He was deeply impressed, and deeply influenced, by the famed German culture of academic freedom he encountered in Göttingen. Indeed, a key theme in the letters to Jefferson reproduced here is that German scholars could explore sensitive topics without having to worry about the institutional consequences in the way that their American counterparts did. Of similar importance to him was what he regarded as the philosophical spirit in which Germans practiced humanistic scholarship. In a letter to Jefferson, Ticknor writes of his desire to see something analogous in America: "I am exceedingly anxious to have this spirit of pursuing all literary studies philosophically—of making scholarship as little drudgery and mechanism as possible transplanted into the U. States, in whose free and liberal soil I think it would, at once, find congenial nourishment. It is a spirit, which in Germany now goes through everything—through theology, history, modern literature, etc."

His assessment would prove to be too optimistic. While Ticknor was still in Germany, studying and seeking out such distinguished men of letters as Goethe (Ticknor was the first American student to make the pilgrimage to Weimar), he received word that the Harvard Corporation had voted to offer him a new professorship—the Smith Professor of French and Spanish Languages. There was some haggling—Ticknor wanted a sizable fund for buying books—but soon the appointment was made, which meant that Ticknor had to "protract" his stay in Europe, as he put it, in order to spend some time in Spain. At Harvard, Ticknor attempted to usher in the spirit he had so admired in Göttingen.

This did not always go over so well, though there were some successes. During Ticknor's first year, his teaching style rankled students almost to the point of mutiny: they openly harassed him. However, he persisted, and when, in the wake of Harvard's student-rowdiness scandal of 1823, the opportunity for policy reform came, he seized it, writing new statues having to do not only with student conduct but also with instruction. More specifically, Ticknor was able to establish that instruction "shall be given by departments," and in turn that "students shall, to a certain degree, have a choice of the studies they are to pursue." And in addition to getting a very limited elective system on the books, Ticknor changed Harvard's policy regarding the grouping of students in recitations and other instructional settings, which, as he put it, now "shall be done according to proficiency," rather than alphabetically.

As the head of the Department of Modern Languages, Ticknor instituted these revisions, and he felt vindicated by the results. The more capable students made rapid progress, and the department's popularity surged as Ticknor lectured not only on French and Spanish literature but on Goethe, Schiller, and Dante as well. Yet in general the faculty failed to comply with the new policies. Although this was a time when others were challenging the classical curriculum on more utilitarian grounds, the bulk of Ticknor's colleagues resisted change. Eventually, the centrality of classical texts was reasserted at Harvard (and more famously at Yale, through the Yale Report of 1828). First, though, President Kirkland largely stopped supporting Ticknor's efforts, and Ticknor's relationship with Harvard suffered. He vacated his chair in the prime of his career; later, the university's library declined to house Ticknor's collection of books, even though it was one of the best private collections in the country. It went instead to the Boston Public Library, an institution that Ticknor helped found.

Ticknor was much admired by later educational reformers, and when his *Life, Letters, and Journals* appeared, posthumously, in 1876, it was widely read and discussed. Upon sending a copy to Thomas Carlyle, Charles Eliot Norton noted that even Ticknor's "defects"—a "lack of imagination and humour"—served him well in his attempt to support important causes by making connections in "conventional society." According to Eliot, Ticknor had the capacity not just to tolerate the small talk and manners one encountered there but also to "take it all" completely "in earnest."

Given Ticknor's creativity as a scholar and professor, Eliot's appraisal seems unfair. The dearth-of-humor part appears more justified, and it also applies to George Bancroft, Ticknor's contemporary and fellow pioneer in establishing Germany (or really Göttingen) as a destination for Americans studying abroad. In fact, it applies even better to Bancroft.

Like Ticknor, Bancroft was a prodigy in the study of classical languages. At sixteen, he graduated with honors from Harvard, where he impressed President Kirkland and Edward Everett, a Latinist who had recently returned from a stint in Göttingen. Everett urged Kirkland to send Bancroft to Göttingen for advanced philological training, and in 1818, a year after his graduation, Bancroft was awarded a three-year fellowship so that he could become (in Kirkland's words) "an accomplished biblical critic, able to expound and defend the Revelation of God."

As had been the case with Ticknor, Bancroft was struck by the freedom and erudition of his instructors in Göttingen. Not long after his arrival, he gushed, "I have come to the land of learning, of literature, of science. I have come to the pure fountains of wisdom, that I may drink of her unpolluted waters and be refreshed." The perception of purity would soon change. Bancroft would point out numerous features of German academic life that seemed to cut two ways. One could rise through the ranks on the basis of scholarly productivity; this, however, encouraged not only real productivity but also the writing of books for the sake of career advancement. And while the robust culture of debate in Germany was to be applauded, it often seemed to go over into attitudes of categorical dismissiveness—no German scholar appreciates the work of his colleagues, Bancroft once complained.

In addition, Bancroft was more of a moralist than Ticknor, and much more attached to the ideal of the scholar as a gentleman. Thus he took offense at many aspects of German intellectual culture, including what he saw as the "indolence" of the great philologist Friedrich August Wolf, once a tremendous workhorse, and the poor hygiene of German scholars and students. Indeed, Bancroft may have been the first American to express outrage over the olfactory experience of the European lecture hall: "When scholars are assembled for a lecture the collection of unpleasant odors is prodigious." The lists he made of the characteristics of German men of learning are, on balance, not very flattering, suggesting as they do that in German letters the "careerist scholars" far outnumber the "philosophical minds," to use Schiller's terminology. Consider this entry: "9. They [German men of letters] regard letters as a trade, are then on a level with mechanics." Or this one: "7. They have no nice feelings, either moral or of good breeding."

Bancroft remained devoted to some of his teachers at Göttingen, particularly the biblical scholar Albert Eichorn and the classicist Arnold Heeren, whose work he later translated. But by the time he took his doctorate, he had grown weary of the place: "In the years I spent at Göttingen I certainly had a good deal to endure. It was like living among the dead. The roughness of the students, the cold hearted rudeness and mutual jealousies of the professors made the life there as solitary as a hermitage." Göttingen's main strength, he concluded, was to push students to "gather genuine learning." It was in Berlin, where Bancroft spent time after leaving Göttingen, that one "learned how to think." In Berlin he became enamored of the "speculative" spirit, especially as it manifested itself in the person of Friedrich Schleiermacher, whose eloquence and independent, probing intellect Bancroft praised to the skies.

Bancroft taught at Harvard for a number of years after returning to the United States, but he never became the biblical scholar Kirkland had hoped he would. Harvard was no Berlin: as a mature scholar, Bancroft found the intellectual environment in Cambridge uninspiring, even stifling. He gave up his position to found a secondary school in Northampton (in an attempt to create gymnasium-style secondary education in America), later went into politics, and channeled the research skills and ideas about national character that he had learned in Germany into a magisterial history of the United States, hence the fact that the field's most prestigious book prize is named in his honor.

TICKNOR'S LETTER TO THOMAS JEFFERSON

Göttingen March 15, 1816—

DEAR SIR,

I have already in my letters from London, and in the letters I have written you from here Oct. 14, Oct. 30, and Novem. 25, told you of so many changes in my plans, that, if I were not sure that you will appreciate my reasons, I should be almost ashamed to write you now to tell you of another. The truth, however is, that I find Göttingen so entirely suited to my purposes—the opportunities and means and inducements to pursue those studies to which I mean to devote my life are so admirable here,—that I have determined to protract my stay in Europe in order to enjoy them one year longer. To this resolution I came on the 27. Jan. in consequence of letters received the day before from home, and as I, of course at the same time determined to defer my visit to France a year longer, I immediately made arrangements for the purchase of your Books in Paris. I could have easily effected this by a literary friend of mine there, but as I knew Mr. Warden's personal respect for you and as you had told me that he is "an excellent bibliograph," I wrote to him on the same 27th of Jan desiring him to procure them. A few days since I received his answer of Feb. 12. in which he very willingly promised to undertake it. To day, I have received your favour of Jan 14. and have instantly written to him and given him your supplement to your catalogue. I hope these arrangements will meet your approbation, and I think they will, as they are the best I could make, though I should much have preferred to purchase them myself, because it is the only opportunity

I may ever have of returning you the many obligations you have conferred on me. This I could have done to great advantage in Holland, where the general poverty and the failing spirit of literature has made the classicks disgracefully cheap; but, then your list was not received or even made out. In Germany, I have thought it best to do nothing, for the strong spirit of recovered independence, tho' not freedom, and the perpetual literary labour of the learned make those old editions of the classicks which you desire very rare, and from 120 to 150 per cent, higher than in Holland and probably 50 or 60 higher than in Paris.—If, however, you should like to have any of the recent editions, which have given a new and more philosophical and acute character to the study of antiquity, Germany and Göttingen will best afford them, or if a year hence you should need anything from France or Italy, I shall eagerly seize the opportunity to procure it, and can safely forward it to you, as I am continually sending books to America.—

The letters, however, which your kindness gave me have embarrassed me much more than the commission for the books. I have already told you that immediately on my arrival here, I sent the one for the Baron de Moll[1] directly to him by one of the professors and since then, I have returned you the one for Mons. De Nemours,[2] as he is already in the U.S. I could easily send the others to France, but La Fayette and Kosciuzko[3] are no longer there and I can neither procure Mons. Say's[4] addresses or even ascertain in what quarter of the world he is. They, therefore, still remain with me waiting for favourable circumstances.

The longer I have continued here, the better I have been satisfied with my situation and the more reasons and inducements I have found to protract my residence. The state of society is, indeed, poor; but the means and opportunities for pursuing the study of the languages particularly the ancient, are, I am persuaded, entirely unrivalled. As I have already written you in my long letter on German literature, I was told even in England and by Dr Parr, England's best and perhaps, vainest classical scholar, that Germany was farther advanced in the study of antiquity than any other nation. This I find to be true. The men of letters here bring a philosophical spirit to the labour of exposition which is wanting in the same class in all other countries. The consequence is that the study of the classicks has taken a new and more free turn within the last forty years and Germany now leaves England at least twenty years behind in the course where before it always stood first. This has been chiefly effected by the constitution of their Universities, where the professors are kept perpetually in a grinding state of excitement and emulation, and by the constitution of their literary society generally, which admits no man to its honours, who has not written a good book. The consequence, to be sure, is that y* professors are more envious and jealous of each other than can be well imagined by one who has not been actually within the atmosphere of their spleen, and that more bad and indifferent books are printed than in any country in the world, but then the converse of both is true; and they have more learned professors and authors at this moment, than England & France put together.

I would gladly hope, that the favour of your correspondence may be continued to me from time to time even after the commission for your books has been executed. If you feel any interest in the state of literature in Germany, which has sprung forth in the last thirty years as unbidden and as perfect as the miraculous harvest of Jason, I can be able to give you occasionally pleasant information—and when I reach France, I shall be able to write to you from the midst of your old friends and from a place associated in your imagination with very many interesting though, perhaps, not always pleasant recollections—If these slight inducements are sufficient with your own kindness to procure me the favour of an occasional letter, I shall feel myself under new obligations to you.—I shall, also, feel it as a great favour, if you will give me your opinion on the prospects of learning in the U.S. and the best means of promoting it—a subject which now occupies much of my attention.—

I pray you to remember me very respectfully and gratefully to your family.—

Your obliged & obed* ser*
GEO: TICKNOR

BANCROFT'S LETTERS TO EDWARD EVERETT

TO EDWARD EVERETT,[5] GÖTTINGEN SEPTEMBER 12 1818:
I have now been in Gottingen nearly a month and have gained some insight into their systems of study. For a knowledge of the courses, which it would be most advantageous for me to hear, I am almost exclusively indebted to your last letter from London. The friends, which I have made here through your intercessions, cannot of course accommodate their advice to my particular views and situation.

When I left America it was not settled very definitely, what plan of study I should pursue. In general it was desired, that I should devote myself to

Philology and Orientalism, and if possible, in a leisure hour, attend such other courses as would afford an agreeable relaxation. All more particular deliberation could better be done, after arriving at the University. Now that I am here, and find the intellectual treasures of the world collected near me, and the most learned instructors around me, by whose labours I can profit, I would gladly make such a use of these advantages, as would enable me on returning home to act an useful and an honourable part in society. To effect this it is necessary to have a definite aim; and indeed to pursue anything to advantage, one must form an exact and comprehensive plan.

On stating my views of study to my friends here, they told me I had better at once arrange the manner, in which I would employ myself for the whole time of residing here; that two or three years are the least number, which can be thought of by one, who wishes to make a respectable progress in Philology; and that the eastern languages would furnish one labour for life. To understand the Hebrew Bible thoroughly and critically two or three other languages must be learned; and these would give me so much occupation that philology must become quite a secondary affair. Or, on the other hand, I may give myself up to classical literature, and at the same time resign the hope of doing much at interpreting the Scriptures. A question then arises in my mind, whether after gaining a fair degree of acquaintance with the Classics, and that chiefly in view of understanding them, I should not strike off into the wide region of Oriental literature?

In deciding on this point, it would be proper to think of the state of learning among us at Cambridge. Criticism in every department receives little enough attention; but most especially in relation to the Eastern languages. Of the forty now studying theology there, all attend a little Hebrew, but most of them for no other purpose than to forget it again. Of the twenty or thirty chapters, which they read, nothing more is attempted than by the help of the Lexicon to make the Original and the English agree. The Oriental department, I suppose, would open a fine and inexhaustible field for labour, would be interesting for the novelties it presented, would give knowledge valuable in itself, necessary to accomplish a theologian and much wanted in America. But it must also be remembered, that in America this branch of learning is very little esteemed, that there are few, who would care to learn anything of it, and that therefore the advantages to be derived from it, would be chiefly a sweet but secret satisfaction.

So far as it respects my immediate occupations I can have no doubt. I shall follow the advice you have given me, and wherever you have expressed an opinion on a doubtful point I shall govern myself accordingly.

I shall hear Dissen[6] on Demosthenes and Aeschines, Köster on Hebrew Grammar, and Welcker[7] (he is the only professor who reads on Latin) on Tacitus. Prof. Benecke[8] takes care of my German, and I have found him after his way kindness indeed. Respecting the choice between young Planck[9] and Eichhorn I am yet undecided. Planck is very weak I believe, and speaks exceedingly fast and low, so that even the Germans lose a great part of his lecture, and I am rather afraid I should lose the whole. I am, too, very desirous of knowing Eichhorn: He is more celebrated at Cambridge than any other of the Gottingen Professors, and it was expected he would be the master, at whose feet I should sit. Yet I should be very unwilling to give my friends any reasonable ground for fearing that I should lose my belief in, or respect for Christianity. I do not myself believe, that my reverence for a religion, which is allied with every early and pleasant association, which as it regards its evidence, has already been the object of my study, and which is connected with all my hopes of happiness and usefulness and distinction, can be diminished by ridicule. The natural effect of observing great talents united with a disposition to mock what so many revere, is to excite indignation or pity. Were Planck well I would hear him at once, and even as it is, I am inclined to do so I have not yet visited Prof E. I believe the best mode will be for me to call on him tomorrow, and if he appear to expect that I should learn from him, to decide upon attending him. If you should hereafter favour me with your opinions about studying Oriental Literature and if tis advised me to do it I suppose it must be done with him. [. . .]

October 1

I have been for some days a regular matriculated student of the University of Gottingen. On the 22nd of September I obtained my *Matrikel.* The process of procuring it is very simple. The doors of the University stand ever open; and all are invited to the rich banquet of learning. Nothing is necessary toward becoming a member of the institution, except to give your name, your country, the occupation of your father, and the studies to which you will devote yourself; self on this being known a paper is immediately handed you by which you become entitled to all the privileges and rights of a citizen of the Georgia Augusta. At the same time you shake hands with the Prorector, by which form you are understood to promise that you will obey the laws of the University. There is particular mention made in the *Matrikel* of duelling, of directly resenting an injury, instead of appealing to the proper authorities, of the preservation of a good character, and pure morals, of the associations called *Landsmannschaften*, and of appearing always in decent clothing. The fees amount to about one Louis d'or. The present Prorector is Consistorial Rath Pott.[10] He appeared particularly pleased on my declaring myself an American, and pointing to the name last entered in his book, which happened to be the name of a Grecian, bade me notice from what distant parts of the globe there were representatives at Gottingen. He then very particularly requested me to visit him, adding that he should have then detained me, to hold a conversation with me but he was involved in business and duties of his office.

October 2

Behold, I have seen a wonder! A learned woman,[11] modest, and who once might have been handsome; a learned woman, Doctor of Philosophy, Master of Arts, and one of the best informed men in the place.

Old Sltizer,[12] who died some ten years ago, was a stern republican abroad and very naturally a tyrant in his own house. (He wrote a very admirable book on the coins of the Russian Empire.) Well—this man married—his wife became pregnant, he was mightily rejoiced, felt sure it was & boy, boasted of the circumstance to his friends, and destined the young man in his own mind for a scholar. His wife was brought to bed, and behold, a little miss came to light. The Professor, however, nought intimidated, still clung to his resolution, and determined to show the world that a woman could master the classics as well as anyone. He accordingly educated her completely as a boy, employing her constantly with her books. As she was really possessed of a vast deal of mind she made great proficiency and he determined that she should join the University. This she actually did; attending lectures, going like the rest of the students with her portfolio under her arm, and differing from them only in this, that she was exceedingly handsome and wore petticoats. Her conduct however, was so perfectly pure and modest, that she never received the least indignity, nor was her character ever impeached. After becoming in this [way] uncommonly learned her father said she must take a degree. This, too, she did, acquitting herself undoubtedly with great honour in the Latin extemporary disputation and of course received, *bona fide*, a doctor's degree.

Shortly after this, to escape this unnatural mode of life, she married and removed to Lübeck; her husband failed to a large amount, and she removed to Göttingen. Here she lives at present, and was visited a great deal but now she is getting on in life and on account of frequent ill health sees not much company. In her character and conversation she is irreproachable and from a long acquaintance with her, I am told one would never hear from her a word that would betray her learning.

TO PRESIDENT KIRKLAND[13]
GÖTTINGEN
September 17 1820

Another semester has just been closed, and now my course at Gottingen is finished. I had hoped to have received a few lines from you, encouraging me in my purpose of joining the University of Berlin for the winter. But though I have not heard from you yet the advantages I shall enjoy there, are certainly so great that there is little room for hesitation. For ancient literature we have at Gottingen three professors; but the eldest is lazy, and does not do his duty; the youngest is a beardless youth of fine promise; but as yet he is only growing learned; while the third, the most learned of the whole, little Dissen, is so sickly and so easily disturbed and brought low, that his good will exceeds his powers of action. (He is now engaged with the new edition of Pindar, and promised me he would make a present of it to the Cambridge library, when completed.) Now at Berlin I am sure of Boeckh,[14] who is perhaps the best scholar in Germany; and Wolf,[15] though eminently slothful, reads lectures in winter; and Buttmann,[16] who is now writing a copious Greek Grammar, exercises the young philologians in interpreting the classics. Apart from all this the lectures here are so calculated as to return every two years, and having remained here two years, I hardly know what lectures to take were I to continue my stay during the winter. I go from Gottingen without much regret. The people here are too cold and unsocial, too fond of writing books and too incapable of conversing, having more than enough of courtesy, and almost nothing of actual hospitality. I admire their industry; but they do not love labour; I consider their vast erudition with astonishment; yet it lies as a dead weight on society. The men of letters are for the most part ill bred; many of them are altogether without manners. Here is Harding,[17] whose name is widely spread as the discoverer of a planet and a capital observer of the stars; but he has not a notion of what a gentleman ought to do on earth; the renowned Stäudlin,[18] the cleverest of all the Gottingen theologians, talks quite as vulgarly as a common man of the 'cursed affair of the queen,' and the 'hellish bad situation of the ministers'; and our excellent Heeren,[19] who has written the most acute book that has ever been written on the commerce of the ancients, hardly knows how to hold commerce with men of his own time. One of the most copious of the professors longs to get some petty office as clerk at Hanover and often exclaims, 'could I once get out of this hell on earth, I would never write a book again.' As it is he writes two octavos a year. And Eichhorn, than whom I have never seen a more amiable or a kinder man speaks often of his labours, in a manner, which does not increase one's respect for him, and seems to think by devoting himself so exclusively to books he has lost the chance of enjoying life, and partaking of the pleasures of the idle. All these things seem to justify the Germans of higher rank in the little respect, with which they treat the learned; but they correspond poorly with the childish ideas I had formed in America of the superior culture and venerable character of the wise in Europe. [. . .]

TO PRESIDENT KIRKLAND

BERLIN

November 5, 1820

[. . .] I have already been here about six weeks, and find abundant cause of joy for having come here. The character of the men of letters is quite the reverse of the character of the Gottingen Professors. There an abhorrence is felt for all innovations; here the new, that is good or promises to lead to good, cannot be too soon adopted. At Gottingen the whole tendency of the courses is, to make the students learned, to fill their memories with matters of fact; here the grand aim is to make them think. At Gottingen experience stands in good repute, and men are most fond of listening to her voice, but at Berlin experience is a word not to be pronounced too often; speculation is looked on as the prime source of truth. At G. the men are engaged in growing learned and writing useful books, which demonstrate their erudition; at Berlin the professors are perhaps quite as learned, but more accustomed to reflect; and you may find many of their books, to have written which a prodigious degree of erudition was required, and which yet do not contain a single citation. Certainly Göttingen is the best place to gather genuine learning; but I hardly think a man would learn there how to use it properly. [. . .]

As to my studies this winter, they will be chiefly a continuance of my former philological ones, to which I add a little philosophy and French and Italian. I need not say, how fine the schools of Prussia are; they are acknowledged to be the finest in Germany. Here in Berlin a great many new ideas are going into application; and the indistinct forebodings of Pestalozzi,[20] and the eloquent discourses of Fichte have not been without lasting fruits. I need not assure you how happy I am in having an opportunity of studying the science of education in a city, where it has been the subject of so much discussion and where the Government have done so much, have done everything they could do, to realize the vast advantages about to result from the reform in the institutions of instruction. No Government knows so well how to create Universities and high schools as the Prussian. The new Academy at Bonn rivals already the oldest Universities. I have taken a course of lectures with Schleiermacher on the science of education; it is the most interesting which I have as yet attended. He brings to his subject a mind sharpened by philosophical meditation and enriched with the learning of all ages and countries. He applies to his subject all his vast acquaintance with the different systems of ethics, and with the human mind; his language is luminous, elegant and precise; his delivery is I think almost perfect. I honour Schleiermacher above all the German scholars, with whom it has been my lot to become acquainted.

My other courses are with Boeckh, Hegel and Wolf, all names of the first rank; though Boeckh is very far from having the genius of Wolf, or Hegel from having the clearness of either.

[...]

CHAPTER 9

American Colleges and German Universities

Richard Theodore Ely

INTRODUCTION TO ELY'S ESSAY

Richard Ely was an economist who helped found the main professional association of his discipline and held professorships at Johns Hopkins, the University of Wisconsin, where his progressive politics almost got him fired, and Northwestern University, where, in 1933, he retired from teaching, having taught for more than fifty years. Ely was also something of a Germanophile. For him as for many Americans of his generation, Germany was a place of academic excellence and innovation. In fact, Ely was known for establishing in the United States the ideas of the German historical school. This was a "historicist" school of economics, which, as he put it, argued that classical economics did not identify unchanging laws but rather described the economic life, for example, "of commercial England in the eighteenth century." Some of the key members of the school—for example, Gustav Schmoller—were known for bringing their politics into the lecture hall, and it was by emulating them in this that Ely nearly lost his job. (Max Weber formulated the ideal of *Wertfreiheit*, or value neutrality in scholarship and especially in teaching, in explicit reaction to Schmoller.) At the time, social scientists in the United States were expected to act otherwise, particularly if they had progressive leanings, as Ely did.

For Ely, Germany was, moreover, a place of bureaucratic efficiency—he reported admiringly on the development of its railway system—and, not least, of fun.

Ely grew up in austere circumstances. His father was an intensely pious man, so pious that he refused to grow barley on the family's farm in upstate New York because he knew it would be used to make beer. This despite the fact that the farm did poorly and needed all the help it could get. During his college years at Dartmouth and Columbia, Ely kept his nose to the grindstone. The transfer to the latter institution was motivated by economic concerns; Ely could live with relatives in New York, which made Columbia the less expensive option. His assiduity would pay off. Ely distinguished himself as a student of literature and philosophy, winning a fellowship for postgraduate study in Germany. It was there, and more specifically in the idyllic town of Heidelberg, that, as he wrote in a letter to his (very alarmed) father, he learned to enjoy life.

Part of the pleasure was the German academic system. Not only did Ely prefer the German system of lectures by experts to the still recitation-oriented American system, which emphasized rote learning; he also remarked on how German professors, in contrast to their American counterparts, treated students as fellow seekers of new knowledge. This, he wrote, made "studying in Germany a pleasure to every real student." Accordingly, Ely went back to Germany as often as he could, and when he became a teacher, he advised his own students—among whom were Thorsten Veblen and Woodrow Wilson—to train at a German university.

But in 1880, when, as a newly minted PhD, Ely was living in Berlin and worrying about his career prospects, the time seemed right for at least a partial debunking of the German university system. It was, after all, the high point of American enthusiasm for German academia. Johns Hopkins, America's first research university, had just been founded, and it was famously indebted to the German model; it soon became known as "Göttingen in Baltimore." In 1879, moreover, more Americans studied abroad in Germany (about six hundred) than in any other year during the century between the end of the Napoleonic Wars and the beginning of World War I. Puncturing the bubble of idealizing and echoing the concerns of many German commentators, including Nietzsche, Ely's essay on American colleges and German universities pointed out several problems with the latter institutions, such as how the storied values of *Lernfreiheit* and *Lehrfreiheit* had been squeezed in the push for vocational training. This push was an effect of a number of factors. During the 1870s, for one thing, the percentage of university students with a degree from a vocational high school increased. For another, the economic downturn of 1873 led to widespread anxieties about university graduates winding up unemployed—Bismarck brooded over the prospect at length, fearing that such a group would spearhead subversive activities—and these worries in turn led some students to use practical concerns to guide their course selection.

Ely was not particularly sympathetic. He argued that instead of making good use of the vast resources at their disposal, and following their intellectual inclinations in a process of self-discovery and self-formation (i.e., *Bildung* as Humboldt had conceived of it), students exercised their freedom to choose what to study (*Lernfreiheit*) as the freedom to choose a career. Having settled on their choice, they cared only about what they needed to do in order to pass their exams and obtain the professional credentials they wanted. Thus the professors' academic freedom (*Lehrfreiheit*), which included the freedom to teach whatever they wanted to, had been compromised. Professors could offer courses in whatever topic they liked, to be sure, but even the best minds and most dynamic speakers were hard-pressed to attract enough students when they wandered into areas that didn't help with exam requirements. Or so Ely maintained. In doing so, he might have noted that German professors had strong material incentives to offer courses that would enroll well, since part of their income came from the fees students paid on a per course basis, and the more students that attended, the greater the professor's "honorarium" would be. (Nonregular faculty derived income for their service to the university solely from the fees.) Ely also claimed that while some students were less focused on entering the workforce, and made full use of their freedom to stay at the university indefinitely, these students tended to slack off rather than fruitfully explore different possibilities.

Upon graduating from college, Ely intended to enter the ministry, and like most American professors of the period, he believed that higher education should involve moral education—the formation of character. His skepticism toward the German model proceeds in part from this belief. While Ely allows that with its rigorous requirements, the German elective system has the advantage of producing competent professionals, he presses his readers to ask themselves: Should anyone really see such a system as a model of higher education worthy of wholesale emulation at American universities?

And even if the German system should be held up as a model, would wholesale emulation have made sense at American universities? The key incongruity between the German and American educational systems, for Ely, was the fact that the German gymnasium provided a foundation of classical learning far superior to the one that could be acquired in American high schools. Of course, this was a problem that had bedeviled Henry Tappan's attempt to put "Prussian educational ideals" into practice in America several decades earlier. For American educational reformers with the same goal, it would remain a great stumbling block, another major reason why these ideals could only be adapted, not adopted.

AMERICAN COLLEGES AND GERMAN UNIVERSITIES

Many excellent articles and addresses on college and university education in the United States and Germany have been written during the last ten years, but the authors have usually taken it for granted not only that all have clear ideas as to the character and purposes of these institutions, but also that perfect harmony exists between these ideas. The discussion has, therefore, turned upon the means of realizing a character and accomplishing ends not plainly defined. Had, however, each educational reformer first obtained a clear conception of the actual "final cause" of American and foreign universities and colleges, and then compared that conception with the desired "final cause," it is safe to assert that the present notions in respect to both would be far less confused.

The comparison universally made is between our colleges and the German universities. It is shown that the condition of higher education in the United States is in a sad state—and about this there can be no doubt; that in Germany, on the contrary, it is in a flourishing one; ergo, let us turn our colleges into German universities. The next question is, How? In answer to this it is explained that in the German universities the studies are all elective and optional; in the colleges of the United States, compulsory. The conclusion is not difficult to be drawn. Make all studies in the colleges elective, and the work is done! The country is provided with a set of first-class universities! The German universities have thus been taken as models, and a sort of blind attempt made to imitate them in the way described. German universities are an acknowledged success, it is true; but what does it mean to pronounce an institution a success? It signifies that a harmony exists between the intentions of its founders and managers and the accomplished results. The questions then naturally arise, What is the purpose of the German university? What is its real distinguishing feature? Then, after having answered these, the further questions, Do American colleges have the same aims? If they do not, is it desirable that they should?

The answer to the first question is not difficult. A German university is, from beginning to end, through and through, a professional school. It is a place where young men prepare to earn their "bread and butter," as the Germans say, in practical life. It is *not* a school which pretends or strives to develop in a general way the intellectual powers, and give its students universal culture. This is the first point which should be clearly understood by all trying to Germanize our institutions. As soon as the student enters the university he makes a selection of some one study or set of studies—law, medicine, or some of the studies included in the "philosophy faculty"—chemistry, physics, Latin, Greek, philosophy, literature, modern languages, etc. If a student pursues chemistry, it is because his chemistry is to support him in afterlife; if Latin and Greek, because he is preparing himself for a position as teacher; so it is with the other branches. The first question a university student asks before selecting a study is, "Of what practical benefit will this be to me?" An opportunity is given to extraordinary talent and genius of developing, however, by allowing a certain freedom in "learning and teaching." There is no regulation to prevent a student of law from hearing a lecture, e.g., on the Agamemnon of Æschylus; but this rarely happens. Each one has the examination in mind which is to admit him into active life, and, as a rule, pursues only the studies required for passing it, and what is more, pursues them no farther than is likely to be demanded. If a smattering of the history of philosophy is required, as in the theological examination in Prussia, the candidate will read the work by Schwegler,[1] but stop there. There are exceptions: some study for the love of study, for the love of science, of truth; but they are few. The professors who teach sciences not required for some examination complain that comparatively few students attend their lectures. Professor Wundt, the distinguished psychologist and philosopher of Leipzig, explains in this way the little attention paid to philosophy by German students. In the philosophical magazine *Mind*, for November, 1877, he compares the German and English universities. "The German student does not," says he, "like his English compeer, reside at the university simply with the object of general scientific culture, but, first and foremost, he pursues a 'Brodstudium.' He has chosen a profession which is to procure him a future living as doctor, practicing lawyer, clergyman, master in one of the higher schools, or the like, and for which he must establish his fitness in an examination at the close of his university career. But how enormously have the subjects of instruction increased in the majority of these professions! . . . It requires either compulsion or a specially lively interest to bring our doctors, lawyers, philologists, to the philosophical lectures. But of late compulsion has for the most part ceased." Professor Wagner, the political economist, of Berlin, has not long since expressed himself quite similarly. He says only a small number of the law students hear his lectures on political economy, or any other lectures which are not absolutely required for examination. In the University of Berlin there are over three thousand matriculated students, and nearly two thousand non-matriculated attendants at lectures; but so celebrated a man as Zeller has only a small number of hearers at his lectures on psychology, because it is a subject required for but few examinations. At Halle in the winter semester 1877–78 only one course of lectures on psychology was announced, that, however, by a clever young man, an author of some philosophical works. Although there are nine hundred students at Halle, the lectures were not delivered, because two could not be found who desired to hear them. The only one who presented himself was the writer, a foreigner, and when he was trying to find number two, and proposed to others to hear the lecture, the answer was, "It is not required for the examination."

This shows how seriously those college professors and trustees have erred who have imagined that they were turning our American colleges into German universities by making the studies elective and optional. The German institution which corresponds to an American college as a school of general intellectual training is the gymnasium, where there is but a minimum of election in the studies; *e.g.*, Hebrew is optional, and the student has perhaps a choice between English and some other study. The Germans suppose that experienced teachers and men of tried ability, who have devoted years to investigating the matter, are better able to judge of the studies advisable for the general development of the intellectual powers of boys than the boys themselves. It would seem that they might be in the right. On the contrary, the essence of the freedom which each university student has of electing his studies is simply the freedom given to men of selecting their own professions. The door through which every German must pass into office or profession is the examination; but the Minister of Instruction and other public authorities prescribe very minutely the studies required for each examination. Each German student is required to have pursued certain sciences, differing according to his intended profession, before he can enter active life. He has only the liberty of pursuing them when, where, and in the order which he will. He selects his own books, professors, and has his own method, lie may be five years in preparing for the examination, or ten, if he chooses to waste time. This is truly a considerable liberty, but far less than it is generally supposed the German students enjoy. Professor Helmholtz, in his inaugural address, delivered October 15, 1877, as rector of the University of Berlin, acknowledges that many German fathers and statesmen have demanded a diminution of even the existing liberty of university life, and adds, farther, that a stricter discipline and control of the students by the professors would undoubtedly save many a young man who goes to ruin under the present system.

There are three departments of our colleges or universities which correspond to three of those of the German universities, and offer no insurmountable difficulty in the perfection of our school system. These departments are those of law, theology, and medicine. The reforms necessary must be evident to men of the respective professions: greater freedom of the schools from the principle of private money-making institutions; a longer and more thorough course of study, as in Germany, where the time required to be passed in previous study for admittance to the professions of law and medicine is about double what it is in the United States; higher requirements for admittance to these professional schools. That here is a place where the government, if not the central, at least that of the separate States, has a duty to perform, no political economist or statesman of note is so given to the *laissez-faire* principle as to deny. All of our States recognize this, and exercise some control as regards physicians and lawyers. If a tailor makes me a poor suit of clothes, no great harm is done: I try another next time. Besides, I can demand samples of his work beforehand, and even if no tailor myself, am not utterly unable to judge of his work. Here the principle of private competition is the only proper one. But the principle of private competition in respect of law and medicine is not sufficient. If a medical quack kills my child, it does not help the matter to reply to my complaints, "Well, try another doctor next time." It is heartless. My child is dead, and nothing can help the matter now. "But you should have known that the man was a humbug," says some one. I should have known nothing of the kind. It is precisely because I do not know, because I am no physician, that I require one. Again, in many small towns there is only one physician, and the people have no choice. It is the same case with lawyers. An ignorant or incapable man may cause me the loss of my property, or even my neck. This "next time" theory helps the matter not at all. It is too late. There is for me no next time. The man appeared to me clever; he talked well, and I tried him. I judged as well as I could, but my not being a lawyer made it impossible for me to be a competent judge of his abilities. The State, then, does its citizens a real service, and one they can not do for themselves, in forcing candidates for the legal and medical professions to submit themselves to an examination by competent authorities, who pronounce upon their fitness for exercising the functions of lawyers or doctors. This principle is recognized by every civilized government in the world, though perhaps nowhere so laxly and negligently as in the United States. What is necessary, then, as regards these professional schools is for the State by proper legislation to raise the standard of requirements, and so assist the colleges and universities in giving us an able and properly educated set of professional men, as in Germany, where actual legal and medical malpractice are exceedingly rare. England has lately been forced to take a step in the right direction by making the requirements for becoming a physician severer. The profession was too open to the principle of free competition, and the abuses became intolerable. One other means of improving these professional schools would be to bring them in closer connection with the college departments, so that a medical or law student should have the liberty of hearing lectures on history, political economy, etc., if he wished. All the different schools should, of course, have one common library. This is the plan pursued on the continent of Europe. It frequently happens, too, that students of different departments have the same studies, and it is a waste of time, money, and force to separate them here. The law student is not the only one who needs to understand "international law," nor the medical student the only one who ought to have some knowledge of physiology and hygiene.[2]

The so-called college department, or "college proper," is the one which offers most difficulty to the reformer, and the one where the most confusion prevails. When the course of study is simply one for general culture, it is not part of a university, in the continental European sense of that term. There is, therefore, in America a want of a school offering opportunities to large and constantly increasing classes of men for pursuing professional studies—a want which is deeply felt, and which sends every year many students and millions of dollars out of the country. Where in the United States can a young man prepare himself thoroughly to become a teacher of the ancient classics? A simple college course is not enough. The Germans require that their teachers of Latin and Greek should pursue the classics as a specialty for three years at university after having completed the gymnasium, which as a classical school would be universally admitted to rank with our colleges. Every college professor of Latin and Greek must admit the need of better preparatory teachers. The poor entrance examinations, when the candidates for admissions do not come from some one of our few old and excellent but expensive academies, like Exeter, Andover, and the Boston Latin School, bear only too strong witness of their previous training. If an American wishes to pursue a special course in history, politics, political economy, mathematics, physics, philosophy, or in any one of many other studies lying outside of the three professions, law, medicine, and theology, he must go to Europe. Even to pursue the study of United States history, the American will do better to go abroad. From Maine to California, from Minnesota to Texas, there is no institution which teaches United States history thoroughly. Many colleges require no knowledge of it, either for entering or graduating. Others imagine that they have done their full duty in demanding a few historical names and dates as condition of admittance. As many—in the country the majority—of our lower schools do not teach history, the result is sad enough. English papers have with reason spoken slightingly of historical instruction in our country. Again, whoever desires, even in theology, medicine, or law, to select some one branch as a specialty, must go to Europe to do so. But these professional schools are already organized, and their needs recognized.

[. . .]

CHAPTER 10

On German Universities

Henry Tappan

INTRODUCTION TO TAPPAN'S TEXTS

The pioneer generation of Americans who studied in Germany—those men who, like George Ticknor, Edward Everett, and George Bancroft, went over just after the Napoleonic Wars—certainly did something to awaken interest in German universities among their compatriots. Indeed, the trail they blazed to the University of Göttingen soon became well worn. Before long, the university had an "American Colony," which in turn had its own fraternity. But what had a far greater influence on the American pedagogical imagination was the 1835 English rendering of a report composed a few years earlier for the minister of education in France: Victor Cousin's highly enthusiastic *Report on the State of Public Instruction in Prussia.* This document piqued the curiosity of many, including that of the man who would emerge as the most ardent champion of the German educational system in mid-nineteenth-century America, Henry Tappan.

Tappan didn't actually study in Germany. He didn't visit Germany's universities, in fact, until he had edged into middle age. In 1838, Tappan was fired from his position as a professor of philosophy at the University of the City of New York (later NYU)—he had run afoul of the administration by protesting against the glacial pace of its reform efforts—and in the 1840s, he traveled widely, visiting universities in England, France, and the German lands. In his telling, the system of higher education he encountered in Prussia more than lived up to the impressions he had formed from afar. An essay that he penned in 1850, and that reflects on the efforts of other American reformers and is excerpted in this volume, enthuses: "In Protestant Germany, what an advance has been made! In no part of the world has university education been so enlarged, and been made so liberal and thorough." Tappan goes on to explain this appraisal:

> We have spoken of the German Universities as model institutions. Their excellence consists in two things: first, they are purely Universities without any admixture of collegial tuition. Secondly, they are complete as Universities, providing libraries and all other material of learning, and having professors of eminence to lecture on theology, law, and medicine, the philosophical, mathematical, natural, philological, and political Sciences, on history and geography, on the history and principles of Art, in fine, upon every branch of human knowledge. The professors are so numerous that a proper division of labor takes place, and every subject is thoroughly discussed. At the University every student selects the courses he is to attend. He is thrown upon his own responsibility and diligence. He is left free to pursue his studies; but, if he wishes to become a clergyman, a physician, a lawyer, a statesman, a professor, or a teacher in any superior school, he must go through the most rigid examinations, both oral and written. Collegial tuition in the German Universities does not exist because wholly unnecessary, the student being fully prepared at the Gymnasium before he is permitted to enter the University. Without the Gymnasium, the University would be little worth.

What Tappan saw, or believed he saw, was Humboldt's ideals of education in action. Having developed a foundational base of knowledge in the classics as gymnasium students, German university students could probe any area of human knowledge, learning from lectures by the top experts of the day, as well as from the awe-inspiring resources of their institutions' libraries. And for Tappan, this process of intellectual exploration—and the maturation of mind and character it fostered—was not at odds with utilitarian ends. Students were "free to pursue" any field in the university's heady atmosphere of reflection and discovery, but in many cases, once they settled on a choice, they had to follow a curriculum designed to make them into credentialed professionals.

Tappan was smitten, and when, after a lengthy and bumpy search, he was appointed the first president of the University of Michigan in 1852, the largest school in the country at the time, he made no secret of his desire to recast the university according to "the Prussian ideals of education." Nor did he make a secret of the difficulties he faced. American secondary schools were a far cry from the gymnasium. One could try to change this: Back then, the University of Michigan had "branches" that were supposed to provide secondary education to several towns, but they, too, lagged far behind the gymnasium. For the foreseeable future, the American university would have to be both college and university. It would have to offer the preparatory foundation of the gymnasium, and also, in order to be a "University worthy of the name," it would have to feature "those more extended studies in science, literature, and the arts, which alone can lead to profound and finished scholarship."

Convinced, as he emphasizes in the work excerpted here, that universities could be built up quickly (with the right sort of state support), Tappan wanted to make rapid progress toward this goal, something he was in fact able to accomplish. During his first five years, he successfully recruited faculty who were interested in research and producing original scholarship; he expanded and strengthened the sciences, hiring a physicist, a civil engineer, and a (German) astronomer; he secured funds for upgrading the library and the scientific facilities; lectures largely supplanted recitations; and the number of students enrolled at Michigan more than doubled, rising to 460 in 1857.

But Tappan's signature reform was to be a level of instruction he called the "University Course," in which college graduates and possibly advanced college students "prepared by previous study" could pursue "the highest knowledge" in a wide range of fields, just as one could, he believed, at German universities. In this way, then, Tappan hoped to make his university "worthy of the name." Or as he put it, the University Course would "form the proper development of the University, in distinction from the College and Gymnasium in operation."

Tappan's University of Michigan has been celebrated as the midcentury American institution that hewed most closely to the German model—and with good reason. But Tappan's attempt at adaptation illustrates the difficulty of that process. As historians have pointed out, Tappan's would-be signature initiative neither corresponded directly to the German system nor directly anticipated the later structure of the American graduate program. The University Course delivered little in the way of specialization or research training. It did indeed represent an improvement over the education delivered by the midcentury college, but it was more like a harbinger of the upper-division undergraduate curriculum than the driver of "finished scholarship" that Tappan had dreamed of.

In addition, the program never got off the ground in the way Tappan hoped it would. He faced opposition at every turn. Despite his background as a clergyman, as well as his belief in the importance of character formation as an aim of higher education, Tappan's European airs aroused suspicion, and he was often accused by the religious colleges in Michigan of promoting a "godless," "amoral" agenda. Many of those colleges pressured the state legislature to shut Tappan's project down. And some state legislators voiced concerns about whether Tappan's reforms were sufficiently American in nature. Only toward the end of Tappan's time at Michigan—he was fired in 1863—did the university offer some of the "postgraduate" courses he had envisioned.

His legacy, however, is substantial. Tappan's actions, as well as writings such as the panegyric to the University of Bonn that follows, won him capable supporters who would continue his work at Michigan and elsewhere. Foremost among them were the historian Andrew Dickson White, who later became Cornell's first president, the classicist Henry Frieze, who had studied in Germany and would repeatedly serve as Michigan's acting president, and Charles Kendall Adams, an undergraduate in Tappan's day, who became a professor of history at Michigan. In 1871, Adams, having done a stint of his own in Germany, instituted seminar-style teaching that resembled the training of advanced students in Germany. And by the end of the 1870s, Frieze and Adams had played a central role in creating PhD programs that had German-style requirements: comprehensive exams and a demonstrated ability to conduct original research. Of course, this, too, was a creative adaptation of the German model, since German universities made no distinction between undergraduate and graduate programs. It's unclear whether such achievements brought Tappan a measure of satisfaction. After his dismissal in 1863, which hurt him deeply, he moved his family to Europe and spent the rest of his life there. He never returned to Ann Arbor.

BONN AND ITS UNIVERSITY

The banks of the Rhine between Cologne and Bonn are flat like those below. We therefore proceeded by the railroad. At Bonn we put up at the Grand Hotel Royal, situated on the bank of the river, near the University, and overlooking the thickly wooded park which stretches in front of it. Our rooms commanded a view beyond the Rhine, up and down the river, and embraced the outline of the *Siebengebirge*—the seven mountains. It was a clear serene summer evening, and the temperature was delightful. Behind the hotel the grounds were tastefully laid out, and on the bank of the river seats were arranged for the guests. Here an admirable military band was performing delicious music. Travellers from all nations were collected, walking and chatting, or seated in groups; while here and there, some individual was lounging apart, quietly whiffing a cigar, resigned to pleasant meditations, and indulging to the full the *dolce far niente.* Among the company there was a plentiful sprinkling of English. Of Americans, besides ourselves, there were two very agreeable southern gentlemen, who had been our companions from Cologne. Every one was in a good humor. We appeared like beings who had left all care behind, and were making a voyage into enchanted regions. Life now was a holiday. Whatever had been, whatever hereafter might be of toil and sorrow, was not remembered or apprehended. The present was to us a pleasure boat upon a summer sea. It was an episode of beauty and joy on the weary way of human life. We were strangers to each other, and we cared not to know each other's names and occupations. We were to each other not like creatures of the common earth, but mysterious beings dropped from kindly skies—angels meeting angels, exchanging smiles and pleasant words, and then passing on, each to his own happy purpose, each full of his own enjoyments. We were on the banks of the legendary Rhine, under the soft twilight of a midsummer evening, "lapped in Elysian airs," and the morrow was full of promise. Is it not well thus sometimes to forget every thing but pleasure? Does not the breath of the beautiful recreate us, and renew our strength to return to the old reality of work?

In this happy mood we went to sleep. In the morning we arose to take a view of Bonn and its University. Bonn is not a large town; it contains only eighteen thousand inhabitants. But it is the more picturesque and agreeable in that it is not a large town. It leaves the hills and trees standing, and does not crowd upon the Rhine as if it were eager to drink up all the water. The Electors of Cologne once resided here. They removed their court from the dense noisy commercial city to this quiet town reposing in the lap of nature. Here no restless improvements are going on; improvement seems to have been accomplished, and to be simply enjoyed. But, nevertheless, improvement is going on here, improvement that never can slumber or pause—the eternal improvement of mind. The palace of the Electors, a quarter of a mile in length, contains the University. Here are the lecture rooms, and the library of 150,000 volumes. It has at present forty professors, and one thousand and fifty students. It enjoys a high reputation. Niebuhr and A. W. Schlegel were professors here. The king of Prussia founded it in 1818, and bestowed upon it the palace of the Old Electors. The University, indeed, constitutes the importance of Bonn. The beauty of the situation, and the literary advantages make it a most desirable place of residence. I walked through the library in mute admiration. It is a noble collection of books. And yet this great and justly celebrated University has been established only thirty-four years. It is therefore a young institution. The idea that Universities must be of slow growth is not justified by the history of Prussia. The University of Berlin was established in 1810. In 1826, the number of matriculated students amounted to sixteen hundred and forty-two, four hundred of whom were foreigners. And yet Prussia has several other flourishing Universities. The whole monarchy equals in square miles only some two of our states, and contains fifteen and a half millions of inhabitants. But Prussia is no less distinguished for common schools and seminaries of every grade. In 1835, there were 21,790 elementary schools, in which two millions of children of both sexes received instruction. About the same time there were one hundred and twenty-four gymnasia, where 24,641 scholars were educated. Let it be remembered that the gymnasia are superior to our colleges. There are many schools, too, in Prussia, specially adapted to mechanics and to various kinds of manufacture and business. Probably no country in the world has an educational system so comprehensive and thorough.

The Universities nourish and bring together men eminent for genius and learning. The kings of Prussia, from Frederick the Great down to the present time, have been the enlightened patrons of learning and learned men. At Berlin, in the immediate vicinity of the Court, are found such men as Humboldt, Savigny, Ranke, Raumer,[1] Ehrenberg, Ritter, Grimm, and Schelling. Here, too, lived Schleiermacher and Neander.[2]

And now this Prussia is an unlimited monarchy: these kings are despots. I have said, in a previous chapter, that despotic governments are beautiful in theory; and I there intimated quite plainly that I deem them such, generally, only in theory. But we must be just. In the educational system of Prussia we have something more than theory. Here is a glorious achievement of an enlightened and energetic despotism. I admit that there are many evils in Prussia, and that the kings are both unwise, and in the wrong, for not granting a constitutional government. But here is a sublime work which they have accomplished for the public good. But, it may be asked, Do you allow this to be an argument in favor of unlimited monarchies? I answer that the government of Prussia is justly entitled to all the argument that can be made out of it. So far, the government may proudly say, Judge us by our fruits. And the only way in which we can nullify the force of the argument is by proving by our works that a republic, too, can create and foster the noblest institutions of learning, can patronize the arts and artists, and learning and learned men.

The immense and peculiar blessings which are enjoyed under a Republic are obvious to all; but it is required, too, that it should be favorable to the highest forms of culture. In order to prove that we are under the most elevated and the happiest conditions of human existence, it is not enough to show that men can be better fed and clothed here than in other lands, and that we enjoy the fairest opportunities for material accumulation; it must be shown, also, that we can develope the grandest forms of humanity itself. We cannot stand still; we must be advancing or deteriorating in national character: we cannot advance without culture; and we cannot have culture without great men as standards of excellence, and as lights to guide us. Now, we have not been without great men—we have had our governing standards and our guiding lights—whether in sufficient degree and number I shall not stop to inquire; but we have had them, and, perhaps, we have them now. But it is certain that in a country so vast as ours, and with destinies so momentous at stake, we want more great men than any other people, for we have a greater work for them to do here than elsewhere—to make a whole people great. It is not only demanded of us as a justification of our institutions that we show ourselves equal to every thing that advances and adorns humanity, but it is the very condition of the perpetuation of these institutions. A Republic like ours must he filled with the light of knowledge, must be permeated by principles of truth and integrity, must be guided by great men, must be filled by a great people—great in character and worth—or it will go to pieces. We are not an inorganic aggregation sustained by a mechanical force, but an organic growth spreading out our branches, bearing fruit, and sustained by a vigorous and sound life within. We want, therefore, both a popular education in the sense of giving a good degree of education to all, and the possibilities and means of the highest forms of education open to all who choose to avail themselves of them. In our country we must open the most auspicious race to man for every thing that meets his wants and destinies and contributes to his perfection.

In popular education we have done much; here we can point to our works with satisfaction: but, in the higher institutions, it must be confessed we are sadly deficient. We have not got in our country one University. One fruitful cause of this deficiency is a current opinion that we are yet too young a country to develope a University system like that which has obtained in Europe, that it must be the slow growth of time, and that when we are prepared for it, we shall have it. But the early youth of our nation is the very season to plant those institutions which shall mine our growth and maturity. Nor is it true that they are necessarily of slow growth. Look at the Universities of Bonn, and of Berlin. We can create universities at once, if we will. Let us show that the spirit of a free people is no less enlightened and mighty than the unlimited monarchy of Prussia.

THE DEVELOPMENT OF EDUCATIONAL SYSTEMS AND INSTITUTIONS

[. . .]

The Educational System of Germany, and particularly in Prussia, is certainly a very noble one. We cannot well be extravagant in its praise. Thorough in all its parts, consistent with itself, and vigorously sustained, it furnishes every department of life with educated men, and keeps up at the Universities themselves, in every branch of knowledge, a supply of erudite and elegant scholars and authors, to the benefit and glory of their country, and the good of mankind.

In comparing the University system of Germany with that of England, it is worthy of remark that Germany has also admirable common-school systems for popular education, while England is strikingly deficient in this respect. In the one case a properly-developed University system has reached its natural result of invigorating general education; in the other the priestly privilege of a cloistered learning is still maintained.

The Colleges of America are plainly copied from the Colleges of the English Universities. The course of studies, the President and Tutors, the number of years occupied by the course, are all copied from the English model. We have seen that in the English Institutions, the name of University alone remained, while the collegial or tutorial system absorbed all the educational functions. In America, while Colleges were professedly established, they soon assumed a mixed character. Professors were appointed, but they discharged only the duty of tutors in the higher grades of study; so that the tutors were really assistant professors, or the professors only tutors of the first rank. Our Colleges also have from the beginning conferred degrees in all the faculties, which in England belongs only to the University. By establishing the faculties of Theology, Law, and Medicine, some of our colleges have approached still more nearly to the forms and functions of a University. By assuming the title of University and College indifferently, as we are prone to do, we seem to intimate that we have some characteristics belonging to both, and that we deem it in our power to become Universities whenever we please. Sometimes the only advance made to the higher position, is by establishing a medical school; which, however, has little other connection with the college than its dependence upon it for conferring the degree of Doctor of Medicine.

If we understand aright the distinction between a College and a University, the latter is not necessarily constituted by collecting together schools under the different faculties. These may be merely collegial schools. A University course presumes a preparatory tutorial course, by which the students have acquired elementary knowledge, and formed habits of study and investigation, to an extent sufficient to enable them to hear the lectures of professors with advantage, to consult libraries with facility and profit, and to carry on for themselves researches into the different departments of literature and science. A University course may be indefinitely extended at the pleasure of the student. He may here undertake the fullest philosophical education possible—passing from one branch of study to another, and selecting courses of lectures according to the state of his knowledge, and the intellectual discipline which he requires; or, having accomplished a satisfactory general education of his powers, he may next, either enter upon professional studies, or devote himself to some particular branch of science as the occupation of his life. In the German Universities any one, whether he designs to give himself wholly to a student's life, or to fit himself for a professor's chair, may, after undergoing the requisite examination, obtain from the faculty to which he belongs, permission to teach, without receiving any compensation, and only as a form of education. The professors extraordinary are selected from these licentiates, and receive a small salary. From these again the professors of the different Faculties are usually selected. Every person of these three classes may lecture upon any subject he pleases: but professors are obliged, besides, to lecture on the branches particularly contemplated in their appointment. In this way at a University alone can the intellectual life be varied and enlarged. A University is literally a *Cyclopaedia* where are collected books on every subject of human knowledge, cabinets and apparatus of every description that can aid learned investigation and philosophical experiment, and amply qualified professors and teachers to assist the student in his studies, by rules and directions gathered from long experience, and by lectures which treat of every subject with the freshness of thought not yet taking its final repose in authorship, and which often present discoveries and views in advance of what has yet been given to the world. In fine, a University is designed to give to him who would study every help that he needs or desires.

A College in distinction from a University is an elementary and a preparatory school. A College may be directly connected with the University, or it may not. Its original connection with the University was partly accidental, and partly necessary. It was necessary to provide convenient habitations for students who flocked to hear the lectures of the doctor or professor. Many of these students might require private tuition, in relation both to preparatory and additional studies, and thus the colleges would become places of separate study under masters appointed for that purpose. This must especially have been demanded in the early period of the Universities, when preparatory schools were not common.

In Germany the Gymnasia are really the Colleges. The education which they furnish is more thorough, we believe, than what is obtained at the Colleges of either England or of our own country. In England, schools like that of Rugby, under the late Dr. Arnold,[3] and in America those schools commonly called *Academies*, and indeed other classical schools, are of the nature of a college, only of a still lower grade, and more elementary. In passing from the classical school to the college the studies are not essentially changed, nor is the kind of discipline. Hence, a student in our country can prepare at the academy for the second, third, and even fourth year of collegial study. In college there may be less of juvenile discipline, and there generally are greater advantages. What gives the college, however, its chief distinction is the power of conferring academical degrees. We may say, therefore, the academy prepares for the college, and the college prepares for a degree. In England the colleges are directly connected with the University. But it appears the University has fallen into desuetude, and colleges alone remain.

In our country we have no Universities. Whatever may be the names by which we choose to call our institutions of learning, still they are not Universities. They have neither the libraries and material of learning, generally, nor the number of professors and courses of lectures, nor the large and free organization which go to make up Universities. Nor does the connection of Divinity, Law, and Medical Schools with them give them this character. For law and medicine a thorough preparatory classical discipline is not required. In this respect the last is the most deficient of the two, and great numbers receive the academical degree of Doctor of Medicine who have never received an academical education. The degree of Doctor of Laws is more sparingly bestowed than any other; and this, as well as Doctor of Divinity, is never bestowed introductory to the entrance upon professional life. The schools of Theology approach more nearly to the University character than any other, since a collegial discipline is generally required preparatory to an entrance therein. The course of study in our colleges, copying from the English, was, at their first institution, fixed at four years. The number of studies then was far more limited than at present, and the scholarship was consequently more thorough and exact. There was less attempted, but what was attempted was more perfectly mastered, and hence afforded a better intellectual discipline. With the vast extension of science, it came to pass that the course of study was vastly enlarged. Instead of erecting Universities, we have only pressed into our four years' course a greater number of studies. The effect has been disastrous. We have destroyed the charm of study by hurry and unnatural pressure, and we have rendered our scholarship vague and superficial. We have not fed thought by natural supplies of knowledge. We have not disciplined mind by guiding it to a calm and profound activity; but, we have stimulated acquisition to preternatural exertions, and have learned, as it were, from an encyclopædia the mere names of sciences, without gaining the sciences themselves.

[. . .]

CHAPTER 11

German Universities: A Narrative of Personal Experience

James M. Hart

INTRODUCTION TO HART'S NARRATIVE

When James Morgan Hart's *German Universities: A Narrative of Personal Experience* appeared in 1874, American professors and college administrators had already said a lot about the German educational system. Indeed, that they had said a lot about the topic had become a topic in its own right. Hart was an English professor who had studied law in Göttingen and Berlin from 1861 to 1864. He had returned for another year in 1872, when he was between jobs (he taught at Cornell, the University of Cincinnati, and again at Cornell). What Hart wanted to add to the mix of writings on the German educational system was a work that would be, as one of his many reviewers put it, a "plain, straightforward account of what a foreign student may do" in Germany, and "what he may best set himself to accomplish." Keyed to a popular audience, and outfitted with some of the trappings of a guidebook, like lists of the top professors in Germany and a "Practical Hints" section, Hart's book has been credited with helping to popularize studying abroad in Germany—or rather, with helping to further popularize it, since it had long been a common practice.

But in addition to giving detailed descriptions of such experiences as sitting for exams, listening to professors lecture, and taking part in the recreational activities favored by German students (the book certainly lives up to its subtitle), *German Universities* has an argumentative component. As the section presented here shows, Hart, whose scholarship was deeply influenced by his encounter with German philology, wants to make a case for the "superiority" of the German system. Though he states upfront that he is not agitating for the blanket adoption of the German model, the implication is that the American system should change—or be changed—to become more like its German counterpart. Indeed, the economist Richard Ely framed his revisionist take on the issue of emulation, which is included in this anthology (136–43), as though it were meant as a direct response to Hart's book, whose insightfulness was lauded, it is worth noting, by none other than Friedrich Paulsen, perhaps the greatest historian of German education.

The two American scholars agreed on a number of points, to be sure, such as the general excellence of German academics, the cost-effectiveness of education in Germany, and the urgent need for educational reforms in America. And both evince great respect for the ideal of *Wissenschaft*, which Hart deftly translates in his introductory paragraph. However, Hart begins by prizing the effects of freedom in studying and freedom in teaching and research (*Lernfreiheit* and *Lehrfreiheit*) in Germany, and by celebrating the freedom of the German university from all, or almost all, "utilitarian" constraints, maintaining that even the disciplines we would today call "preprofessional" (e.g., law) are taught from a theoretical approach, rather than from a practical one. Ely starts off by challenging precisely those positions.

Both authors permit themselves large, programmatic generalizations based mostly on anecdotal evidence (a common feature of debates about academia that has persisted to the present day). Taken together, their writings convey a sense of the range of students' experiences at late nineteenth-century German universities, as well as a sense of the range of the attitudes toward the German university among the young American scholars who earned degrees there. For anyone interested in the kind of filtering that went on in the minds of Americans reporting on German universities, Hart's and Ely's appraisals invite a more thorough comparison. What could be very revealing indeed is a comparative assessment of them, one that draws on not only memoirs of student years in Germany, a vast resource that tends to be long on nostalgia, but also a thorough scholarly account of the students, teaching conditions, and practices of knowledge production at German universities during the *Kaiserreich*. But that scholarly work remains to be written.

EXCERPT FROM *GERMAN UNIVERSITIES*

What Is a University?

To the German mind the collective idea of a university implies a *Zweck*, an object of study, and two *Bedingungen*, or conditions. The object is *Wissenschaft*, the conditions are *Lehrfreiheit* and *Lernfreiheit*. By *Wissenschaft* the Germans mean knowledge in the most exalted sense of that term, namely, the ardent, methodical, independent search after truth in any and all of its forms, but wholly irrespective of utilitarian application. *Lehrfreiheit* means that the one who teaches, the professor or *Privatdocent*, is free to teach what he chooses, as he chooses. *Lernfreiheit*, or the freedom of learning, denotes the emancipation of the student from *Schulzwang*, compulsory drill by recitation.

If the object of an institution is anything else than knowledge as above defined, or if either freedom of teaching or freedom of learning is wanting, that institution, no matter how richly endowed, no matter how numerous its students, no matter how imposing its buildings, is not, in the eye of a German, a *university*. On the other hand, a small, out-of-the-way place like Rostock, with only thirty-four professors and docents, and one hundred and thirty-five students, is nevertheless as truly a university as Leipsic, where the numbers are one hundred and fifty and three thousand respectively, because Rostock aims at theoretical knowledge and meets the requirements of free teaching and free study. The difference is one of size, not of species.

If we examine the list of lectures and hours of universities like Leipsic, Berlin, and Vienna, we shall be overwhelmed, at first sight, with the amount and the variety of literary and scientific labor announced. The field seems boundless. All that human ingenuity can suggest is apparently represented. On examining more closely, however, we shall find that this seemingly boundless field has its limits, which are very closely traced and which are not exceeded. Strange as it may sound to the American, who is accustomed to gauge spiritual greatness by big numbers and extravagant pretensions, a German university, even the greatest, perceives what it can do and what it *can not do*.

It is not a place "where any man can study anything." Its elevated character makes it all the more modest. It contents itself with the theoretical, and leaves to other institutions the practical and the technical. The list of studies and hours for Leipsic in the semester 1872–3 fills thirty octavo pages. In all that list we shall discover scarcely one course of work that can be called in strictness practical. A German university has one and only one object: to train thinkers. It does not aim at producing poets, painters, sculptors, engineers, miners, architects, bankers, manufacturers. For these, the places of instruction are the Art Schools of Dresden, Munich, Düsseldorf, the Commercial Schools at Bremen, Hamburg, Berlin, Frankfort, the Polytechnicums at Hanover, Frankenberg, Stuttgart, etc. Even in the professions themselves, theory and practice are carefully distinguished, and the former alone is considered as falling legitimately within the sphere of university instruction.

Taking up the four faculties in order: theology, law, medicine,[1] philosophy, and watching them at work, we shall perceive that the evident tendency of their method is to produce theologians rather than pastors, jurists rather than lawyers, theorizers in medicine rather than practitioners, investigators, scholars, speculative thinkers rather than technologists and school-teachers. Yet every pastor, lawyer, doctor, teacher, botanist, geologist has passed through the university course. What is meant, then, by the assertion that the university gives only theoretical training? Do not the practical men in all the professions receive their professional outfit at the university and can receive it nowhere else? The seeming discrepancy is to be explained only by considering the university as a permanent, self-supporting institution, a world in itself, existing for itself, rather than a mere ladder by which to ascend from a lower to a higher plane. Self-supporting, I mean, of course, in the sense that the university is a detached organism assimilating and growing in accordance with its own laws. In a pecuniary sense, it is wholly or almost wholly dependent upon state subvention. The distinction, subtle as it may appear, is essential in forming a just conception of the character of university work. The university supplies itself with its educational staff exclusively from its own graduate members, who pass their entire lives within its precincts. The professors, assistant-professors, docents whose names one reads in the catalogue of Berlin or Leipsic or Heidelberg are one and all, with scarcely an exception, men who started in life as theoreticians and never made the effort to become practitioners. To them the university was not a mere preparatory school, where they might remain long enough to get their theoretical training, and then turn their backs upon it forever. On the contrary, it was an end, a career in itself. They have always been university men, and never expect to become anything else. In this place I must guard against being misunderstood. The reader would receive a very unfair impression of Göttingen, for instance, if he were to infer, from what has been said, that the Göttingen faculty is made up exclusively of Göttingen graduates. Quite the reverse is the case. Probably two thirds come from elsewhere. As a rule, the young *Privatdocent* receives his first call as professor from a university where he has not been known as a student. There exists in this respect complete parity among the German institutions of learning. The feeling which prompts an American college to prefer its own graduates for professors is something quite unknown in Germany. I leave it to the reader's judgment to decide which of the two systems is better: that of liberal selection, or that of "breeding-in." When I speak of a university as recruiting exclusively from its graduates, I mean neither Berlin nor Leipsic nor Heidelberg in particular, but the twenty universities of the German empire regarded as one body, the members of which are perfectly co-ordinate. Professors and docents, and even students, pass from one to another with a restlessness, we might say, that would be surprising in

America, but which is looked upon in Germany as a matter of course. It is the exception, not the rule, when a man passes his entire career as instructor in one place. The key-note of the system is simply this. To those who are connected with the university in any instructional capacity whatever, it is an end and not a means, a life and not a phase of life, a career and not a discipline. The professors are not selected from among the leading lawyers, pastors, doctors, teachers, scientists of the country or province. When a chair already existing becomes vacant, or a new chair is created, and the question of filling it comes up, the Senatus Academicus does not scrutinize the bench or the bar or the gymnasium for an available man. It endeavors to ascertain who is the most promising *Privatdocent*, either in its own midst or at some other seat of learning, the young man who has made his mark by recent publications or discoveries. The newly organized university of Strassburg is a signal instance in point. Within two years after the close of the French war, Strassburg was opened with a full corps of instructors in all the departments. The total number at present is eighty. Yet of these eighty not one, so far as I can ascertain, is what might be called a practitioner. They are all full or half-professors or docents called from other institutions of learning. One who is familiar with the muster-roll of the universities can resolve the Strassburg list into its elements, saying: This man came from Berlin, that one from Vienna, that one from Würzburg, and so on. The reader will probably say: Is not this the case in America also? Are not our college professors all college graduates? To which the answer must be: Not in the same way, not to the same extent. How many of our college professors have been professors, and nothing else? How many have qualified themselves directly for the respective chairs which they occupy, by a life of special study? How many of them formed the resolve while still students, to lead a college life forever, to devote themselves exclusively to instructing others in turn, either at their own Alma Mater or at some other college? I do not have in view such institutions as Yale and Harvard, old, well endowed, fed from the rich soil of New England culture. I mean the typical American college as it exists in the Middle, Southern, and Western States. How many of the professors have been in business, or tried their skill at farming, engineering, journalism? Has or has not the professor of Latin served an apprenticeship as mathematical tutor, or kept a boarding-school for young ladies? How few of the hundreds and thousands of men, from New York to San Francisco, calling themselves professors, can say with a comfortable degree of pride: I selected my specialty in youth, I have pursued it without intermission, without deviation ever since, and I have produced such and such tangible evidences of my industry as a specialist.

No, the reader may rest assured that the character and atmosphere of a German university differ radically from the character and atmosphere of the typical American college. It is a difference of kind, not merely of degree. Comparisons, according to the popular adage, are odious. Yet, even at the risk of giving offense, I take the liberty of drawing a comparison that may serve, perhaps, to throw some light on this vital point. At all events, the comparison shall be a just one. Marburg, in Hesse, has at present 430 students; Princeton, my Alma Mater, has 420. The numbers, then, are almost identical. Each is located in a small country town. Yet Princeton has, all told, not more than 18 professors and tutors; Marburg has 62. Among them are men renowned throughout the world for their original investigations. The same might be said, indeed, of the Princeton faculty, but only with grave restrictions. No one professor at Princeton has the opportunity of working either himself or his students up to his or their full capacity. The instruction goes by routine, each professor contributing his quota to the supposed general development of all the students in a body. At Marburg there is the fourfold division of faculties; there are students pursuing theology, law, medicine, classic philology, modern philology, the natural sciences, history, orientalia. Each instructor has his select band of disciples, upon whom he acts and who re-act upon him. There is the same quiet, scholarly atmosphere, the same disregard for bread-and-butter study, the same breadth of culture, depth of insight, liberality of opinion and freedom of conduct, that one finds in the most favored circles of Leipsic, Berlin, Heidelberg, or Vienna. During every hour of the two months that I passed at Marburg, I was made to feel that a German university, however humble, is a world in and for itself; that its aim is not to turn out clever, pushing, ambitious graduates, but to engender culture.

This condition is both cause and effect. Many of the students who attend the university do so simply with a view to becoming in time professors. The entire *personnel* of the faculty is thus a close corporation, a spiritual order perpetuating itself after the fashion of the Roman Catholic hierarchy. Inasmuch as every professional man and every school-teacher of the higher grades has to pass through the university, it follows that the shaping of the intellectual interests of the country is in the hands of a select few, who are highly educated, perfectly homogeneous in character and sympathies, utterly indifferent to the turmoils and ambitions of the outer-world, who regulate their own lives and mould the dispositions of those dependent upon them according to the principles of abstract truth. The quality of university education, then, is determined by its object, and that object is to train not merely skillful practitioners, *but also future professors*. In fact, the needs of the former class are subordinated to the needs of the latter. In this respect, the faculty acts, unconsciously, in accordance with the promptings of the instinct of self-preservation. If thorough scientific culture is an essential element in national life, it must be maintained at every cost. The slightest flaw in the continuity of spiritual descent would be as dangerous as a break in the apostolic succession of the church. Every inducement, therefore, must be held out to young men to qualify themselves in season for succeeding to their present instructors. The lectures and other instruction must be adapted to train and stimulate *Privat-docenten*, for they are the ones who are to seize and wear the mantles of the translated Elijahs. For every professor dead or removed, there must be one or two instantly ready to fill his place.

This is not the *avowed* object of the university course. One might pass many years in Germany without perceiving it stated so bluntly. Yet I am persuaded that it is at bottom the determining factor in the constitution of university life. It will explain to us many incidental features for which there is elsewhere no analogy; for instance, the sovereign contempt that all German students evince for everything that savors of "bread-and-butter." The students have caught, in this respect, the tone of their instructors. Even such of them as have no intention of becoming *Privat-docenten* pass three and four years of their life in generous devotion to study pure and simple, without casting a single forward glance to future "business." All thought of practical life is kept in abeyance. The future practitioners and the future theoreticians sit side by side on the same bench, fight on the same *Mensur*, drink at the same *Kneipe*, hear the same lectures, use the same books, have every sentiment in common; hence the perfect *rapport* that exists in Germany between the lawyer and the jurist, the pastor and the theologian, the practicing doctor and the speculative pathologist, the gymnasial teacher of Latin and Greek and the professed philologist. Hence the celerity with which innovating ideas spread in Germany. Let a professor in the university of Tübingen, for instance, publish a work on some abstruse, difficult topic, in which he threatens to overturn previous theories and notions. Why is it that in a month or two the book provokes a tempest of assent or dissent from far and near? Simply because every practical man in that line, every lawyer, or doctor, or pastor, as the case may be, has been initiated so far into the theory of his profession as to be able to detect at a glance the full purport of the new departure. Let the book contain but a single mis-statement of an historic fact or an established principle of natural science, and a hundred angry reviewers pounce upon it and hold it up to public condemnation. Whereas, in this country, and even in England also, the grossest blunders pass unchallenged. Our reviewers are either ignorant or indifferent.

To repeat, the university instruction of Germany does not attempt to train successful practical men, unless it be indirectly, by giving its students a profound insight into the principles of the science and then turning them adrift to deduce the practice as well as they can from the carefully inculcated theory. Its chief task, that to which all its energies are directed, is the development of great thinkers, men who will extend the boundaries of knowledge.

Viewed from this point, then, the two conditions, *Lehrfreiheit* and *Lernfreiheit*, are not only natural and proper, but are absolutely essential. Were the object of higher education merely to train "useful and honorable members of society," to use the conventional phrase of the panegyrists of the American system, the German universities might possibly change their character. In place of professors free to impart the choicest results of their investigations, they might substitute pedagogues with text-books and class-books, noting down the relative merits and demerits of daily recitations. In place of students free to attend or to stay away, free to agree with the professor or to differ, free to read what they choose and to study after their own fashion, they might create a set of undergraduates reciting glibly from set lessons and regarding each circumvention of the teacher as so much clear gain. But the Germans know perfectly well wherein the value of their university education lies. They know that speculative thought alone has raised Germany from her former condition of literary and political dependence to the foremost rank among nations. The gain is not without its sacrifice. Many a young man who, under another method, might be drilled into a tolerable alumnus, falls by the way-side through idleness and dissipation. For one who succeeds, two or three fail. Yet the sacrifice is unavoidable. If German thought is to continue in its career of conquest, if the universities are to remain what they are, the training-ground of intellectual giants, the present system of freedom must be maintained.

The professor has but one aim in life: scholarly renown. To effect this, he must have the liberty of selecting his studies and pushing them to their extreme limits. The student has but one desire: to assimilate his instructor's learning, and, if possible, to add to it. He must, therefore, be his own master. He must be free to accept and reject, to judge and prove all things for himself, to train himself step by step for grappling with the great problems of nature and history. Accountable only to himself for his opinions and mode of living, he shakes off spiritual bondage and becomes an independent thinker. He must think for himself, for there is no one set over him as spiritual adviser and guide, prescribing the work for each day and each hour, telling him what he is to believe and what to disbelieve, and marking him up or down accordingly.

[. . .]

* Part 3 *

American Adaptations

CHAPTER 12

The Morrill Act

INTRODUCTION TO THE MORRILL ACT

The United States has many state universities but no national university. Until the creation of the Department of Education, in 1980, the funding and administration of education was normally regarded as a local matter. Perhaps as a consequence, when the federal government has turned its attention to education, the results have been monumental, and often far beyond what legislators imagined. Few people expected that more than seven million veterans would take advantage of the tuition provisions of the Servicemen's Readjustment Act of 1944 (the GI Bill), or that the passage of the National Defense Education Act of 1958, a response to the launch of the Soviet satellite Sputnik, would trigger massive growth in academic fields well outside the Act's main targets of funding.

So the Morrill Act, named for Justin Smith Morrill, a congressman from Vermont who was dedicated to improving the education of farmers—or, as he put it, "the industrial classes"—ended up making possible the establishment and enhancement of universities across the nation. Actually, there were two Morrill Acts. The first was signed into law in 1862. Congress had passed a similar bill in 1859, but it was vetoed by James Buchanan. In 1862, though, Lincoln was president, and southern states were no longer represented. Federal power was exclusively in the hands of the North. The Morrill Act was one of the many acts of nation-building the Civil War Congress undertook, including creation of the first national system of taxation and the first national currency. A second Morrill Act, in 1890, increased the amount of federal subvention of colleges benefiting from the act.

The Morrill formula was unusual: states were granted an amount of federal land, determined on a per capita basis, the income from the rent or sale of which could be used to endow "at least one college" providing education in "agriculture and the mechanic arts." (Hence the use of the term "land-grant" to describe these institutions.) Crucially, Morrill insisted that this practical instruction be combined with studies in the traditional liberal arts and sciences.

States made themselves eligible for the act's provisions by adapting existing colleges to its terms or by establishing new public universities (which annual financial support provided by the 1890 act made sustainable). Among the major research institutions that came into existence under the terms of the act were Cornell University and the University of California, both of which opened in 1868. (UC was created by amalgamating the existing College of California with an institution endowed by land-grant revenues.) But the act's broadest effects were the addition of scientific schools to existing institutions, such as Columbia and Princeton, and the funding of schools of agriculture and mining (A&Ms) and engineering. Morrill did not quite realize his wish to elevate education in practical subjects to the status of the liberal arts, but, like the National Defense Education Act almost a century later, he set in motion a tide that lifted many boats.

TRANSCRIPT OF MORRILL ACT (1862)

Chap. CXXX.—AN ACT Donating Public Lands to the several States and Territories which may provide Colleges for the Benefit of Agriculture and Mechanic Arts.

Be it enacted by the Senate and House of Representatives of the United States of America in Congress assembled, That there be granted to the several States, for the purposes hereinafter mentioned, an amount of public land, to be apportioned to each State a quantity equal to thirty thousand acres for each senator and representative in Congress to which the States are respectively entitled by the apportionment under the census of eighteen hundred and sixty: Provided, That no mineral lands shall be selected or purchased under the provisions of this Act.

SEC. 2. And be it further enacted, That the land aforesaid, after being surveyed, shall be apportioned to the several States in sections or subdivisions of sections, not less than one quarter of a section; and whenever there are public lands in a State subject to sale at private entry at one dollar and twenty-five cents per acre, the quantity to which said State shall be entitled shall be selected from such lands within the limits of such State, and the Secretary of the Interior is hereby directed to issue to each of the States in which there is not the quantity of public lands subject to sale at private entry at one dollar and twenty-five cents per acre, to which said State may be entitled under the provisions of this act, land scrip to the amount in acres for the deficiency of its distributive share: said scrip to be sold by said States and the proceeds thereof applied to the uses and purposes prescribed in this act, and for no other use or purpose whatsoever: Provided, That in no case shall any State to which land scrip may thus be issued be allowed to locate the same within the limits of any other State, or of any Territory of the United States, but their assignees may thus locate said land scrip upon any of the unappropriated lands of the United States subject to sale at private entry at one dollar and twenty-five cents, or less, per acre: And provided, further, That not more than one million acres shall be located by such assignees in any one of the States: And provided, further, That no such location shall be made before one year from the passage of this Act.

SEC. 3. And be it further enacted, That all the expenses of management, superintendence, and taxes from date of selection of said lands, previous to their sales, and all expenses incurred in the management and disbursement of the moneys which may be received therefrom, shall be paid by the States to which they may belong, out of the Treasury of said States, so that the entire proceeds of the sale of said lands shall be applied without any diminution whatever to the purposes hereinafter mentioned.

SEC. 4. And be it further enacted, That all moneys derived from the sale of the lands aforesaid by the States to which the lands are apportioned, and from the sales of land scrip hereinbefore provided for, shall be invested in stocks of the United States, or of the States, or some other safe stocks, yielding not less than five per centum upon the par value of said stocks; and that the moneys so invested shall constitute a perpetual fund, the capital of which shall remain forever undiminished, (except so far as may be provided in section fifth of this act,) and the interest of which shall be inviolably appropriated, by each State which may take and claim the benefit of this act, to the endowment, support, and maintenance of at least one college where the leading object shall be, without excluding other scientific and classical studies, and including military tactics, to teach such branches of learning as are related to agriculture and the mechanic arts, in such manner as the legislatures of the States may respectively prescribe, in order to promote the liberal and practical education of the industrial classes in the several pursuits and professions in life.

SEC. 5. And be it further enacted, That the grant of land and land scrip hereby authorized shall be made on the following conditions, to which, as well as to the provisions hereinbefore contained, the previous assent of the several States shall be signified by legislative acts:

First. If any portion of the fund invested, as provided by the foregoing section, or any portion of the interest thereon, shall, by any action or contingency, be diminished or lost, it shall be replaced by the State to which it belongs, so that the capital of the fund shall remain forever undiminished; and the annual interest shall be regularly applied without diminution to the purposes mentioned in the fourth section of this act, except that a sum, not exceeding ten per centum upon the amount received by any State under the provisions of this act may be expended for the purchase of lands for sites or experimental farms, whenever authorized by the respective legislatures of said States.

Second. No portion of said fund, nor the interest thereon, shall be applied, directly or indirectly, under any pretence whatever, to the purchase, erection, preservation, or repair of any building or buildings.

Third. Any State which may take and claim the benefit of the provisions of this act shall provide, within five years from the time of its acceptance as provided in subdivision seven of this section, at least not less than one college, as described in the fourth section of this act, or the grant to such State shall cease; and said State shall be bound to pay the United States the amount received of any lands previously sold; and that the title to purchasers under the State shall be valid.

Fourth. An annual report shall be made regarding the progress of each college, recording any improvements and experiments made, with their cost and results, and such other matters, including State industrial and economical statistics, as may be supposed useful; one copy of which shall be transmitted by mail free, by each, to all the other colleges which may be endowed under the provisions of this act, and also one copy to the Secretary of the Interior.

Fifth. When lands shall be selected from those which have been raised to double the minimum price, in consequence of railroad grants, they shall be computed to the States at the maximum price, and the number of acres proportionally diminished.

Sixth. No State while in a condition of rebellion or insurrection against the government of the United States shall be entitled to the benefit of this act.

Seventh. No State shall be entitled to the benefits of this act unless it shall express its acceptance thereof by its legislature within three years from July 23, 1866:

Provided, That when any Territory shall become a State and be admitted into the Union, such new State shall be entitled to the benefits of the said act of July two, eighteen hundred and sixty-two, by expressing the acceptance therein required within three years from the date of its admission into the Union, and providing the college or colleges within five years after such acceptance, as prescribed in this act.

SEC. 6. And be it further enacted, That land scrip issued under the provisions of this act shall not be subject to location until after the first day of January, one thousand eight hundred and sixty-three.

SEC. 7. And be it further enacted, That the land officers shall receive the same fees for locating land scrip issued under the provisions of this act as is now allowed for the location of military bounty land warrants under existing laws: Provided, their maximum compensation shall not be thereby increased.

SEC. 8. And be it further enacted, That the Governors of the several States to which scrip shall be issued under this act shall be required to report annually to Congress all sales made of such scrip until the whole shall be disposed of, the amount received for the same, and what appropriation has been made of the proceeds.

CHAPTER 13

The Utility of Universities

Daniel Coit Gilman

INTRODUCTION TO GILMAN'S ESSAY

When Johns Hopkins died on December 24, 1873, he left a will that would change the shape of American higher education. The Baltimore investor and director of the Baltimore and Ohio Railroad Company had put half of his $7 million estate in the hands of twelve trustees, who had the vague charge of founding the "Johns Hopkins University." The certificate of incorporation stated simply that the university's purpose was to promote education in the state of Maryland. At the time Hopkins's bequest was the largest philanthropic gift in US history.

Ten of the twelve named trustees had attended college, and they all embraced Hopkins's challenge and immediately set out to educate themselves on the state of American higher education. Some trustees quickly became critical of an American education system that, as one put it, had "erected a temple without a dome, a column without a capital, a spire without a pinnacle." The United States lacked an institution devoted to the most advanced forms of learning and knowledge.

As part of their planning, the trustees invited several of the leading university reformers to meet with them and discuss the future of American higher education, including James B. Angell of Michigan, Charles Eliot of Harvard, and Andrew White of Cornell. (Both James McCosh of Princeton and Noah Porter of Yale declined the invitations.) Thus, in the summer of 1874, Eliot traveled to Baltimore to meet with the trustees. After one trustee asked him whether the future university should dedicate itself to a "higher degree of education" than had thus far been possible in the United States, Eliot advised them to delay making Hopkins a postgraduate institution. "The post-graduate course," he warned, "is a matter far off for you. Wait until you have fully organized the undergraduate college before tackling graduate education." The trustees did not listen.

The trustees also conferred with the same leaders about a university president. Eliot and his colleagues all recommended the same man: Daniel Coit Gilman. Gilman had graduated from Yale College in 1852 with a degree in geography, and after serving in St. Petersburg as an attaché and dabbling in postgraduate studies at Harvard and Yale, he returned to Yale's Scientific School, renamed Sheffield Scientific School in 1861, the subordinate and separate institutional home of subjects not included in the classical college curriculum. Following several years in various administrative posts, including librarian and fund-raising positions, Gilman was appointed professor of physical and political geography. After declining presidencies at the Universities of Wisconsin and California and having lost out to Noah Porter in 1871 for Yale's top job, Gilman finally accepted entreaties to become the University of California's first president in 1872. The University of California had been established by combining the resources of the College of California and the Agricultural Mining and Mechanical Arts College. Gilman's brief tenure in Oakland was marked by a public feud over competing visions of the new university and whether it should focus on teaching the classical college curriculum, modern sciences, or agriculture.

The University of California had to plan its future without Gilman, however, who left in 1875 to become the first president of Johns Hopkins University. But before he had even arrived in Baltimore, the plans for a new university committed to graduate education, which he and the trustees had designed, had become the object of a dispute carried out in the pages of Baltimore's leading newspapers. The university's benefactor, Johns Hopkins, claimed one, had been committed to "education for the people and not sinecures for the learned." The purported plans for a university devoted exclusively to postgraduate education were a manifest refusal to honor Hopkins's intentions. A further controversy followed in the fall of 1876, when Gilman invited Thomas Huxley, a vocal proponent of Darwinism, to deliver a series of public lectures. Gilman, asserted one paper—wrongly, as it turned out, since the university opened with a ceremony replete with Christian prayer—had invited a Darwinist to lecture, instead of a minister to pray, at the opening of the new Johns Hopkins University.

When Gilman sent his letter accepting the office of president, he included a second letter outlining his ideas for a nonsectarian and nonpolitical institution committed to the free pursuit of truth. "The institution we are about to organize," he wrote, "would not be worthy of the name university if it were to be devoted to any other purpose than the discovery and promulgation of truth; and it would be ignoble in the extreme if the resources which had been given by the Founder without restrictions should be limited to the maintenance of ecclesiastical differences or perverted to the promotion of political strife. As the spirit of a University should be that of intellectual freedom in pursuit of the truth and of the broadest charity toward those from whom we differ in opinion it is certain that sectarian and partisan preferences should have no control in the selection of teachers and should not be apparent in the official work." The "spirit" and defining character of the new university in Baltimore was to be one of "intellectual freedom" and a refuge from "sectarian and partisan" prejudices. For Gilman, academic freedom was the distinguishing feature of a real university, that is, an institution that strove above all for scientific knowledge. And echoing German traditions of *Lehrfreiheit* and *Lernfreiheit*, he embraced the dual aspect of academic freedom: the freedom of professors to study and teach what they wanted, and of students to follow their interests. Those notions of academic freedom also distinguished the university from the college. For Gilman, the former focused on graduate education and the pursuit of knowledge, whereas the latter focused on undergraduate education and the moral formation of students.

Despite suggestions that Hopkins would focus only on the "highest" levels of learning, it opened in 1876 with both a college and a postgraduate university. In many ways the college continued the classical curriculum, including required courses on moral philosophy—listed as "Logic, Ethics, and Psychology" and taught with Noah Porter's *Elements of Moral Science*. But the university was something distinct and new in the history of American higher education. Hopkins was the first American university to offer substantial post-college graduate fellowships. The purpose, as the trustees wrote, was to give scholars of "promise" the opportunity to "prosecute further studies, under favorable circumstances, and likewise to open a career for those who propose to follow the pursuit of literature and science." In its first year, the graduate fellowship program received 152 applications and, after planning on only 10, offered 20 fellowships to students from across the United States, including 3 who had PhD's from German universities.

THE UTILITY OF UNIVERSITIES

An Anniversary Discourse, February 22, 1885

To be concerned in the establishment and development of a university is one of the noblest and most important tasks ever imposed on a community or a on a body of men. It is an undertaking which calls for the exercise of the utmost care, for combination, cooperation, liberality, inquiry, patience, reticence, exertion, and never-ceasing watchfulness. It involves perplexities, delays and risks. Mistakes cannot possibly be avoided; heavy responsibility is never absent. But history and experience light up the problem; hope and faith give animation to the builders when they are weary and depressed. Deeply moved by these considerations, I desire to bring before you, my colleagues in this work, without whose labors all would be a failure, you who are trustees, and you who are teachers, before the citizens of Baltimore and before this company of students pressing forward to take the places of authority in the work of education and administration—before you all, I wish to bring some aspects of university life, which, if not new, may perhaps be stated in terms which are fresh, with illustrations drawn from our own experience.

[. . .]

Why is it that universities are so highly esteemed? What are the advantages which follow their foundation? Remembering that a university is the best organization for the liberal education of individuals, and the best organization for the advancement of science, apply the double test, what is done for personal instruction, and what is done for the promotion of knowledge, and you will be able to judge any institution which assumes this name.

Ask, first, if it is a place of sound education. Are the youth who are trained within its walls honest lovers of the truth—are they learned, are they ready, are they trustworthy? When they leave the academic classes, do they soon find a demand for their services? Do they rise in professional life? Are they sought for as teachers? Do they show aptitude for mercantile, administrative, or editorial life? Do they acquit themselves with credit in the public service? Do the books they write find publishers? Do they win repute among those who have added to the sum of human knowledge? Have they the power of enjoying literature, music, and art? Can they apply the lessons of history to the problems of our day? Are they always eager to enlarge their knowledge? Do they become conservative members of society, seeking for progress by steady improvements rather than by the powers of destruction and death? Are they useful, courteous, cooperative citizens, in all the relations of life? Do the charities, the churches, the schools, the public affairs of the community, receive their constant consideration? Are there frequent manifestations among them of unusual ability in science, in literature, in oratory, in administration? As the roll of the alumni increases and the graduates are counted by hundreds and not by scores, does it appear that a large proportion are men of honorable, faithful, learned, and public-spirited character? These are the questions by which, as the years go on, a university is to be tested; to sum all questions in one, is it proved to be a place for the development of manliness?

I beg leave to dwell a little longer upon this text, because I think there is danger of its importance being overlooked. The material resources of a university, the aggregate numbers who attend its courses, its numerous buildings, its great collections, appeal to everybody; only those who look at results are competent to give a conclusive opinion, and their opinion cannot be formed in one decade. A generation is the briefest period for a fair review. When the year of our Lord 1900 comes, this foundation will be a quarter of a century old. To that remote tribunal we appeal for judgment on our work of today. But we may anticipate this final verdict, and ascertain by our own inspection and inquiry what is done in any institution for the education of youth, what opportunities are afforded, how those advantages are regarded by the most intelligent young men, and what kind of scholarship is developed at the termination of the academic course.

Here let me protest against the common method of estimating intellectual work by numerical standards alone. I have heard it said that some men are possessed by a statistical devil. They can only think in figures; they will ask, in respect to a new acquaintance, how much is he worth; of a library, how many volumes there are; of an orchestra, how many pieces; of a college, how many students. I have known the expenses of an institution made a dividend and the number of scholars the divisor, the quotient representing the cost of each pupil. All this is wrong, absolutely wrong. If such a standard were allowable, the largest number of scholars taught by the cheapest teacher would be the greatest success. It is not the number but the quality of students which determines the character of a high school. It is important to count; it is better to weigh.

Having spoken of what the university does for individuals, let us consider its second function. It benefits society as well as individual men. It renders services to the community which no demon of statistics can ever estimate, no mathematical process ever compute. These functions may be stated as the acquisition, conservation, refinement, and distribution of knowledge.

These carefully chosen words I proceed to explain.

1. It is the business of a university to advance knowledge; every professor must be a student. No history is so remote that it may be neglected; no law of mathematics is so hidden that it may not be sought out; no problem in respect to physics is so difficult that it must be shunned. No love of ease, no dread of labor, no fear of consequences, no desire for wealth, will divert a band of well-chosen professors from uniting their forces in the

prosecution of study. Rather let me say that there are heroes and martyrs, prophets and apostles of learning, as there are of religion. To the claims of duty, to the responsibilities of station, to the voices of enlightened conscience, such men respond, and they throw their hearts into their work with as much devotion and as little selfishness as it is possible for human nature to exhibit. By their labors, knowledge has been accumulated, intellectual capital has been acquired. In these processes of investigation the leading universities of the world have always been engaged.

This is what laboratories, museums, and libraries signify. Nothing is foreign to their purpose, and those who work in them are animated by the firm belief that the advancement of knowledge in any direction contributes to the welfare of man. Nor is research restricted to material things; the scholars of a university are equally interested in all that pertains to the nature of man, the growth of society, the study of language, and the establishment of the principles of intellectual and moral conduct.

2. Universities are conservative. They encourage the study of the history, the philosophy, the poetry, the drama, the politics, the religion,—in fine, the experience of antecedent ages. Successors of the ancient monasteries, they keep alive in our day the knowledge of ancient languages and art, enrich the literature of our mother-tongue, hold up to us the highest standards of excellence in writing, and enable us to share in the thoughts of the noblest of our race. Let me especially remind you that to the universities men turn instinctively for light on the interpretation of the Scriptures. When new manuscripts are discovered, or new versions are proposed, or new monuments are unearthed, it is to the universities, where the knowledge of ancient and remote tongues has been cherished, that the religious world looks for enlightenment and guidance. Their dominant influence is highly spiritualizing; I would even go further and say that it is truly religious. I am not unmindful that within the academic circles men are found whose spiritual insight is but dim,—so it is in all other circles,—but I assert, without fear of contradiction, that the influence of study is, on the whole, favorable to the growth of spiritual life, to the development of uprightness, unselfishness, and faith, or in other words, it is opposed to epicureanism and materialism. In belief there are tides, as there are in the ocean, ebb and flow, flow and ebb; but the great ocean is there, with its deep mysteries, unchanging amid all superficial disturbances. Faith, with all its fluctuations, is as permanently operative in human thought as knowledge.

3. Universities are refining. They are constantly, by laborious processes, by intricate systems of cooperation, and by ingenious methods, engaged in

eliminating human errors and in submitting all inherited possessions to those processes which remove the dross and bring out the gold. No truth which has once been discovered is allowed to perish, but the incrustations which cover it are removed. It is the universities which edit, interpret, translate, and reiterate the acquisitions of former generations in both literature and science. Their revelation of error is sometimes welcomed, but it is generally opposed; nevertheless the process goes on, indifferent alike to plaudits or reproaches. If their lessons are hard to the beginners, they lead the persevering to high enjoyment.

4. Universities distribute knowledge. The scholar does but half his duty who simply acquires knowledge. He must share his possessions with others. This is done, in the first place, by the instruction of pupils. Experience has certainly demonstrated that, with rare exceptions, those men are most learned who produce most. The process of acquiring seems to be promoted by that of imparting. The investigator who is surrounded by a bright circle of friendly inquisitors and critics finds his best powers developed by this influence. Next to its visible circle of pupils, the university should impart its acquisitions to the world of scholars. Learned publications are therefore to be encouraged. But beyond these formal and well-recognized means of communicating knowledge, universities have innumerable less obvious, but not less useful, opportunities of conveying their benefits to the outside world.

These general principles I propose to illustrate by asking you to go with me around the circle of the sciences, that we may observe the part which universities have taken or should take in respect to various departments of knowledge.

Let me begin by saying that a university should discover and teach all that can be known of the human body. If you ask me why this is so important, I reply, in order that every one may be able to lead a healthier, stronger, and more rational life than is now possible for the want of more knowledge. Hospitals are essential to alleviate sufferings which have been encountered; physical training is of great value; but still more important to humanity is the laboratory in which are studied the laws of life. A celebrated physiologist declares that a "hundred years of life is what Providence intended for man," and others tell us that most of our minor ailments may easily be avoided, and the number of efficient days may be largely increased. Science has proved that many diseases which used to scourge the civilized world may be prevented, and it has recently brought us within reach of new discoveries which will still further interrupt the progress of pestilence. The employment of anesthetics has marvelously alleviated the sufferings of humanity. The causes and remedies of cerebral excitement and degeneration have never been understood as now, and the possibilities have never been so great for the restoration to their normal activity of the powers which have been alienated. In view of these great results and of these anticipations, it is clearly the duty of a university to study all the forms and functions of life which are manifested in organisms lower than man, all the laws which govern animal and vegetable growth, all that can possibly throw light on human physiology.

Those who are devoted to research of this kind, revealing with their microscopes the structure and the life-histories of the minutest organisms, are constantly, and in most unexpected ways, coming upon new illustrations of the plan of creation, which have an important bearing upon the welfare of man. They are the interpreters of nature and the benefactors of humanity; and I do not hesitate to add that if there is any branch of learning which at the present time deserves the most generous support, it is surely biology, because of its obvious relations to the health and happiness of every human being. I cannot but think that those who oppose its study will be ranked in future years among the obscurantists of the nineteenth century.

Next, I mention, as the subject for university study, psychology, the nature of man's soul, the characteristics of his mental and moral activity. This science has lately made great progress; it has improved its methods and enlarged its scope. Those who are devoted to it appreciate the inherited experiences of the human race, and are not indifferent to the lessons which may proceed from intuition and introspection; they study all the manifestations of intellectual and spiritual life; but, on the other hand, they are not afraid to inquire, and they know how to inquire, into the physical conditions under which the mind works; they watch the spontaneous, unconventional actions of children; they investigate the laws of heredity; they examine with curious gaze the eccentricities of genius, and with discerning, often with remedial eye, the alienation of human powers; and they believe that by a combination of these and other methods of research among which experiment has its legitimate place, the conduct of the human understanding and the laws of progressive morality will be better understood, so that more wholesome methods of education will be employed in schools of every grade. They acknowledge the superiority of the soul to the body, and they stand in awe before the mysteries which are as impenetrable to modern investigators as they were to Leibnitz and Spinoza, to Abelard and Aquinas, to Aristotle and Plato,—the mysteries of man's conscious responsibility, his intimations of immortality, his relations to the Infinite.

I do not know whether philosophy is on a "return to Kant," or to common sense, but I believe that, standing firm on the postulates, God, soul, and immortality, it will in years to come disentangle many perplexities, brush away heaps of verbal accumulations, and lead the mind to purer and nobler conceptions of righteousness and duty. I go even further, and, as I believe that one truth is never in conflict with another truth so I believe that the ethics of the New Testament will be accepted by the scientific as well as the religious faculties of man: to the former, as law; to the latter, as gospel.

In confirmation of these views, let me quote to you the language of that one among us who is best qualified to speak upon this subject:

> The new psychology, which brings simply a new method and a new standpoint to philosophy is, I believe, Christian to its root and center; and its final mission in the world is not merely to trace petty harmonies and small adjustments between science and religion, but to flood and transfuse the new and vaster conceptions of the universe and of man's place in it—now slowly taking form, and giving to reason a new cosmos, and involving momentous and far-reaching practical and social consequences—with the old scriptural sense of unity, rationality, and love beneath and above all, with all its wide consequences. The Bible is being slowly re-revealed as man's great text-book in psychology, dealing with him as a whole, his body, mind, and will, in all the larger relations to nature and society, which has been so misappreciated simply because it is so deeply divine, That something may be done here to aid this development (continues the lecturer) is my strongest hope and belief.[1]

The study of society engages the earnest interest of another set of men, and the apparatus of their laboratory includes archaeological and historical memorials of the activity of the race. The domain of history and political science has never been cultivated as it is in modern times. The discovery of primeval monuments and the interpretation of long hidden inscriptions, the publication of ancient documents once hidden in monasteries and governmental archives, the inquiry into primitive forms of social organization, the development of improved modes of research, the scientific collection and classification of facts which illustrate the condition of ancient and modern communities, and especially the interest awakened in the growth of institutions and constitutions, give to this oldest of studies the freshest interest. Papers which have lately been printed on rudimentary society among boys, on the laws of the mining-camp, on the foundations of a socialist community, on the differences between parliamentary and congressional government, on the derivation of modern customs from the ancient beginnings of the Aryan people, on the nature of communism, and many more such themes, afford illustrations of the mode in which the historical student among us, following the lines of Stubbs,[2] Maine,[3] Freeman,[4] Seeley,[5] Bluntschli,[6] Roscher,[7] and other celebrated workers, is advancing historical science and developing the true historical spirit. The aim of all these inquiries is to help on the progress of modern society by showing how the fetters which now bind us were forged, by what patient filing they must be severed, and at the same time to work out the ideal of a society in which liberty is everywhere, but "liberty sustained by law."

Languages and literature have always received attention in universities, and will always be dominant, for reasons which are as enduring as language itself. We study tongues that we may know the men of other climes and other days; we study literature to enjoy it. As an aid to intercourse with people of other nations, and for the purpose of keeping up with the record of modern science, nobody doubts that the study of modern languages is to be encouraged; but if we really would own the inheritance which is our birthright, if we wish to appreciate the masterpieces of literature if it is well to put ourselves in sympathy with mankind, to laugh with those who have laughed, and weep with those who have wept, we must not be restricted to the writings of to day. In science, it has been said, read the newest and latest; not so in literature but the best. Isaiah and John, Homer and Aeschylus, Cicero and Virgil, the Nibelungenlied and Chaucer, Dante and Petrarch, are as full of life, beauty, instruction, and entertainment to us as to former generations. But from the classical standard of excellence this busy world would soon depart, were it not that in every university there are scholars keeping bright the altar-fires, and warming us with the glow of their enthusiasm whenever we come under their influence, sharpening, too, our wits by their critical acumen.

It is not uncommon nowadays to hear objections to classical education, usually from those who have never had it, and declamations against dead languages, usually from those who have never learned them. But the humanists may unquestionably leave it to the geologists to fight the battle for antiquity. The latter assure us that the older the fossils the more instructive their lessons; indeed, so much importance is attached to ancient animal life that the national government, with great liberality, encourages its study by promoting explorations, museums, and costly publications. Be it so; but let not the nation which does this forget that men are of "more value than many sparrows"; that the oldest literature is not old or dead, but fresh and living in comparison with the bones of the cave dwellers; and, that though a megatherium is wonderfully instructive, an ancient epic or a drama is equally worthy of attention.

Jebb,[8] in his "Life of Bentley," asserts that "probably the study of classical antiquity, in the largest sense, has never been more really vigorous than it is at the present day." We might add that classical poetry has never been so popular;

else why these innumerable editions and translations? Why, after Worsley,[9] Butcher,[10] Bryant, and their predecessors, are we reading aloud and smiling over the immortal Odyssey, as it is given to us in the rhythmical prose of Palmer? This is a good sign; only it is well to remember that reading translations is not reading Greek, and, as Jebb goes on to say, we must not forget the difference between "the knowledge at second-hand" which the intelligent public can possess, and "the knowledge at first hand" which it is the business of the libraries and professorships of a university to perpetuate.

If the defenders of classical study would confine their argument to the line which was lately followed by Butcher, they would silence their opponents. "To Greece," he says, "we owe the love of science, the love of art, the love of freedom—not science alone, art alone, or freedom alone, but these vitally correlated with one another and brought into organic union. . . . The Greek genius is the European genius in its first and brightest bloom. From a vivifying contact with the Greek spirit, Europe derived that new and mighty impulse which we call progress."

But I must not pass from the subject without a word upon the study of language in general, that faculty of the human race which was never half understood until the universities of Germany entered upon the study of comparative philology, by the introduction of the study of Sanskrit. With this new torch they have thrown a flood of light upon the nature of speech, the history of our race, the brotherhood of nations, and the development of ideas which lie at the basis of all Indo-European civilization.

The Shemitic tongues have long been subjects of university study, especially Hebrew and Arabic—the former so much esteemed as the language of the Old Testament that it used to be spoken of as the language of Paradise, and the latter being regarded as a key to the ideas and religion, the ancient literature and science, of one of the largest families of men. Of late years the domain of Shemitic study has been widened; libraries long hidden have been exhumed on the sites of ancient Babylon and Nineveh; records, the very existence of which was unknown at the beginning of this century, written in characters to which there was then but the slightest clue, are now read and printed and studied as a part of the history of mankind. Assyrian becomes a language of university study, not, indeed, for many scholars, but for a few, and the bearing of their discoveries is so important upon the language and history of the Hebrews that one of the most learned of English theologians has recently said that, in respect to certain of the obscurer passages of the Old Testament, the world must wait for the light which will come from Assyriology.

Certainly, if the history of mankind is worth studying, if the lessons of the past are of value, language and literature, the ancient, the modern, the primitive, and the cultivated, will never be neglected among the studies of an enlightened community.

When we turn from man to his environment, we soon perceive that mathematics lies at the basis of all our knowledge of this world. To count, to measure, and to weigh are steps in civilization, and as we extend our powers in these directions, we find that even the distance and mass of the planets, the form of the earth, the velocity of light, the mechanical equivalent of heat, and the unit of electrical resistance may be accurately ascertained, and the results, with many of the ideas which they involve, may become a part of the intellectual possessions of every educated person. Yet when we reflect that hardly any branch of knowledge is so depreciated by the average man as the modern advancement of pure mathematics, we must believe that its influence upon civilization is not sufficiently considered.

Professor Cayley,[11] in a recent address, alluded to the connection of mathematics with common life, on the one hand, and with the deepest questions of philosophy,—for example, the metaphysical ideas of time and space, on the other. As to its utility, he declared that he would defend this science, as Socrates defended justice, quite irrespectively of worldly advantages; and then he proceeded to show the relations of mathematics to the certainty of knowledge, and to emphasize the idea that mathematical science is not built upon experience, but upon certain fundamental assumptions, which are, indeed, found to be in conformity with experience. I wish that every student, however remote his studies may be from mathematical text-books, would turn to the opening passages of this discourse, and steady his own mental equilibrium by the assurance that the science which is most exact, and most satisfactory in its reasonings, is based upon fundamental postulates which are assumed and not proved by experiment. "In the theory of numbers," he says, "these are very remarkable instances of propositions observed to hold good for very long series of numbers, and which are nevertheless untrue."

If you persist in taking the utilitarian view, and ask me what is the good of Mr. Glaisher's[12] determination of the least factors of the missing three out of the first nine million numbers, the volume containing the sixth million having lately been published; or if you put a much more comprehensive question, as to the use of the Abelian functions, I shall be forced to say, I do not know; and if you press me harder I shall be obliged to express my conviction that nobody knows; but I know, and you know, and everybody may know who will take the pains to inquire, that the progress of mathematics underlies and sustains all progress in exact knowledge.

Whewell,[13] the author of the "History of Inductive Sciences," has brought out very clearly the fact that "the opening of Greek civilization was marked by the production of geometry, the idea of space was brought to a scientific precision; and likewise the opening of modern European civilization was distinguished by the production of a new science, mechanics, which soon led to the mechanics of the heavens, and this step, like the former, depended on men arriving at a properly distinct fundamental idea, the idea of force." Henry Smith,[14] arguing for the value of his favorite study to mankind, points out the injury which would come to the intellectual strength of any nation "whose notions of the world and of the things in it were not braced and girt together with a strong framework of mathematical reasoning. It is something," he continues, "for men to learn what proof is and what it is not. The work in mathematics at Alexandria or Syracuse, two thousand years ago, is as perfect in its kind, and as direct and unerring in its appeal to our intelligence, as if it had been done yesterday at Berlin or Göttingen by one of our own contemporaries." In kindred language, Cayley, working forward as well as backward, and not unmindful, let us hope, of the Sylvestrian school upon this side of the Atlantic, in which he had been a teacher and a guest, thus concluded the address from which I have already quoted:

> Mathematics have steadily advanced from the time of the Greek geometers. Nothing is lost or wasted; the achievements of Euclid, Archimedes, and Apollonius are as admirable now as they were in their own days. Descartes's method of coordinates is a possession forever. But mathematics have never been cultivated more zealously and diligently, or with greater success, than in this century—in the last half of it or at the present time; the advances made have been enormous, the actual field is boundless, the future full of hope. In regard to pure mathematics we may most confidently say:
>
> "Yet I doubt not through the ages one increasing purpose runs, And the thoughts of men are widened with the process of the suns."

Many who hesitate to assent to these views of the relation of pure mathematics to civilization have no question whatever in lauding applied mathematics, especially astronomy and physics; and no wonder, for within the memory of this generation the world has gained these five results of physical science: steam locomotion, telegraphy, telephony, photography, and electric lighting. The first three, it may be said, have revolutionized the methods of human intercourse; the fourth has multiplied infinitely the means of communicating knowledge to the brain by what Sir William Thomson,[15] following John Bunyan, has termed the eye-gate; and the fifth, still in its dawn, includes possibilities of illumination which we are not likely to exaggerate. But I have no time to eulogize these recent gains of civilization; every word I can spare must be given to emphasize the fact which is most likely to be forgotten, that these wonderful inventions are the direct fruit of university studies. I do not undervalue the work of practical men when I say that the most brilliant inventor who ever lived has been dependent upon an unseen company of scholars, the discoverers and the formulators of laws which he has been able to apply to methods and instruments. Nor do I forget that Faraday,[16] like Shakspere, was not a university man. But I mean to say that the manifold applications of science, about which everybody is talking, are only possible because of the abstract studies which universities promote. The electromagnetic inventions, which are now so multiform, are only possible because scores of the greatest intellects of the century, one after another, have applied their powers of absolute reasoning to the interpretation of phenomena which could have been elucidated in any part of the world, and at any epoch of the past, if only the right methods had been employed. As long as universities held aloof from experimental sciences, these discoveries were not made; but when laboratories for investigation were established, an alliance was formed by mathematics and physics, and a new type of intellectual workers was produced, men whose hands were as cunning to construct and make use of instruments as their brains were cunning to develop the formulae of mathematics. Take the splendid list of leaders who have followed Franklin and Rumford.[17] They may be called the school of Sir Isaac Newton, so much of their inspiration is due to him. Not all were trained in academic walls; but not one failed to derive help from the advantages which universities provide and perpetuate.

One of the greatest of these men, Sir William Thomson, has lately been here. He was invited to come because it was believed that he, more than any other foreigner, could give an impulse to the study of physics in this country. His lectures were on a subject so remote from ordinary thought that I do not suppose its announcement conveys to those who are unfamiliar with the present position of physical inquiries the least idea of what the lecturer was to talk about. Nevertheless so great was the attraction of his powers that a large company—two or three from England, one from Japan, several from beyond the Alleghanies, and many from this neighborhood, most of them teachers and professors of physics—here assembled daily for a month to catch what they could of his learning and his enthusiasm. His words were taken down and have been given to the public in the form of lecture notes, and have thus reached already the principal seats of learning abroad and at home; but the chief results of his visit will be seen, as the years go on, in the increased devotion of his followers to their science, and in their emulation of his enthusiasm and concentration. Could I give you a more interesting example of the way in which a university may encourage physical science?

Notwithstanding all the progress in physics and astronomy which has been made during a century, those who know the most about these subjects will assure us that they are but at the alphabet of their science. Read the address of the astronomer of Princeton, on a recent occasion, in which he enumerates the impending problems of astronomy; or that of one of our own staff, when he reviews the condition of electrical science, and declares that "as the region of the unknown is infinitely greater than the known, there is no fear of there not being work for the whole world for centuries to come"; and he adds (to please, I suppose, the practical men) that, in the applications of science, "the telephone, the telegraph, and electric lighting are but as child's play to what the world will see."

Chemistry is the child of the nineteenth century. The atomic theory, which lies at the foundation of all modern investigations, was announced by Dalton[18] (that English Friend after whom it would not be amiss to name our chemical laboratory "Dalton Hall," as a tribute alike to his eminence and to the society in which our founder was also trained)—Dalton's law, I say, was announced between 1804 and 1808, so that we can trace more distinctly than in most sciences the exact influences under which chemistry has grown up. Alchemy, the search for gold or for the philosopher's stone, never became a science, and contributed very little to the good of man; but when the universities of Europe, with their trained observers, their methods of accurate work, their habit of publication, and especially their traditional principles of cooperative study, directed their attention to the fundamental laws of atomic combination, the science of chemistry grew with rapidity, and with benefits to mankind which can never be enumerated. To no man were its early days more indebted than to Liebig,[19]—"of organic chemistry the very source and fountainhead,"—good as a thinker, good as an investigator, good as a lecturer, but better still, as one of his most illustrious pupils has informed us, "in the peripatetic teaching of his laboratory."

"It was at the small University of Giessen," says Hofmann, from whom I have just quoted, that "Liebig organized the first educational laboratory that was ever founded. This school forms an epoch in chemical science. It was here that experimental instruction such as now prevails in our laboratories received its earliest form and fashion; and if we are proud of the magnificent temples raised to experimental science in all our schools and universities, let it never be forgotten that they all owe their origin to the prototype set up by Liebig half a century ago." The world appreciates the results which have proceeded from these laboratories; let it also be remembered that they were the creation, not of industrial fabrics, not of mercantile corporations, not even of private enterprise, but of universities, and that the motive which inspired their founders and directors was not the acquisition of wealth, but the ascertainment of fundamental law.

The science, which began with the century, is going forward more rapidly than ever. Yet, if we examine a recent exposition of the principles of theoretical chemistry, we may discover that here, as in mathematics and in physics, the most expert perceive that the field which is open to investigation is much vaster than that which has been surveyed. Here, as everywhere else, the higher one ascends the greater his horizon. What good is to come to men from these researches it would not be wise to predict; but we may reflect on what has recently occurred. Within the last few months a boon has been conferred on humanity, so great that all the cost of all the laboratories of all the lands in Christendom would have been a small price to pay for so precious a pearl. It came into the world, never again to leave it, unheralded, unexpected, from the laboratory of science, to deaden for a few moments and then restore to life the organs of the sight, so that operations on the eye, hitherto dreaded, may be performed without the slightest pain. The chemists may modestly say that this discovery was an accident, not to be compared in significance with the discovery of Avogadro's law. That may be so, yet this sort of accident does not happen in Africa, or the Fiji Islands; it "happens" where there are universities and laboratories, and trained men able and ready to observe phenomena, and discover and apply principles.

In this rapid review, I have hardly introduced a theme which would be more appropriate for a volume than for a discourse. I have not spoken of the study of the structure of the earth, the physics of the globe, the laws of storms, the constituent rocks and minerals of the earth, the record of life hidden in ancient strata, the living kingdoms of animals and plants, the distribution of the races of men, the progress of archaeology, or of innumerable subdivisions in the great branches of human knowledge. Such a task would be beyond my powers; I have only attempted to suggest what each one of you may study for the rest of your lives, as you watch the growth of universities and the progress of knowledge. I have purposely avoided all questions pertaining to professional and technical education.

A few miles east of one of my former homes—the settlement of Berkeley in

California—there is an isolated peak of moderate height, from the top of which you may survey an area equal to that of the State of New York. From Mount Shasta on the north to Mount Whitney on the south, you may trace the jagged, often snow-white, crest which bears the name of Sierra Nevada. Here and there a peak rises a little higher than its neighbors, and can be identified from the lookout; but human vision cannot see the chains beyond the chains, nor the marvelous valley Yosemite and the beautiful Lake Tahoe, which are sheltered within the nearest range of hills. All that the eye can distinguish on the horizon are a few of the loftiest summits, as it turns toward the east, and a glimpse of the Farallones Islands, as it turns toward the west. So today, from a hill not very high, we have looked upon a broad area, distinguishing only the chief features of the landscape; but we have seen the mountains and the sea.

CHAPTER 14

Opening Exercises

G. Stanley Hall

INTRODUCTION TO HALL'S INAUGURAL ADDRESS

The construction of major research universities virtually overnight and essentially from scratch, almost inconceivable today, is one of the notable features of the post–Civil War expansion of American higher education. In some cases, the provisions of the 1862 Morrill Act, which made funds available for endowments, was a key factor. But in other cases, the creation of these new institutions was made possible by the existence of individuals wealthy enough to finance an entire university, and by the almost complete absence of the protocols of faculty governance. This gave university presidents (and, sometimes, university funders) a free hand in hiring and firing faculty and allocating resources. The two went together. There are individuals today who are wealthy enough to underwrite the creation of a university, but they and their chosen administrators would have much less control over how their money was spent.

The private universities that sprang up in the last third of the nineteenth century are therefore forever associated with two names: a funder and a president. Johns Hopkins, named for its benefactor, a Baltimore financier, and headed by Daniel Coit Gilman, opened its doors in 1876. Stanford, named in memory of the son of its founder, Leland Stanford, opened in 1891; its first president was David Starr Jordan. The University of Chicago opened a year later. The money came from John D. Rockefeller; the president was William Rainey Harper. Hopkins and Chicago were academic powerhouses almost from the start; building up Stanford took a little longer. But there was one major train wreck among the start-ups, Clark University.

The school's benefactor, Jonas Clark, had made his fortune selling goods to California gold miners. He and Leland Stanford were friends. Like the

Stanfords—and unlike Rockefeller—Clark took an active interest in the institution whose bills he was paying. He chose as his president G. Stanley Hall, one of the great academic careerists of the era. Hall was a farm boy from Massachusetts; he started out at Williams, from which he graduated in 1867, and followed a winding educational path, ending up by receiving Harvard's first PhD in philosophy, in 1878.

Hall worked in the profession's hottest new discipline, experimental psychology. He had spent years in Germany, studying with the leading figures in the field. At Harvard, he was a student of William James, and, before becoming president of Clark, he taught at Hopkins. He was a disciple of Daniel Coit Gilman and the German university model. His belief in the paramount importance of scientific research was almost mystical. He talked about "the holy fervor of investigation" and called the researcher "the Knight of the Holy Spirit of truth."

Hall's inaugural address, in 1889, articulates many beliefs he shared with his presidential peers, especially faith in the economic rewards to the nation of an investment in pure science. The address also signals some of the reasons the Clark experiment failed. Jonas Clark turned out not to be so benign a patron as Hall imagined, and the city of Worcester, Clark's hometown, did not rise to the occasion financially, as Clark and Hall had both hoped it would. Clark opposed Hall's intention to make the university a graduate school (Gilman had had the same intentions at Hopkins, but abandoned it), and Hall's decision to have only five departments—mathematics, physics, chemistry, biology, and psychology—was out of keeping with the general, and ultimately winning, conviction that the modern university should teach everything.

And there was the problem of Hall's personality. He had a habit of making promises he either could not or did not intend to keep. His faculty quickly grew discontented, and this enabled William Rainey Harper to raid the place. By 1892, two-thirds of Clark's senior faculty and three-quarters of the junior faculty had resigned. Half of them went to Chicago. By the terms of Clark's will, the trustees were obliged to create Clark College, which they did in 1902, but Hall prevented it from being combined with the graduate program. That finally happened after his retirement, in 1920.

OPENING EXERCISES, OCTOBER 2, 1889

Clark University, Worcester, Mass.

We are here to mark in a simple way, as befits its dignity, a rare event which we hope and pray may prove not only the most important in the history of this favored city but of forever growing significance for our state and nation, for culture and humanity.

Located with great forethought in a city whose culture ensures that enlightened public sentiment so needful in maintaining the highest possible academic standards, in a city whose wealth and good will, we trust, are as fair a promise as can anywhere be given or asked of that perpetual increase of revenue now required by the rapid progress of science—in a city central among the best colleges of the East, whose work we wish not only to supplement but to stimulate, whose higher interests we hope to serve, and whose good will and active co-operation we invite, governed by trustees of eminence in the nation as well as in the state who ask no sectarian and no political questions of their appointees, whose influence without and whose counsels within are of inestimable and well appreciated value; consecrating ourselves to the toil of science at an hour so peculiarly critical and so opportune in the university development of the country, I must believe that not only every intelligent inhabitant of Worcester, but every unbiased friend of higher education everywhere, will wish to add to our already unexpectedly large endowment of public and private good will at home and abroad his and her hearty, ungrudging and reiterated God-speed.

Just because, instead of the easy and wasteful task of repeating what is already well done about us, we strive to take the inevitable next step and to be the first, if we can, upon the higher plane; because we must study not only to utilize all available experience wherever we can, but to be wisely bold in innovations wherever we must; because there will be indifference and misconception from friends who do not see all the importance of our work at first; because there are difficulties inherent in the very nature of that work itself as great as the work is needed, we must go slowly and surely, establishing but few departments at first, and when they are made the best possible, adding new and most related ones as fast as we can find the men and money to support them. We must prolong the formative period of foundation, and must each and every one realize well that we are just entering upon years of unremitting toil, in which patience and hope will be tempered with trial. But our cause is itself an inspiration, for it is in the current of all good tendencies in higher education, and of the ultimate success of what is this day begun, there is not a shadow of doubt or of fear.

Our history begins more than twenty years ago, in the plans of a reticent and sagacious man, whose leave we cannot here await to speak of, who in affluence maintains the simple and regular mode of life inbred in the plain New England home of his boyhood;—plans that have steadily grown with his fortune and that have been followed and encouraged with an eager and growing interest, which extended to even minor items by the devoted companion of his life. Besides a large fund already placed to our account, he has given his experience and unremitting daily care, worth to us large sums in economies, and resulting in well appointed buildings and a solidity of materials and a thoroughness of workmanship which I believe are without a parallel of their cost and kind in the country. Not only in the multifarious work of the university office, its methods of estimates, orders, book-keeping, of individual accountability for all books, apparatus, supplies and furniture, but in the larger questions of university polity without and effective administration within, in the definition of duty for each officer, the strict subordination and the concentration of authority and responsibility sure to appeal to all who have the instinct of discipline, and which are exceptionally needful where the life of science is to be so free, and the policy so independent; in the express exemption, too, of all instructors who can sustain the ardor of research from excessive teaching and examination, in the appointment of assistants in a way to keep each member of the staff at his best work and to avoid the too common and wasteful practice in American universities of letting four thousand dollar men do four hundred dollar work, in the ample equipment of each department, that no force be lost on inferior tools—in all these and many other respects the ideal of our founder has been to make everywhere an independent application of the simplest and severest but also the largest principles of business economy.

As business absorbs more and more of the talent and energy of the world, its considerations more and more pervading if not subordinating, whether for better or worse, not only the arts, the school, the press, but all departments of church and state, making peace and war, cities or deserts, so science is slowly pervading and profoundly modifying literature, philosophy, education, religion and every domain of culture. Both at their best have dangers and are severe schools of integrity. The directness, simplicity, certainty and absorption in work so characteristic of both are setting new fashions in manners, and even in morals, and bringing man into closer contact with the world as it is. Both are binding the universe together into new unities and imposing a discipline ever severer for body and mind. When their work, purified of deceit and error, is finished, the period of history we now call modern will be rounded to completeness, culture will have abandoned much useless luggage, the chasm between instruction and education will be less disastrous, and all the highest and most sacred of human ideals will not be lost or dimmed but will become nearer and more real.

When one who has graduated with highest honors from this rigorous school of business, after spending eight years of travel abroad studying the means by which knowledge and culture, the most precious riches of the race, are increased and transmitted, and finding no reason why our country, which so excels in business, should be content with the second best in science, devotes to its services not only his fortune at the end of his life, but also years yet full of exceptional and unabated energy, we see in such a fact not only the normal, complete, if you please, post-graduate ethical maturity of an individual business life, but also a type and promise of what wealth now seems likely to do for higher education in America. It is no marvel that our foundation has already been so often so conspicuously and so favorably noted in authoritative ways and places in an European land where, if monarchy should yield to a republic, university culture could not penetrate its people as it now does. It is thus a more typical and vital product of the national life at its best than are foundations made by state or church in which to train their servants. In thus giving his fortune to a single highest end as sagaciously and actively as he has acquired it, may our founder find a new completeness of life in age, which Cicero did not know, and taste

—"all the joy that lies
In a full self-sacrifice."

The very word science, especially when used in its relation to business, is too often degraded by cheap graduates who are just fit to look after established industrial processes, but are useless if competition finds or needs new and better ones; who certify to analyses of commercial products that good chemists know are impossible; who, if international competition in manufactures were more free, would give place to better trained, perhaps German, experts still faster than they are doing; who, in criminal, medical, and patent law suits often have the address to carry judge and jury against far better chemists, but who have no conception of the higher quality and more rigorous methods of their own science; who make chemistry, physics and geology mercenary, culinary, the servants instead of the masters of industrial progress, and the very "life-springs of all the arts of peace or war." This evil, although so great and common that even the best men in other professions too rarely see the high ideal culture power of real science, is yet only incidental and temporary.

A good illustration of the high and normal technological value of pure science is at hand in dyeing, one of the most scientific among the many and increasing chemical industries. England furnishes nearly all the raw, formerly valueless, material for coal tar colors, out of which Germany made most of the seventeen and a half million dollars' worth manufactured in 1880. England bought back a large fraction of the colored goods, and Germany made the profits because she could furnish the best training in pure chemistry. It is for this reason that she is driving other countries out of the field in other leading chemical industries. The great factories there employ from two or three to more than a score each of good, and often the best, university trained chemists at large salaries and the best of these spend a good part of their time in original research in the factory laboratories. The prospect of these lucrative careers has had very much to do in filling the chemical laboratories of the universities with hundreds of students and the German government (best that of Prussia) has met the demand by erecting and equipping new and sometimes magnificent laboratories at nearly all of her universities. New artificial processes of making organic products of commerce have freed thousands of acres of land where they were formerly grown, and have made new industries and often impaired old ones. Many professors of chemistry make large outside incomes, nearly all are sanguine; some even declare that before very long leading drugs, and even food that will equal if not actually excel nature's products, will be made artificially. The leading professor in one of the largest chemical laboratories of Germany told me in substance that he no longer went after outside technical work, but now made it a virtue to wait for it to seek him, and it has been strongly urged that even the government should take steps to prevent the migration of German chemists to the universities of other countries, lest Germany lose her pre-eminence in chemical industries.

This remarkable contact of the marvelous new business life and energy of Germany, particularly of North Germany, (which in both suddenness and vigor equals any of the wonderful developments in this country), with staid and tranquil academic ways, has had some marked reverberations and given new direction and impetus to other studies in some other departments where it is not directly felt. It has led to the erection and equipment by the government of great technological schools, and has shown to business men and employers that no course in the sciences which underlie technology can be too advanced, prolonged or severe to be practical. Where ought the value and significance of such a training be better appreciated than here in the land of Fulton, Morse, Bell and Edison?

There are, however, eminent chemists in Germany and many more in surrounding European countries, who deplore what they call the irruption of the technical spirit into the universities. They fear the proximity of the factory and the patent office to the university laboratory has narrowed the field of view and made methods of research relatively less severe, they complain that in their teaching they must hasten over inorganic chemistry, neglecting all the other elements for the carbon compounds, and that there are almost no inorganic chemists in Germany; that in choosing between several substances inviting research, one of which promises great commercial value and the other none, strict scientific impartiality is lost; that in the eagerness for practical results, problems are attempted too complex for the present methods of experimenters who are trying to "eat soup with a fork," as one sadly told me, and that thus while published researches are more numerous they are less thorough and have introduced many formulae that neither prove nor agree, so that much work now accepted must be done over again and far more thoroughly; that even Liebig set a bad example in this respect, and that many new products of which university chemists boast are so inferior to those of nature as to be really adulteration.

What I have tried to illustrate mainly in the field of one science is more or less true under changed ways and degrees in the sphere of others. The sciences are also at the very heart of modern medical studies. Biology explores the laws of life upon which not only these studies but human health, welfare and modern conceptions of man and his place in nature so fundamentally rest. The law of the specific energy of nerves, e.g., which Helmholtz says equals in importance the Newtonian law of gravity, and more than anything else made physiology the science which has had so large a share in raising the medical profession in Germany to a position in the intellectual world such as it never had before, doing for it in some degree what chemistry has done for dyeing, and even instruments like the ophthalmoscope, which almost created a department of medical practice, or the spectroscope, now indispensable in the Bessemer process, sugar refining, in wine and color-dye tests, the detection of photographic sensibilators, in the custom house and in two important forms of medical diagnosis,—all these, to cut short a long list of both epoch-making laws and important instruments, are the direct products of whole souled devotion to unremunerative scientific research.

It is hard for medical students to realize that they can not understand hygiene, forensic medicine, pharmacology, and toxicology without a rigorous drill in chemistry; that they must know physics to understand the diagnostic and therapeutic use of electricity, ophthalmology, otology, the mechanism of the bones, muscles, circulation, etc.; that zoology is needed to teach sound philosophic thought, generic facts about the laws of life, health, reproduction and disease. These, and sometimes also sciences like mineralogy, anthropology, and psychology, are required in Europe, with much more rigor than is common with us, of every medical student. Thus doctors, like technologists, cannot know too much pure science. An eminent medical practitioner in Europe compares young physicians who slight the basal sciences of their profession and pass on to the clinical, therapeutic and practical parts, to young men who grow prematurely old and sterile. The phrase of Hippocrates, "Godlike is the physician who is also a philosopher," is still more true and good in its larger, more modern and looser translation, viz., exalted is the physician who knows not only the most approved methods of practice, but also the pure sciences which underlie and determine both the dignity and value of his profession.

Medical instruction on the one hand must select as its foundation those sciences and those parts of the sciences most useful in meeting man's great enemy, disease. It needs far more anatomy than physics and little mathematics, astronomy or geology. Technical instruction on the other hand is and must be so organized as to reflect the state of industry. It properly lays more stress upon chemistry with its many applications than upon biology, which has far fewer; more upon electricity than upon molecular physics; and more upon organic than inorganic chemistry. The university, which is entirely distinct from and higher than any form of technical or professional instruction can be, should represent the state of science *per se*. It should be strong in those fields where science is highly developed, and should pay less attention to other departments of knowledge which have not reached the scientific stage. It should be financially and morally able to disregard practical application as well as numbers of students. It should be a laboratory of the highest possible human development in those lines where educational values are the criterion of what is taught or not taught, and the increase of knowledge and its diffusion among the few fit should be its ideal. As another puts it, "The more and better books, apparatus, collections and teachers, and the fewer but more promising students, the better the work." In Europe, besides its duty to science the university must not fail of its practical duty to furnish to the state good teachers, preachers, doctors, advocates, engineers and technologists of various kinds. Here a university can if it chooses do still better and devote itself exclusively to the pure sciences. These once understood, their applications are relatively easy and quickly learned. The university must thus stand above, subordinate and fructify the practical spirit, or the latter will languish for want of science to apply.

The important facts that are both certain and exact, and the completely verified laws, or well ordered, welded cohesion of thought that approach such mental continuity as makes firm, compactly woven intellectual or cerebral tissue, are so precious in our distracted and unsettled age, that it is no marvel that impartial laymen in all walks of life are coming to regard modern science in its pure high form as not only the greatest achievement of the race thus far, but also as carrying in it the greatest, though not yet well developed, culture power of the world, not only for knowledge but also for feeling and conduct. It is of this power that universities are the peculiar organs; to them is now committed the highest interests of man; from them and from science now comes the light and advancement of the world. They became and remained the asylums of free thought and conviction when Rome and all other privileged orders declined, and their germs were brought and piously and early planted on these shores by our fathers. The term is not only "the noblest in the vocabulary of science," but universities are the chief nurseries of talent, where is kept alive the holy fervor of investigation that in its passion for truth is fearless of consequences and has never been more truly and loftily ideal than now, when its objects of study are often most crassly material. It is their quality more than anything else that determines not only the status of the medical and all technological professions, but also whether the legal profession is formal, narrow, mercenary and unlearned as it seems now in danger of becoming in Germany, because even the German universities, despite their great preeminence in all other respects, are by general consent of the most competent Germans themselves relatively weak in those departments which underlie the practice of law or broadly based on history and social or economic science informed in administrative experience, and culminating in judicial talent and statesmanship. Universities largely determine whether a land is cursed by a factious, superstitious, half-cultured clergy, or blessed by ministers of divine truth, who understand and believe the doctrines they teach; who attract and enlarge the most learned and penetrate the life of the poor and ignorant, quickening, comforting and informing in a way worthy the Great Teacher himself; and making their profession as it should be—the noblest of human callings.

Compared with our material progress, we are not only making no progress, but are falling behind in higher education. It has been estimated that but five per cent. of the practicing physicians of this country have had a liberal education, and that sixty per cent. of our medical schools require practically no preliminary training whatever for admission, while European laws require a university training for every doctor before he can practice. Again, we apply science with great skill but create or advance it very little indeed. Should the supply of European science which now so promptly finds its way here and fertilizes and stimulates to more or less hopeful reaction our best scholars, and upon which we live as upon charity, be cut off by some great war or otherwise, the unbalanced and shortsighted utilitarian tendencies now too prevalent here would tend toward the same stagnation and routine which similar tendencies unchecked long ago wrought out in China. We all most heartily believe in and respect technical and applied science and all grades of industrial education, but these are as much out of place in a truly academic university as money-changers were in the temple of the Most High.

But yet the fact that these and other evils and difficulties are now so widely seen and so deeply felt, that endowments for higher education seem now the order of the day, that the largest single endowment in this country has already so effectively begun so many reforms in scarcely more than a decade in Baltimore; that churchmen, statesmen and business men now need only to see their own interests in a way a little larger and broader, as they are now tending to do, to co operate more actively than they ever have done in strengthening our best foundations—such considerations sustain the larger and more hopeful view that our country is already beginning to rise above the respectable and complacent mediocrity still its curse in every domain of culture, and will show that democracy can produce—as it must or decline—the very highest type of men as its leaders. The university problem seems to be fairly upon us. We now need men in our chairs whose minds have got into independent motion; who are authorities and not echoes; who have the high moral qualities of plain and simple living and self-sacrificing devotion to truth, and who show to this community and the country the spectacle of men absorbed in and living only for pure science and high scholarship, and are not mere place-holders or sterile routine pedagogues, and all needed material support is sure to come.

A word so characteristic here that it might stand upon our very seal, is concentration. Of this our founder, in declining to scatter his resources among the countless calls from individuals, institutions and causes, from excellent to vicious, and refusing us as yet, in the one work he has set out to accomplish, no needed thing, sets an example. We have selected a small but closely related group of five departments, and shall at first focus all our means and care to make these five the best possible. Neither the historical origin nor the term university have anything to do with completeness of the field of knowledge. The word originally designated simply a corporation with peculiar privileges and peculiarly independent to do what it chose. We choose to assert the same privilege of election for ourselves that other institutions allow their students, and offer the latter in choosing their subjects a larger option between institutions. The continental habit of inter-university migration also on the part of students, if once adopted here, would, no doubt, stimulate institutions no less than it has stimulated competing departments in the same university. Our plan in this respect implies a specialization as imperatively needed for the advanced students, as it would we admit, be unfortunate for students still in the disciplinary collegiate stage. If our elementary schools are inferior to the best in Europe, and if our fitting schools are behind the French Lycée, the German Gymnasium and the great English schools it is our universities that are comparatively by far the weakest part of our national system. The best of these best know that 50 or 100 instructors cannot do the work of 350; that they cannot hope at present to rival European governments which erect single university buildings, costing nearly four million dollars each, as at Berlin and Vienna, nor equal the clinical opportunities of large European cities with poorer populations and more concentrated hospital systems. Our strongest universities are far too feeble to do justice to all the departments, old and new, which they undertake. Our institutions are also too uniform; the small and weak ones try to copy every new departure of the stronger ones as the latter copy the far stronger institutions in Europe. If the best of them would do work of real university grade, they should specialize among the fields of academic culture, doing well what they do, but not attempting to do everything, the American system might yet come to represent the highest educational needs of the country. In contrast with the present ideal of horizontal expansion and the waste of unnecessary duplication, we believe our departure will be as useful as it is new.

Again, concentration is now the master word of education. In no country has the amount of individual information been so great, the range of intelligence so wide, the number of studies attempted by young men in colleges and universities so large for the time and labor given to each, the plea for liberal and general, as distinct from special and exclusive studies, been so strong. This is well, for general knowledge is the best soil for any kind of eminence or culture to spring from, and because power, though best applied on a small surface, is best developed over a large one and not in brains educated, as it were, in spots. More than this our utilitarian ideal of general knowledge is far more akin to that of Hippias, who would make his own clothes and shoes, cook his own food, etc., or to that of Diderot, who would learn all trades, than to the noble Greek ideal of the symmetrical all-sided development of all the powers of body and mind. The more general knowledge the better; but everything must shoot together in the brain. In the figure of Ritcher, the sulphur, saltpeter, and charcoal must find each other or the man makes no powder. The brain must be trained to bring all that is in it to a sharp focus without dispersive fringes. The natural instinct of every ambitious youth is to excel, to do, or make or know something better than any one else, to be an authority, to surpass all others, if only in the most accuminated specialty. Learning thus what true mental freedom is, he is more docile in all other directions.

If it be extravagant to say that no minds are so feeble that they cannot excel, if they concentrate all their energies upon a point sufficiently small, nothing is more true than that the greatest powers fail if too much is attempted. This is not only a wise instinct that makes for economy, but in the parliamentary committee rooms, in corporation meetings, in the court room, in business, in science, in the sick chamber, the modern world in nearly every department is now really governed by experts—by men who have attained the mastery that comes by concentration. The young man who has had the invaluable training of abandoning himself to a long experimental research upon some very special but happily chosen point was typically illustrated in a man I knew. With the dignity and sense of finality of the American senior year quick within him, his first teacher in Germany told him to study experimentally one of the score of muscles of a frog's leg. He feared loss and limitation in trying to focus all his energies upon so small and insignificant an object. The mild dissipation of too general culture, the love of freedom and frequent change, aided by a taste for breezy philosophic romancing, almost diverted him from the frog's leg. But as he progressed he found that he must know in a more minute and practical way than before—in a way that made previous knowledge seem unreal—certain definite points in electricity, chemistry, mechanics, physiology, etc., and bring them to bear in fruitful relation to each other. As the experiments proceeded through the winter, the history of previous views upon the subject were studied and understood as never before and broader biological relations gradually seen. The summer, and yet another year were passed upon this tiny muscle, for he had seen that its laws and structure are fundamentally the same in frogs and men, that just such contractile tissue has done all the work man has accomplished in the world, that muscles are the only organ of the will. Thus, as the work went on, many of the mysteries of the universe seemed to centre in his theme; in fact, in the presence and study of this minute object of nature he had passed from the attitude of Peter Bell, of whom the poet says,

> "A cowslip by the river's brim
> A yellow cowslip was to him,
> And it was nothing more,"

up to the standpoint of the seer who "plucked a flower from the crannied wall," and realized that could he but understand what it was, "—root and all and all in all, he would know what God and man is." Even if my friend had contributed nothing in the shape of discovery to the great temple of science, he had felt the *omne tutit punctum* of nature's organic unity, he had felt the profound and religious conviction that the world is lawful to the core; he had experienced what a truly liberal education, in the modern as distinct from the mediaeval sense, really is. We may term it non-professional specialization.

Perhaps the most thorough and comprehensive government reports ever made in any language are those of the English parliamentary commissioners on endowments. The first of these occupied nearly nineteen years and fills nearly two-score heavy folio volumes. In all, about twenty thousand foundations, new and centuries old, large and small, devoted to a vast variety of uses, good and questionable, were reported. The conclusions drawn from this field of experience, which is far richer and wider in England than elsewhere, was that of all the great popular charities, higher education has proven safest, wisest and best, and that for two chief reasons—first, because the superior integrity and ability of the guardians who consented to administer such funds, the intelligence and grateful appreciation of those aided by them, and the strong public interest and resulting publicity—all three combined to hold them perpetually truest to the purpose and spirit of the founders; and secondly, because in improving higher education, all other good causes are most effectively aided. The church can in no other way be more fundamentally served than by providing a still better training for her ministers and missionaries. Charity for hospitals and almshouses is holy, Christ-like work, but to provide a better training for physicians and economists, teaches the world to see and shun the causes of sickness and poverty. Sympathy must always tenderly help the feeblest and even the defective classes, but to help the strongest in the struggle for existence is to help not them alone but all others within their influence.

Of all the many ways of supporting the higher education, individual aid to deserving and meritorious students is one of the most approved. In the University of Leipzig, e.g., four hundred and seven distinct funds can aid eight hundred and forty-nine students. Of these funds the oldest was established in 1325, and they are increasing in number, more new ones having been given between 1880 and 1885 than in any entire decade before. In size they range from thirty-five thousand to fifty dollars, in Berlin from one hundred and forty thousand to one of less than forty dollars. In cases where conditions are specified the most frequent limitation is to students from a certain locality and next to those of a certain family. By the older founders students of theology were more often preferred, but the more recent funds are for medicine, law, philology and pure science, and a fund of over two hundred thousand lately given the University of Marburg is for advanced students in those sciences which underlie medicine. These funds are often given, named for, held and sometimes awarded by churches or their pastors, magistrates, heads of fitting schools, boards of education, representatives of prominent families, for students of their name, the donor himself or herself, individual professors etc., subject of course to satisfying the university examiners. Many are tenable for one, more for three, and some for five and six years. The funds must be invested with pupilary security, and with interest commonly less than four per cent. In Cambridge and Oxford provision is made for nearly 1,000 fellows and eight hundred scholars, not to mention the exhibitions at Oxford. The fellowships are more lucrative and are designed for more advanced men than are provided for in the German universities, the fellows aiding the master in internal administration. In England, besides the religious and other founders, as in Germany, the great historic industrial and mercantile corporations provide many of the fellowships and scholarships, particularly those of the sixteenth and seventeenth centuries, and they are granted by bishops, curates, heads of business corporations, masters of the great schools, heads or fellows of colleges. In France, where these foundations were swept away by the revolution, stipends and bursaries are provided annually by the Government. New appropriations for the most advanced students of all was the secret of the remarkable *École Pratique des Hautes Études*, founded in 1868, of which a recent report just printed for the Exposition says, condensing its substance, that its purpose has always been to foster scientific zeal with no shade of temporal interest, that it restored the almost obliterated idea of higher education, gave unity to scientific interests throughout France, and made her feel the scholarly desiderata of the age, made young professors not only well instructed, but trained in good methods, that although its profound researches are not manifest to the public, has given a more scientific character to all the faculties, and rendered a service to the state out of all proportion to its cost. In France individuals co-operate with the state in this work.

Has there ever been devised a form of memorial to and bearing the names of husbands, wives, children or parents, by which even the smallest funds could be bestowed in a way more lastingly expressive of the individuality, spirit and the special lines of interest of the donor, more worthy the dead and more helpful to the highest ends of life? Since the first endowment of research in the Athenian Porch and Grove, thousands and thousands of donations of this sort have borne tangible witness to the sentiment so often and vividly taught by Plato that in all the world there is no object more worthy of reverence, love and service than eugenic, eupeptic, well-bred, gifted young men, for in them is the hope of the world.

The more advanced our standards are to be, the fewer will be our students, and the more expensive their needed outfit of books and apparatus. If we divide our running expenses only by the number of students our present fellowships and scholarships allow us to receive out of our two hundred and fifty applicants, the amount we spent per student, the first year will probably be without a parallel. Besides this, for a number of students with important researches on hand we are expending hundreds of dollars each for their individual needs, and should be glad to do so for more as good men. The best students very often graduate with empty pockets, but with their zeal and power at its best, and when an extra year or two would make a great difference in their entire career. Also, as the field of knowledge grows more complex, the economy of energy needed for concentration is impossible without the leisure secured by comfortable support.

Connected with all the protection, exemptions and privileges so dearly prized and tenaciously clung to by the mediaeval universities, there have always been dangers sometimes grave and not yet entirely obviated. The new charity is often popularly called a science as well as a virtue. Its axiom is that no man has a right to give doles to beggars without satisfying himself personally or through some agency to that end that his gift will do good and not harm to the recipient. History, and I may add personal observation, shows that the same general law holds true to some extent in universities. I believe they should not award fellowships to men fresh from college (save in the very rarest cases), unless they are able to guide and direct as well as to follow their work in every detail. A fellow should be encouraged and stimulated by a daily and familiar intercourse with the professors. His methods, reading and researches should be kept at their best and the entire resources of the institution should be a soil for his most rapid and helpful growth. Students thus served, even if their gratitude does not prompt them, as in some late instances in Germany, to study, revive and try to conform with piety to the ideal of ancient and almost forgotten donors, whose provisions they enjoyed, will not be lacking in appreciation. To appoint a man to use such funds in electing among undergraduate courses, or to take his chances among the confusing multifarious subjects offered in foreign institutions, is, I believe, in most cases of small utility, and in some cases that I know, positively harmful. May the methods of exclusion we are studying be so effective that neither our precious funds nor the precious energy of our instructors be wasted upon the idle, stupid or unworthy students, now too often exposed in vain for four years to the contagion of knowledge.

"Education used to be a question for ladies and for schoolmasters," said a French statesman last spring, but it is now not only a question of state on which the support of all great institutions depends, but the great question into which all others issue if profoundly discussed or studied. So greatly do republics need the whole power of education, and so serious is their struggle for existence against ignorance and its attendant evils, that it has well been said that the problem whether this form of government be permanent is at bottom a question of education. But monarchies are no less dependent upon the education of their leaders and servants. In his famous address declaring that if Germany was ever to be free and strong, it must be by becoming the chief educational state of Europe, must realize the platonic republic in which the education of its youth was the highest care of the rulers, Fichte laid down the policy which has been one of the chief causes of the wonderful development of that country. Moreover, evolution, which shows that even life itself is but the education of protoplasm cells and tissues, that the play-instinct in children and the love of culture in adults, not only measure the superfluous individual energy over and above that required by the processes necessary to life, but are perhaps largely the same, also makes it plain that the hunger for more and larger education of life is but the struggle of talent to the full maturity and leadership which is its right.

For myself I have no stronger wish or resolve than that in the peculiarly arduous labors I expect, I may never forget that this institution should be a means to these high purposes and not degenerate to an end in itself: and may it be as true of our graduates to remotest time, as it is of us in a unique way and degree to-day, that we could not love Clark University so much, loved we not science and education more.

CHAPTER 15

The Relations of the National and State Governments to Advanced Education

Andrew D. White

INTRODUCTION TO WHITE'S SPEECH TO THE NATIONAL EDUCATIONAL ASSOCIATION

America's state universities are not just uniquely American institutions; they stand out as such. Here, for example, is the impression that the British historian Tony Judt formed as a young academic in the early 1970s and endorsed shortly before his death in 2010:

> By far the best thing about America is its universities. Not Harvard, Yale *e tutti quanti:* though marvelous, they are not distinctively American—their roots reach across the ocean to Oxford, Heidelberg, and beyond. Nowhere else in the world, however, can boast such *public* universities. You drive for miles across a godforsaken Midwestern scrubscape, pockmarked by billboards, Motel 6s, and a military parade of food chains, when—like some pedagogical mirage dreamed up by nineteenth-century English gentlemen—there appears . . . a library! And not just any library: at Bloomington, the University of Indiana boasts a 7.8 million-volume collection in more than nine hundred languages, housed in a magnificent double-towered mausoleum of Indiana limestone.[1]

Indeed, where else in the world does one encounter anything like the spectacle Judt describes? And who knows? Maybe the best (distinctively American) thing about America is its public universities. Maybe they're even "by far" the best thing about America.

But while it's true that the sponsor of the Morrill Act insisted on combining practical studies with the traditional liberal arts, the emergence of so many land-grant universities into the form Judt admired—that is, as massive oases of learning where the resources from the land grants were concentrated—was not merely a function of his mandate or of homegrown thinking about higher education. Many factors contributed to this process, and not the least important of them was the vision of education articulated by Andrew Dickson White, who found crucial inspiration in the universities of England, France, and, above all, Germany. He once wrote about the University of Berlin that there he encountered "the ideal of a university, not only realized, but extended and glorified."

White, Cornell's first president and more than anyone else the architect of that university, began contemplating possibilities for educational reform when he was an undergraduate at Yale, in the early 1850s. For him, the "Yale system" of rote learning in history and the focus on narrow questions of grammar, or "gerund grinding," as he liked to say, in the study of classical literature, was deeply unsatisfying, even stifling. He longed for courses that would "set students thinking" but rarely encountered them.

In Paris and especially Berlin, where he studied after graduating from Yale, White found the situation to be very different. Like many other "new administrators," to use Laurence Veysey's phrase for the men who created a version of the research university in the United States, White became enamored of the German system, though not in a besotted way. White's autobiography in fact contains a memorably unflattering account of a lecture by the great historian Leopold von Ranke, who taught for many years at the University of Berlin. In White's telling, Ranke muttered to himself as he stared up at the ceiling and slowly slid off his chair, while a crowd of students trying to take notes looked on in bewilderment. But that was an anomaly. Many of the professors he heard were more comprehensible, and it was thrilling to listen to someone lay out new ideas about a topic, rather than present facts from someone else's book. Also thrilling was the freedom to focus on a field in which one was genuinely interested. It would be an understatement to say that the continental lecture system, as well as the elective system, impressed White. He returned to the States profoundly committed to both.

After spending six years as a professor of history at the University of Michigan, where he had the opportunity to witness Tappan's reforms, White was elected to the New York State Assembly. Given his background, he was a natural fit for the committee on education, and it was in his capacity as the chairman of that committee that he was able to influence the marshaling of Morrill Act funds in New York. With the state-supported German universities in mind, and against fierce opposition from the New York colleges and universities angling for part of what seemed like a windfall, White campaigned for a concentration of resources in a great university, where scholars and scientists would be brought together with the infrastructure they needed to carry out their work effectively.

White was hardly the first reformer to point out that the proliferation of "sectarian" colleges and universities, that is, schools whose confessional allegiances helped to determine hiring and shape curricula, had caused an unproductive scattering of resources. As White emphasized in the speech that follows, which he gave in 1874 to the National Educational Association, many schools received collections of books and natural materials that they couldn't use because they couldn't find an expert of the right denomination to hire to work with them. Nor was White alone in arguing that when religious authorities intervened into debates about science, they tended to obstruct intellectual progress, though White went further than most in arguing the case, penning a large work on the topic. But White was in a rare position to do something about these problems, especially after winning the Quaker farmer and businessman Ezra Cornell, his fellow assemblyman, for his side.

Together they would withstand innumerable attacks, which included charges of political corruption—this was the time of Tammany Hall—and godlessness, and they were able to push through a bill that called for the centralization of state Morrill Act revenues that White deemed so crucial, with Cornell pledging half a million dollars of his own money, as well as the land for a campus. And thus, in 1865, Cornell University was brought into being.

With his background in agriculture, and being from humble origins, Cornell wanted the university that bore his name to be both accessible and broad in its offerings. He is supposed to have said, "I would found an institution where any person can find instruction in any study." Of course, the goal of breadth, of bringing together vocational fields and the traditional liberal arts, had already been set forth in the Morrill Act. White's accomplishment was that in honoring this mandate and Cornell's wishes, while also pursuing his own long-held aims, he created a model for making the balance work. White instituted elective study and designed two large divisions, one for the liberal arts and one for applied and professional fields, which he called the Division of Special Sciences and Arts. However, White put his own field, history, into the Division of Special Sciences, in part because he believed history to be of use to future statesmen, and in part to make the crucial "equivalence" among the more and less traditional areas of study seem not just formal but also substantive.

White was not an innovator in the area of graduate education. Yet from the beginning, he had his sights set on academic excellence, and he aggressively recruited top-flight researchers in both the humanities and the sciences. Generally White did so with the support of existing faculty, whom he was adept at handling, though not always with the backing of the board of trustees, a body with which he was known to clash.

White also threw himself into the task of building cutting-edge academic facilities. But he managed to devote himself, at the same time, to establishing the vocational fields. Somewhat ironically, the initial agriculture program flopped; Cornell was a pioneer, however, in other areas, such as industrial chemistry and veterinary science. With Ezra Cornell essentially guaranteeing that students of limited means would be able to work their way through school, and with White, who shared many of Cornell's progressive commitments, supporting him in this, young men from around the state took notice. In October of 1868, Cornell enrolled 412 students, all of whom had passed the entrance exam. It was the largest entering class in the history of American higher education.

But White's efforts as an educational leader were not limited to Cornell. While serving as its first president, White also became the first president of the American Historical Association. And he agitated for what he took to be the productive uses of the Morrill Act revenues in states other than New York, as well as for vastly increased national and state government support for higher education. Only in this way, he argues in the speech excerpted below, could America develop a system of universities that would educate the broad public—the country's most vital resource, as he saw it—to be innovators in areas ranging from statecraft to engineering. Only in this way could America come to have what Germany had and thus equip itself to compete effectively on the world stage. Here, too, White faced resistance and objections. Indeed, these amount to a catalog of the critical responses that the great transformation of American higher education in the late nineteenth century called forth. What would happen to all the small colleges if such centers of learning were created? If universities were dependent on government support, wouldn't they have to go into the business of political lobbying, and wouldn't that be a bad thing? Would modern universities devoted to the pursuit of secular knowledge produce men of sound character? And here, too, White had answers that would prove influential.

THE RELATIONS OF THE NATIONAL AND STATE GOVERNMENTS TO ADVANCED EDUCATION

Among all the modern nations, two stand pre-eminent for faith in public education, and for energy in providing it.

Of these, I name first the German nation. In the midst of great calamities and trials, and long years of hard work, and under administrations economical to parsimony, she has developed a system, which, for half a century, has won the admiration of the world by its intellectual triumphs, and which, in the past ten years, has aroused the world's wonder by its political and social triumphs.

Next I name the United States, where, in sight of all mankind, popular education is lifting a nation above all the efforts of demagogues in the field, in the senate-house, and in the press.

In one thing these two nations have adopted the same policy, and obtained the same results. Each has made abundant provision for primary and secondary education in public schools, and both have found in this a source of triumphs both in peace and war, which have placed them in the foremost rank among modern nations.

But in the other half of the system,—in provision for advanced education, in high scientific and industrial schools and universities,—they have followed courses directly opposite, and with directly opposite results.

Germany has carried out her fundamental principle logically. Having started with the idea that the people of a nation should provide for the education of the nation, it has stopped at no imaginary line: it has provided for the education of the whole people,—for the young in primary and secondary schools; for those more advanced, in technical schools and universities. The result is now before the world.

Forth from these institutions have come a majority of the greatest leaders of modern thought and practice,—not only great theologians and lawyers and physicians and historians, and general scholars, but great engineers, physicists, chemists, and naturalists—strong in developing the material resources of the nation. Nor have they done less for liberty than for civilization.

In a State whose central administration is thoroughly orthodox, and exercises strong political control, these universities are strongholds of freedom in politics and religion. In the halls of the University of Berlin, within a stone's throw of the palace of the rigidly orthodox Frederick William IV., might be heard during his entire reign the free utterances of men opposed to every religious or political doctrine which the king thought essential. From the palace window, where the Emperor William loves to stand, can be seen in the university lecture-rooms, on the opposite side of the street, professors putting forth ideas fatal to absolute monarchy.

Bear in mind, too, that this is not the result of centuries of work,—a result impossible in a new country.

Though some of the German universities are on very old foundations, they have been remodelled to suit modern needs, and are in reality new: the greatest of all, the University of Berlin, is younger than the majority of our American colleges which have most reputation; and the greatest of her institutions for advanced instruction in the applied sciences have grown up within twenty years.

The result has been great, politically, intellectually, and morally. These universities, supported by the whole people, and for the whole people, stand far above any others in the world.

The United States, agreeing with Germany in the general line of her public school policy and primary education, has pursued an entirely different path in regard to university policy and advanced education.

While making primary and secondary education a matter of National and State concern, it has left its advanced education, in the main, to various religious sects. It has allowed an utterly illogical imaginary line to be drawn, below which the State provides for education gladly and fully, above which she turns the whole matter over to the sectarian spirit of the country. While the United States has pushed the roots of its public school system down into the needs and feelings of the whole people, and thus obtained a deep rich soil, which has given sturdy growth, it has pushed the roots of advanced education down into the multitude of scattered sects, and has obtained a soil wretchedly thin, and a growth miserably scant.

For the first result of this policy as to advanced education was, that as sects multiplied, the so-called colleges and universities multiplied. Now, while the main condition of primary education is diffusion of resources, the main condition of advanced education is concentration of resources. England sees this, and has but four universities; imperial Prussia sees it, and has eight; the United States has not seen it, and the last Report of the Bureau of Education shows that we have over three hundred and sixty institutions bearing the name of "college" and "university."

The most evident result has been the impoverishment of the whole system. With very few exceptions, these colleges and universities are without any thing approaching complete faculties, without libraries giving any idea of the present condition of knowledge, without illustrative collections for study, without laboratories for experiment, with next to no modern apparatus and instruments. This is true of the whole country; but it is more sadly true of those States outside of the original thirteen.

The next striking result has been a lasting injury to those engaged in the work of advanced instruction. Many noble men stand in the faculties of those colleges and universities,—men who would do honor to any institution of advanced learning in the world. After much intercourse with university professors of various nations, I feel assured that I have never seen any who surpass in natural strength and earnestness very many in our own country; and I have heard this remarked more than once by thoughtful American fellow-students while sitting in foreign university lecture-rooms. These men of ours would, under a better system, develop admirably the intellectual treasures of our people and the material resources of our country; but cramped by want of books, want of apparatus, want of every thing needed in advanced instruction, cramped above all by the spirit of the sectarian college system, very many of them have been paralyzed.

I know whereof I speak. Within the last twenty years I have seen much of these institutions, and within the last seven years I have made it a duty to watch them closely; and I freely confess that my observations have saddened me. Go from one great State to another, in every one you shall find that this unfortunate system has produced the same miserable results,—in the vast majority of our States not a single college or university worthy of the name; only a multitude of little sectarian schools with pompous names and poor equipments, each doing its best to prevent the establishment of any institution broader and better.

The traveller arriving in our great cities generally lands in a railway station costing more than all the university edifices of the State; and he sleeps in a hotel in which there is embarked more capital than in the entire university endowment for millions of people.

[. . .]

Such is the main outline of the development of the American system of college instruction; and, if its result is in the main unsatisfactory, its present condition is mortifying.

This system of advanced education is now an old one. The time has arrived when it may be fully and fairly judged. It is not a new or young plant, as many fondly suppose: it has been developing more than two hundred years. By this time, if ever, we may expect a great, strong growth, a luxuriance in bloom and fruitage. But what do we see? Let me sum up with a few facts universally acknowledged. As to universities, our prevailing sect system has failed in two hundred and fifty years to develop one which ranks with institutions bearing that name in the other great civilized nations, some of them of far more recent creation than our own. The University of Berlin is younger than a multitude of our American colleges; it was brought up to its highest pinnacle by a nation crushed by military disaster and by financial burdens; yet no one will claim that we have an institution to compare with it.

As to schools of mechanical and civil engineering, we are developing some which are doing excellent work; but we have not as yet one which will take rank with the multitude of such schools on the continent. To say nothing of such institutions as the French École Polytechnique, we have no advanced schools to compare with recent creations at Stuttgart, Carlsruhe, and Zurich.

As to laboratories, all these years of work in America, mainly shaped by the prevailing system, have failed to give us one to compare for a moment with several recently erected at Leipsic, Berlin, Heidelberg, Munich, and elsewhere, by government aid.

As to museums of the mechanic arts, all our collections combined would be as the small dust in the balance, when compared to the Conservatoire des Arts et Metiers.

As to art collections bearing on the various industries, if we were to add together all that our American system has accumulated, and multiply the sum by thousands, we should have nothing to approach the schools recently created by the English Government at South Kensington. As to various branches of instruction, we have many men in all departments equal to the best in Europe; but for want of a university system to give scope to their ambition, they have almost entirely lacked opportunity. American students have been forced to pursue their most advanced studies abroad. Even as to that which is nearest us,—no full professorship of American history exists in our land. To study this history, young men have gone to sit at the feet of Laboulaye[2] at Paris, Neumann at Berlin, and Kingsley[3] at English Cambridge. It is in view of such a meagre growth in over two hundred years under the prevailing system, that I present the following as the fundamental proposition of this paper:—

The main provision for advanced education in the United States must be made by the people at large, acting through their National and State legislatures, to endow and maintain institutions for the higher instruction, fully equipped, and free from sectarian control.

And first, I argue that *the past history and present condition of the higher education in the United States arouse a strong presumption in favor of making it a matter of public civil action, rather than leaving it to the prevailing system of private sectarian action.*

The history already given certainly arouses a presumption against the existing system; but that presumption is greatly strengthened by noticing what has been done, under the beginning of the plan I now advocate,—the plan under which the citizens of the various States of the United States have taken advanced education into their control.

Look briefly over this history of a better effort. The first good attempt to give to this country a true university, as distinguished from the American deterioration of the English college, was made by State action in the creation of the University of Virginia.

The prevailing sectarian system profited not at all by this example. The great universities of Germany grew into their modern state, nurseries of the love of learning and the love of freedom; but the sectarian college system of America went on multiplying the usual poor imitations of English colleges, when public civil action was again resorted to, and gave the beginning of another university: the combined bounty of the National and State Government, wisely administered, gave to the country the University of Michigan.

As to scientific and technological instruction, our country waited for years after such advanced instruction was given in Europe: but there came only scattered and feeble efforts; and the first great and comprehensive system which gave a college for applied science to every State in the Union was established by the congressional act of 1862, supplemented by the various acts of the State legislatures.

As to the illustration of natural science, the one collection in the United States that has acknowledged rank throughout the world is the one fostered by the wise and careful bounty of the State of Massachusetts at Cambridge.

And as to education in morals, that very education of what is best in man, which is claimed as the especial *raison d'être* of the prevailing sectarian system, the only institution which is generally recognized as strong enough to impress upon its whole teaching a sense of duty sufficiently deep to hold its own against the immoral tides of these times, the only one, which, when graduates of all other institutions fail, is, by common consent, appealed to, to give managers to our railways who will not plunder, investigators of our mines who will not lie, negotiators with our Indians who will not cheat, is the Government College at West Point.

But I argue next, *that careful public provision by the people for their own system of advanced instruction is the only republican and the only democratic method.*

While I hail with joy supplementary private gifts when not used as fetters, I maintain that there can be no system more unrepublican than that by which a nation or a state, in consideration of a few hundreds of thousands of dollars, delivers over its system of advanced instruction to be controlled and limited by the dogmas and whimseys of living donors or dead testators. In more than one nation, dead hands, stretching out from graves closed generations gone, have lain with a deadly chill upon institutions for advanced instruction during centuries. More than one institution in our own country has felt this grip and chill. The progress of civilization in the Old World since the French Revolution of 1789 has tended more and more to the building up of its education in accordance with the needs of living men rather than the anticipations of dead men. My position is simply, that, if we ought to govern ourselves in any thing, we ought to govern ourselves in this; and that if, in matters of far less importance, we will not allow our rights, duties, and wants to be decided upon by this or that living man, we certainly ought not, in a matter of such vast importance as the higher education of our children, to allow our rights, duties, and wants to be decided upon by this or that dead man.

Again: I argue that *public provision, that is the decision and provision by each generation as to its own advanced education, is alone worthy of our dignity as citizens.*

What would be thought of a State which refused to build its State-house from its State treasury, and on the ostensible ground that private giving is good for the donor, and honorable to the State, begged individuals to build it? Should we not have a result exactly typical of what is exhibited in the prevailing system for advanced instruction? We should probably, if fortunate enough to get any thing at all, find, after a century, an edifice perfectly typical of what has been given us under our similar system in advanced education,—a Roman tower of brick here; a Gothic spire of stone there; a Greek pediment of wood here; a Renaissance cupola of iron there; a Doric column of porphyry next a Corinthian column of sandstone; no fitting approaches, because no one had given any thing so humble; halls too small, and doorways too narrow, and windows askew in accordance with this or that dead man's whimsey.

But this is the least. Suppose that we really get our building thus constructed, what would be thought of the policy which should leave the State building thus erected to be controlled forever, as to its occupancy and use, by living and dead donors, ancient and modern, and by their medley of ideas, religious and secular, forcible and feeble, crude and thoughtful, shrewd and absurd? And, if this system is incompatible with State and National dignity as regards a mere pile of stone and mortar, how much more so, when there is concerned the building of an edifice made of the best brains and hearts of living men, and the control of a great system of advanced education, in all its branches, for the entire nation, for all generations!

Again: I argue that *by public provision can private gifts be best stimulated.*

We have had in our country many noble examples of munificence toward institutions for advanced instruction; but no one thing seems to have stimulated them so much as the public endowments, which have aroused discussion, and afforded objects to which citizens of all creeds could contribute as a patriotic duty.

Take, as an example, the congressional grant of 1862, to national colleges for scientific and industrial instruction. The recent reports of the United States Commissioner of Education show that gifts have been aggregated about these nuclei to the amount of over eight million dollars. Let me refer to an example within the State of New York. The national grant was concentrated upon one institution, the Cornell University. This encouraged thoughtful and liberal men to hope that something worthy of the State might be built upon that foundation; and the result is, that in eight years there have been added to that original endowment private gifts to the value of over a million, five hundred thousand dollars; and, so far as I can learn, none of these gifts would have been made but for the nucleus afforded by the national grant.

I argue next, that *by liberal public grants alone can our private endowments be wisely directed or economically aggregated.*

No one conversant with the history of advanced instruction in this country can have failed to note the ineffably absurd way in which large gifts for advanced instruction have been frittered away under the prevailing system.

There is hardly a State in the Union where the sums, large and small, that have been scattered among a multitude of petty sectarian institutions called colleges and universities, would not have produced one institution of great public value, had these gifts been directed to one object and aggregated about one nucleus.

Compare two Western States lying near each other,—Ohio and Michigan. The State of Ohio has had every advantage over its northern neighbor as to population, soil, wealth, communication with the seaboard, and priority of complete occupation; but, as regards advanced education, it stumbled into the policy of scattered denominational colleges supported by sectarian beggary.

The State of Michigan took its national grant, developed upon that a State University; and from time to time its State legislature has added judiciously to it. Now look at the results. The great State of Ohio has within its borders not one college or university well equipped in any respect,—not one which rises above the third or fourth class. On the other hand, the State of Michigan has a noble university of the very first rank, with over a thousand students; and, what is of vast importance, the presence of such an institution has strengthened the whole system of public instruction throughout the State. No State has a more admirable series of primary schools and high schools; and her normal school ranks among the best, and so does her agricultural college. The system has been pronounced by thoughtful men from other States the best in the Union; and the whole secret of its excellence is, that, by wise and liberal legislation stimulus and direction were given to private endowment. The difference between the two States I have named is, that in Michigan a public endowment gave statesmanlike direction to private endowment; while in Ohio all was frittered away and scattered between the clamors and intrigues of sects and localities.

So much for the direction of endowments: look now at their aggregation. Take the facts as they stand: I will mention cases well known. A weak denominational college in one of our States has received from a friend a great telescope worthy of the greatest institution in the world; but hardly any one else has given the institution any thing: there is no gift of a well-equipped observatory, or provision for an observer; and the telescope might as well be in Japan.

On the other hand, another denominational college has received the gift of a splendid observatory; but no one has added a gift of money for a telescope and other instruments. So the prevailing system gives you at one college a useless telescope, and at another a useless observatory.

I know of another denominational institution which has received a splendid geological collection; but as it has no provision for a geological laboratory, or for a geological professor, the collection, for all scientific purposes, is a mere illusion.

I know another denominational institution, which received from a denominational friend a splendid herbarium; but from the day it was received it has never been used, for the reason that no other member of the denomination has provided a professorship of botany.

I know another institution of this kind, which has received an excellent collection in mineralogy; but all appeals from the denomination to which it belongs have failed to secure an endowed professorship of metallurgy; and it would be money saved, had the collection never been taken out of the earth.

Compare this with the example I have just mentioned. The nation gave a moderate grant for a university to the State of Michigan: the State legislature added to it judiciously. Thus was built up one great institution. The result is, that from various parts of the State, and from other States, gifts have been aggregated about the nucleus thus formed. Thus was provided both a telescope and an observatory; thus has its library been enlarged; thus were developed its illustrative collections. They are a matter of State concern and State pride; and individual gifts come in from all sides more and more to supplant public gifts.

The same, in a less degree, may be seen in several other universities: the only difficulty in these cases is, that public gifts have been too small to give the public system a fair and full trial.

[. . .]

CHAPTER 16

The University and Democracy

William Rainey Harper

INTRODUCTION TO HARPER'S SPEECH AT THE UNIVERSITY OF CALIFORNIA

One of William Rainey Harper's many assets as a university president was his skill at recruiting faculty, and one of his many coups as a recruiter was his "raid" on Clark University in 1892. The action badly damaged Clark, a fledging institution at the time, and left its president, G. Stanley Hall, reeling. But Hall proved to be resilient. He built Clark back up, and he was eventually able to appreciate Harper's accomplishments. Not long before Harper's death in 1906, Hall reflected on what Harper had achieved. In a letter to John D. Rockefeller, who contributed the seed money for the University of Chicago and recruited Harper to be its first president, Hall observed that early on, academic administrators on the East Coast had greeted Harper's innovations with skepticism. With good reason, however, attitudes toward Harper had shifted in the direction of approval. Hall's own take was that Harper would "go down in the history of education as a man who marks a great and salutary epoch." A little more than a century later, that seems about right.

Today Harper's University of Chicago looks like the culminating feat of the period of watershed reforms and reorganization in American higher education ushered in by the Morrill Act and the end of the Civil War. With an intrepid, "we'll find a way to pay for it" attitude and an evangelical sense of purpose, Harper combined the proposals and initiatives of other university reformers with his own abundant ideas.

The result was a game changer—a late nineteenth-century American research university that perhaps more than any of its peers served as a model for American universities in the first half of the twentieth century. During Harper's time as founding president, which stretched from 1891 to 1906, the University of Chicago invented the quarter system to allow for year-round classes, as well as more flexibility for its faculty; it established an undergraduate program that entailed two years of general study in the liberal arts followed by two years of more focused study in a field chosen by the student; it set up and successfully recruited top talent for an array of graduate programs (Harper's highest priority, at least early on); it built professional schools; it created correspondence courses and satellite campuses.

An acclaimed scholar of the Old Testament, Harper earned his PhD at Yale under the supervision of W. D. Dwight, one of the "new men," a group of professors who valued systematic, cutting-edge research—most, including Dwight, had studied in Germany—and who did much to alter the culture of scholarship at Yale in the 1860s and 1870s. Harper shared their values. Indeed, he frequently expressed his admiration for the German university model and its culture of research. And what initially intrigued Harper about the prospect of a Rockefeller-sponsored university in the Midwest was the idea that it would be a research-oriented school along the lines of Johns Hopkins.

But Harper was also committed to the ideal of expert knowledge as a public good. As he established himself as a Bible scholar, he helped develop adult education programs, taught in a variety of extra-academic settings, gave many public lectures, and encouraged his listeners to send him questions and comments—one of Harper's colleagues at Yale claimed that Harper received more correspondence than the rest of the faculty combined. It was clear that any university he led would be selective in some ways and inclusive in others.

In his rhetoric, too, Harper achieved a balance. Actually, he achieved multiple balances. In "The University and Democracy," a speech given at the University of California, Berkeley in 1899, Harper insisted that the university, defined as a corporation of equals united in their search for truth, needed total freedom from political and ecclesiastical control in order to carry out its mission, something it had not always had. But this mission gave the modern university a political calling, since it is the search for truth that brings enlightenment, and in order to function properly, democracy needs enlightened leadership. And because democracy is a providential gift, the university's free, nonecclesiastical mission has an ethical and, indeed, spiritual component that lends itself to being expressed in the language of Christianity. Harper declared that the university is "the agency established by heaven to proclaim the principles of democracy." The university is thus also "the prophet" and "the priest" of democracy.

In making such pronouncements, Harper was responding to a fraught context. This was a moment when the leaders of many universities with a religious heritage felt moved, or pressured, to reconsider the place of that heritage in the mission of their university, and to cast their aims in more secular terms. But there was also pushback, and Harper had to deal with that, especially in the late 1890s. The University of Chicago was new, to be sure, but it nevertheless had a religious heritage. For many of the people involved in its founding, including Rockefeller, the point was to continue and improve upon the work of the "old" University of Chicago, a Baptist institution that had fallen into insolvency. By 1899, conservative Baptists had become frustrated with Harper's focus on programs where distinguished scholars trained graduate students to be cutting-edge researchers, and they expressed their displeasure. "Democracy and the University" can be read as Harper's answer, as a justification of open inquiry in the face of such opprobrium. Yet the speech, which has little to say about expert knowledge, also reflects a subtle but crucial shift in his priorities. With the outbreak of the Spanish-American War, it seemed that America had left behind an era of rebuilding and entered the world scene as the great example, and bringer, of democracy. And what grew more important in Harper's estimation was the four-year liberal arts education that would form young men into thoughtful leaders needed for rising to this challenge.

Despite some of his suggestions to the contrary—he once remarked that "a man who was Dean and who gave no instruction would merely be a clerk"—Harper "reveled in planning," i.e., in mapping out strategies for institution-building; and the enthusiasm that breathes through his writings on the complexities and challenges of the "business side" of the modern university rivals that of his famous "democracy" speech. Where Harper failed to find a balance was in his life. His sense of obligation weighed on him, and he pushed himself relentlessly. Moreover, concerns about money eventually weighed on him, too. All this may or may not have contributed to his early death from cancer, but it certainly made him suffer. Not long before he gave his soaring Berkeley address, Harper wrote to an old friend, "The pressure is tremendous. I cannot myself understand how I can stand it. My only consolation is that it will not last forever."

THE UNIVERSITY AND DEMOCRACY

[. . .]

The three birth-marks of a university are, therefore, self-government, freedom from ecclesiastical control, and the right of free utterance. And these certainly give it the right to proclaim itself an institution of the people, an institution born of the democratic spirit.

Such being its origin, we may ask ourselves whether it has essentially changed its nature in the development through which ten or more centuries have carried it. The proper restriction of the term must, however, be first applied. What is a university today? I accept, with modification, a common definition: a self-governing association of men for the purpose of study; an institution privileged by the state for the guidance of the people; an agency recognized by the people for resolving the problems of civilization which present themselves in the development of civilization. According to this definition, therefore, only those institutions are universities in which adults are associated (thus excluding elementary and secondary schools, and likewise colleges conducted for the training of boys and girls in various stages of advancement); in which definite and distinct effort is put forth to guide the people in the decision of questions which from time to time confront them, and to furnish leaders in the different callings in whom the people may have full confidence; in which facilities are furnished and encouragement afforded to grapple with the great problems of life and thought, in the worlds of matter and of mind, with the sole purpose of discovering truth, whatever bearing that discovery may have upon other supposed truth. This requires men of the greatest genius, equipment of the highest order, and absolute freedom from interference of any kind, civic or ecclesiastical.

In this connection it is worth while to note Thomas Jefferson's conception of the functions of the University:

> (1) To form the statesmen, legislators, and judges, on whom public prosperity and individual happiness are so much to depend; (2) to expound the principles and structure of government, the laws which regulate the intercourse of nations, those formed principally for our own government, in a sound spirit of legislation, which banishing all unnecessary restraint on individual action, shall leave us free to do whatever does not violate the equal rights of another; (3) to harmonize and promote the interests of agriculture, manufactures, and commerce, and by well-informed views of political economy to give a free scope to the public industry; (4) to I develop the reasoning faculties of our youth, to enlarge their minds, cultivate their morals, and instil into them the principles of virtue and order; (5) to enlighten them with mathematical and physical sciences, which advance the arts, and administer to the health, the subsistence, and comforts of human life; (6) and generally to form them to habits of reflection and correct action, rendering them examples of virtue to others, and of happiness within themselves.

The university is naturally the seat of the highest educational work; but again the word "highest" requires definition. It is the highest function of the university to prepare leaders and teachers for every field of activity. It will include, therefore, the work of the college, the secondary school, and the elementary school (with the kindergarten work), if this work is conducted either, on the one hand, as practice work in connection with which teachers may be trained, or, on the other hand, as laboratory work in connection with which effort is being made to work out the solution of important problems, or to secure a more perfect type of work. The sympathies of the true university will be so broad as to bring it into touch with educational problems of every kind.

The university is, further, an integral part of the public-school system. The state, by granting its charter, makes it a public institution, whether its support comes from the state itself or from private funds. As a public institution, it may not detach itself from the various forms of educational or legislative work conducted under state patronage. Its ideals control the development of all that falls below it. The university, therefore, may not stand aloof; nor may the colleges and schools shut themselves away from its strong and revivifying influence. There may be no organic connection. In most cases such organic connection is unnecessary. The bond is spiritual, and as such stronger than merely formal connection could possibly become.

The university is also an institution of the people. It must, therefore, be "privileged" and, in many instances, supported by the people. In the latter case, it must be influenced by the changes which the people may undergo in their opinions. But the people must remember that when, for any reason, the administration of their institution, or the instruction in any one of its departments, is changed by an influence from without, whenever effort is made to dislodge an officer or a professor because the political sentiment of the majority has undergone a change, at that moment the institution has ceased to be a university; and it cannot again take its place in the rank of universities so long as there continues to exist to any appreciable extent the factor of coercion. The state has no more right than the church to interfere with the search for truth, or with its promulgation when found. The state and church alike may have their own schools and colleges for the training of youthful minds, and for the propagation of special kinds of intelligence; and in these it may choose what special coloring shall be given to the instruction. This is proper, for example, in the military schools of the state, and in the theological schools of the church. But such schools are not universities. They do not represent the people; they do not come out of the people.

The university touches life, every phase of life, at every point. It enters into every field of thought to which the human mind addresses itself. It has no fixed abode far away from man; for it goes to those who cannot come to it. It is shut in behind no lofty battlement; for it has no enemy which it would ward off. Strangely enough, it vanquishes its enemies by inviting them into close association with itself. The university is of the people, and for the people, whether considered individually or collectively.

[. . .]

Democracy has been given a mission to the world, and it is of no uncertain character. I wish to show that the university is the prophet of this democracy and, as well, its priest and its philosopher; that, in other words, the university is the Messiah of the democracy, its to-be-expected deliverer.

The university is the prophet—that is, the spokesman—of democracy. Democracy, if it continue, must include the masses and maintain their sympathy and interest. But as a system it is the product of a long period of evolution, and, as such, is not a simple system. It is, indeed, already somewhat cumbersome and complex. The principles which underlie it need constant and repeated statement by those whose statement will make deep impression. Although intended to be the expression of the popular mind, it is the outcome of movements which have been in operation fifty centuries or more. It is the result of the operation of laws of life which antedate the existence of man himself. Of the history of these movements and of the character of these laws the popular mind is for the most part ignorant. This history must be told over and over again, and the principles made very plain, that all who hear may understand.

But democracy has not yet been unified. Unmistakable traces exist of past ages. The weight of the multitude which it must carry renders progress slow in any case. And without unity the doctrine of equality may not exert its full force. Spokesmen who understand this unity and appreciate its necessity in the economy of democratic progress must proclaim it far and near, until no ear shall have failed to hear the proclamation, no heart shall have failed to heed its clear injunction. The elements which together make this unity must be drawn together and held together by influences that shall outnumber and outweigh those pitted on the other side.

The truth is, democracy has scarcely yet begun to understand itself. It is comparatively so young and untried, and the real experiment has been of so short a duration that it could not be otherwise. Democracy needs teachers who shall say, *Know thyself*; messengers who shall bring light to shine upon dark places. There is great danger that the next step, at any time, may be a wrong step. Some such have already been taken; and history shows the terrible cost of being compelled to go back and start anew. Democracy is now able to walk alone, but not infrequently something occurs which leads us to think that there has not yet been time enough to learn how a fair and even balance may at all times be maintained.

Democracy seems to be in the ascendency; but the impartial student of the situation sees many and great fields not yet occupied, while those already occupied are hardly more than nominally possessed. We have democracy in government, to be sure, but if it is a good thing in government, it must be equally good in social relations of various kinds, in art and literature and science. That its influence has been exerted in these fields no one will dispute. But of no one of them may it be said to have taken full possession. And even in the realm of government, how slight comparatively among the nations is the progress of the last century! The occupation of these fields—not by conquest, but by invitation—would greatly strengthen democracy in the places now occupied. Who will persuade the nations to prepare the invitation? Who will induct democracy into these new fields of arts and literature and science? There must be teachers who know democracy and at the same time literature or science, and who, in due time, will bring about the union which promises to the world so much for human welfare.

Democracy has great battles yet to fight. Every step forward is in the face of deadliest opposition. Her enemies are those who sit on thrones and command great armies. Christianity may be democratic, but the church is too frequently hostile to the application of democratic principles. These battles, moreover, must be fought with words, not swords. The pen is far the more effective weapon. There will be many battles; some of them will be long drawn out. The mutterings of war may now be heard in many quarters, but in the end prophetic weapons will win the victory, and "the kings shall shut their mouths, for that which had not been told them shall they see, and that which they had not heard shall they consider" (Isa. 52:15).

Sometimes, too, democracy grows despondent. Borne down by the weight of opposition, overcome by the power of those who for personal ends would see her humbled in the dust, she cries: "My way is hid from the Lord; my judgment is passed over from my God." Discouragement and despair lead to utter demoralization and failure. Under such circumstances, the words of the comforter are needed. Who can measure the density of the darkness and distress which have settled down upon the minds and hearts of the great multitude of men and women in our great cities, for whom, as individuals, there is no hope in life save perhaps that of bare existence until kindly death shall call them away? Yet these it is who constitute the multitude that is called democracy.

"And they look unto the earth and behold distress and darkness, the gloom of anguish, and into thick darkness they are driven away; and they pass through it hardly bestead and hungry; and it comes to pass that, when they are hungry, they fret themselves, and curse their king and their God and turn their faces upward." But now the prophet's voice is heard: "But there shall not always be gloom to her that was in anguish . . . the people that have walked in darkness shall see a great light." And they shall rejoice; for all oppression shall be removed, and all war shall cease, and a new government shall be established—a government of justice and righteousness which shall endure forever. It is the prophetic voice speaking to a downcast, downtrodden people—a democracy despondent.

At times, furthermore, democracy is corrupt. Under the guise of loyalty to her best interests, those in whose hands she has intrusted herself in loving kindness assault and seduce her. Shame and reproach fall upon her. She must be cleansed and purified before she may again take up her great and glorious work for all the world with a certain hope of success. She has exhibited a fatal weakness; the result will be ruinous. Sharp and stern words must be spoken by the prophet, whose keen eye sees the situation and its dangers. No pity may be extended, no word of sympathy, until the evil has been mended. The lesson is bitter and full of shame; but the effect will be for good, if the chastisement is severe enough. The clear voice of prophetic rebuke must be heard, whenever corruption rears its head to public gaze.

Democracy surely has a mission; and if so, that mission, is in a word, *righteousness.* It is an interesting fact that all the great religious truths were worked out in the popular mind before they were formulated by the thinkers. The world is waiting for the working out of the doctrine of national righteousness through democracy, and no effort to formulate the doctrine beforehand will avail. But the day is coming when the thought will have become tangible enough to be expressed. The popular mind will not be able to do this service. The prophet, whose discerning eye reads the thought in the heart of democracy itself, expressed in heartthrobs reaching to the very depths of human experience—the prophet, I say, will then formulate the teaching which will make earth indeed a paradise.

The democracy, as an institution, needs interpretation. The past must be interpreted in order that its lessons may be learned, its mistakes avoided. The greatest danger is that there shall be failure to maintain the closest connection with the past. This is necessary for the sake of comparison. Without such comparison we may never know our own position. Every event of past history has contained a message. Every life has been an utterance. These events and lives are to be treated as object lessons which we are to contemplate, and by contemplation to learn how righteousness may be found. The rise and fall of nations, the growth and decay of institutions, the temporary influences of great characters as interpreted in the light of the present, constitute the basis for all better understanding and all better execution of the democratic idea.

The present itself must be known and interpreted. Its currents and cross-currents, while in large measure the result of forces set in movement far up the stream, must be estimated anew with each fresh dawn of day. The shallows and depths are never the same on two successive days. The charts noting danger signals must be prepared with each turn of the tide of public opinion. And, on the other hand, the slightest turn in the direction of promise is to be encouraged. It is often the smallest variation from the ordinary that proves to be the precursor of greatest reform; for true reform always begins with the thin edge of the wedge. If the present be cared for, the future will take care of itself.

But the future of democracy must be considered. Mounting the watch-tower of observation, the true leader of democracy will make a forecast of the tendencies, in order to encourage his followers by holding up the glory that awaits them, or, by depicting the disaster that is coming, to turn them aside from a policy so soon to prove destructive.

In ancient days, the man who interpreted the past, who measured the present, and who foretold the future was called a prophet. The university, I contend, is this prophet of democracy—the agency established by heaven itself to proclaim the principles of democracy. It is in the university that the best opportunity is afforded to investigate the movements of the past and to present the facts and principles involved before the public. It is the university that, as the center of thought, is to maintain for democracy the unity so essential for its success. The university is the prophetic school out of which come the teachers who are to lead democracy in the true path. It is the university that must guide democracy into the new fields of arts and literature and science. It is the university that fights the battles of democracy, its war-cry being: "Come, let us reason together." It is the university that, in these latter days, goes forth with buoyant spirit to comfort and give help to those who are downcast, taking up its dwelling in the very midst of squalor and distress. It is the university that, with impartial judgment, condemns in democracy the spirit of corruption which now and again lifts up the head, and brings scandal upon democracy's fair name.

The university is the prophet who is to hold high the great ideal of democracy, its mission for righteousness; and by repeated formulation of the ideal, by repeated presentations of its claims, make it possible for the people to realize in tangible form the thought which has come up from their deepest heart. The university, I maintain, is the prophetic interpreter of democracy; the prophet of her past, in all its vicissitudes; the prophet of her present, in all its complexity; the prophet of her future, in all its possibilities.

Among the prophets of olden times, some were mere soothsayers who resorted to the ministrations of music in order to arouse themselves to excited frenzy. Some were dreaming seers, as much awake when sleep settled down upon their eyes as they were asleep to all that was about them in their waking moments. Some were priests whom the prophetic spirit had aroused, but had not wholly subjugated. Some were the greatest souls the world ever knew, whose hearts were touched by the spirit of the living God, whose eyes were open to visions of divine glory, whose arms were steeled by the courage born of close communion with higher powers. It is just so with universities. Some are universities only in name; some, forgetting the circumstances of their birth, may indeed be arrayed against democracy. But the true university, like the true prophet, will be faithful to its antecedents and, therefore, faithful to democracy.

But the university is also the priest of the democracy. But a priest is found only in association with religion. Is democracy a religion? No. Has democracy a religion? Yes; a religion with its god, its altar, and its temple, with its code of ethics and its creed. Its god is mankind, humanity; its altar, home; its temple, country. The one doctrine of democracy's creed is the brotherhood, and consequently the equality of man; its system of ethics is contained in a single word, righteousness.

In this religion there is much of Judaism, and likewise much of Christianity. This was to be expected, for it was Jeremiah of olden time who first preached the idea of individualism, the idea that later became the fundamental thought in the teaching of Jesus Christ, the world's greatest advocate of democracy; while the supplementary idea of solidarity, the corollary of individualism, was first preached by Ezekiel, and likewise later developed into Christianity.

The prophet in history has always been a hero; he has been applauded for his boldness and for his idealistic visions. The priest, on the other hand, has generally been thought a cunning worker, and while his shrewdness has been appreciated, his ambition has been feared and dreaded. In modern times, as in most ancient days, the prophets and the priests have become more and more closely identified in spirit and in work; but the difference is still a marked one.

The religion of democracy is an eclectic religion. It has absorbed many of the best features of various religions and systems of philosophy. It is a broad religion, including a wide variety of belief and practice. It is, nevertheless, a definite religion, representing a clearly defined tendency of expression, both in feeling and in action. It is a worldwide religion; but the world in great part must be changed before its acceptance will be general.

It is the prophet that has to do with creed and ethics, and these have already been considered. The priest is concerned with the religious cultus or practice, and finds his chief occupation in the upbuilding and preservation of the practice. His work is the work of service. He is the mediator between the individual and the ideal, whether abstract or concrete, which constitutes his God. For the god of each individual is that individual's highest conception of man, his ideal man. The priest of democracy's religion is therefore a mediator between man and man; for man is the constituent element in democracy, and humanity is the ideal of all its aspirations.

The service of the priest includes, likewise, the bringing into a close communion, each with the other, of the individual and his God, the cultivation of a deep and lasting communion between the two. This service represents still further the act of consecration on the part both of the priest and the worshiper—consecration to the highest and holiest conceptions of truth and life. It is the priest who himself trained in all the mysteries of a religious cultus, himself the custodian of the traditions of the past, inducts those who are of a kindred feeling into those strange mysteries and their inherited treasures.

The university, as priest, is a mediator between man and man; between man and man's own self; between mankind and that ideal inner self of mankind which merits and receives man's adoration. The university, like the priest, leads those who place themselves under its influence, whether they live within or without the university walls, to enter into close communion with their own souls—a communion possible only where opportunity is offered for meditative leisure. The university guild, of all the guilds of workingmen, has been the most successful in securing that leisure for contemplation, consideration of society and of nature, without which mankind can never become acquainted with itself. And for this reason the university is in deep sympathy with every legitimate effort, made by other guilds of workingmen, to secure shorter hours of labor and longer hours for self-improvement. Communion with self, study of self, is, where rightly understood, communion with God and study of God.

The university, furthermore, performs priestly service for democracy in the act of consecration which is involved in her very constitution. And here the old and the modern views of education are combined. The university isolates itself from everything that would tend to draw her from the predetermined service which she has undertaken. Her purpose is a fixed one, and nothing may cause her to swerve from it. She has devoted herself with a consecration received from heaven to the cause of lifting up the folk of her environment—an act of consecration than which none is more holy. But now, though separated thus from all the world for the world's sake, she puts herself in touch with this same "all the world," and no gate or portal fails to greet her entrance. Set apart, and consecrated to the service of every kind of man, she leads those who will follow her to consecrate themselves to the cause of liberty and truth and righteousness, in home, in country, and throughout the world.

The university is the keeper, for the church of the democracy, of holy mysteries, of sacred and significant traditions. These are of such character that if touched by profane hands they would be injured. But the initiated are given free access, and every man who will may receive initiation. No effort is made to exclude; every effort is made rather to include in the list of the initiated the whole world; for the mysteries are such only to those who have not yet been brought to see. Home, country, and humanity—it is for these and with these that this priestly activity is put forth.

[. . .]

* Part 4 *

Undergraduate Education in the University

CHAPTER 17

The New Education

Charles William Eliot

INTRODUCTION TO ELIOT'S ARTICLE

Although he later said that he did not write "The New Education" as a job application, two months after the article appeared in the *Atlantic Monthly*, Charles William Eliot was appointed president of Harvard. He was inaugurated in October 1869, the youngest president in Harvard's history—he was thirty-five—and he would become the longest serving. He stepped down in 1909. Eliot belonged to a postwar generation of university presidents that included Andrew Dickson White, at Cornell; James Burrill Angell, at Michigan; and Daniel Coit Gilman, at Johns Hopkins. These men—along with a younger cohort that included David Starr Jordan, at Stanford, and William Rainey Harper, at Chicago—transformed the antebellum college into the modern research university.

Eliot became associated with almost all the elements of that transformation, from the abandonment of the role of in loco parentis and the institution of undergraduate electives to the establishment of graduate schools in the arts and sciences. In these areas, he did not lead the way; other educational leaders were there before him. But he did have one original idea when he came into office, and that idea underwrote the most important reform in the history of American higher education. It was to make the bachelor's degree a prerequisite for admission to professional school.

When Eliot became president, only 78 of the 306 students enrolled in Harvard Medical School and 61 of the 120 students at Harvard Law School had college degrees. These were, comparatively, respectable numbers. As Eliot pointed out in "The New Education," at Michigan, 19 of the 411 medical students and none of the 367 law students had prior degrees. Scientific education

(Eliot was trained as a chemist) was just as bad—"the refuge of shirks and stragglers," Eliot called it. Students could enter scientific schools as teenagers and obtain terminal degrees after taking courses mainly in a single specialty.

Eliot worried that in an expanding nation—the transcontinental railroad was completed the year he became president—young men were able to enter the professions without any education beyond the few years they spent getting vocational training. The thinness and general laxness of professional education was a threat to national prosperity, but the attractiveness of a professional career was a threat to the college. Eliot's reform elevated the value of a professional school degree; it also tied the college to the fortunes of the rising professional class. It took some time for the reform to succeed: Harvard Medical School did not require a bachelor's degree for admission until 1901. But Eliot brought into being the system of elite education that the United States maintains today: liberalization before professionalization. Eliot made the liberal arts college the gateway to the higher-status professions.

The crucial element in Eliot's vision of the modern university was a bright-line separation between undergraduate and graduate education. The latter was practical and guided by a utilitarian rationale, but the former was scholarly and disinterested—the pursuit of knowledge for its own sake. "The practical end should never be lost sight of by student or teacher in a polytechnic school," Eliot wrote, "and it should very seldom be thought of or alluded to in a college. . . . The practical spirit and the literary or scholastic spirit are both good, but they are incompatible. If commingled, they are both spoiled." Eliot thought that the two-stage higher education system he envisioned would be unique. "The American college is an institution without parallel," he wrote; "the American university will be equally original." It still is.

THE NEW EDUCATION

Its Organization

"What can I do with my boy? I can afford, and am glad, to give him the best training to be had. I should be proud to have him turn out a preacher or a learned man; but I don't think he has the making of that in him. I want to give him a practical education; one that will prepare him, better than I was prepared, to follow my business or any other active calling. The classical schools and the colleges do not offer what I want. Where can I put him?" Here is a real need and a very serious problem. The difficulty presses more heavily upon the thoughtful American than upon the European. He is absolutely free to choose a way of life for himself and his children; no government leading-strings or social prescriptions guide or limit him in his choice. But freedom is responsibility. Secondly, being thus free, and being also in face of prodigious material resources of a vast and new territory, he is more fully awake than the European can be to the gravity and urgency of the problem. Thirdly, he has fewer means than any other, except the English parent, of solving the problem to his son's advantage. It is one hundred and thirty years since the first German practical school (*Realschule*) was established, and such schools are now common. Sixty years ago, in France, the first Napoleon made great changes, mostly useful ones, in methods of education. For more than a generation the government schools of arts and trades, arts and manufactures, bridges and highways, mines, agriculture, and commerce, have introduced hundreds of well-trained young men every year into the workshops, factories, mines, forges, public works, and counting-rooms of the empire. These young men begin as subalterns, but soon become the commissioned officers of the army of industry.

The American people are fighting the wilderness, physical and moral, on the one hand, and on the other are struggling to work out the awful problem of self-government. For this fight they must be trained and armed. No thoughtful American in active life reaches manhood without painfully realizing the deficiencies and shortcomings of his own early training. He knows how ignorance balks and competition overwhelms, but he knows also the greatness of the material prizes to be won. He is anxious to have his boys better equipped for the American man's life than he himself was. It is useless to commend to him the good old ways, the established methods. He has a decided opinion that there are or ought to be better ways. He will not believe that the same methods which trained some boys well for the life of fifty or one hundred years ago are applicable to his son; for the reason, that the kind of man which he wants his son to make did not exist in all the world fifty years ago. So without any clear idea of what a practical educations is, but still with some tolerably distinct notion of what it is not, he asks, "How can I give my boy a practical education?"

Thanks to the experience gained during the last twenty years in this country, it is easier to answer this question than it used to be. Certain experiments have been tried whose collective results are instructive. There have been found many American parents willing to try new experiments even in the irrevocable matter of their childrens' [*sic*] education, so impressed were they with the insufficiency of the established system. It requires courage to quit the beaten paths in which the great majority of well-educated men have walked and still walk. A boy who is brought up in a different way from his peers and contemporaries, with different information, habits, and associations, suffers somewhat both in youth and manhood from the mere singularity of his education, though it may have been better than the common. If it were the custom for all young men, whose parents were able to let them spend one third of the average human span in preparation for the rest, to study Chinese ten years or more; if scraps of Chinese had the same potent effect on the popular imagination as have classical quotations in Parliament, and selections from Plutarch in Congress; if, in short, acquaintance with Chinese were the accepted evidence of having studied till twenty-one or twenty-five years of age before beginning to earn a living,—it might well be matter of serious consideration for a careful parent, whether his son had not better devote the usual number of years to the study of that tongue.

Without a wide-spreading organization, no system of education can have large success. The organization of American colleges and their connections is extensive and inflexible. Endowed institutions offer teaching at less than its cost. A large number of professors trained in the existing methods hold firm possession, and transmit the traditions they inherited. Then there are the recognized text-books, mostly of exquisite perverseness, but backed by the reputation of their authors and the capital of their publishers. Lastly, the colleges have regular inlets and outlets. They are steadily fed by schools whose masters are inspired by the colleges, and they as regularly feed all the real and all the so-called learned professions.

The new education must also be successfully organized, if it would live. A system of education which attracts no great number of boys, which unites its disciples in no strong bonds of common associations and good-fellowship, and which after years of trial, is not highly organized with well-graded schools, numerous teachers, good text-books, and a large and increasing body of attached alumni, has no strong hold upon the community in which it exists. Let us see what has been done towards this organization.

We wish to review the recent experience of this country in the attempt to organize a system of education based chiefly upon the pure and applied sciences, the living European languages, and mathematics, instead of upon Greek, Latin, and mathematics, as in the established college system. The history of education is full of still-born theories; the literature of the subject is largely made up of theorizing; whoever reads it much will turn with infinite relief to the lessons of experience. But it should be observed that it is experience in mass, the experience of a generation, and not individual experience, which is of value. To have been a schoolmaster or college professor thirty years only too often makes a man an unsafe witness in matters of education: there are flanges on his mental wheels which will only fit one gauge. On the other hand, it must be acknowledged that conservatism is never more respectable than in education, for nowhere are the risks of change greater. Our survey of the institutions which represent the new education in this country will be absolutely impersonal; the merits of different systems are to be discussed, not the characters or qualifications of the men who have invented, or worked under, these systems. This limitation of the discussion is judicious, from all points of view; for in no country is so little attention paid by parents and students to the reputation of teachers for genius and deep learning as in our own. Faradays, Rumfords, and Cuviers would get very few pupils here, if their teachings were unmethodical and objectless—if, in short, they taught under a bad general system. Spasmodic and ill-directed genius cannot compete in the American community with methodical, careful teaching by less inspired men. This American instinct seems, on the whole, to be a sagacious one. Nevertheless, it is only when genius warms and invigorates a wise and well-administered system, that the best conditions are attained.

We must begin our survey with the institutions of highest grade, because from the parent's point of view the higher school necessarily determines in large measure the nature of the lower school, just as the shape, weight, and bearings of a superstructure determine the form and quality of its foundations. The foundation-plan is the last to leave a careful architect's office. In choosing a preparatory school, the careful parent will consider to what it leads; above all, he will make sure that the school is not an *impasse.* The higher and lower institutions are, indeed, mutually dependent if the admission examinations of the colleges and polytechnic schools seem, on the one hand, to sharply define the studies of the preparatory schools; on the other hand, it is quite as true that the colleges and advanced schools are practically controlled in their requisitions by the actual state of the preparatory schools. They can only ask for what is to be had. They must accept such preparation as the schools can give.

Institutions which exist only on paper, or which have been so lately organized that their term of actual work is only counted by months, will not be alluded to. The agricultural colleges begotten by Congress are all in this category. A large school can hardly get under way in less than four or five years. Three kinds of institutions or organizations for giving the new education are to be distinguished: the scientific "schools" connected with colleges; the scientific "courses" organized within college; and the independent "schools" especially devoted to non-classical education. These three organizations will be considered in succession.

The greater part of the "scientific schools" of the United States are connected with colleges. Such are the Sheffield Scientific School of Yale College, the Lawrence Scientific School at Harvard College, the Chandler Scientific School of Dartmouth College, and the School of Mines of Columbia College. Two considerations seemed to justify this connection: first, the natural desire to utilize the libraries, collections, and cabinets of apparatus already belonging to the colleges; and, secondly, the expectation of engaging the professors of the colleges in the work of the new schools. It was thought that an unnecessary duplication of buildings, equipments, and salaries might thus be avoided. These advantages have been in part realized, but only in part. The scientific schools have needed separate buildings, and to a large extent separate apparatus and separate professorships; but the college libraries have been a gain to them, and some courses of lectures, delivered to undergraduates of the colleges, have been open to students of scientific schools, though not always much resorted to by them. Except at Dartmouth, the aid of the college professors has been more apparent than real, because, being greatly overtasked with college work, these professors have had little time or energy to spare for the scientific schools.

A decided disadvantage is to be offset against any advantages which the scientific schools may have gained from their association with established colleges. A new system of education, crude, ill-organized, and in good degree experimental, has been brought into direct comparison and daily contact with a well-tried system in full possession of the field. The foundling has suffered by comparison with the children of the house. Even where there have been no jealousies about money or influence, and no jarrings about theological tendencies or religious temper, the faculty and students of the scientific school have necessarily felt themselves in an inferior position to the college proper as regards property, numbers, and the confidence of the community. They have been in a defensive attitude. It is the story of the ugly duckling.

An impression prevailed at the outset, that a scientific school was to be a professional school in the same sense as a law or medical school, and that graduates of the colleges would continue their studies in the scientific schools precisely as they do in the schools of law, medicine, and theology. The men who projected the Harvard and Yale schools were evidently under this impression.[1] Experience has shown that the scientific schools proper are not recruited in this manner to any considerable extent. Between 1846 and 1868 there have appeared on the rolls of the Lawrence Scientific School the names of one hundred and sixty-four persons who had already received some degree or other before they joined the school; but most of these persons remained but a short time in the school. Since the foundation of the school, only twelve graduates of Harvard College have thought it worth their while to take a degree of Bachelor of Science at the Lawrence Scientific School; and only ten other persons have possessed any other degree at the time of receiving the degree of Bachelor of Science. Between 1847 and 1868 there have appeared on the rolls of the Yale Department of Philosophy and the Arts (of which department the Yale Scientific School made the chief part) the names of one hundred and sixty-nine persons who had received a degree of some sort before they joined the school. This number is much more considerable in proportion to the whole number of students than in the Lawrence Scientific School, and requires some explanation. During the greater part of the existence of the Yale Department of Philosophy and the Arts, the two departments, or divisions, of engineering and chemistry, together constituting the Yale Scientific School, have made up the bulk of the department, as they have at Harvard. But at Yale there has all along been something else. Instruction of a higher character than that given in the college proper has been steadily offered in the classics, Sanscrit and other Oriental languages, the modern languages, philosophy, history, mathematics, and physics. A small number of graduates of Yale and other colleges have each year availed themselves of these opportunities. Exactly how many it is not possible to learn from the annual catalogues, because students in the Department of Philosophy and the Arts (which included, as a subdivision, the Scientific School) have not always been classified on the catalogue. In some years the discrimination was made. Thus it appears that in

1853–54	there were	3	such advanced students who already held the degree of A.B.
1854–55	" "	9	
1855–56	" "	8	
1856–57	" "	7	
1857–58	" "	3	
1858–59	" "	2	
1859–60	" "	10	
1860–61	" "	8	

What was true in these years was doubtless true to a greater or less extent in all. The greater number of persons possessed of degrees when they became members of the Yale Department of Philosophy and the Arts have been, not members of the scientific school proper, but men who were really taking a post-graduate course of instruction in philology, philosophy, history, or pure science. For the benefit of these persons the degree of Doctor of Philosophy was created in 1860. It is true that, of the 169 persons who held degrees at the time of joining the Yale Department of Philosophy and the Arts, few remained long. Since the foundation of the department, only eight graduates of Yale College have taken the degree of Bachelor of Philosophy; only twelve have taken the degree of Doctor of Philosophy; and no other person have possessed any other degree at the time of receiving these. The other scientific schools have not fared better, in this respect, than those of Harvard and Yale. The Chandler School, at Dartmouth, gave 104 degrees of Bachelor of Science between 1854 and 1864, but not one of these bachelors possessed any degree. The Columbia School of Mines has received a certain number of Columbia Bachelors of Arts as special students; but as this school was only founded in 1864, and has undergone material modifications since the start, the average quality of its graduates is yet to be determined.

Whatever, therefore, may have been the anticipations of their founders, it is evident that, as a matter of fact, the scientific schools, as they have been actually conducted, have not attracted college graduates in any considerable number. They have not been professional schools in the same sense as the schools of law, medicine, and theology; nor speaking generally, have they been schools of higher grade than the colleges, in respect to the average quality of their students. The methods of instruction at some of them have been such as are suitable for advanced students; but the methods have been in advance of the students.

In plan, these scientific schools are not all alike. They agree in requiring no knowledge of Latin and Greek for admission, and in excluding the dead languages from their schemes of instruction, but in many essential respects they differ widely. Thus, the minimum age of admission is eighteen at the Cambridge School, seventeen at the Columbia School, sixteen at the Sheffield School; and fourteen at the Chandler School. The requisites for admission are very various, and the schemes of study and methods of instruction are not the same at any two of these four schools. Each school must be examined by itself.

The history of the development of the Department of Philosophy and the Arts in Yale College is so full of instruction as to justify us in dwelling upon it at some length; it is at once an epitome of the past history of scientific instruction in this country, and a prophecy of its future. The department was established in 1847, at a time when a thrill of aspiration and enthusiasm seems to have run through all the New England colleges. As at Harvard in 1846, and at Columbia in 1864, it was a laboratory of applied chemistry which was really the principal feature of the new scheme; but at Yale, advanced instruction in philology, philosophy, and pure science, suitable for graduates, was also offered. In the five years from 1847 to 1852 the average annual number of students was only about sixteen. In 1852 a department of engineering was added to the department of chemistry; and a degree of Bachelor of Philosophy was offered to students who remained two years in *either* department, and passed satisfactory examinations in three branches of study within the same department. The two departments of chemistry and engineering were entirely distinct. A student might take the degree in either department without knowing anything of studies pursued in the other. As there was no examination for admission, and only a narrow, one-sided, two years' course of study in either department, it is not surprising that the degree of Bachelor of Philosophy soon came to be slightly considered; it really stood for very little culture. In the eight years from 1852 to 1860 the average annual number of students was about forty-seven. A slight change for the better occurred in 1858, when candidates for a degree were required to pass an examination in French or German.

Thus far the Yale Scientific School had borne a strong resemblance to what the Lawrence Scientific School of Cambridge then was, and has always remained; but in 1860 the teachers in the Yale Department of Philosophy and the Arts, dissatisfied with the fruits of their labors, took a great step in advance.

They first systematized the post-graduate instruction in philosophy, philology, and science by offering the degree of Doctor of Philosophy to Bachelors of Arts, Science, or Philosophy, who after two additional years of study should give good evidence of high attainment in two distinct branches of learning. Candidates for this degree, not already Bachelors, were required to pass an admission examination equivalent to that required for the bachelor's degree, the three bachelor degrees taking equal rank. This Doctor's degree has been given thirteen times since 1861. The existence of this programme of instruction at Yale, unpretentious but genuine, and perseveringly offered to a few real students, taken in connection with the facts, that one hundred and sixty-nine persons possessed of degrees have studied something additional to the ordinary college course in this Yale Department of Philosophy and the Arts since its foundation; that one hundred and sixty-four persons possessed of degrees have been members of the Lawrence Scientific School within the same period; that the Columbia School of Mines has received a few persons possessed of degrees; and that young Americans go every year to Europe, in search of better educational facilities than they suppose their own country to afford them,—proves that there is a small but steady demand in the older American communities for instruction higher than that of the ordinary college course, and yet different from that of the law, medical, and theological schools. This legitimate success at Yale, on a really high level, if also on a modest scale, points the way to improvements which ought soon to be made at all the more important American "universities," which will then better deserve their ambitious title.

At the same time, the Yale instructors in the Department of Philosophy and the Arts reorganized completely the Scientific School by constituting, first, a three years' "general course" of studies, embracing mathematics, physical science, modern languages, literature, history, political economy, and commercial law; secondly, a special course in chemistry, which included French, German, English, botany, physical geography, physics, history of the inductive sciences, geology, and logic, besides the chemistry; and, thirdly, a special course in engineering, which included French and German, and lectures upon astronomy, chemistry, physics, mineralogy, and geology, besides the studies which bear most directly upon engineering. These two special courses at first covered but two years; but in 1862 the first year of the general course was required of all candidates for a degree in the chemical department; and in 1864 a three years' course of study was definitely adopted as the plan of the whole school. Other special departments have since been added to the original ones of chemistry and engineering, but the fundamental plan of the school is essentially unchanged since 1864. A year's course of general studies precedes a two years' course in some one of seven different departments. These departments are chemistry and mineralogy, natural history and geology, engineering, mechanics, agriculture, mining, and a selected course in science and literature. The studies of these seven departments are in large measure common; but there is nevertheless a very decided divergence into different ways at the beginning of the second year of the school, according to the student's bent or to his choice of a profession. Since 1864 every candidate for the degree of Bachelor of Philosophy has been required to pass successfully through a three years' course of carefully selected studies,—a generous course, embracing mathematics, English, French, and German, moral, mental, and political philosophy, and history, besides a large variety of scientific subjects. This scheme is of course analogous to that of the common American college, with a large elective element in the last two years. The classics are omitted, the course is only three years long instead of four, and the studies of the last two years have a distinctly practical or professional turn; but there is the same regular course of studies leading to a degree, the same movement by classes, and a range of subjects as extensive as in the common college course. It should be said that, in 1864, the Congressional grant to promote the giving of instruction in agriculture and the mechanic arts, so wisely given to Yale College by the Connecticut Legislature, began to influence for good the development of the Scientific School.

Another marked change in the policy of this school deserves attention. Up to 1860 there was no real examination for admission. Anybody, no matter how ignorant, could join the chemical department; and, in the engineering department, some acquaintance with algebra, geometry, and plane trigonometry was all that was required. No previous knowledge of chemistry was expected of students entering the laboratory. The Yale school did not differ from the Cambridge school in this respect. In fact, the Lawrence Scientific School had no other requisites for admission than those above mentioned until this year (1868). In 1860 the Yale Scientific School established an examination for admission to any department of the school. This examination comprised arithmetic, algebra, geometry, plane trigonometry, the elements of natural philosophy and chemistry, English grammar, and geography. The same preparation in Latin as for the college proper was also recommended to the candidate for admission to the Scientific School. This admission examination has been but slightly modified since 1860. The history of the United States has been substituted for chemistry, and Latin is about to be insisted upon as a qualification for admission.[2]

The changes in the Yale school since 1860 have all had one aim, namely, to raise the grade of the school by getting in a better class of students, and then teaching them more and better. The methods of a professional school have been abandoned as unsuitable, and those of a college have been taken up; but the apparent declension is a real elevation. For a loose-jointed, one-sided scheme has been substituted one which is both methodical and comprehensive. It is interesting to see that the improvement has been appreciated. The average annual number of students in the period from 1847 to 1852 was sixteen; in the period from 1852 to 1860 it was forty-seven, but the average attendance was largest in the earlier years of this period; since 1860 the annual number of students has steadily risen from thirty-eight, the number of that year, to one hundred and twenty-two in 1867–68. Nineteen teachers now take an active part in the work of instruction. Every legitimate effort is made to carry as many students as possible through the regular course, and bring them up to the standard fixed by the examination for the degree. Effort in this direction is needed; for numbers of students resort to the school for brief periods, to their own injury and that of the school. Since the foundation of the school, only one hundred and twenty-eight degrees of Bachelor of Philosophy have been given.

The Lawrence Scientific School at Cambridge is, and always has been, what the Yale school also was at first,—a group of independent professorships, each with its own treasury and its own methods of instruction. The several departments are so distinct that the student in one department has no necessary connection with any other. Each student is, as it were, the private pupil of some one of the professors, and the other professors are no more to him than if they did not exist. The pupils of the professor of chemistry, the pupils of the professor of engineering, the pupils of the professor of comparative anatomy, and at rare intervals a pupil in mineralogy or botany, make up the school. The assistants in the Museum of Zoölogy help to swell the number of students enrolled in the annual catalogue. There is no common discipline, and no general course of co-ordinated studies which all candidates for any degree must pass through. A young man who has studied nothing but chemistry, or nothing but engineering, and who is densely ignorant of everything else, may obtain the sole degree given by the school,—that of Bachelor of Science. There appears never to have been any examination for admission, except that some knowledge of algebra, geometry, and trigonometry has been required, before a student could join the department of engineering. It has been the practice to receive students into the chemical laboratory without requiring any previous knowledge of chemistry, or indeed of anything else. Nominally, students have not been admitted until they were eighteen years of age, but practically this rule has proved quite elastic. The degree of Bachelor of Science can be obtained in any one department by residing at least one year at Cambridge, and passing the examination of that single department. This examination has usually been passed after a residence of from eighteen to thirty months. This system, or, rather, lack of system, might do for really advanced students in science, for men in years and acquired habits of study,—in fact, the school has been of great service to a score or two of such men,—but it is singularly ill adapted to the wants of the average American boy of eighteen. The range of study is inconceivably narrow; and it is quite possible for a young man to become a Bachelor of Science without a sound knowledge of any language, not even his own, and without any knowledge at all of philosophy, history, political science, or of any natural or physical science, except the single one to which he has devoted two or three years at the most.[3]

The annual number of students in the Lawrence Scientific school, thus composed of five or six distinct departments, has fluctuated irregularly between a maximum of eighty (in 1854–55) and a minimum of forty-nine (in 1867–68). The average annual attendance may be said to have been sixty-four,—the majority being students of engineering. Of this number only very few entered more than one department, and but a small proportion remained long enough in the school to finish satisfactorily even that course of study. In fifteen years (1851–65 inclusive) only one hundred and forty-six degrees of Bachelor of Science were given.

The two schools thus far considered are the oldest scientific schools, connected with colleges, in the country, and they have had the prestige of connection with the two leading colleges in the United States. Their experience has been various, and is of great value for the guidance of new enterprises.

In 1852 the Chandler Scientific School at Dartmouth College was founded. The age of admission was put at fourteen; and the requisites for admission were very low, being little more than a decent grammar-school training. A regular course of studies, covering three years, and ending in a degree of Bachelor of Science, was laid down at the start, and was extended to four years in 1857. It must be confessed that the humble starting-point of the course necessarily lowers the character of the whole; but, nevertheless, the range of studies is considerable. English, French, and German, mathematics, the elements of several sciences, and sundry subjects in history, philosophy, and logic, make part of the course. The fourth year is the only one which presents any elective elements; it is divided into a course for civil engineering, a commercial course, and a general course. Up to 1864 the average annual number of students in the Chandler Scientific School was less than forty. Since that year it has materially increased, reaching sixty-three in 1867–68. Dartmouth College has lately received two gifts which will materially add to its resources, and enable it to elevate the character of its scientific instruction. Sylvanus Thayer,[4] Brigadier-General of Engineers, U.S.A., has given the college fifty thousand dollars as a foundation for a school of architecture and engineering; and the New Hampshire Legislature has wisely transferred to the college the Congressional grant in aid of technical instruction in agriculture and the mechanic arts.

The Chandler Scientific School has labored under the serious disadvantage of having too intimate a connection with the college proper. It has borne another name, and offered instruction of a lower character than that of Dartmouth College. It cannot be said to have had a distinct faculty. Some of the teachers in the college have given a part of their time to the subordinate course. It has been distinctly in a position of inferiority.

The Columbia School of Mines was founded in 1864, with a somewhat narrower scope than the schools thus far described. Its object was to give instruction in those branches of science which relate to mining and metallurgy; and, perhaps unintentionally, it held out to persons engaged in mining and metallurgical enterprises the hope that graduates of the school would be competent forthwith to conduct works, whether new or old.[5]

It was doubtless intended to suggest that the three years' course of study laid out in the school programme would give an adequate preliminary training to young men, who, after some years of experience in actual works, would become competent to conduct mining and metallurgical enterprises. It is to be regretted that the paragraph of the catalogue in which the objects of the school are announced, taken in connection with a very recent statement[6] by the President of Columbia College, and a passage[7] in a circular lately issued by the school, still gives some support to the erroneous notion that young men can be made competent at any school, no matter how good, to take up immediately the charge of great enterprises in mining, manufacturing, or road and bridge building.

A technical school lays the best foundation for later; if well organized, with a broad scheme of study, it can convert the boy of fair abilities and intentions into an observant, judicious man, well informed in the sciences which bear upon his profession; so trained, the graduate will rapidly master the principles and details of any actual works, and he will rise rapidly through the grades of employment; moreover, he will be worth more to his employers from the start than an untrained man. Nevertheless, after the school, a longer or shorter term of apprenticeship upon real works of engineering, mining, building, or manufacturing will be found essential for the best graduates of the best technical schools. When people are content with the services of the last graduates of the medical school as family physicians, when the youngest bachelors of laws are forthwith retained with heavy fees for important cases, it will be time enough to expect that young men who have just completed their school training for the difficult professions of the engineer, manufacturer, miner, or chemist, will be competent at once to take charge of mines, manufacturing establishments, or large works of engineering. No matter how good the polytechnic, scientific, technological, or mining schools may be, it is a delusive expectation that their graduates will be able to enter at once the highest grades of employment, and assume the direction of practical affairs upon a large scale immediately upon leaving the schools. Common sense brings any one who considers the magnitude of the investments necessary in mining and metallurgical works to this conclusion. Young men of twenty to twenty-four are seldom equal to great money responsibilities.

The Columbia School of Mines was organized during one of the periodical hot turns of the intermittent mining-fever to which the American people is subject. It began in 1864–85 with twenty-nine students; but in the following year the catalogue bore the names of eighty-nine, while eight professors and four assistants took part in the work of instruction. About one half were special students, mostly of chemistry or assaying, who did not follow the regular course of instruction, and indeed remained but a short time in the school. Not a few students took merely a six weeks' or two months' course of instruction in assaying. In the next year (1866–67) there were one hundred and five students in the school, of whom thirty-eight were special students; twenty-five out of the one hundred and five held degrees, mostly Columbia degrees of Bachelor of Arts. In the year 1867–68 there were one hundred and nine students in the school, of whom forty-four were special; twenty-one out of the one hundred and nine held the degree of Bachelor of Arts. Beside the professors attached to other departments of Columbia, who give a portion of their time to the School of Mines, four professors and eight assistants in chemistry, drawing, and metallurgy are exclusively devoted to the School of Mines. The course of study has undergone some change since the beginning in 1864. It was originally a single three years' course; but within the last year a preparatory year has been added, which practically makes the whole course four years long, and during the last two years of the four a considerable elective element has been introduced into the course. The minimum age for entrance was originally eighteen, and is now seventeen. The requisites for admission are arithmetic and the elements of algebra and geometry. The studies of the first year are required of all students; in the second year the mathematics and chemistry become elective; in the third and fourth years each student chooses one of four courses, namely, mining engineering, metallurgy, geology and natural history, and chemistry. The majority of the studies in these four courses are common to all; but there are, nevertheless, considerable divergences. The degree of Engineer of Mines or Bachelor of Philosophy is conferred on those students who, at the end of the course, pass satisfactory examinations. Students are expected to visit mines and works during the vacations, and report upon them in full, with all necessary drawings and specimens.

The principal subjects in which instruction is given are mathematics, mining, engineering, chemistry including mineralogy, geology, and metallurgy. French and German are included in the programme of studies; but, singularly enough, it appears, from President Barnard's Report for 1868, that the provision for instruction in the modern languages is very defective. Drawing is also required; but there is only one "assistant" in drawing against six in chemistry. The tabular view of exercises and the list of officers indicate that the teaching of chemistry and the allied subjects occupies a very large, and indeed the most important, place in the work of the school.

We come now to the examination of the scientific or English "courses" organized within colleges. These courses run parallel with the classical course of instruction which it has been the primary object of the American colleges to provide. They are cast in the same mould as the classical course; but the metal is of a different composition. The experiment of conducting parallel classical and scientific courses in one and the same institution is by no means a new one. It is merely being tried afresh on a large scale and under new conditions in this country, after having failed in Europe. In Brown University, Union College, and the University of Michigan, for example, there have existed for several years two or more parallel courses,—one the common semi-classical course; the other, or others, constructed on the same frameworks as the classical course by simply replacing Latin and Greek, or Greek alone, by living European languages, and at the same time expanding a little the mathematical and scientific instruction. A student may choose either course, but not two; at the end of one course he will probably be a Bachelor of Arts; at the end of the other, a Bachelor of Science or Philosophy.

At Union College the second course is called "scientific," but the graduates in it take the degree of Bachelor of Arts. One feature in the announcement of Union College touching the scientific course is amusing. When Latin was the common speech of scholars, diplomas were naturally written in that language, as being the most generally intelligible; and the custom, though it has lost much of its original significance, is observed to this day in American colleges. But unfortunately, the graduates of the scientific course of Union College are not supposed to understand Latin, although they receive the degree of Bachelor of Arts. Under these circumstances, the authorities of Union College have had a happy inspiration. Since a diploma would evidently be worthless unless expressed in some foreign language or other, Union College announces that the diploma for students of the scientific course is expressed in French. The authorities of Union are countenanced in this absurdity by the Chandler School at Dartmouth. By far the larger number of students at Union choose the classical course. The great falling off in the number of students resorting to Union College since 1860,[8] to whatever cause or causes it may be due, is sufficient to prevent any friend of the system from quoting that college, at any rate, in its support. There exist at Union an engineering department and a chemical department distinct from the college proper; but the number of students in both has been and is small. It should be said, however, that, while the college as a whole has been rapidly losing students, the chemical department has increased its numbers.

At Brown University (Providence), an English and scientific course was introduced into the college plan as early as 1846. It was soon lost to sight in the loose and exaggerated elective system which prevailed there for some years. But it has reappeared in the shape of a three years' course of instruction, parallel with the Freshman, Sophomore, and Junior years of the regular college curriculum, and ending with the degree of Bachelor of Philosophy. The classics may be omitted altogether, or one dead language may be studied instead of two. This course is simply a shorter and less comprehensive course of study than the regular course for the degree of Bachelor of Arts; and the degree of Bachelor of Philosophy must, of course, be regarded as of less value than the other. The inferior course of study is less attractive than the classical course. Though the students of the two courses are entered in the same classes, and, to a large extent, pursue the same studies in the same class-rooms under the same teachers, the number of students who aim at the superior degree of Bachelor of Arts is much larger than the number of those who are content to be Bachelors of Philosophy.

At the University of Michigan the scientific courses as they stand in the programmes are essentially the ordinary college four years' course, with the suppression of both Latin and Greek, or of Greek alone; the gaps being filled in with modern languages, drawing, and a little additional mathematics. A course in civil engineering is made out by converting the Senior year into a year of special instruction in geology, mechanics, and engineering. A course in mining engineering is arranged by introducing into the last two years of the scientific course certain studies which have a direct bearing upon that profession. The students in these various courses are united in most of their studies, separated in comparatively few. Scientific students and classical students appear in the same classes, Senior, Junior, Sophomore, and Freshmen; but the classical students receive the degree of Bachelor of Arts, the scientific students the degree of Bachelor of Science, Civil Engineer, or Mining Engineer. The students of the classical course are decidedly in the majority, especially in the Junior and Senior years.

The simultaneous carrying on of what should be such different courses of instruction within the same walls, in the same community of students, and by one and the same corps of instructors, is, we believe, very disadvantageous to both systems of training. Such a combination has been thoroughly tried in the Lycées of France, and has completely failed and been abandoned. In Germany it has seemed expedient to separate the two courses, even during the school-boy period; and for the higher instruction of both systems entirely separate institutions have been found necessary. The fact is, that the whole tone and spirit of a good college ought to be different in kind from that of a good polytechnic or scientific school. In the college, the desire for the broadest culture, for the best formation and information of the mind, the enthusiastic study of subjects for the love of them without any ulterior objects, the love of learning and research for their own sake, should be the dominant ideas. In the polytechnic school should be found a mental training inferior to none in breadth and vigor, a thirst for knowledge, and genuine enthusiasm in scientific research, and a true love of nature; but underneath all these things is a temper or leading motive unlike that of a college. The student in a polytechnic school has a practical end constantly in view; he is training his faculties with the express object of making himself a better manufacturer, engineer, or teacher; he is studying the processes of nature, in order afterwards to turn them to human uses and his own profit; if he is eager to penetrate the mysteries of electricity, it is largely because he wants to understand telegraphs; if he learns French and German, it is chiefly because he would not have the best technical literature of his generation sealed for him; if he imbues his mind with the profound and exquisite conceptions of the calculus, it is in order the better to comprehend mechanics. This practical end should never be lost sight of by student or teacher in a polytechnic school, and it should very seldom be thought of or alluded to in a college. Just as far as the spirit proper to a polytechnic school pervades a college, just so far that college falls below its true ideal. The practical spirit and the literary or scholastic spirit are both good, but they are incompatible. If commingled, they are both spoiled.

It is not to be imagined that the mental training afforded by a good polytechnic school is necessarily inferior in any respect to that of a good college, whether in breadth, vigor, or wholesomeness. Certain it is that an average graduate of the Zurich Polytechnicum or the Paris École Centrale has a much better title to be called "learned"[9] than most graduates of American colleges and professional schools. He has studied more, harder, and to better effect, though in a different spirit. But the two kinds of education cannot be carried on together, in the same schedules, by the same teachers. The classical course will hurt the scientific, and the scientific the classical. Neither will be at its best. The experience of the world and common sense are against such experiences as those of Brown, Union, and Michigan. Nevertheless, they may be good temporary expedients during a transition period, or in crude communities where hasty culture is as natural as fast eating. They do good service in lack of better things.

The incompatibility of the practical spirit and the literary spirit, which has here been dwelt upon, may appear to some to limit unduly the number of subjects proper to be taught in college. The tendency to the practical side of every subject which befits a good polytechnic school would be improper in a college; but the same subjects may to a very great extent be taught in both. One and the same subject may be studied in two very unlike frames of mind. We have only desired to urge the incompatibility of one temper with another temper, both being good in their separate places.

Another unjust inference might be drawn from what has been said of the impossibility of carrying on two long courses of instruction of different aims and essence within the same schedules of hours and terms and the same walls. It might be inferred that the applied sciences are necessarily unfit to be taught or studied in a university, taking the word in its best sense. It cannot be said too loudly or too often, that no subject of human inquiry can be out of place in the programme of a real university. It is only necessary that every subject should be taught at the university on a higher plane than elsewhere. Even scholars are apt to be intolerant of this subject or that in university schemes; one can see no sense in archæology; another condemns natural history as being without practical applications, useless for training, and frightfully absorbent of money; a third finds pure science wholesome meat, but applied science utilitarian chaff. It is impossible to be too catholic in this matter. But the American university has not yet grown out of the soil, and we are rather meeting a theoretical than a practical objection. The incidental remark may be permitted, that a university, in any worthy sense of the term, must grow from seed. It cannot be transplanted from England or Germany in full leaf and bearing. It cannot be run up, like a cotton-mill, in six months, to meet a quick demand. Neither can it be created by an energetic use of the inspired editorial, the advertising circular, and the frequent telegram. Numbers do not constitute it, and no money can make it before its time. There is more of the university about the eight or ten Yale graduates who are studying in the Yale Department of Philosophy and the Arts, than in as many hundred raw youths who do not know more than a fair grammar school may teach. When the American university appears, it will not be a copy of foreign institutions, or a hot-bed plant, but the slow and natural outgrowth of American social and political habits, and an expression of the average aims and ambitions of the better educated classes. The American college is an institution without a parallel; the American university will be equally original.

[...]

CHAPTER 18

Inaugural Address

Noah Porter

INTRODUCTION TO PORTER'S INAUGURAL ADDRESS, YALE UNIVERSITY

In the 1820s, American colleges from Harvard and Brown to the Universities of Michigan and Vermont considered revising their prescribed, classical college curricula after increasingly widespread worries that they were antiquated. One of the most notable responses, for its provenance as well as its rhetorical sting, was the Yale Report of 1828. Drafted by Yale College president Jeremiah Day and Professor of Latin and Greek James Kingsley, the report responded directly to critics clamoring for the end of a curriculum organized around "dead languages." The proper end of college, they wrote, was to provide the "discipline and the furniture of the mind; expanding its powers, storing it with knowledge." It should "fix" attention and "direct the train of thought." It should, in short, form what was commonly referred to in eighteenth- and nineteenth-century works of moral psychology as the mental faculties and develop "habits of thinking." And, argued Day and Kingsley, a prescribed curriculum focusing on Latin and Greek literature and language provided "the most effectual discipline" of the mental faculties and, more broadly, the best character for young men.

Forty years after the 1828 report, Yale was still struggling to reconcile the classical college with modern scholarship and public demands for a more socially relevant curriculum. When Yale's president, Theodore Dwight Woolsey, announced he would retire in 1871, a struggle for the future of Yale and its classical curriculum broke out. One group of alumni, "Young Yale," fought to extricate their alma mater from the influence of what they termed the "narrow-minded" and "uncultivated" Congregational ministers of Connecticut. The young upstarts pushed for Daniel Coit Gilman, a Yale alumnus and professor of geography in the Sheffield Scientific School. Yale's Corporation, still champions of the classical college curriculum and the 1828 report, chose Noah Porter, professor of moral philosophy and metaphysics.

Although Porter would ultimately defend the classical curriculum, he was no mere gentleman scholar. He was an active thinker and writer who sought to bring together Scottish commonsense philosophy with German idealism. Among his works was *The Human Intellect*, a systematic account of faculty psychology and the latent capabilities of the mental faculties around which most classical college curricula had been organized. Like his eighteenth- and nineteenth-century predecessors, Porter described the purpose of college as the discipline of the mind and soul rather than the acquisition of specialized knowledge or, as he put it, the mere "accumulation of facts." Colleges should form moral and mental character.

In his inaugural address as president of Yale College in 1871, Porter struggled to clarify the relationship between modern science and Christianity and also the relationship between the modern research university and the traditional college. Like many of his contemporaries, he insisted that there was no conflict between religion and science, because both pursued the same truth.

But he had no such irenic confidence in the ultimate harmony of the research university and the college. These, he asserted, were two distinct institutions. Critics of the classical curriculum wanted to turn Yale College into a university in order to "invest it with the dignity, the privileges, and, above all, with the freedom, which are supposed to belong to an institution with the more high sounding name." But a university, he warned, required a college and the "discipline" and the formation it provided. The division was clear—the college would form young, moral men; the university would advance knowledge.

INAUGURAL ADDRESS, 1871

I need make no apology for selecting as my theme the Higher Education of the country. An occasion like the present would, under any circumstances, require me to speak of this subject in some of its aspects. It cannot be avoided at the present time, when the entire theory of Higher Education is so generally and so actively discussed. Never, perhaps, did this subject occupy the thoughts of so many persons and occupy them so earnestly. It certainly never excited more active controversy, or provoked more various or confident criticism, or was subjected to a greater variety of experiments than with us in these passing years. The remark is not infrequently made that college and university education are not merely agitated by reforms; they are rather convulsed by a revolution,—so unsettled are the minds of many who control public opinion, so sharp is the criticism of real or imagined defects in the old methods and studies, and so determined is the demand for sweeping and fundamental changes.

[. . .]

In entering upon the discussion of our theme, we observe, *First: the Higher Education should be conversant with the Past.* This is one of its special distinctions and imperative obligations. It does not describe its sole or its whole duty, but a class of duties which are prominent and characteristic. It is sometimes made a ground of reproach against this education and the men devoted to it, that they are so greatly occupied with the past; as if the one function to which above all others they are set apart were not to master its gathered *acquisitions* and its instructive wisdom. An education which despises the past is necessarily limited and narrow. It is judged and condemned already by the ignorance and effrontery of its pretensions. Institutions and teachers of culture that profess to concern themselves little with what has been thought and done in other generations are convicted of incompetency by their own announcements.

The Past with which this education should concern itself includes, first of all, those positive and permanent acquisitions which man has produced in previous generations and transmitted to the present,—*i.e.* whatever man has learned to be true of the universe of matter and of spirit, and whatever he has invented or created in appliances for his comfort, in machinery for his labors and locomotion, and in products of art for his wonder and delight. To this we should add as no less important all those principles, traditional and recorded, concerning man's duty and destiny, embracing ethics and theology; concerning his political and social relations, constituting legal and political science; concerning the courtesies and amenities of life, comprehending what we call civilization. Here belong those works of literature which the world has not been willing to let die. All these are the products of the past, its gathered accumulations which, whatever be their nature and however they are preserved and transmitted, nothing but barbarism or anarchy could forget or destroy. To preserve some of these products the lower and more diffused culture is sufficient. Others can be preserved and transmitted only by selected guardians,—who receive them into careful hands, teach others to understand and value and improve them, and thus transmit them with added wealth and beauty to the generation that follows.

But besides these products of the activities of the past there are also *the records of these activities* themselves. It is with these preeminently that the higher education should concern itself. Foremost we name history proper, as it opens for us its pictured and admonitory pages—the history of deeds and of men, with the events that stir the imagination, and inspire to imitation, with its inciting and warning examples of character, and the incidents that illustrate and enforce those truths which men are continually disposed to forget. Next the history of thought and speculation—so sadly and so often the history of confusion and of error—the history of philosophy of every sort, physical, political, ethical, theological, and metaphysical. Connected with this, and most important, is the history of speech, or the study of language, which in its structure and changes is of itself so instructive a reflex of human thought and emotion and so important a record of human civilization. This study of what *man has been and attempted* in the past is fully as important for education as is the mastery of what man has *learned and proved*. To assert as many do, and to imply as more would hastily infer, that the past can teach us nothing, except the positive truths and products which survive it, is to overlook the most important functions of education and of knowledge—its offices in stimulating thought and awakening activity, its capacity to enlarge the mind by comparative judgments and to enrich it with permanent principles.

[. . .]

It has become a doctrine with not a few that there is a natural antagonism between culture and practical success, that exact learning and refined tastes are incompatible with eminence in the conduct of affairs. The doctrine has been converted into the heresy, that in a republic which in theory is controlled by principles and insight, special reliance on either is a disqualification for public trusts. More marvelous still in a community which rests on popular education, the doctrine is studiously propagated that the higher learning is antagonistic to the lower.

We have no time to show that no ignorance can be more stupid and no heresy more malignant and destructive. The lessons of history—both the earlier and the more recent—are distinct and vivid that in a republic like ours, wealthy, proud, and self-confident, there can be neither permanence nor dignity if the best knowledge and the highest culture of the world do not influence its population and its institutions. It becomes a serious question, then, how the learning and culture of the country can be more successfully provided for and made generally accessible. Something may be done by organizing learned societies for historical, geographical, political, and sociological research, by special and public libraries, by institutes for learned lectures, by museums of archaeology, natural history, and art, by laboratories and observatories, and by detached schools of technology and physics. Many such institutions and societies have already been founded. Not a few have been largely endowed at the suggestion of individual caprice or local pride. They are all admirable in their way and useful in their sphere, but they neither supersede nor in any considerable degree supplement the universities and colleges. They rather lean upon these for support, and refer to them as authorities. They must be devoted chiefly to the accumulation of appliances for the special or the occasional student, rather than to the organized and persistent pursuit of science and learning. If now and then an ample foundation, abundant leisure, and a well-appointed establishment invite to special researches, there is wanting the sense of responsibility and of social excitement which are essential to the highest success. Learning and culture rarely thrive so well as when prosecuted by a society of men who can stimulate and aid one another by their diverse aptitudes and tastes and acquisitions.

Assuming that our colleges are preeminently fitted to be the *seats of learning* in such a country as ours, the question is most important *what more can be done to make them more eminent and influential in this regard*. It is safe to say in reply that it is not desirable to attach to them chairs or foundations devoted exclusively to research with no obligations to instruction. The experience of the English universities has shown that life endowments with limited or uncertain duties of instruction, have not accomplished so much for the higher learning of the country as they would have done had the incumbents been held to constant and active service in teaching. The duty of communicating need not interfere with activity in learning. It rather imparts a present and pressing interest to research. It gives clearness and method and fixedness to what is learned. Even if the line of study is higher than the line of instruction, the habits which are inspired in the class-room are favorable to solid and sober acquisition. To communicate with the living voice and in the presence of those waiting to learn, awakens a life and interest in the teacher which the preparation of the written essay or learned paper can never inspire. On the other hand, the duties of teaching need not interfere with the time and interest which study requires. How can the demands of the two be adjusted? Let the college be so well endowed as to allow its younger teachers sufficient time for study while it imposes on them special duties of discipline and instruction. As age advances, and the attainments are more conspicuous, let the duties of instruction be lightened. If graduate classes are formed and university work is undertaken, let this work be assigned to the older and more eminent. Let special and advanced students never be set aside by the pre-occupations of elementary teaching,—but let the accomplished professor never cease to instruct so long as health and life permit. The example is not infrequent in the German universities of veterans in Philology like Böckh, in History like Ranke, in Physics like Karl Ritter,[1] in Theology like Nitszch[2] and Twesten,[3] in Philosophy like Brandis,[4] in Law like Mittermaier,[5] appearing in the lecture-room and going from the lecture-room to the study to prosecute the researches which have made them authorities in the world of learning and lights to mankind. These examples, and the successful working of the German theory, teach a twofold lesson: that the university is the fittest place for undergraduates to further the higher learning of the country, and that in the university the man of research should continue to be active as an instructor. The plan which has been developed in Yale College of attaching university schools or classes to the undergraduate curriculum, and of encouraging college professors to enter upon higher teaching, is eminently fitted to make them learned men, and at the same time efficient and successful instructors. It will also contribute to the learning and culture of the country by arousing the desire for research and culture among the students.

[...]

From the relation of the higher education to the past, we pass to its concern with the present, and observe that this education should never be so devoted to the generations which are gone as to forget the generation which is now thinking and acting. The learning which it acquires it does not acquire for the gratification of a few erudite students, or the satisfaction of a few curious critics, but for the service of the present age. While a college cannot teach except it also learns from the past, it cannot teach unless it understands and sympathizes with the generation which it attempts to instruct. While it is true that certain truths and principles are the same for all the generations, it is also true that every age has its own methods of conceiving and applying them, its own difficulties in accepting what is true and in refuting what is false, its own forms of scientific inquiry, and its own forms of literary expression. This is eminently true of our country in these our times. Its intellectual activity is unlike that of any other country or of any other period. From the phases of scientific and of popular activity with which the whole country is moved from time to time, the higher institutions may not estrange themselves, in their devotion to the routine of academic instruction or the prosecution of learned researches. It is not impossible now and then that they should fall behind the science and speculation, the philology and literature of their own day, through their exclusive occupation with the thinking and literature of past generations. They do well also to remember that though learned, they have no monopoly of learning; though scientific, they do not necessarily lead or even follow the science of their time; though devoted to literary criticism and research, there is a busy world of historians and poets and essayists, whose energetic activity is moving forward or backward, upward or downward, the thought, the diction, and the principles of a progressive generation. The private student and the amateur scientist and philologist have sometimes leisure and resources which the college professor cannot command. Now and then, from some quarter unlooked for, there springs up a genius in speculation or literature, who sets the learned world in a maze of wonder at his strength and his audacity. It is unfortunate for the prestige of the college and the cause of learning, if the incumbent of any of its departments falls behind the knowledge and the discussions of the times. If the mathematician, the physicist, the philologist, the critic, the historian, or the metaphysician of the university is not master of the acquisitions and the discussions which have been reached in his own sphere, his college is weakened and dishonored. It not only suffers in reputation, but it must fail to prepare its pupils adequately for the field of thought and activity into which they are to be ushered. Unless the teacher is alive to the thinking of the present he cannot prepare his pupils fully to meet it,—to accept whatever in it is true and good, and to reject whatever is erroneous and evil. Moreover, if he is ignorant of the present, his pupils cannot be, even while they sit under his teachings. They come into his class-room fresh from the exuberant life of a new generation. He may ignore or despise it. They do not. They sympathize with its knowledge and its ignorance, they share in its wisdom and its folly. If he understands and cares for neither, he is so far unfitted to counsel and guide them. But if they are made aware that he understands the great world without the college as well as the little world within, they will listen to his instructions with respect.

[. . .]

Indeed, of all the later studies of the college and the advanced studies that follow, it is indispensable that the teacher should be a man who judges the present by the past, and makes the present illustrate the past. President Woolsey has been none the less efficient as an instructor, because he has brought his reading and his thought to bear upon questions of social morals and international complications.

There is special need at the present moment that the student should sympathize with the present generation, because he is sometimes reproached with being out of sympathy with it, and because the present so pressingly needs all the energy and skill which culture and learning can apply to elevate and correct it. If the professors of our higher institutions sometimes cease to sympathize with present movements, it is never true of their pupils. For this very reason the necessity is so much the more imperative that their teachers should also understand these movements,—that they may prepare their pupils to meet them; if in the direction of the truth that they should welcome them, if of error that they should know why they withstand them. The standing reproach against university life, that it tends to withdraw its pupils from the thought and activities of their times, is, however, refuted by the history of universities in every generation,—from the days when Luther reflected in his own struggling heart the thoughts and feelings which were moving the men of his time, down to the present moment when the speculations of Mill and of Buckle have penetrated into the common rooms of Oxford, and agitated the colleges where Wesley[6] and Whitefield,[7] Pusey[8] and Newman,[9] Arnold[10] and Whately[11] half anticipated and half created the revolutions of popular thought and feeling with which their names are connected. But while the university should wisely adapt itself to the needs and changes of the present, it should never humor its caprices nor conform itself to its unreasonable demands. It should in some sense be the teacher of the public as well as of its own pupils. It is in no sense the servant of public opinion when public opinion is superficial or erroneous,—but it is called to be its corrector and controller. Especially in matters of education should it neither pander to popular prejudices nor take advantage of popular humors. If there is any sanctuary where well-grounded convictions should find refuge, and where these should be honored, it is in a place devoted to the higher education; especially if these convictions concern the very function for which its members are called to serve at its altar. We would not recall the times when the most weighty questions in theology and law were submitted to a council of university professors, but the days will be degenerate indeed when university professors have no convictions, or fail to assert them concerning the higher education, whether they do or do not suit the humor of the hour.

The higher education in mastering the past and sympathizing with the present, will wisely forecast and direct the future. The men whom it trains are men of the future, and to a large extent have the future of the country in their hands. Hence the relations of this education to the future take up into themselves and control its relations to the present and the past. The aims and duties of its directors are briefly comprehended in the positions: as students, they should add to the science of the past; as teachers they should train to the highest intellectual capacity and achievement as well to the noblest impulses and perfection.

The duty of adding to the knowledge of one's time will scarcely be questioned. It needs little illustration or enforcement in an age of intellectual enterprise which sees little that is true which is not new, and of moral hardihood which has almost forgotten its reverence in the ardor of its hopes. The time was when the learned classes and their institutions were content to repeat traditional lore,—when logic, philology, and theology were the exclusive spheres of intellectual activity and the sole instruments of culture, and when these sciences were taught and learned in a mechanical spirit. In those times one age was very like another, and the education of one generation was the dull and traditionary transcript of that which went before. To a certain extent this is still true of the English schools and colleges. But since the modern comparative and critical spirit has breathed life into philology and history; since philosophy, ethics, and theology have been searched by solvents of a potency never before dreamed of; since even logic and revelation are challenged at every turn concerning their right to be;—since the new sciences of nature have astonished the world by their achievements, and have become romantic almost to insanity in their aspirations; since literature itself fills the popular mind with the most daring promises and the boldest denials, it is impossible that the best thought and learning should not be occupied with the future.

We hardly need assert that no teacher at the present day deserves the name who is not prepared to revise his opinions, and if need be to change them. The spirit of progress and of growth animates all circles, and it should breathe a vigorous and hopeful life into every university. The eye of every instructor should look hopefully and eagerly forward, to greet every new discovery, to welcome every new truth, and to add to past contributions by new experiments, invention, and thought. In all these investigations by which the higher education would add to scientific truth, whatever may be the subject matter which they concern, and whatever may be the consequences to cherished faiths and opinions, its spirit should be free. But the freest inquirer is the most remote from rashness and conceit. The bravest confidence in truth is commonly measured by docility, candor, and reverence.

Leaving this point we pass to the duty of training to the highest intellectual power and achievement. Two principles must be regarded as unquestioned: The higher education should aim at intellectual culture and training rather than at the acquisition of knowledge, and it should respect remote rather than immediate results.

The highest education should propose intellectual training as its chief object. That education is conceived in the wisest spirit and is in the best sense the most liberal which values permanent intellectual power and culture above any accumulation of facts, any knowledge of words or phrases, or any dexterity in action or in speech. No one will deny that training is reached by acquiring knowledge, but knowledge in the best sense is more than the accumulation of facts, whatever these may be, whether words, events, paradigms, or dates. Facts as such do not constitute knowledge, but only facts as held in a method and as related to principles and laws. Facts as such do not even enrich the mind, but only those facts which stimulate the imagination, which elevate the feelings, which illustrate principles, and regulate the life. Moreover, in all the stages of education many of the tasks are purely preparative and disciplinary. The most earnest stickler for knowledge made easy and self-propelling, must confess that in childhood alphabets and paradigms and derivations and syntactical rules must be painfully learned before they can be understood and applied. As we advance, nomenclatures and classifications must be matured, and by and by mathematical distinctions must be discerned and made familiar, at the cost sometimes of reluctant attention; skill and accuracy in working problems and reading French and German, even if we let alone Latin and Greek, must be acquired before the mind is able or is pleased to walk, or it may be to soar, along or above the heights of analysis and speculation. The truth cannot be set aside nor denied, that in the elementary stages of every branch of knowledge, from the mastery of the alphabet upwards, intellectual labor must be enforced largely for the sake of its remote results, and these results often appear only as enhanced skill or capacity.

Studies for discipline, so obtrusive in the lower education, cannot be avoided in the higher. The methods and appliances of teaching have not yet been so far perfected, nor have the minds of our pupils been so far quickened or elevated by preliminary training, as to enable us to dispense with many studies which are especially disciplinary, and in a degree unattractive. The elements of every science, even of the sciences of nature, the grammar of every new language, bring with them drudgery and work, which excite no high intellectual, emotional, or practical interest. It is urged that inasmuch as all study and acquisition must be disciplinary, it can matter little what studies are pursued, whether the modern or the ancient languages, whether the mathematics or natural history, whether physics and philosophy or experimental research; and therefore each student should select what he fancies, or believes he can use. We cannot accept the doctrine that all studies are equally disciplinary in their influence and effect, or that a selection of the most quickening and useful cannot be made by teachers better than by pupils. In such selection regard should be had to the time allowed for higher culture, as well as to the aptitudes and tastes and future employments of the student.

We confess that a long course of disciplinary study, sternly enforced and with much of routine and drudgery, with a feeble apprehension or positive doubt of its usefulness, and a slowly awakened sense of intellectual advantage, is often wearisome to the student, and not always grateful to the teacher. For this reason it is greatly desired that every curriculum, especially the classical or humanistic, should be administered with an intellectual spirit so overmastering as to be irresistible by the most inert and torpid; that the study of language and of literature as it proceeds should be constantly more and more quickening to thought; that as the pupil wakens into habits of inquiry and glows with curiosity, every lesson shall more than meet his wants, and kindle new ardor for the next. The great mass even of our best students can never become strongly interested in the minutiae of grammar or the niceties of philology; but there are few who cannot be kindled to the appreciation of the classical writings, as literature. The discipline of grammar should not be dispensed with, but discipline ceases to be useful when it has exhausted its power to interest. We trust the time is not far distant when a better and more uniform preparation in the classics, and the mastery of the elements of French and German before entering college, shall make more feasible the more intellectual and aesthetic study of the ancient and modern languages and literature; when a manlier faith in the work of the college shall pervade the college and the community, and a spirit of self-culture and self-improvement shall enforce study without the friction or the complaint of marks and conditions. But even then—in that millennium which the prophets of the new dispensation declare to have already come in the schools which they have reared—the external law and examination will not cease to be required; rather, will they be hailed and responded to as the best auxiliaries and incentives to the law written on the heart.

To relieve the college system of the difficulties adverted to, the plan of elective studies has been proposed—not of elective courses or schools, of which we have spoken and which the college provides—but the choice of studies from time to time, to be directed by the real or fancied aptitudes or preferences of the pupil, and the possible relation of these studies to his future profession or career. We grant for this plan a temporary satisfaction to the more earnest students and the more ardent enthusiasm which attends the continued prosecution of a favorite study. But we cannot overlook the very serious evils to which it is exposed. The majority of undergraduate students have neither the maturity nor the data which qualify them to judge of the relative value of studies or their bearing on their future employments. The few who have a definite career, or pronounced tastes, may be misled by their feelings to judge in the direction which is most injurious because for the present it is more pleasing. The plan involves the certain evil of breaking into the common life of the class and the college as well as of unprofitable expenditure and insuperable complexity.

A still more serious objection to a wide range of elective studies in the college is found in its tendency to limit the cycle of the studies acknowledged to be liberal, and to contract the period of university education. We urge in this connection that the higher education of this country ought in its forecast of the future, to contemplate a longer rather than a shorter period of time for its completion. Its guardians should see that no projects for shortening this period should be introduced under the plausible pretext of greater liberality in respect to the methods or the matter of study and instruction. It would be most unfortunate should the impression prevail that the highest general or liberal education this country should aspire after or furnish, must be given in the so-called college as distinguished from the graduate school, and no arrangements should be made for the completion of any of these liberal studies, after taking the first degree—most unfortunate, indeed, if the rush and pressure of practical life should crowd itself behind that degree, and high culture in the college should be estimated by extraordinary proficiency in one or two specialities of science, letters, or philosophy—after which comes the practice and application of what has been learned. The more urgent is this noisy tumult of life without, and the stronger its pressure against the doors of the college, the greater need is there that certain studies which have little relation to this life should be attended to, and the less occasion that those should be anticipated which will absorb all the energies of life. We prefer the theory of liberal culture which assumes that an increasing rather than a diminishing number of our choicest youth of leisure will continue their literary and scientific studies, and thus be able to dignify and adorn their life by habits of systematic research and of earnest literary activity—that some who are devoted to business will acquire the strength to withstand the absorbing cares and the insatiable greed of money getting; that here and there a professional man may be saved from the narrowness which the exclusive claims of his calling must engender if science, and literature, and history are not actively attended to. What this country demands is a larger number of educated men who are elevated and refined by a culture which is truly liberal; men whose convictions are founded in manifold reading and comprehensive thought; men with the insight which comes only from a larger converse with history, a profound meditation on the problems of life and speculation, and a catholic taste in literature. The more such men mingle in the concerns of life, the more do they soften our controversies and dignify our discussions, refine upon our vulgarities and introduce amenities into our social life. They are needed in our politics and literature, at the bar and in the pulpit, in our newspapers and journals. We have plenty of cheap glitter, of tawdry bedizenment and showy accomplishments; plenty of sensational declamation, coarse argument, and facile rhetoric; much moral earnestness which needs tolerance and knowledge, and religious fervor which runs into dogmatism and rant. We need a higher and more consummate culture, in some of the men at least whom we educate for the work of life, and for this reason the arrangements for university education should contemplate a prolonged period of study.

Instead, then, of providing university studies for undergraduate students, we desire to make our undergraduate departments preparatory for university classes and schools. These undergraduate departments are two: the old classical college—the Yale College which is known as the germ of all its offshoots—and the Sheffield School with its modern and scientific curriculum of three years. Both these are feeders to the University proper. This consists of the professional schools for Theology, Law, and Medicine, and what answers to the department of Philosophy in a German university, making the analogy of the two almost complete. The Philosophical Department, so far as organized, includes the classes and courses of study for graduate students in the Scientific School (as the Schools of Engineering and Chemistry), a school of Philology fully organized, a school of Mathematics and Physics, and a partially organized school in which History and English literature, and Politics are taught, which it is hoped may be organized as a School of the Moral and Political Sciences. To these should be added, as not least significant, the School of the Fine Arts. This is our scheme of an organized university. It presupposes undergraduate instruction and discipline, and superadds additional study and reading in regular classes, under able instructors. It is no more than just to say that these arrangements have been responded to by the attendance of as many students as our most sanguine hopes could have contemplated. This scheme of classes looking towards a university degree, is capable of indefinite expansion according to the demands of science and letters, the resources of the university in money and men, and the appliances of books and collections. It invites to the founding of university professorships, of which more than one is fully endowed and most ably filled, the incumbents of which may not only lend honor to the institution in their appropriate spheres, but may give valuable instruction and incitements to undergraduate pupils.

Thus far we have considered culture and discipline in their relations to the intellect. But the intellect is not the whole of man, nor do his intellectual powers or acquisitions alone determine his value to himself and the community—much less that which is higher than his value, his worth. This is measured by his character, as indicated by his aspirations and his motives. We cannot if we would avoid the ethical and religious aspects of the higher education.

To form the character is a legitimate end of education of every kind, and the higher its rank the more important is it that its moral and religious results should be the best conceivable. A college or university, a majority of whose pupils should deny duty and God in theory, or dishonor both by characters that were atheistic and vicious—whose private lives should be profligate and selfish, and whose public morality should be venal and false—would do more to corrupt the country, not only its morality but its intellectual tone, than a formidable array of pulpits and newspapers could withstand. Could the vile creatures among us who now affront the day by the factitious glare of wealth and office, by any possibility assume the charms which high education and refined culture might impart, they would become in very deed the scourges of God to the community. If an institution of learning, with pupils trained to such characters, could continue to exist without perishing from its own rottenness, it would be a fountain of corruption and death in the social structure. Should atheism be taught in it as a scientific theory, and a materialistic psychology logically compel to the denial of conscience; should all domestic ties be unloosed by a scientific demonstration, and social obligations be dissolved at the word of some demigod of genius, the devastation would be none the less real and none the less appalling because it was accomplished by the necessities of science or ordered by the dicta of philosophy. The wail of the sufferers would be none the less heart-rending, because the requiem of the world's aspirations and hopes was inspired and chanted by some genius in whom poetry and music were said to be incarnate. The present aspects of society at home and abroad, in the small and the large, are compelling thoughtful men to ask, whether the practical relaxation of the bonds of duty, especially among men of culture and education, is not the result of a more or less distinctly acknowledged theoretical skepticism. And yet under this practical pressure it is still questioned by not a few doctrinaires in education, whether any direct and positive instruction or influence in ethics or religion is compatible with the independence of the student and the catholicity of science. It is, of course, conceded, that the rules and influences of public morality and Christian civilization should be practically recognized and enforced, but it is contended that neither ethical nor Christian truth should be set forth in the forms of science, or made the matter of academical instruction. These it is urged should be left to the family and the church, and with the operation of either the college or the university should not concern itself. We hold the opposite opinion. In giving our reasons for it we premise that we have special reference to students in the college as distinguished from students in the university, students in a condition of pupilage and living in a closely-knit society. How far our principles apply to university schools and classes can be readily inferred. For convenience we separate ethical from religious truth. That ethical truths and ethical relations are appropriate subjects for scientific investigation cannot be questioned. They are assumed in politics and law. They cannot be excluded from the sciences of natural right and social obligation. They are constantly obtruding themselves in those discussions which fill so large a space,—and so many of which conduct to action,—in our modern thinking. The questions of reform and of progress with which political economy and sociology are concerned, all involve ethical principles either true or false. We contend that every man who assumes to think and decide for himself should have well-grounded convictions upon these subjects, which he can state and defend with scientific clearness. Duty is the one art which every man has occasion to practice, and he that by culture is trained to have reasons for his beliefs and acts, must use his intellect to guide him here. But the scientific and literary devotee is exposed to the danger of overlooking these truths as truths of science in the more obtrusive and absorbing claims of his favorite studies. Receiving them as taught by common sense and enforced by conscience, and therefore bestowing upon them little intellectual activity, he finds and requires no place for them in his scheme of rational knowledge. Exciting little of that curiosity which the novelties of science and letters arouse, they elicit few earnest questionings, and consequently no positive and well-grounded responses. Such a man may retain his practical faith, but he gives it no intellectual respect because it excites little intellectual activity. Perhaps he surrenders it without question, at the sudden call of some scientific theory, or under the potent charm of some favorite author. Scientific theories of matter and life all have ethical consequences and an ethical significance. The laws of the physical universe either witness to duty and immortality or they fail to suggest either, according to our interpretation of them. History, literature, and criticism necessarily involve ethical principles and relations. Our philosophy of history, our estimates of literature, our canons of criticism, our choices of favorite authors, involve ethical faiths and sympathies, and these must react with subtle and irresistible energy upon the intellectual habits and the intellectual tone. Any education must be defective and narrow which does not concern itself with ethical principles and their relations to science, to literature, and life.

That a high tone of practical ethics should be enforced by the college discipline and the college life, will be universally allowed. First of all, the discipline of the college should have moral aims and a moral significance. Any regime which holds to thorough and honest intellectual work, which is ready to expose pretension and dissipate shams, trains indirectly but effectively to honest dealing, to uprightness before God and downrightness before man. To hold the student to minute fidelity in little things is an enforcement of one of the most significant maxims of the Gospel. A discipline that is indulgent and inconstant and fitful, that does not enforce its own rules, nor respect its own aims, not only is unjust to the intellectual training of its pupils, but insensibly lowers the tone of their characters by failing to train them to self-control, to obedience, to industry, and patient application. The quiet and mechanical working of a good system of college discipline contains within itself the most effective moral influences. In its administration, however, the spirit should never be sacrificed to the letter, nor its moral import be strangled by technical preciseness. Whether it is applied to the scholarship or the character, it should be felt to be kind and noble and elevating. It should be strict without being over precise, impartial but not ungenerous, exacting but not petty, rigid but not suspicious.

[...]

The Religious and Christian character of our higher education is intimately related to the ethical. If science and literature involve ethical relations, they also involve those which are religious. If the sentiments and obligations of the conscience give dignity and interest to both, much more do those which connect man with God and Immortality. The Christian history occupies the foremost place in modern progress and development, and whether it is credible and true must be decided by every man who concerns himself with history at all. The Christian faith and sentiments and morals and civilization, have so far penetrated and leavened the principles of modern life that criticism must face the question whether the Christ from whom these have proceeded be an impostor, a myth, a romance; or the central object of the world's faith and reverence, the inspirer of its best and purest emotions, the foundation of its immortal hopes. In respect to all these points, the instructions and the influence of every institution of higher learning must be Christian or anti-Christian, as the impression of the characters and teachings of its instructors is positive or negative. The more positive this impression is the better will it be for the education which the institution gives. The more Christian a college or university is, other things being equal, the more perfect and harmonious will be its culture, the more philosophical and free its science, the more exact and profound its erudition, the richer and more varied its literature. We should be treacherous to our faith did we not believe this and act accordingly. We rejoice that this is still the judgment of so many who influence public opinion. We desire more instead of less of Christianity in this university. We do not mean that we would have religious take the place of intellectual activity, for this would tend to dishonor Christianity itself by an ignorant and narrow perversion of its claims to supremacy. We do not desire that the sectarian or denominational spirit should be intensified. With this the liberalizing spirit of Christian culture has the least sympathy. The more truly Christian a university becomes, the less sectarian will be its spirit and influence. But we desire that all science should be more distinctly connected with that thought and goodness which are everywhere manifested in the universe of matter and of spirit; that the scientific poverty of the atheistic materialism should be clearly proved to the understanding as well as felt to be repellent to the heart; that the starveling character of the fatalistic theory of history may be decisively set forth, and the ignoble tendencies of a godless and frivolous literature may be amply illustrated. We desire that the place and influence of Christ and Christianity in reforming the domain of speculation and of action, of letters and of life, should be distinctly, emphatically, and reverentially recognized. In all this we are not untrue to the catholicity and authority of science, for we avow ourselves ready to reexamine every question of faith in the light of the newest researches and the freshest speculation, and, if need be, to modify our belief by the issue. But we have no such distrust concerning the results as to provide in any of our arrangements for the necessity of gradually or suddenly abandoning a positive and historical Christianity. As devoted to scientific thought we claim to be as free as the most untrammeled. We would cast off our Christianity as a filthy garment if we loved it better than we love the truth. We have no favors for our faith to ask of science, and no patronage to solicit from erudition. On the other hand, we have no fears from either. As students in literature we would cherish the most catholic tastes and sympathies: nor need we fear to do so when from Lucretius to Goethe there comes up the sad and unbroken testimony, that the absence of faith and worship weakens and withers the most gifted genius. In the light of our past history and what are to be the pressing demands of this country, we assert the opinion that Yale College must and will be forever maintained as a Christian university. Would that it were provided with a chapel that in the strength and beauty of its architecture worthily represented the place which Christianity holds in the esteem of its guardians and friends.

We hold that the earnest and Christian daily worship of a college household elevates and invigorates the community, even though to some extent it may be unconscious of this influence. The varied discussion and enforcement of the themes of Christian truth and duty, when managed with simplicity and skill, cannot but educate the mind to the widest and most stimulating thought, as well as refine it to the seriousness, tenderness, and pathos which are the appropriate results of culture.

[. . .]

CHAPTER 19

Liberty in Education

Charles William Eliot

INTRODUCTION TO ELIOT'S ESSAY

With a few prominent exceptions, since 1945 the American undergraduate curriculum has had three components: the major (or concentration), general education, and electives. Each component has its own history; together, they were intended to square (or triangulate) what educational leaders believed to be the principal desiderata of the academic experience: training in a specialty, exposure to a variety of subjects of individual interest, and the acquisition of "what every educated person needs to know."

These are not entirely commensurable goals. In fact, each of the three components was designed as the corrective to one of the others. The major was a reaction to electives, and general education was a reaction to the major. But the elective was the first piece of the modern curriculum to come into being.

Electives were themselves a reaction to the highly prescribed curriculum of the antebellum college. Before 1870, most college courses were required, often with specific assigned texts; and everything, even the few electives, was taught by class. At Harvard in 1868–69, for example, each class had its own set of required courses. All freshmen had to take Latin, Greek, mathematics, French, elocution, ethics, and Greek history. Every student had to master texts by Edward Gibbon and Dugald Stewart. Seniors had to take courses in history, philosophy, economics, and composition, along with a limited choice of electives.

With the arrival of Charles William Eliot as Harvard's president, in 1869, this quickly changed. Electives had been tried at other schools before Eliot came on the scene—successfully under Andrew White at Cornell, not so successfully under Francis Wayland at Brown—and they had been experimented with at Harvard. Before his appointment, Eliot seems to have been skeptical of the idea, but he converted in time for his inauguration, and (much to the annoyance of White) he soon became the most vocal and visible champion of the elective system. By 1872, he had opened college courses to all students regardless of class (in some cases, students needed the permission of the instructor); by 1900, the only requirements for a Harvard AB were knowledge of a foreign language and a course in expository writing.

Eliot's essay "Liberty in Education" (1885) is a characteristic manifesto. It appeals to the complexity and uniqueness of the individual student, to the constantly evolving state of modern scientific knowledge, and to the ability of young people to choose for themselves—part of Eliot's attack on the doctrine of in loco parentis. Elsewhere, Eliot described the elective system as "in the first place an outcome of the Protestant Reformation. In the next place, it is an outcome of the spirit of political liberty."

Eliot's faith that a set of courses a student has selected for himself or herself will have "more theoretical and practical merit for his case than the required curriculum of my college days" was just the nineteenth-century faith in laissez-faire: free individual choice conduces to optimal outcomes. "Artificial regulation is superfluous," as Eliot put it. Eliot sincerely believed this philosophy, but the elective system met a practical, even political, need as well. It was the system required by the commitment to the idea that the university should include research on, and therefore instruction in, every subject that is amenable to scholarly inquiry.

The most radical assertion in "Liberty in Education" is this: "All branches of sound knowledge are of equal dignity and equal educational value." This should still astonish us as a general proposition. Can it possibly be true? Yet it remains a doctrinal principle of the modern university. Curricula, even general education curricula, are obliged to reflect the full range of academic specialties that the academy houses. Constraints on student choice are often regarded as impermissible value judgments about the relative worth of different fields. At the bottom of this state of affairs is the faith that training in *any* academic field of inquiry produces in students the habits of mind a liberal education is supposed to instill. On this view, it's the habits of mind, and not the content of courses, that are the true take-aways of the undergraduate academic experience. If that's what you believe, then the free elective system is the ideal model.

LIBERTY IN EDUCATION

How to transform a college with one uniform curriculum into a university without any prescribed course of study at all is a problem which more and more claims the attention of all thoughtful friends of American learning and education. To-night I hope to convince you that a university of liberal arts and sciences must give its students three things: (1) Freedom in choice of studies, (2) Opportunity to win academic distinction in single subjects or special lines of study, (3) A discipline which distinctly imposes on each individual the responsibility of forming his own habits and guiding his own conduct. These three subjects I shall take up in succession, the first of them taking the greater part of the time allotted me.

1. *Of freedom in choice of studies.*

Let me first present what I may call a mechanical argument on this subject. A college with a prescribed curriculum must provide, say, sixteen hours a week of instruction for each class, or sixty-four hours a week in all for the four classes, without allowing for repetitions of lectures or lessons. Six or eight teachers can easily give all the instruction needed in such a college, if no repetitions are necessary. If the classes are so large that they need to be divided into two or more sections, more teachers must be employed. If a few extra or optional studies, outside of the curriculum, are provided, a further addition to the number of teachers must be made. Twenty teachers would, however, be a liberal allowance for any college of this type; and accordingly there are hundreds of American colleges at this moment with less than twenty teachers all told. Under the prescribed system it would be impossible for such a college to find work for more teachers, if it had them. Now there are eighty teachers employed this year in Harvard College, exclusive of laboratory assistants; and these eighty teachers give about four hundred and twenty-five hours of public instruction a week without any repetitions, not counting the very important instruction which many of them give in laboratories. It is impossible for any undergraduate in his four years to take more than a tenth part of the instruction given by the College; and since four fifths of this instruction is of a higher grade than any which can be given in a college with a prescribed curriculum, a diligent student would need about forty years to cover the present field; and during those years the field would enlarge quite beyond his powers of occupation. Since the student cannot take the whole of the instruction offered, it seems to be necessary to allow him to take a part. A college must either limit closely its teaching, or provide some mode of selecting studies for the individual student. The limitation of teaching is an intolerable alternative for any institution which aspires to become a university; for a university must try to teach every subject, above the grade of its admission requirements, for which there is any demand; and to teach it thoroughly enough to carry the advanced student to the confines of present knowledge, and make him capable of original research. These are the only limits which a university can properly set to its instruction—except indeed those rigorous limits which poverty imposes. The other alternative is selection or election of studies.

The elective system at Harvard has been sixty years in developing, and during fourteen of these years—from 1846 to 1860—the presidents and the majority of the faculty were not in favor of it; but they could find no way of escape from the dilemma which I have set before you. They could not deliberately reduce the amount of instruction offered, and election of studies in some degree was the inevitable alternative.

The practical question then is, At what age, and at what stage of his educational progress, can an American boy be offered free choice of studies? Or, in other words, At what age can an American boy best go to a free university? Before answering this question I will ask your attention to four preliminary observations.

1. The European boy goes to free universities at various ages from seventeen to twenty; and the American boy is decidedly more mature and more capable of taking care of himself than the European boy of like age.
2. The change from school to university ought to be made as soon as it would be better for the youth to associate with older students under a discipline suited to their age, than with younger pupils under a discipline suited to theirs—as soon, in short, as it would be better for the youth to be the youngest student in a university than the oldest boy in a school. The school might still do much for the youth; the university may as yet be somewhat too free for him: there must be a balancing of advantages against disadvantages; but the wise decision is to withdraw him betimes from a discipline which he is outgrowing, and put him under a discipline which he is to grow up to. When we think of putting a boy into college, our imaginations are apt to dwell upon the occasional and exceptional evil influences to which his new freedom will expose him, more than upon those habitual and prevailing influences of college companionship which will nourish his manliness and develop his virtue; just as we are apt to think of heredity chiefly as a means of transmitting vices and diseases, whereas it is normally the means of transmitting and accumulating infinitely various virtues and serviceable capacities.
3. A young man is much affected by the expectations which his elders entertain of him. If they expect him to behave like a child, his lingering

childishness will oftener rule his actions; if they expect him to behave like a man, his incipient manhood will oftener assert itself. The pretended parental or sham monastic regime of the common American college seems to me to bring out the childishness rather than the manliness of the average student; as is evidenced by the pranks he plays, the secret societies in which he rejoices, and the barbarous or silly customs which he accepts and transmits. The conservative argument is: a college must deal with the student as he is; he will be what he has been, namely, a thoughtless, aimless, lazy, and possibly vicious boy; therefore a policy which gives him liberty is impracticable. The progressive argument is: adapt college policy to the best students, and not to the worst; improve the policy, and in time the evil fruits of a mistaken policy will disappear. I would only urge at this point that a far-seeing educational policy must be based upon potentialities as well as actualities, upon things which may be reasonably hoped for, planned, and aimed at, as well as upon things which are.

4. The condition of secondary education is an important factor in our problem. It is desirable that the young men who are to enjoy university freedom should have already received at school a substantial training, in which the four great subdivisions of elementary knowledge—languages, history, mathematics, and natural science—were all adequately represented; but it must be admitted that this desirable training is now given in very few schools, and that in many parts of the country there are not secondary schools enough of even tolerable quality. For this condition of secondary education the colleges are in part responsible; for they have produced few good teachers, except for the ancient languages; and they have required for admission to college hardly anything but the elements of Greek, Latin, and mathematics. But how should this condition of things affect the policy of an institution which sees its way to obtain a reasonable number of tolerably prepared students: Shall we stop trying to create a university because the condition of secondary education in the country at large is unsatisfactory? The difficulty with that policy of inaction is that the reform and development of secondary education depend upon the right organization and conduct of universities. It is the old problem: Which was first created, an egg or a hen? In considering the relation of college life to school life, many people are confused by a misleading metaphor—that of a building. They say to themselves: on weak foundations no strong superstructure can be built; schools lay the foundations on which the university must build; therefore, if preparatory schools fail to do good work, no proper university work can subsequently be done. The analogy seems perfect,

> but has this fatal defect: education is a vital process, not a mechanical one. Let us, therefore, use an illustration drawn from a vital function, that of nutrition. A child has had poor milk as an infant, and is not well developed; therefore, when its teeth are cut, and it is ready for bread, meat, and oatmeal, you are to hold back this substantial diet, and give it the sweetened milk and water, and Mellin's Food, which would have suited it when a baby. The mental food of a boy has not been as nourishing and abundant as it should have been at school; therefore when he goes to college or university his diet must be that which he should have had at school, but missed. Education involves growth or development from within in every part; and metaphors drawn from the process of laying one stone upon another are not useful in educational discussions. Harvard College now finds itself able to get nearly three hundred tolerably prepared students every year from one hundred or more schools and private tutors scattered over the country; and she is only just beginning to reap the fruit of the changes in her own policy and discipline which the past eighteen years have wrought. Schools follow universities, and will be what universities make them.

With these preliminary suggestions I proceed to answer the question, At what age can an American boy best go to a university where choice of studies is free? and to defend my answer. I believe the normal age under reasonably favorable conditions to be eighteen. In the first place, I hold that the temperament, physical constitution, mental aptitudes, and moral quality of a boy are all well determined by the time he is eighteen years old. The potential man is already revealed. His capacities and incapacities will be perfectly visible to his teacher, or to any observant and intimate friend, provided that his studies at school have been fairly representative. If his historical studies have been limited to primers of Greek, Roman, and American history, his taste and capacity for historical study will not be known either to his teacher or to himself; if he has had no opportunity to study natural science, his powers in that direction will be quite unproved; but if the school course has been reasonably comprehensive, there need be no doubt as to the most profitable direction of his subsequent studies. The boy's future will depend greatly upon the influences, happy or unhappy, to which he is subjected; but given all favorable influences, his possibilities are essentially determined. The most fortunate intellectual influences will be within his reach, if he has liberty to choose the mental food which he can best assimilate. Secondly, at eighteen the American boy has passed the age when a compulsory external discipline is useful. Motives and inducements may be set vividly before him; he may be told that he must do so and so in order to win something which he desires or values; prizes and rewards near or remote may be held out to him; but he cannot be driven to any useful exercise of his mind. Thirdly, a well-instructed youth of eighteen can select for himself—not for any other boy, or for the fictitious universal boy but for himself alone—a better course of study than any college faculty, or any wise man who does not know him and his ancestors and his previous life, can possibly select for him. In choosing his course he will naturally seek aid from teachers and friends who have intimate knowledge of him, and he will act under the dominion of that intense conservatism which fortunately actuates civilized man in the whole matter of education, and under various other safeguards which nature and not arbitrary regulation provides. When a young man whom I never saw before asks me what studies he had better take in college, I am quite helpless, until he tells me what he likes and what he dislikes to study, what kinds of exertion are pleasurable to him, what sports he cares for, what reading interests him, what his parents and grandparents were in the world, and what he means to be. In short, I can only show him how to think out the problem for himself with such lights as he has and nobody else can have. The proposition that a boy of eighteen can choose his own studies, with the natural helps, more satisfactorily than anybody else can choose them for him, seems at first sight absurd; but I believe it to be founded upon the nature of things, and it is also for me a clear result of observation. I will state first the argument from the nature of things, and then describe my own observations.

Every youth of eighteen is an infinitely complex organization, the duplicate of which neither does nor ever will exist. His inherited traits are different from those of every other human being; his environment has been different from that of every other child; his passions, emotions, hopes, and desires were never before associated in any other creature just as they are in him; and his will-force is aroused, stimulated, exerted, and exhausted in ways wholly his own. The infinite variety of form and feature, which we know human bodies to be capable of, presents but a faint image of the vastly deeper diversities of the minds and characters which are lodged in these unlike shells. To discern and take due account of these diversities no human insight or wisdom is sufficient, unless the spontaneous inclinations, natural preferences, and easiest habitual activities of each individual are given play. It is for the happiness of the individual and the benefit of society alike that these mental diversities should be cultivated, not suppressed. The individual enjoys most that intellectual labor for which he is most fit; and society is best served when every man's peculiar skill, faculty, or aptitude is developed and utilized to the highest possible degree. The presumption is, therefore, against uniformity in education, and in favor of diversity at the earliest possible moment. What determines that moment? To my thinking, the limit of compulsory uniform instruction should be determined by the elementary quality and recognized universal utility of the subjects of such instruction. For instance, it is unquestionable that every child needs to know how to read, write, and, to a moderate extent, cipher. Therefore primary schools may have a uniform programme. One might naturally suppose that careful study of the mother-tongue and its literature would be considered a uniform need for all youth; but as a matter of fact there is no agreement to this effect. The English language and literature have hardly yet won a place for themselves in American schools. Only the elements of two foreign languages and the elements of algebra and geometry can be said to be generally recognized as indispensable to the proper training of all young people who are privileged to study beyond their seventeenth year. There is no consent as to the uniform desirableness of the elements of natural science, and there is much difference of opinion about the selection of the two foreign languages, the majority of educated people supposing two dead languages to be preferable, a minority thinking that living languages are permissible. The limit of that elementary knowledge, of which by common consent all persons who are to be highly educated stand in need, is therefore a narrow one, easily to be reached and passed, under respectable instruction, by any youth of fair ability before he is eighteen years old. There, at least, ceases justifiable uniformity in education. There, at least, election of studies should begin; and the safest guides to a wise choice will be the taste, inclination, and special capacity of each individual. When it comes to the choice of a profession, everybody knows that the only wisdom is to follow inclination. In my view, the only wisdom in determining those liberal studies which may be most profitably pursued after eighteen is to follow inclination. Hence it is only the individual youth who can select that course of study which will most profit him, because it will most interest him. The very fact of choice goes far to secure the cooperation of his will.

I have already intimated that there exist certain natural guides and safeguards for every youth who is called upon in a free university to choose his own studies. Let us see what these natural aids are. In the first place, he cannot help taking up a subject which he has already studied about where he left it off, and every new subject at the beginning and not at the middle. Secondly, many subjects taught at the university involve other subjects, which must therefore be studied first. Thus, no one can get far in physics without being familiar with trigonometry and analytic geometry; chemical analysis presupposes acquaintance with general chemistry, and paleontology acquaintance with botany and zoology; no one can study German philosophy to advantage unless he can read German, and no student can profitably discuss practical economic problems until he has mastered the elementary principles of political economy. Every advanced course, whether in language, philosophy, history, mathematics, or science, presupposes acquaintance with some elementary course or courses. Thirdly, there is a prevailing tendency on the part of every competent student to carry far any congenial subject once entered upon. To repress this most fortunate tendency is to make real scholarship impossible. So effective are these natural safeguards against fickleness and inconsecutiveness in the choice of studies, that artificial regulation is superfluous.

I give, in the next place, some results of my own observation upon the working of an elective system; and that you may have my credentials before you I will describe briefly my opportunities of observation. I had experience as an undergraduate of a college course almost wholly required; for I happened upon nearly the lowest stage to which the elective system in Harvard College ever fell, after its initiation in 1825. During the nine years from 1854 to 1863 I became intimately acquainted with the working of this mainly prescribed curriculum from the point of view of a tutor and assistant professor who had a liking for administrative details. After a separation from the University of six years, two of which were spent in Europe as a student and four at the Massachusetts Institute of Technology as a professor, I went back as president in 1869 to find a tolerably broad elective system already under way. The wishes of the governing boards and external circumstances all favoring it, the system was rapidly developed. Required studies were gradually abolished or pushed back; so that first the Senior year was made completely elective, then the Junior, then the Sophomore, and finally in June last the Freshman year was made chiefly elective. No required studies now remain except the writing of English, the elements of either French or German (one of these two languages being required for admission), and a few lectures on chemistry and physics. None of the former exclusive staples, Greek, Latin, mathematics, logic, and metaphysics, are required, and no particular combinations or selections of courses are recommended by the faculty. I have therefore had ample opportunity to observe at Harvard the working of almost complete prescription, of almost complete freedom, and of all intermediate methods. In Europe I studied the free university method; and at the Institute of Technology I saw the system—excellent for technical schools—of several well-defined courses branching from a common stock of uniformly prescribed studies.

The briefest form in which I can express the general result of my observation is this: I have never known a student of any capacity to select for himself a set of studies covering four years which did not apparently possess more theoretical and practical merit for his case than the required curriculum of my college days. Every prescribed curriculum is necessarily elementary from beginning to end, and very heterogeneous. Such is the press of subjects that no one subject can possibly be carried beyond its elements; no teacher, however learned and enthusiastic, can have any advanced pupils; and no scholar, however competent and eager, can make serious attainments in any single subject. Under an elective system the great majority of students use their liberty to pursue some subject or subjects with a reasonable degree of thoroughness. This concentration upon single lines develops advanced teaching, and results in a general raising of the level of instruction. Students who have decided taste for any particular subject wisely devote a large part of their time to that subject and its congeners. Those who have already decided upon their profession wisely choose subjects which are related to, or underlie, their future professional studies; thus, the future physician will advantageously give a large share of his college course to French, German, chemistry, physics, and biology; while the future lawyer will study logic, ethics, history, political economy, and the use of English in argumentative writing and speaking. Among the thousands of individual college courses determined by the choice of the student in four successive years, which the records of Harvard College now preserve, it is rare to find one which does not exhibit an intelligible sequence of studies. It should be understood in this connection that all the studies which are allowed to count toward the A.B. at Harvard are liberal or pure, no technical or professional studies being admissible.

Having said thus much about the way in which an American student will use freedom in the choice of studies, I desire to point out that a young American must enjoy the privileges of university life between eighteen and twenty-two, if at all. From two thirds to three fourths of college graduates go into professions or employments which require of them elaborate special preparation. The medical student needs four years of professional training, the law student at least three, the good teacher and the skilful architect quite as much. Those who enter the service of business corporations, or go into business for themselves, have the business to learn—a process which ordinarily takes several years. If a young man takes his A.B. at twenty-two, he can hardly hope to begin the practice of his profession before he is twenty-six. That is quite late enough. It is clearly impossible, therefore, that the American university should be constructed on top of the old-fashioned American college. The average Freshman at Harvard is eighteen and two thirds years old when he enters, and at the majority of colleges he is older still. For the next three or four years he must have freedom to choose among liberal studies, if he is ever to enjoy that inestimable privilege.

Two common objections to an elective system shall next have our attention. The first is often put in the form of a query. Election of studies may be all very well for conscientious or ambitious students, or for those who have a strong taste for certain studies; but what becomes, under such a system, of the careless, indifferent, lazy boys who have no bent or intellectual ambition of any sort? I answer with a similar query: What became of such boys under the uniform compulsory system? Did they get any profit to speak of under that regime? Not within my observation. It really does not make much difference what these unawakened minds dawdle with. There is, however, much more chance that such young men will get aroused from their lethargy under an elective system than under a required. When they follow such faint promptings of desire as they feel, they at least escape the sense of grievance and repugnance which an arbitrary assignment to certain teachers and certain studies often creates. An elective system does not mean liberty to do nothing. The most indifferent student must pass a certain number of examinations every year. He selects perhaps those subjects in which he thinks he can pass the best examinations within the smallest amount of labor; but in those very subjects the instruction will be on a higher plane than it can ever reach under a compulsory system, and he will get more benefit from them than he would from other subjects upon which he put the same amount of labor but attained less success. It is an important principle in education, from primary school to university, that the greater the visible attainment for a given amount of labor the better; and this rule applies quite forcibly to a weak student as to a strong one. Feeble or inert students are considerably influenced in choosing their studies by the supposed quality of the teachers whom they will meet. As a rule they select the very teachers who are likely to have the most influence with them, being guided by traditions received from older students of their sort. It is the unanimous opinion of the teachers at Cambridge that more and better work is got from this class of students under the elective system than was under the required.

Having said thus much about the effects of free choice of studies upon the unpromising student, I must add that the policy of an institution of education, of whatever grade, ought never to be determined by the needs of the least capable students; and that a university should aim at meeting the wants of the best students at any rate, and the wants of inferior students only so far as it can meet them without impairing the privileges of the best. A uniform curriculum, by enacting superficiality and prohibiting thoroughness, distinctly sacrifices the best scholars to the average. Free choice of studies gives the young genius the fullest scope without impairing the chances of the drone and the dullard.

The second objection with which I wish to deal is this: free choice implies that there are no studies which are recognized as of supreme merit, so that every young man unquestionably ought to pursue them. Can this be? Is it possible that the accumulated wisdom of the race cannot prescribe with certainty the studies which will best develop the human mind in general between the ages of eighteen and twenty-two? At first it certainly seems strange that we have to answer no; but when we reflect how very brief the acquaintance of the race has been with the great majority of the subjects which are now taught in a university the negative answer seems less surprising. Out of the two hundred courses of instruction which stand on the list of Harvard University this year it would be difficult to select twenty which could have been given at the beginning of this century with the illustrations, materials, and methods now considered essential to the educational quality of the course. One realizes more easily this absence of accumulated experience on considering that all the natural sciences, with comparative philology, political economy, and history, are practically new subjects, that all mathematics is new except the elements of arithmetic, algebra, and geometry, that the recent additions to ethics and metaphysics are of vast extent, and that the literatures of the eighteenth and nineteenth centuries have great importance in several European languages. The materials and methods of university education always have been, and always will be, changing from generation to generation. We think, perhaps with truth, that the nineteenth century has been a period of unprecedented growth and progress; but every century has probably witnessed an unprecedented advance in civilization, simply because the process is cumulative, if no catastrophes arrest it. It is one of the most important functions of universities to store up the accumulated knowledge of the race, and so to use these stores that each successive generation of youth shall start with all the advantages which their predecessors have won. Therefore a university, while not neglecting the ancient treasures of learning, has to keep a watchful eye upon the new fields of discovery, and has to invite its students to walk in new-made as well as in long-trodden paths. Concerning the direct educational influence of all these new subjects the race cannot be said to have much accumulated wisdom.

One presumption of considerable scope may, however, be said to be established by experience. In every new field of knowledge the mental powers of the adventurers and discoverers found full play and fruitful exercise. Some rare human mind or minds must have laboriously developed each new subject of study. It may fairly be presumed that the youth will find some strenuous exercise of his faculties in following the masters into any field which it taxed their utmost powers to explore and describe. To study the conquests of great minds in any field of knowledge must be good training for young minds of kindred tastes and powers. That all branches of sound knowledge are of equal dignity and equal educational value for mature students is the only hopeful and tenable view in our day. Long ago it became quite impossible for one mind to compass more than an insignificant fraction of the great sum of acquired knowledge.

Before I leave the subject of election of studies, let me point out that there is not a university of competent resources upon the continent of Europe in which complete freedom of studies has not long prevailed; and that Oxford and Cambridge have recently provided an almost complete liberty for their students. In our own country respectable colleges now offer a considerable proportion of elective studies, and as a rule the greater their resources in teachers, collections, and money, the more liberal their application of the elective principle. Many colleges, however, still seem to have but a halting faith in the efficacy of the principle, and our educated public has but just begun to appreciate its importance. So fast as American institutions acquire the resources and powers of European universities, they will adopt the methods proper to universities wherever situate. At present our best colleges fall very far short of European standards in respect to number of teachers, and consequently to amplitude of teaching.

As yet we have no university in America—only aspirants to that eminence. All the more important is it that we should understand the conditions under which a university can be developed—the most indispensable of which is freedom in choice of studies.

2. *A university must give its students opportunity to win distinction in special subjects or lines of study.*

The uniform curriculum led to a uniform degree, the first scholar and the last receiving the same diploma. A university cannot be developed on that plan. It must provide academic honors at graduation for distinguished attainments in single subjects. These honors encourage students to push far on single lines; whence arises a demand for advanced instruction in all departments in which honors can be won, and this demand, taken in connection with the competition which naturally springs up between different departments, stimulates the teachers, who in turn stimulate their pupils. The elaborate directions given by each department to candidates for honors are so many definite pieces of advice to students who wish to specialize their work. It is an incidental advantage of the system that the organization of departments of instruction is promoted by it. The teachers of Latin, of history, or of philosophy, find it necessary to arrange their courses in orderly sequence, to compare their methods and their results, and to enrich and diversify as much as possible the instruction which they collectively offer. Many European universities, but especially the English, offer honors, or prizes, or both of these inducements, for distinguished merit in specialties; and the highly valued degree of Ph.D. in Germany is a degree given for large attainments in one or two branches of knowledge, with mention of the specialty. The Harvard faculty announced their system of honors in 1866–67, and they certainly never passed a more effective piece of legislation. In 1879 they devised a lesser distinction at graduation called honorable mention, which has also worked very well. To get honors in any department ordinarily requires a solid year and a half's work; to get honorable mention requires about half that time. The important function of all such devices is to promote specialization of work and therefore to develop advanced instruction. It is unnecessary to point out how absolutely opposed to such a policy the uniform prescription of a considerable body of elementary studies must be.

3. A university must permit its students, in the main, to govern themselves.

It must have a large body of students, else many of the numerous courses of highly specialized instruction will find no hearers, and the students themselves will not feel that very wholesome influence which comes from observation of and contact with large numbers of young men from different nations, States, schools, families, sects, parties, and condition of life. In these days a university is best placed in or near the seat of a considerable population; so that its officers and students can always enjoy the various refined pleasures, and feel alike the incitements and the restraints, of a highly cultivated society. The universities of Rome, Paris, Vienna, Berlin, Leipsic, Christiania, Madrid, and Edinburgh forcibly illustrate both of these advantages. These conditions make it practically impossible for a university to deal with its students on any principle of seclusion, either in a village or behind walls and bars. Fifteen hundred able-bodied young men living in buildings whose doors stand open night and day, or in scattered lodging-houses, cannot be mechanically protected from temptations at the university any more than at the homes from which they came.

Their protection must be within them. They must find it in memory of home, in pure companionship, in hard work, in intellectual ambition, religious sentiment, and moral purpose. A sense of personal freedom and responsibility reinforces these protecting influences, while the existence of a supervising authority claiming large powers which it has no effective means of exercising weakens them. The *in loco parentis* theory is an ancient fiction which ought no longer to deceive anybody. No American college, wherever situated, possesses any method of discipline which avails for the suppression or exclusion of vice. The vicious student can find all means of indulgence in the smallest village, and the worst vices are the stillest. It is a distinct advantage of the genuine university method that it does not pretend to maintain any parental or monastic discipline over its students, but frankly tells them that they must govern themselves. The moral purpose of a university's policy should be to train young men to self-control and self-reliance through liberty. It is not the business of a university to train men for those functions in which implicit obedience is of the first importance. On the contrary, it should train men for those occupations in which self-government, independence, and originating power are preeminently needed. Let no one imagine that a young man is in peculiar moral danger at an active and interesting university. Far from it. Such a university is the safest place in the world for young men who have anything in them—far safer than counting-room, shop, factory, farm, barrack, forecastle, or ranch. The student lives in a bracing atmosphere; books engage him; good companionships invite him; good occupations defend him; helpful friends surround him; pure ideals are held up before him; ambition spurs him; honor beckons him.

CHAPTER 20

The New Departure in College Education, Being a Reply to President Eliot's Defence of It

James McCosh

INTRODUCTION TO MCCOSH'S ARTICLE

There was a self-consciously rearguard resistance to the institution of the elective system. Two conservative educators in particular criticized the change in the philosophy of undergraduate education: Noah Porter, the president of Yale, and James McCosh, the president of Princeton. Porter gave his reasons in his inaugural address, in 1871: "The majority of undergraduate students have neither the maturity nor the data which qualify them to judge of the relative value of studies or their bearing on future employment," he said. He was aiming at one of the core principles backing Charles William Eliot's embrace of electives: the belief that young people are the best judges of their own interests. ("The manners and customs of the Yale Faculty are those of a porcupine on the defensive," Eliot commented in a letter to Daniel Gilman, the president of Johns Hopkins, in 1880.)

McCosh, too, was skeptical about students' ability to discipline themselves. Under a system that allows them to choose their own course of study, he argued in "The New Departure in College Education," in 1885, students "can choose the branches which will cost them the least study, and put themselves under the popular professors who give them the highest grades with the least labor." In other words, students will cherry-pick the easiest courses. (The term back then was "snap.")

In the end, Porter and McCosh were obliged to open the curricular doors at Yale and Princeton to electives. And the great elective debate did end with the defeat of the adherents of the doctrine of in loco parentis, which is the doctrine to which Porter and McCosh's objections belong. By the beginning of the twentieth century, the elective system had become an established feature of the college curriculum. (At Princeton, in 1900, more than half the curriculum was still prescribed; Yale finally adopted an elective system in 1904.)

But there was pushback. For McCosh was not wrong. On the contrary: a self-study at Harvard, carried out in 1902, when expository writing was the only course required for graduation, discovered that students overenrolled in introductory lecture classes, that most of them failed to take a wide variety of courses, and that the amount of time spent studying was "discreditably small." Fifty-five percent of the class of 1898 had taken only introductory courses for four years. Students were clearly taking advantage of the curricular freedom Eliot had given them, and using their bonus time to pursue social activities rather than, as Eliot had imagined, to explore new areas of intellectual interest.

The reaction against electives was one of the things that led to Eliot's replacement as president of Harvard by A. Lawrence Lowell, in 1910, and to the widespread adoption of the major, or concentration. (The major seems to have been introduced in 1885 by David Starr Jordan, then the young president of Indiana University, later the first president of Stanford.) The major was usually combined with a distribution requirement, which forced students to take courses in every major area of academic study—the pedagogically minimalist "breadth and depth" model. These reforms did not revive the old classical curriculum, but they put some bones into the undergraduate experience.

THE NEW DEPARTURE IN COLLEGE EDUCATION, BEING A REPLY TO PRESIDENT ELIOT'S DEFENCE OF IT (1885)

I have been drawn into this three-cornered debate by no merit or demerit of mine.[1] I was told by the Nineteenth Century Club that the President of Harvard was to advocate what was called his "new departure," and I was invited to criticize it. I have noticed with considerable anxiety that departure as going on for years past without parents or the public noticing it. I am glad that things have come to a crisis. Fathers and mothers and the friends of education will now know what is proposed, what is in fact going on, and will have to decide forthwith whether they are to fall in with and encourage it, or are to oppose it.

I asked first what the question was. President Eliot has shaped it as follows: "In a university the student must choose his studies and govern himself." I saw at once that the question thus announced was large and loose, vague and ambiguous, plausible to the ear, but with no definite meaning. But it commits its author to a positive position and gives me room to defend a great and good cause. The form is showy but I can expose it; I can prick the bubble so that all may know how little matter is inside. On the one hand I am sorry that the defence of solid and high education should have devolved on me rather than on some more gifted advocate. But on the other hand I feel it to be a privilege that I am invited to oppose proposals which are fitted, without the people as yet seeing it, to throw back in America (as Bacon expresses it) "The Advancement of Learning."

I will not allow any one (without protest) to charge me with being antiquated or old-fashioned or behind the age—I may be an old man but I cherish a youthful spirit. For sixteen years I was a professor in the youngest and one of the most advanced universities in Great Britain, and I have now been sixteen years in an American college, and in both I have labored to elevate the scholarship. I act on the principle that every new branch of what has shown itself to be true learning is to be introduced into a college. My friends in America have encouraged me by generously giving me millions of money to carry out this idea. I am as much in favor of progress as President Eliot, but I go on in a different, I believe a better way. I adopt the new, I retain what is good in the old. I am disappointed, I am grieved when I find another course pursued which allows, which encourages, which tempts young men in their caprice to choose easy subjects, and which are not fitted to enlarge or refine the mind, to produce scholars, or to send forth the great body of the students as educated gentlemen.

Freedom is the catch-word of this new departure. It is a precious and an attractive word. But, O Liberty!, what crimes and cruelties have been perpetrated in thy name! It is a bid for popularity. An entering Freshman will be apt to cheer when he hears it—the prospect is so pleasant. The leader in this departure will have many followers. The student infers from the language that he can study what he pleases. I can tell you what he will possibly or probably choose. Those who are in the secrets of colleges know how skillful certain students are in choosing their subjects. They can choose the branches which will cost them least study, and put themselves under the popular professors who give them the highest grades with the least labor. I once told a student in an advanced stage of his course, "If you had shown as much skill in pursuing your studies as in choosing the easiest subjects you would have been the first man in your class." I am for freedom quite as much as Dr. Eliot is, but it is for freedom regulated by law. I am for liberty, but not licentiousness, which always ends in servitude.

I am to follow the President of Harvard in the three roads which he has taken; placing positions of mine face to face with his:

I. FREEDOM IN CHOOSING STUDIES.
II. FREEDOM IN CHOOSING SPECIALTIES.
III. FREEDOM IN GOVERNMENT.

I.

Freedom in Choosing Studies. I am for freedom, but it must be within carefully defined limits. First, a young man should be free to enter a university or not to enter it. He is to be free to choose his department in that university, say Law or Medicine, or the Academic terminating in the Bachelor or Master's Degree. But, having made his choice, is he to have all possible freedom ever after? At this point the most liberal advocate of liberty will be obliged to tell the student, "We are now required to lay some restraints upon you," and the youth finds his liberty is at an end. He has to take certain studies and give a certain amount of time to them, say, according to the Harvard model, to select four topics. He goes in for Medicine: he may make his quartette Physical Geography, which tells what climate is; and Art, which teaches us to paint the human frame; and Music, which improves the voice; and Lectures on the Drama, which show us how to assume noble attitudes. These seem more agreeable to him than Anatomy and Physiology, than Surgery and Materia Medica, which present corpses and unpleasant odors. I tell you that, though this youth should get a diploma written on parchment, I would not, however ill, call him in to prescribe to me, as I might not be quite sure whether his medicines would kill or cure me. Or the intention of the youth is Engineering in order to make or drive a steam engine, and he does not take Mathematics, or Mechanics, or Graphics, or Geodesy; but as unlimited choice is given him, he prefers drawing and fieldwork—when the weather is fine, and two departments of gymnastics—now so well taught in your colleges—boxing and wrestling. I tell you I am not to travel by the railway he has constructed. But he has a higher aim: he is to take a course in the Liberal Arts and expects a Master's Degree; but Greek and Mathematics and Physics and Mental Philosophy are all old and waxing older, and he takes French to enable him to travel in Europe, and Lectures on Goethe to make him a German scholar, and a Pictorial History of the age of Louis XIV, and of the Theatre in ancient and modern times. This is a good year's work, and he can take a like course in each of the four years; and if he be in Yale or Princeton College, he will in Spring and Fall substitute Base Ball and Foot Ball, and exhibit feats more wonderful than were ever performed in the two classical countries, Greece and Rome, at their famous Olympian Games and Bull Fights.

I have presented this designedly rude picture to show that there must be some limits put to the freedom of choice in studies. The able leader of the new departure, with the responsibilities of a great College upon him, and the frank and honest gentleman, who has such a dread of a Fetish—the creature of his own imagination—will be ready to admit that in every department of a University there should be a well considered and a well devised curriculum of study. It is one of the highest and most important functions of the governing bodies to construct such a scheme. It should have in it two essential powers or properties.

First, there should be branches required of all students who pursue the full course and seek a degree. This is done in such departments as Engineering and Medicine and should be done in Arts. The obligatory branches should be wisely selected. They should all be fitted to enlarge or refine the mind. They should be fundamental, as forming the basis on which other knowledge is built. They should be disciplinary, as training the mind for further pursuits. Most of them should have stood the test of time and reared scholars in ages past. There will be found to be a wonderful agreement among educated men of high tastes as to what these should be.

There should be included in them the eight studies on which examinations are held in order to entrance into Harvard College. These are 1, English; 2, Greek; 3, Latin; 4, German; 5, French; 6, History; 7, Mathematics; 8, Physical Science. This is the scheme of preparatory studies just issued by Harvard. It seems to me to require too much from our schools. It will prevent many teachers who have hitherto sent students to college from doing so any more. Teachers in smaller towns and country districts will have to look to this. If the scheme is carried out fewer young men will come up to our colleges from such places. They will find that they cannot get French and German and physical apparatus in the schools available to them. Some of the branches had better be reserved for college, where they will be taught more effectively. But passing this by as not just to our present point, I put all these cardinal studies in the branches which should be required in a college.

In the farther courses of a college other obligatory studies should be added, such as Biology, including Botany and Zoology, Geology, Political Economy or better Social Science, and at least three branches of Mental Science, Psychology, Logic, and Ethics. All these by a wise arrangement could be taught in the three or four years at school and the four years of college. They should be judiciously spread over the years of school and college training; a certain number of them in each successive year for every student. They should advance with the age and progress of the student. They should follow one another in logical order from the more elementary to the higher, which presuppose the lower. Thus Mathematics should come before Physics, and Biology before Geology, and Psychology before Logic and Ethics.

Education is essentially the training of the mind—as the word *educare* denotes—the drawing forth of the faculties which God has given us. This it should especially be in a University, in a *Studium Generale*, as it used to be called. The powers of mind are numerous and varied, the senses, the memory, the fancy, judgment, reasoning, conscience, the feelings, the will; the mathematical, the metaphysical, the mechanical, the poetical, the prosaic (quite as useful as any); and all these should be cultivated, the studies necessary to do so should be provided, and the student required so far to attend to them, that the young man by exercise may know what powers he has and the mental frame be fully developed. To accomplish this end the degrees of Bachelor of Arts and of Master of Arts were instituted. These titles have acquired a meaning. For centuries past tens of thousands of eager youths have been yearly seeking for them and the attainments implied in them. True, the standard adopted in some colleges has been low—some who have got the diploma could not read the Latin in which it is written; still it has a certain prestige and a considerable attractive power. It indicates, as to the great body of those who possess it, that they have some acquaintance with elevated themes, that in short they have some culture. I do not wish to have this stimulus withdrawn. I have been laboring for the last thirty-two years to elevate the requirements for the degree. But let it retain its meaning and carry out its meaning thoroughly. Let it be an evidence that the possessor of it has some knowledge of literature, science, and philosophy.

I have no objection that other degrees be instituted, such as Bachelor of Literature, Bachelor of Science, but only on one condition, that examinations be deep, that they be rigid, that they imply a knowledge of the principles as well as of the details of the branches taught, that they cultivate the mind and elevate the tastes as well as fit men for professions. But let us retain in the meanwhile the old Bachelor and Master Degrees, only putting a new life into them. They should not be given to one who knows merely English and German, or one who knows merely chemistry and physics, still less to one who knows merely music and painting. Eminence in these has no right to assume, or in fact steal, the old title. Let each kind of degree have its own meaning and people will value it accordingly. But let A.B. and A.M. abide to attract youths to high general scholarship.

Under this Academic Degree I would allow a certain amount of choice of studies, such as could not be tolerated in professional departments, as Law or

Medicine. But there are branches which no candidate for the degree should be allowed to avoid. There should be English, which I agree with President Eliot in regarding as about the most essential of all branches, it being taught in a scientific manner. There should be Modern Languages, but there should also be Classics. A taste and a style are produced by the study of the Greek and Latin with their literatures, which are expressively called Classic. It may be difficult to define, but we all feel the charm of it. If we lose this there is nothing in what is called our Modem Education to make up for the loss. President Eliot has a high opinion of German Universities, but the eminent men in their greatest University, that of Berlin, have testified that a far higher training is given in the Classical Gymnasia than in the scientific Real Schule.[2]

There should be physical science, but there should also be mental and moral science required of all. In knowing other things our young men should be taught to know themselves. When our students are instructed only in matter they are apt to conclude that there is nothing but matter. Our colleges should save our promising youths, the hope of the coming age and ages, from materialism with its degrading consequences. We must show them that man has a soul with lofty powers of reason and conscience and free will, which make him immortal and enable him so far to penetrate the secrets of nature, and by which he can rise to the knowledge of God.

We in Princeton believe in a Trinity of studies: in Language and Literature, in Science, and in Philosophy. Every educated man should know so much of each of these. Without this, man's varied faculties are not trained, his nature is not fully developed and may become malformed.

A college should give what is best to its students, and it should not tempt them to what is lower when the higher can be had. Harvard boasts that it gives two hundred choices to its students, younger and older.[3] I confess that I have had some difficulty in understanding her catalogue. I would rather study the whole Cosmos. It has a great many perplexities, which I can compare only to the cycles, epicycles, eccentricities of the old astronomy, so much more complex than that of Newton. An examination of students upon it would be a better test of a clear head than some of their subjects, such as "French Plays and Novels." As I understand it, one seeking a degree, may, in his free will choose the following course:

In Sophomore Year—

1. French Literature of the Seventeenth Century.
2. Mediæval and Modern European History.

3. Elementary Course in Fine Art, with collateral instruction in Water-coloring.
4. Counterpoint (in music).

In Junior Year —

1. French Literature of the Eighteenth Century.
2. Early Mediæval History.
3. Botany.
4. History of Music.

In Senior Year—

1. French Literature of the Nineteenth Century.
2. Elementary Spanish.
3. Greek Art.
4. Free Thematic Music.[4]

There are twenty such dilettanti courses which may be taken in Harvard. I cannot allow that this is an advance in scholarship. If this be the modern education, I hold that the old is better. I would rather send a young man, in whom I was interested, to one of the old-fashioned colleges of the country, where he would be constrained to study Latin, Greek, Mathematics, Rhetoric, Physics, Logic, Ethics, and Political Economy, and I am persuaded that his mind would thereby be better trained and he himself prepared to do higher and more important work in life. From the close of Freshman year on it is perfectly practicable for a student to pass through Harvard and receive the degree of Bachelor of Arts, without taking any course in Latin, Greek, Mathematics, Chemistry, Physics, Astronomy, Geology, Logic, Psychology, Ethics, Political Economy, German, or even English! (If, as President Eliot insists, a knowledge of our mother-tongue is the true basis of culture, what is to be said of this?)

Secondly. It should be an essential feature of the course for a degree that the attendance of the student on lectures and recitations should be obligatory. This is a very important matter. The student may have freedom in his choice, but having made his election he should be bound to attend on the instruction imparted. He should not be allowed to attend the one day and stay away the next. A professor should not be subjected to the disadvantage of only a portion of his students, say a half or a third, being present at any one lecture, and of the students who attend, not being the same continuously. Parents living far away from the college-seat should have some security that their sons professing to be at college are not all the winter skating on the ice, or shooting canvasback-ducks on Chesapeake Bay.

But it is said that if a student can stand an examination, it is no matter where he gets his knowledge. There is an enormous fallacy lurking here. I admit that a youth may make himself a scholar without being at a college or submitting to its examinations. But if he goes to college let him take all its advantages. One of these is to be placed under a continuous course of instruction in weekly, almost daily, intercourse with his professors, keeping him at his work and encouraging him in it. It is thus that the academic taste, thus that the student spirit with its hard work is created and fostered.

I have had thorough means of becoming acquainted with those systems in which there is no required attendance; and I testify that they do not tend to train high scholars. Everything depending on a final examination, the student is sure to be tempted to what is called cramming. A student once told me what this led to in his own experience. In five of the branches taught to his class, he spread his daily studies over the year; but in one he trusted to cramming. I said to him, "Tell me honestly what is the issue." He answered, "In the five branches I remember everything and could stand another examination to-day, but in the one—it happened to be botany—it is only four weeks since I was examined on it, but my mind is a blank on the whole subject."

I know that in Germany they produce scholars without requiring a rigid attendance, and I rather think that in a few American colleges, they are aping this German method, thinking to produce equally diligent students. They forget that the Germans have one powerful safeguard which we have not in America. For all offices in Church and State there is an examination by high scholars following the college course. A young man cannot get an office as clergyman, as teacher, as postmaster, till he is passed by that terrible examining bureau, and if he is turned by them his prospects in life are blasted.[5] Let the State of Massachusetts pass a law like the Prussian, and Harvard may then relax attendance, and the State will do what the colleges have neglected to do.[6]

II.

Specialties in Study.—Men have special talents, and so they should have special studies provided for them. They are to have special vocations in life, and college youth should so far be prepared for them. Every student should have Obligatory studies, but he should also be allowed Elective studies. The branches of knowledge are now so numerous and literature is so wide and varied, that no one can master it all; should he try to do so, he would only be "a jack of all trades and a master of none."

The student should have two kinds of electives provided for him. He may be allowed to take subjects which could not be required of all, such, for example, as Sanscrit, Anglo-Saxon, the Semitic Tongues, and in science, Histology and Physical Geography. No college should make these obligatory, and yet considerable numbers of students would prize them much and get great benefit from them, to fit them for their farther study and life-work. Or, the student, after taking certain elementary branches, should have higher forms of the same provided for him, and be encouraged to take them. Of all the rudimentary branches or cardinal studies, there should be a course or courses required of all in order to make them educated gentlemen, but there should be advanced courses—Electives, to produce high scholars in all branches, literary, linguistic, scientific, philosophic. All students should know several of the highest languages, ancient and modern, but there should be advanced linguistic studies, and especially a science of Comparative Language. I defy you to make all master Quaternions, or Quantics, or Functions, but these should be in the college for a select few. All should be taught the fundamental laws of the human mind, but there should also be a number entering into the depths and climbing the heights, of the Greek, the Scotch, and the German philosophies.

I hold that in a college with the variety there should be a unity. The circle of the sciences should have a wide circumference but also a fixed centre. In every year there should be certain primary and radical studies required of every student, with all the while a diversity in his electives. This I take the liberty of saying is the difference between Harvard and Princeton. In Harvard there are now in no year any studies obligatory on all except a part of Freshman year studies—everything is scattered like the star dust out of which worlds are formed. Greek is not obligatory; Mathematics are not obligatory; Logic and Ethics are not obligatory. In Princeton a number of disciplinary branches are required, and so many are required in each year to give us a central sun with rotating planets. In Nature, as Herbert Spencer has shown, there is differentiation which scatters, but there is also concentration which holds things together. There should be the same in higher education. In a college there may be, there should be specialists, but not mere specialists, who are sure to be narrow, partial, malformed, one-sided, and are apt to become conceited, prejudiced, and intolerant. The other day a gymnast showed me his upper arm with the muscle large and hard as a mill-stone. It is a picture of the mental monstrosities produced by certain kinds of education. The tanner insists that "there is nothing like leather," and the literateur that there is nothing like language; while the mathematician assures you that there is nothing to be believed except what can be demonstrated; leading Goethe to say, "As if, forsooth, things only exist when they can be mathematically demonstrated. It would be foolish in a man not to believe in his mistress' love because she could not prove it to him mathematically; she can mathematically prove her dowry but not her love."

Dr. Eliot tells us he has found great difficulties in combining the Prescribed and the Elective Courses. In my thirty-two years' college teaching I have met with no such difficulty. On the contrary I have found them working in harmony. Thus I have found the Prescribed study in Greek helping me in the Elective History of Philosophy.[7]

It is now shown that all science is correlated, and every one thing depends on every other. Humboldt had his "Cosmos," and Mr. Grove[8] his "Correlation of the Forces," and the Duke of Argyll[9] has his "Unity of Nature." Nature is a system like the solar, with a sun in the centre and planets and satellites all around, held together by a gravitating power which keeps each in its proper place, and all shining on each other. You cannot study any one part comprehensively without so far knowing the others. In like manner, all the parts of a good college curriculum should be connected in an organic whole. Make a man a mere specialist and the chance is he will not reach the highest eminence as a specialist. The youth most likely to make discoveries is one who has studied collateral subjects; the well gushes out at a certain point because the rains have descended on a large surface and entered the earth, and must find an outlet.

I may here point out the evils little noticed arising from a boy having too many choices; they say two hundred in Harvard. I believe that comparatively few young men know what their powers are when they enter college. Many do not yet know what their undeveloped faculties are; quite as many imagine that they have talents which they do not possess. Fatal mistakes may arise from a youth of sixteen or eighteen committing himself to a narrow-gauge line of study, and he finds when it is too late that he should have taken a broader road.

A young man, we may suppose, when he enters college leaves out Greek, attracted by a popular teacher of French. When he has done so he finds, as he comes to junior year, that a voice, as it were, from God, calls him to preach the gospel of salvation. Then he comes to see his mistake, for if he has to be an expounder of Scripture, he must know the language of the New Testament, and to attain this he must go back two or three years to school, and, unwilling to do this, he gives up studying for the ministry. The Churches of Christ will do well to look to this new departure, for they may find that they have fewer candidates for the office of the ministry. The Colleges may have to look to this, for the churches furnish to them the most constant supply of students. For myself, I fear that the issue will be an unfortunate division of colleges into Christian and infidel.

A like result may follow from other unfortunate choices, as we say, from young men "mistaking their trade." One who might have turned out a splendid teacher devotes himself to metaphysics and neglects classics and mathematics. Another who might have become a statesman has avoided logic and political economy, being allured by music and plays. The boy has turned away from mathematics to find that in his future study and professional work he absolutely needs them.

III.

Self Government.—I hold that in a college, as in a country, there should be government; there should be care over the students, with inducements to good conduct, and temptations removed, and restraints on vice. There should be moral teaching; I believe also religious teaching—the rights of conscience being always carefully preserved. But one part of this instruction should be to inculcate independence, independence in thinking, independence in action and self-control. The student should be taught to think for himself, to act for himself. If he does not acquire this spirit, no external authority will be able to guide and restrain him. I abhor the plan of secretly watching students, of peeping through windows at night, and listening through key-holes. Under the spy system, the students will always beat their tutors. The tricky fellows will escape, while only the simple will be caught.

But is there, therefore, to be no moral teaching, no restraint on conduct? Are students to be allured away from their homes, hundreds and thousands of miles away, from California, Oregon, and Florida, to our Eastern colleges, and there do as they please—to spend their evenings according to their inclinations, to keep no Sabbaths, and all the while get no advice, no warning from the college authorities? They see a student going into a liquor store, a dancing saloon, a low theatre, a gambling-house. Are they to do nothing? Are they precluded from doing anything? A student is seen drunk. What are you to do with him? "The law is not made for the righteous man, but for the lawless and disobedient." Have you no law to reach him? You have no right to discipline him. It is an interference with his freedom. He is a man, and not a boy, and he should resent it. He is able to guide himself. His widowed mother lives a thousand miles away, and cannot reach him. He continues in this course. Are you to allow him to remain in the institution to ruin himself and corrupt others? You answer, we will send him away. But you cannot do so (so I hope) without evidence, and this implies that horrid thing, discipline. But you dismiss him. I have been obliged to dismiss students on rare occasions. It is a terrible ordeal to me. I have sometimes felt more than the student himself. And when the father comes to me, the father trying to suppress the bursting feeling, and the mother in agony which cannot be restrained, I am crushed, I am prostrated. But my creed is, prevention is better than punishment. Surely, if we have the right to dismiss and expel (I never expelled a student), we have the liberty to instruct, to advise, to remonstrate, nay, to discipline. I have some painful scenes to pass through in the government of a college, but I have had more pleasant ones. I have to testify that three-fourths, I believe nine-tenths, of the cases of discipline I have administered have ended in the reformation of the offender. I have been gratified by many fathers and mothers thanking me for saving their sons from ruin. Scores of graduates, when they meet me, have said, "I thank you for that sharp rebuke you gave me; you gave it heartily, and I was irritated at the time, but now I thank you as heartily, for I was arrested thereby when rushing into folly."

It is time that fathers and mothers should know what it is proposed to do with their sons at college. The college authorities are in no way to interfere with them. They are to teach them Music and Art, and French Plays and novels, but there is no course in the Scriptures—in their poetry, their morality, their spirituality. The President of Harvard recommends that all colleges should be in great cities. Students are to be placed in the midst of saloons, and gambling-houses, and temples of Venus, but meanwhile no officer of the college is to preach to them, to deal with them. Suppose that under temptation the son falls. I can conceive a father saying to the head of the institution, "I sent my son to you believing that man is made in the image of God, you taught him that he is an upper brute, and he has certainly become so; I sent him to you pure, and last night he was carried to my door drunk. Curse ye this college; 'curse ye bitterly,' for you took no pains to allure him to good, to admonish, to pray for him." I was once addressed by a mother in very nearly these words. I was able to show that her son had come to us a polluted boy from an ungodly school, and that we had dealt with him kindly, warned him solemnly, disciplined him, given notice of his conduct to his mother, and prayed for him. Had I not been able to say this conscientiously I believe I would that day have given in my resignation of the office I hold, and retired to a wilderness to take charge of myself, feeling that I was not competent to take care of others.

It is a serious matter what we are to do to provide religious studies in our colleges. Professor Huxley[10] knows that there is little or nothing in our ordinary school books to mould and form the character of children, and so, as member of the London School Board, he votes for the reading of the Scriptures in the schools, not that he believes them, but because they are fitted to sway the mind,—which I remark they are able to do, because they are divine. Everybody knows that science alone is not fit to form or guard morality; and

Herbert Spencer[11] is very anxious about this transition period, when the old has passed away (so he thinks) and the new morality is not yet published. Emerson stood up manfully for the retention of prayers in Harvard University. Are we now in our colleges to give up preaching? to give up Bible instruction? to give up prayers? But I am on the borders of the religious question, on which I now formally propose that *This club should have another meeting in which President Eliot will defend the new departure in the religion of colleges and I engage with God's help to meet him.*[12]

In closing, I have to confess that I regard this new departure with deep anxiety. The scholarship of America is not yet equal to that of Germany or Great Britain. Some of us are anxious to raise it up to the standard of Europe. We are discouraged by this plan of Harvard to allow and encourage its students to take branches in which there is so little to promote high intellectual culture. We know what a galaxy of great men appeared in Harvard an age ago, under the old training. I know that it is keenly discussed, within the college itself, whether there is anything in the present and coming modes of dissipated instruction to rear men of the like intellectual calibres. Has there been of late any great poem, any great scientific discovery, any great history, any great philosophic work, by the young men of Cambridge? I observe that the literary journals, for which our young writers prepare articles, have now fixed their seat in New York rather than Boston.

The wise leaders of the new departure do not propose to fight against religion. They do not fight with it, but they are quite willing to let it die out, to die in dignity. They have put severe learning on a sliding scale, not it may be in order to a sudden fall, but insensibly to go down to the level of those boys who do not wish to think deeply or study hard. I am glad things have come to a crisis. Let parents know it, let the churches know it, let all America know it, let scholars in Europe know it, let the world know it—for what is done in Harvard has influence over the world. But some timid people will say, "Tell it not in the lands whence our pious fathers came that the college whose motto is *Pro Christo et Ecclesia* teaches no religion to its pupils. Tell it not in Berlin or Oxford that the once most illustrious university in America no longer requires its graduates to know the most perfect language, the grandest literature, the most elevated thinking of all antiquity. Tell it not in Paris, tell it not in Cambridge in England, tell it not in Dublin, that Cambridge in America does not make mathematics obligatory on its students. Let not Edinburgh and Scotland and the Puritans in England know that a student may pass through the once Puritan College of America without having taken a single class of philosophy or a lesson in religion. But whatever others may do, *I say, I say*, let Europe know in all its universities—I wish my voice could reach them all—that in a distinguished college in America a graduate need no longer take what the ages have esteemed the highest department of learning; and I believe that such an expression of feeling will be called forth, that if we cannot avert the evil in Harvard we may arrest it in the other colleges of the country.

CHAPTER 21

On the Future of Our Educational Institutions*

Friedrich Nietzsche

INTRODUCTION TO NIETZSCHE'S LECTURES

During the last decades of the nineteenth century, the German education system was thought to be the best in the world. The British critic, poet, and school inspector Matthew Arnold believed it was, and he would certainly not have had much trouble finding Germans who agreed with him. Germany's schools and universities were, understandably, a source of national pride. Its elementary schools educated a greater percentage of the population than their British and French counterparts. The German gymnasium, the main secondary school, was known for its rigorous instruction, especially in classical languages. And German universities were celebrated for their devotion to the ideal of research and for fruits of that devotion: major innovations across the disciplines, from cutting-edge chemistry laboratories to philological texts and collections still used today. Foreign students flocked to Germany not only to master new forms of knowledge but also to learn, as J. G. Fichte had put it, how to learn.

Of course, not all foreign students were fully won over by the German system; but the sharpest criticisms came from home. Throughout the Second Empire, there was, indeed, much handwringing over the entire educational system. It wasn't that most of the worries were new. Rather, they had become

* Excerpt translated by Damion Searls from Friedrich Nietzsche, "Ueber die Zukunft unserer Bildungsanstalten," in *Friedrich Nietzsche: Kritische Studienausgabe,* ed. Giorgio Colli and Mazzino Montinari, vol. 1 (Munich: Deutscher Taschenbuch Verlag, 1999). A version of this lecture appeared as Lecture V in Friedrich Nietzsche, *Anti-Education*, trans. Damion Searls, ed. Paul Reitter and Chad Wellmon (New York: New York Review Books Classics, 2015).

more intense and widespread as certain tendencies, like academic specialization, had grown more prominent, and as major changes had taken place. An expanding government apparatus and the resulting labor needs (the state bureaucracy employed close to 2 million people in 1914, as over against a little more than half a million at the beginning of the *Kaiserreich*); the acceleration of Germany's industrial boom in the years after unification in 1871, as well as the economic bust that quickly followed it; the pressures that attended arriving on the scene as a world power—these are just a few of the developments that lent added urgency to the debate about education, whose central question a leading historian of the topic has described as follows: "How should the elite classical schools of the mid-nineteenth century be reformed to meet the needs of the rapidly approaching twentieth century?" This is a useful formulation, but it also warrants qualifying. Many of the participants in the debate would have found it misleading, because for them, the problem was that Germany's schools and universities had ceased to be truly elite, in the sense of excellent and exclusive, and were becoming worse in the turbulent young *Reich*.

Friedrich Nietzsche was one such participant. His chief contribution to the schools debate came in the form of a series of lectures, *On the Future of Our Educational Institutions*, which he held in Basel's city museum in the winter of 1872. From his post in Basel—at the time, Nietzsche was a young classics professor and gymnasium teacher there—he had grown increasingly disillusioned with "the whole Prussian system of education." His disillusionment had multiple sources. Nietzsche's devotion to the philosopher Arthur Schopenhauer had a part in this; when, as a student, Nietzsche began reading Schopenhauer, it had the effect of making him feel that his own style was "dead" and, in turn, that the gymnasium had failed him. At least as important were Nietzsche's Wagnerian commitments, which were as passionate then as they would ever be. Wagner's aim of regenerating modern culture by tapping into the "true German spirit," a term Nietzsche invokes more than once in the Basel lectures, was a primary standard by which Nietzsche measured the worth of cultural undertakings and institutions, including the schools, and in his estimation, the schools measured up less and less.

What Nietzsche spelled out is a vision of education in which disciplined yet also passionate study of the classical world unlocks the transformative power of genius. But he presented this ideal as being terribly hard to realize. As Jacob Burckhardt, who attended the first lecture, observed, Nietzsche's focus was on the many trends he regarded as pulling against "true education." Not the least of them was the drive to open up the system of education and mix practical and classical education at the secondary level. For according to Nietzsche, genius could be nourished only in the most exclusive settings.

The German educational system was in fact becoming more inclusive, though more slowly than Nietzsche suggested. In 1880, a very small percentage of primary school students went on to a gymnasium—3 percent, to be precise. Yet the number of gymnasium students was growing at a rate that outpaced that of population growth. In 1859, there were 133 gymnasiums within the territories that would be united after the Franco-Prussian War; there were 205 at the time of unification, with the student population rising from 38,000 to 59,000. Furthermore, who got to attend a gymasium was determined, to Nietzsche's chagrin, much more by wealth than by talent: he wanted the educational system to be both aristocratic and meritocratic.

The classical gymnasium, meanwhile, lost its status as the sole path to the university. Starting in 1870, a student could also get there with a diploma from the more vocationally oriented high schools, which in the early 1880s became knows as *Realgymnasien.* One consequence of this was that ever-greater percentages of university students opted to study nonhumanities fields. The barbarians had arrived at the gates, or so it seemed to Nietzsche and a host of his contemporaries, such as Heinrich von Treitschke and Karl Hillenbrand. Not only that, the barbarians, along with everyone else, were being besieged by a culture of distraction that at once stemmed from and contributed to the decline of the schools. But Nietzsche wasn't without hope. In his Basel lectures, he claims that "nature" is on the side of a correction, which may require the wholesale destruction of the prevailing system of education. Still, it wouldn't be fair to describe the tone of the lectures as sanguine. Like many other commentators, Nietzsche put the accent on what he perceived to be the erosion of the highest sort of *Bildung*. In at least one way, then, Nietzsche's Basel lectures provide us with a representative sample of the education debate of his day.

In other ways, however, *On the Future of Our Educational Institutions* is a bracingly unusual work. Nietzsche was quite prescient in recognizing the danger for academic freedom posed by both surging German nationalism after 1871 and the Prussian state's apparent desire to express its status as a world power through all the institutions under its control. In places, the lectures anticipate Max Weber's writings of fifty years later on the decline of academic freedom in Germany (as a result of the state's new heavy-handedness in regulating academic affairs). Furthermore, rather than offering the tables and graphs that filled most calls for reform, Nietzsche made his case through a fictional dialogue set in the woods outside of Bonn, the city where he spent his first year as a university student. The participants are two students, one of whom is the narrator (and supposedly Nietzsche himself), an elderly philosopher, and the philosopher's much younger companion, a gymnasium teacher who is considering leaving the profession out of a sense of futility. The narrator's elaborate descriptions of the sylvan setting make the lectures feel at times like a literary experiment. Furthermore, the philosopher is more a Schopenhauer figure than a Socratic one, and it's not hard to see why his and his disciple's diatribes against the broadening of the education system have failed to resonate among scholars (or why they entertained Nietzsche's high-culture-loving audiences in Basel). First published posthumously, *On the Future of Our Educational Institutions* is far from being Nietzsche's most influential writing. Yet for all that, one of the guiding ideas of the lectures is a rather supple "thesis," to use the term with which Nietzsche presents it in the introduction to the planned book version of the lectures.

Nietzsche's point is that "two seemingly opposed" developments, the "widening and narrowing" of education, are actually phenomena that complement each other, driven as they are by the same modern spirit. Both are catastrophically inimical to the flourishing of individual geniuses, the force the lectures frame as the one that might redeem modern culture. Both the broader, more practical version of education and the cult of specialization at German universities make education into something calculable, into a matter of amassing measurable, marketable skills or sets of data. Thus both take education away from what counts for Nietzsche as true education—the adventure of seeing how far the most talented youth can go in cultivating their highest mental faculties by immersing themselves in the culture of ancient Greece.

With its emphasis on the self-formation through the study of antiquity, as well as on the need for this process to enjoy a high degree of freedom from practical ends, Nietzsche's educational ideal has neohumanist components that evoke the thinking of Wilhelm von Humboldt. But Nietzsche's position also has a pronounced anti-Humboldtian side, because where Humboldt believed that the process of self-formation required not only freedom from external constraints but also internal freedom—the intellectual freedom of individual students—Nietzsche saw the process as requiring the extreme obedience and subordination once brought forth, in his telling, by Greek students. Like the neohumanists of Humboldt's day, Nietzsche thought that the way to *Bildung* went through Greece, but his Greece was very different from theirs.

In a cruel twist, precisely the study of philology at German universities had come to block the path to that crucial resource for renewal in a nihilistic age: the living inspiration of the classical world. Empirical knowledge of ancient Greece (and Rome as well) could be useful, Nietzsche allowed, but with few exceptions, philologists buried the classical world under mountains of facts and determinations about textual authenticity that had no value for the formation of geniuses—and thus for life—in the present day. Thus, instead of helping Germans access the true spirit of antiquity, philologists did the opposite. As the philosopher's companion puts it, "Philologists founder and die due to the Greeks—we can live with that loss. But for antiquity itself to die due to the philologists!"

Nietzsche was hardly the only one to level this kind of criticism. Goethe and Schiller bemoaned how the pedantry of German scholars drained the life from classical culture. Friedrich Schelling worried that classical study was becoming "more and more a matter of industry," and less about actual thought and intellection. In the 1830s, the Berlin philologist August Böckh, who famously defined his discipline as the attempt "to understand" how human experience "has been understood," expressed concern over how the detail fetishism of an ascendant rival mode of philology ("word philology") was "fragmenting" the scholarly discussion of the ancient world, when the point was to identify principles that cut across different areas of knowledge. J. J. Bachofen, a student of Böckh's whom Nietzsche knew in Basel and admired, decried not only the success of Böckh's rivals but also what he took to be the Prussianization and industrialization of philology through the efforts the renowned classicist Theodor Mommsen. Beginning in 1858, Mommsen used his position at the Prussian Academy of Sciences to promote his vision of big philology, or what a collaborator termed the "large scale production of the sciences" (*Grossbetrieb der Wissenschaften*), which involved teams of researchers cataloging vast amounts of data.

But Nietzsche went further than these critics. In the Basel lectures he began to develop the idea that academic knowledge diminishes life rather than enhances it, tying the entrenchment of this knowledge to interlocking but also self-reinforcing cycles. It was a shift in values—a loss of faith in the power of genius—that allowed philologists to treat classical antiquity as mere grist for the mill of *Wissenschaft*: Philologists were for Nietzsche the consummate modern skeptics. The philological treatment of antiquity, which has shaped the approaches of gymnasium teachers, has in turn had the effect of alienating students even further from a salutary belief in the power of the classical world, to the point where classical material had become "dead." Meanwhile, journalism has seized the space left open by a hyperspecialized *Wissenschaft* that has lost sight of the bigger picture, with the result that students and teachers alike turn to journalism for reflection on the large questions, which has only made it even more difficult for them to have a productive relationship with antiquity. In this context, those few who have a drive for true education must suffer. The mindless drudgery of academic philology is, according to Nietzsche, sometimes nothing other than the means through which these few try to anesthetize their thwarted drive.

Nietzsche's characters hold the state largely responsible for this situation, but the speculations about the state's motivations for undermining true *Bildung* go beyond the idea that the state wants to use the educational system to train bureaucrats and good earners and to produce work that will add to its symbolic might. Anticipating Nietzsche's theory of inversion in *On the Genealogy of Morals*, the old philosopher claims that the state and its allies have purposely redefined *Bildung* in such a way that the rare few who have the impulse for true *Bildung* will fail to thrive. According to the old philosopher, the state knows that these few are a revolutionary force in society, and it fears them. The state's reformulation of *Bildung* is, then, a way that weaker minds maintain control over stronger ones—slave pedagogy.

The lectures also have much to say about the relationship between modernity and the humanities. They are withering on the subject of the incipient culture of mass entertainment and the leveling of established hierarchies in modernity. But rather than constructing a culture-versus-anarchy dualism in the style of Matthew Arnold, whose *Culture and Anarchy* appeared in 1869, Nietzsche's Basel lectures challenge us to think through the complex predicament of the humanities in modern society. They prompt us to question how the very forces that allowed the humanities to become established and flourish in new ways—secularization, institutional rationalization, democratization, etc.—also came to imperil the best the humanities had to offer.

No longer was Nietzsche merely dissatisfied with the limits of academic knowledge, as he had been during his student days. With *On the Future of Our Educational Institutions*, academic knowledge has become one of the great issues of modernity, and that this was so would be one of Nietzsche's great themes, an aspect of his work that influenced generations of German thinkers.

The section of the text excerpted here comes from the fifth of five lectures, the lecture that deals most concertedly with German universities. It was held on March 23, 1872.

ON THE FUTURE OF OUR EDUCATIONAL INSTITUTIONS (EXCERPT)

I continued my comrade's speech: "In fact," I said, "it seems to me that everything you criticize the gymnasium for—no doubt rightly—is only a necessary means to foster a kind of independence in its students, or at least a belief that they are independent. This is the intended purpose of the German essays you discussed earlier: the individual must learn to make use of his opinions and ideas early on, so that he can walk without crutches later. That is why he is encouraged to produce original work so early, and write criticism and make sharp judgments even earlier. If Latin and Greek cannot inspire students with a passion for distant antiquity, then at least, given the way these studies are pursued, they can awaken the scholarly feelings, the desire for a rigorous causality of knowledge, the passion to uncover and discover. How many students have been seduced forever by the charms of science and scholarship as a result of a new way of reading that they found in the Gymnasium and snatched up with eager young fingers! The Gymnasium student has to study all sorts of things and collect all kinds of knowledge, and this no doubt gradually creates an instinct that will then lead him to study and collect independently at the university in similar ways. In short, we believe that the goal of the Gymnasium is to prepare and accustom its students to live and learn later as independently as they were previously compelled to live and learn in the Gymnasium."

The philosopher laughed at this, not entirely good-naturedly, and said: "What a fine example of independence you have just given me. And it is just this independence that so horrifies me and makes the presence of the students of today so disagreeable to me. Yes, my good friends, you are prepared, you are mature, you are complete—Nature broke the mold after she made you, and your teachers have every right to rejoice in you. What freedom, certainty, and aplomb your judgments show, how new and fresh your insights are! You sit in judgment, and every culture in every age runs away; your scholarly feelings are kindled, and the flame blazes out of you—look out, everyone, make sure you don't get burned! And then, if I consider your professors too, I see the same independence once again, taken to an even more powerful and more charming level. Never was there an era so rich in magnificent independences, and never has slavery of all kinds been so hated—including, of course, the slavery of education and culture!

"Permit me, though, to judge this independence of yours by just that standard—culture—and see how your universities measure up as purely cultural institutions. If someone from another country wants to find out more about our university system, his first pressing question will be: How do your students participate in the university system? We will answer: By means of the ear—as listeners. The foreigner is amazed: 'Purely by listening?' he asks again. 'Purely by listening,' we answer again. The student attends lectures. Whenever he speaks, or sees, or walks, or is with someone else, or makes art—in short, insofar as he lives and breathes—he is independent, i.e., not dependent on the educational institution. It very often happens that the student writes something down while he is listening. These are the moments when he is attached by an umbilical cord to the university. He can choose what he wants to hear; he does not necessarily have to believe what he hears; he can shut his ears if he does not want to hear. This is the 'acroamatic' method of instruction.[1]

"The teacher, then, speaks to listening students. Whatever else he thinks or does is separated from the students' perception by a monstrous chasm. Often, the professor reads while he speaks. In general, he wants to have as many listeners in attendance as possible, but in desperate cases he contents himself with few, almost never with just one. One speaking mouth plus many ears and half as many writing hands: that is the academic system from the outside—that is the educational machinery of the university in action. Moreover, he who possesses this mouth is separated from, and independent of, the owners of those many ears, and this double independence is glorified as 'academic freedom.'[2] To make this freedom still greater, the one can more or less speak whatever he wants, and the others can listen to more or less whatever on offer they want, except that, behind both parties, a modest distance away, stands the state with a certain attentive, supervisory look on its face—making sure to remind everybody from time to time that *it* is the aim, the purpose, and indeed the embodiment of this whole strange speaking and listening process.

"We, who must be permitted just this once to regard this astonishing phenomenon solely insofar as it represents an educational institution, will then inform the inquiring foreigner that what our universities call 'education' and 'culture' pass from mouth to ear, and that all forms of educational training are merely, as I have said, 'acroamatic.' But since the listening, and even the choice of what is to be listened to, are left to the independent decision of the academically free-minded student, and since the latter, in turn, can deny all credibility and authority to everything he hears, all educational upbringing in the strict sense is left to the student himself, and the independence it was thought desirable to aim at in the Gymnasium now struts about in its most brilliant plumage, presenting itself, with the greatest pride, as 'independent academic education.'

"Oh happy age, when youths are wise and cultured enough to teach *themselves* how to walk![3] Oh incomparable Gymnasiums that cultivate independence, whereas other eras believed that what should be cultivated was dependence, discipline, subordination, and obedience, and that every conceit of independence should be forestalled! Now, my good friends, do you see why, from the standpoint of education, I regard today's universities as mere extensions of the Gymnasium? The culture provided by a Gymnasium education steps through the gates of the university as something complete and whole, with its own particular, demanding claims: *it* requires, *it* legislates, *it* passes judgment. So do not fool yourselves about the cultured student: insofar as he believes himself to have received the blessings of education, he remains the Gymnasium schoolboy shaped by his teacher's hands, who, having left the Gymnasium after his period of academic isolation, is thereby removed from any and every further process of formation and guidance toward culture, so as to live entirely on his own and free from then on.

"Free! Put this freedom to the test, you connoisseurs of human nature! A structure built on the soft soil of our present Gymnasium culture, on crumbling foundations, it stands crooked and vulnerable to the breath of the whirling tempest. Look at this free student, herald of educational independence, and divine him from his instincts, know him from his desires! What do you think of his education when you measure it by these three yardsticks: his need for philosophy, his instinct for art, and, finally, by the standard of Greek and Roman antiquity, the categorical imperative incarnate of all culture?

"Man is so beset by the most serious and difficult problems that, when he is made to see them the right way, he quickly arrives at sustained philosophical wonder: the only fertile soil in which a deeper, nobler education can grow. Most often, it is his own experiences that lead him to these problems, and especially in his tempestuous youth almost every personal incident shimmers in a double reflection: as an example of everyday triviality, and at the same time an example of an eternal, astonishing problem, deserving of explanation. At that age, when one sees one's experiences encircled with metaphysical rainbows, so to speak, man is at the peak of his need for a guiding hand, because he has suddenly and almost instinctively been convinced of the double meaning of existence and has lost the firm footing of the beliefs and received opinions he once cherished.

"This great need is only natural, but clearly it is seen as the worst enemy of all from the perspective of the beloved independence that the cultured youth of today is supposed to be groomed for. All those young men of 'the modern age' who have already fallen into the lap of 'self-understanding' are eager to suppress and cripple this need for guidance, divert it or deform it, and their favorite method is paralyzing this natural philosophical impulse through so-called 'historical education.' A still-recent system that has already gained scandalous, worldwide fame has found the formula for this self-destruction of philosophy, and now, in any historical consideration of things, we can already see so much reckless naiveté in making the unreasonable 'reasonable' and calling the blackest of black 'white' that one is often tempted to quote this line of Hegel's as a parody: 'Can what is counter to reason be actual?'[4] Alas, what goes against the dictates of reason is today precisely what seems 'actual'—active in the world—and using this type of actuality as an explanation of history is now seen as the quintessence of 'historical education.' The philosophical instincts of our youth have pupated into this—and the peculiar philosophers of our universities seem to have sworn to reinforce our young academics' belief in it.

"Gradually, a profound exploration of the same eternal problems has come to be replaced by a historical, in fact a philological, pondering and questioning: What did this or that philosopher think or not think, and is this or that text rightly ascribed to him or not, and even: is this or that reading of a classical text preferable to the other. Nowadays the students in our university philosophy seminars are encouraged to ponder emasculated philosophical considerations such as these, whereas I myself have long since been accustomed to see such scholarship as a branch of philology, and to judge its practitioners according to whether or not they are good philologists. As a result, of course, *philosophy itself* is banished from the university altogether—and with this, our first question about the cultural value of the universities has been answered.

"The relation between these same universities and *art* cannot be admitted without shame, for they stand in no relation whatsoever. There is not a single trace of artistic thinking, learning, striving, or comparing to be found there, and no one would seriously claim that the university's voice is raised to promote the important national artistic projects. Whether an individual professor happens to feel personally inclined toward art, or an endowed chair is established for aesthetic literary historians, is not the point—the fact remains that the university as a whole is not in any position to impose strict artistic discipline on its academic youth. It simply lets whatever happens happen, willy-nilly. This is a particularly incisive rebuke to the university's arrogant claim to be the highest educational institution.

"Our academic 'independents' carry on with their lives without philosophy, without art: why then would they have any interest in getting mixed up with the Greeks and Romans, whom no one has any reason to pretend to respect any more, and who, moreover, sit majestically alien on remote, nearly inaccessible thrones? Thus the universities of today, quite logically, pay no attention at all to these utterly extinct cultural impulses, and they establish their philological professorships solely to rear up future generations of exclusively philological minds, who are then in turn responsible for the philological preparation of Gymnasium students—a life-cycle which benefits neither the philologists themselves nor the Gymnasiums, but which does serve to belie for a third time the university's claim to be what it so proudly proclaims itself as: a cultural institution.[5] For take away the Greeks (never mind the Romans) together with philosophy and art and where is the ladder you can use to ascend to culture? If you try to climb without these aids, then I must inform you that all your erudition will weigh on your shoulders as a heavy burden rather than give you wings and bear you aloft."

[. . .]

* Part 5 *

Diversity and Inclusion: Female University Students

CHAPTER 22

Diversity and Inclusion: Introduction

Throughout the nineteenth century, scholars and students, both in Germany and abroad, associated German research universities with intellectual community, academic freedom, and the endless pursuit of knowledge. But in the last decades of the century, critics at home and elsewhere began to consider whether these ideals were fitting for women. Were *Wissenschaft* and *Bildung* less than universal? Were they and the institutions with which they were bound up exclusively male?

The new university of the nineteenth century, as imagined by Fichte, Humboldt, Schelling, and Schleiermacher, did not extend its reforms to include women. It remained a strictly male intellectual community: German universities had never allowed women to matriculate. Beginning in the 1860s, however, a broad reform movement began to address the state of women's education. By the end of the first decade of the twentieth century, all German universities admitted women. But the calls for educational reform did not begin with a focus on university education for women; they aimed at improved secondary education for young girls.

Before 1800, German states had few schools for girls that provided any sort of formal education beyond the elementary level, and there were no schools that provided anything comparable to the Latin schools and, later, gymnasiums for boys. Between 1800 and 1870, however, state support for women's education increased markedly. By 1872 the newly established German Empire could boast 165 municipal or state-supported higher schools for girls. But these, too, paled in comparison to the quality, rigor, and orientation of the higher schools for boys. The schools for girls ended at age fifteen or sixteen, compared to eighteen or nineteen for boys. Latin, Greek, mathematics, and science were not included in the curricula for girls; instead, the higher schools for girls focused on sewing, drawing, and dancing. They were finishing schools that trained young girls for their future domestic lives, not for entrance to German universities or a future profession.

In 1872, 164 teachers, almost all of whom were men, gathered in Weimar to discuss possible reforms for the higher schools for girls. The group rejected the curriculum of the traditional humanist gymnasium and endorsed instead a more "realist" curriculum that included modern languages but no science and little math. Although the group embraced the exalted language of *Bildung*, the purpose of such an education for women was sharply distinguished from that of an education designed for men. Women needed to be educated and cultivated to ensure, as the conference's final report put it, that the "German husband would not be bored."

In the 1860s, some women began to attend university lectures as auditors, and at least two foreign women, both Russian, earned doctoral degrees in 1874 at the University of Göttingen. But by 1880 almost all German universities had cracked down on the mostly informal arrangements that allowed women to audit courses, and in 1886 Prussia even issued a decree reiterating the ban on female students. Reform efforts did not regain momentum until the late 1880s, when various advocacy groups, old and new, such as the Women's Welfare Association, the German Women's Association, and the Women's Reform Association, began to submit petitions to both state and national legislatures.

One of the most significant of these petitions was submitted to the Prussian Ministry of Education in October 1887; it was written by a group organized by Helene Lange, a Berlin teacher and leader of the insurgent women's movement in Germany. Although the ministry rejected its main points, and it never even reached the floor of the Prussian House of Deputies, the petition left its mark. It was accompanied by "Higher Schools for Girls and Their Mission," a widely circulated essay that came to be known as the "Yellow Brochure." Lange reiterated the petition's calls for more female teachers in the upper grades and more advanced training for them. However, what distinguished Lange's brochure from the other petitions and reform tracts of her day was not its particular demands, none of which were especially radical at the time, but the way in which she explicitly connected the question of women's education to the broader cultural and social questions concerning women. Lange argued that women's education was not only a matter of individual equality with men; it was also one of a basic social need. Lange was acutely aware that arguments based on claims about fundamental, even natural differences between men and women had historically been used to exclude women from higher education. Her answer was to chart a kind of middle course. Without dismissing the rhetoric of natural differences, she insisted that for the good of both women and society, women should have an intellectually substantive education. She asserted that women had distinct social duties to educate future generations, especially concerning religious and ethical matters. Lange would go on to establish *Realkurse* in Berlin that sought to educate women through a general education program of coursework in math, science, history, modern languages, and Latin. Similar courses, many of which sought to prepare women to take the Abitur,[1] were developed across Germany throughout the 1890s.

After the initial flurry of petition activity, a series of gradual changes began to alter the situation of higher education for women. In the mid-1890s, Prussia, for example, issued a number of decrees stipulating changes in the curricula and requirements for more female teachers in the higher schools for girls. Most importantly, however, these decrees, in Prussia and elsewhere, signaled an increased state interest in regulating standards and quality for the higher schools for girls.

Such shifts took place within a context in which educational inclusion was a burning, if vexed, issue. Between 1873 and 1910, the number of government bureaucrats in Germany quadrupled. The state was well aware of its labor needs, and through various policy measures it facilitated access to a university education among groups that had traditionally been excluded, e.g., graduates of *Realschulen*. In some ways, it was actually harder to be a poor university student in the 1880s than it had been in the 1780s, since the standards of living had changed and the amount of time required to achieve a university degree had as well. But for the growing lower middle classes, the state created a new system of financial aid, which, along with a relaxing of admissions standards, helps to explain why after 1870 university enrollments in Germany expanded at a rate that far exceeded that of population growth. This development occasioned much concern, and not only among people who, like Nietzsche, thought that the "widening" of the educational system would undermine its quality. Against the background of the boom-and-bust economy of the *Gründerzeit*, Bismarck worried about the prospect of debt-saddled unemployed university graduates giving intellectual help to "those fighting against the social order," and he enjoined his ministers to curtail their efforts at making higher education more accessible.

Others resisted inclusiveness not out of anxieties about social unrest or maintaining academic excellence but rather because they wanted to protect the distinction that being university trained conferred on them—this despite the fact that some of the same people prized Humboldt's ideal of *Bildung* for its inclusive and meritocratic ethos. The medical profession, for example, was quite open about its motivation for resisting measures that would allow *Realschule* graduates, who hadn't studied Greek, to become physicians: loss of prestige. Meanwhile, the political makeup of academia in Germany was changing, and this had important consequences for the debate about inclusion. Although the situation on the ground was complex—W. E. B. Du Bois singled out attending Heinrich von Treitschke's lectures as a high point of his time in Germany—the ascendance of chauvinists like Treitschke and Heinrich von Sybel to a tone-setting role encouraged anti-inclusion attitudes. More precisely, it encouraged opposition to the sharp rise, postunification, in the Jewish and foreign student populations at Germany universities. Many students in the latter group were women, and their status as double outsiders made for particularly fascinating perspectives on the student experience: we have provided samples of their recollections in the following section.

With respect to women, the forces driving toward inclusion prevailed, up to a point. In the 1890s, the situation for women hoping to study in universities changed appreciably. The year 1894 saw the University of Göttingen begin to allow female auditors. In 1900, the German state of Baden opened university matriculation to all women who had taken the Abitur and even denied a request from the University of Freiburg to create separate classes for women. Despite protests from universities in Munich and Erlangen, Bavaria allowed women to matriculate in 1903.

But Prussian universities, especially the storied University of Berlin, continued to bar women from admission. Many male academics, some of them leading scholars of the day, acknowledged the basic legitimacy of the women's movement and its demands for more and better education for women, but they questioned whether the university was the proper place to achieve these ends. Were women capable of the tireless pursuit of knowledge? "As much as I recognize the necessity for this concession to new conditions [i.e., admitting women to universities]," wrote Friedrich Paulsen, the famed historian of German education, "I cannot deny that I do not look for such great intellectual progress to result from it as some others seem to expect. The history of the sciences and arts hardly leaves any room for doubt that real creative activity has, in general, been bestowed by nature in a larger measure upon the male than upon the female."[2] There were also concerns about how the inclusion of women would affect the social lives of students and their storied rituals. For many German professors, the university could be conceived of only as a male community not least because, as Treitschke once put it, "women didn't drink beer like men." This was no trivial remark; for many university graduates and particularly for those who, like Treitschke, had belonged to a fraternity, rituals of male bonding made up a crucial part of the student experience, so crucial that it was hard to conceive of people who couldn't take part in them as actual students.

After decades of frustrated reform efforts, the Prussian education minister issued a decree in 1908 allowing women to be admitted to universities. It was typical of this process that there was a catch. The minister stipulated that professors would be allowed to exclude women from their own lectures "under extraordinary circumstances." The gains, nevertheless, were real. By 1914, 7.5 percent of the students enrolled at Prussian universities were women.

CHAPTER 23

Higher Schools for Girls and Their Mission: Companion Essay*

Helene Lange

Germany's higher schools for girls were created by private efforts, in an attempt to respond to a need that gained prominence at the end of the previous century and the beginning of the present one. This need had made itself felt, most keenly, at a time when intellectual life in Germany had become rejuvenated and German national literature bloomed. "Women who were intensely receptive to the beauty of our emerging classical literature and who saw themselves as the heralds of a new age—it was such women who founded new institutions of learning and taught that the loftiest longings of the female heart should be satisfied."[1]

Like all private efforts, the success of these schools was only guaranteed by the character of those who supported them. On the one side, one could expect, and one in fact encountered, complete dedication to what had been freely undertaken; one also encountered individual and collective, and for that reason sustained, engagement, ingenuity, and energy. But on the other side, there was an unjustified attitude of acceptance toward all kinds of modish foolishness, which was brought about, in part, by the financial instability of these new institutions and their ultimate dependence on public support.

To make this process more systematic, and because of the obvious social benefits of having well-run higher schools for girls, the state soon took it upon itself to found such schools, with individual communities following suit. These were to serve as models for the private schools. Since the schools founded by

* From Helene Lange, "Die höhere Mädschenschule und ihre Bestimmung, Begleitschrift," in *Kampfzeiten: Aufsätze und Reden aus vier Jahrzehnten* (Berlin: Herbig, 1928).

the state and communities didn't rely on the goodwill of the public, one didn't need to worry about responses of the kind mentioned above. On the other hand, even the directors of the state and community-run schools were quite limited in their authority. They weren't free to choose their own personnel or to design their own curricula, and they were not in a position to put the most creative ideas into practice.

These new schools are in one respect fundamentally different from the private schools. While the influence of women is of great importance in the latter, it is minimal in the former. The power to determine the curriculum as well as the highest administrative and instructional positions—all these belong to men in the new schools. And this situation appears to be of little concern for most people, even though the point of the undertaking is the educational development and social progress of women.

The results of these new schools have been somewhat disappointing—not what one had hoped for. The cause of this was thought to be undue borrowing from the boys' school model. Thus, the attempt was made to create a firmer foundation for girls' schools by developing and debating theories about the nature of female education. A definitive theoretical basis for the organization of higher schools for girls had just come into view, when in 1872, a conference of girls' schools pedagogues took place in Weimar. Its organizer was Dr. G. Krehenberg of Berlin; its purpose was to justify the goal of higher schools for girls in a position paper dedicated to the German government. In its "second thesis" the paper defined this goal as follows: Higher schools for girls have as their mission making it possible for young women to participate in German intellectual culture—broadly conceived—as they are entitled to. This goal corresponds to the task *Gymnasien* and *Realschulen* pursue with boys and young men. But this will not be accomplished by merely imitating those institutions; rather, it must be achieved through a mode of organization that takes into account a woman's nature and life's purpose. Only in this kind of organization will we find the future of schools for girls.

There is little to object to in this assertion, but it is also purely formal. What it actually means depends on how one defines "a woman's nature and life's purpose." Strikingly, the position paper discusses this important point in none of its individual theses. Yet the reasoning behind thesis two is telling; indeed, it gives us a clear sense of the definition with which the Weimar conference was operating. "Our aim," we read, "is to make possible for women an education that is equal to that of men in its methodological and thematic breadth, so that German men aren't bored at home, and held back in their devotion to elevated topics, by the narrow-mindedness and provinciality of German women.

Rather, German women should stand by the side of German men with an understanding of and warm feeling for such topics." Women should be educated, so that they don't bore men! This is too close to Rousseau's idea that women exist for the pleasure of men to be an acceptable sentiment here in Germany, where we have much worthier views about pedagogy and education. Thesis three proceeds from the following premise: "higher schools for girls should strive to develop harmoniously the intellect, one's emotional disposition, and the will, understood in the national-religious sense of the term, building in doing so on a realistic-aesthetic foundation." We would be inclined to agree, but the thesis quickly becomes contradictory, making the initial demands seem impossible to achieve. For the thesis also frames the forming of a "noble personality" in women as its central aim. How can one speak of developing faculties harmoniously when one ultimately has such a one-sided goal, when one does not develop the personality for its own sake?

This reasoning served to provide a principled justification for the practice of keeping female teachers as far as possible from the most important positions in the instruction of girls, a practice that had previously been helped by a lack of good evidence. Because it is men themselves who know best how much education is needed for them to avoid feeling bored at home, and on the other hand, for them not to be made uncomfortable (the Weimar paper demands for women only "an understanding of and warm feeling for" the elevated topics that interest men, not the ability to form an independent judgments about such topics, and certainly not the ability to pursue them effectively)—because of this, it was only logical that women would assist with the most elementary instruction, and men would be the ones responsible for the further development of the will.

The one-sidedness of the Weimar paper, which, moreover, was concerned mostly with the surface-level features of the higher schools for girls and the directors and teachers employed there, elicited strong resistance—especially in private school circles, whose existence and achievements it mostly ignored. The Berlin Association of Higher Girls' Schools expressed just this objection in a second position paper, which was also dedicated to the German government. This paper rests on very solid ground and makes a strong case for the influence of women in schools for girls, yet the arguments it put forth had little practical effect. The government believed it had to ascribe greater credibility to the Weimar position, which was represented by the same people who run public schools for girls. Thus a more detailed reckoning here with this position might seem pointless, and yet we will return to it repeatedly.

Fourteen years have passed since that conference in August.[2] An entire generation has passed through school. And what are the results? Only one party is completely satisfied, even if not with all of the results, to be sure, but with the direction that the higher schools for girls have taken, namely, the academically trained directors and teachers who work in them.

If we only listen to what they write and discuss in their assemblies, then the higher schools for girls are flourishing and developing in the proper direction, even if some areas need to be developed further. But if one listens to the fathers and above all to the mothers of our young girls, if one listens to public opinion, and, finally, if one considers without prejudice the results of our upper girls' schools, then one is left with deep doubts about the effectiveness of the system that has been implemented in these schools.

We want to refrain from anecdotal criticisms; individual mistakes will always be made. But we cannot lose sight of the essential duty of a girls' school: to educate, to educate to an inner richness, as Pestalozzi says. And this duty is not being fulfilled. Our schools do not educate. They do not help parents raise modest women of noble morals. All they do is teach. Nor can we lose sight of the fact that in most cases this teaching consists of an unpedagogical, excessive burden of positivistic material and false systematization, so that what young girls come to know is in many cases scattered, superficial, and incomplete. Our primary complaint is this: Our young girls experience only a small portion of what men learn thoroughly. And this small portion is seldom experienced in a way that might spark their interest and prepare them for a more in-depth encounter in the future, or for the important prospect of thinking for themselves. Instead, this small portion of what could be learned is simply left behind as so many assorted positive facts or ready-made judgments. Without any connection to an inner life, these facts and judgments are quickly forgotten. And the young girls are left only with the conceited feeling of "having had" and of being able to engage in critique.

This type of teaching explains the inability of our schools to promote true education. Whatever reason can grasp only superficially cannot contribute to the development of an ethical personality. It can never be related to internal and external life. And in the hours of instruction in which an immersion might be possible and a thorough lingering with the subject matter occurs—in religion and German class, for example—the desired effect never materializes for different reasons. The male teachers are too unfamiliar with the spheres of thinking and obligations of the young girls sitting before them to give practical value to the beautiful sayings and sentences in which endless wisdom resides. And thus many of our young girls accustom themselves to a form of bookkeeping. They indulge in "beautiful thoughts" and feelings in the school; they follow the religious-aesthetic observations of their teachers with a sensitivity that may even surprise them. But they do this while neglecting their small circle of domestic and moral duties. They look down on their peers who may live in less refined circles. The fact that there is and must be a close connection between such circles and their real, daily lives will only occur to them if it is relentlessly demonstrated from a knowing hand in relation to their own duties.

We will have occasion to return to this point later, but first we need to unearth the causes of the phenomena we have just described. How have our girls' schools, which are not forced into such things through exams or "administrative authorities," come to have such an excess of positive material, with ready-made formulas about things that for children are completely impenetrable? The result is that that their intellectual and moral capacities wane, and only automata are educated.

The next and most obvious reason lies in the curriculum proposed at the August conference, which, as already noted, has formed the basis of instruction in our higher schools for girls. The curriculum was oriented, as Luise Büchner[3] rightly notes, "to the idea of finishing or completing a girl's education." Büchner, who was asked by the Culture Ministry to comment on the "minutes [of the conference]," continues: "And this could never make for anything spirited or lively," "the material to be learned and the time allotted to study it are incommensurate." With almost every object of study, one wants to cry out Too Much! By the age of sixteen—after which the young girl could potentially take care that her German husband is not bored—the young girl should "have had" everything that constitutes the essential content of a general education, because a continuing education, even if desirable, was not seen as obligatory. Such an education is not considered to be the responsibility of a school. A great deal of its actual content, still inaccessible to children, is provided in the form of ready-made opinions, and an overview oftentimes compensates for insight. [. . .] If one wants "to prepare" a person by the age of sixteen, then only a homunculus can come about.

The excessiveness of our higher schools for girls, however, is only a symptom of a deeper defect. As stated above, we should look for the deeper cause of our young girls' poor education in the faulty view of the vocation of women. Already seventy-seven years ago, Betty Gleim[4] warned of that great truth, namely, the prejudice that "the woman exists for the sake of man, and only has value in so far as she pleases and serves man (and this despite the Christian teaching of the equality of the sexes)." But she was neither heard nor heeded.

[. . .]

As long as a woman is not educated simply for her own sake—that is, as a human and into a human; as long as she is educated, according to Rousseau's dubious views concerning the education of women in Germany, only for the sake of man; as long as the intellectually dependent woman is considered the best woman, because she can above all else meet her future husband's desires, the direction of which it is impossible to predict, with a "warmth of feeling"—as long as all this is so, the German education of women will not change. For many men, this will seem like no great travesty, because their own satisfaction will thereby be secured.

[. . .]

But the situation is different. It concerns not just women—their destiny is inextricably bound up with that of the next generation. And with this the great cultural duty of women becomes clear, a duty that lacks nothing in greatness and beauty compared to that of men. It is a duty that we have no interest in trading with men. While men explore and shape the external world, mold it according to their own sensibility and will, try to coerce time, space, and matter, the education of our future humanity lies in our hands, the care of the most noble characteristics, those that make the human human: morality, love, godliness. We should cultivate in children the world of the mind and teach it to recognize the proper value of all things, to respect the divine as higher than the temporal, the moral as higher than the sensible. We should also teach the mind to think and act.

Can anyone believe that the education which the schools now provide our girls is a suitable preparation for the fulfillment of this duty?

CHAPTER 24

Women at the German Universities: Letters to the Editor of the *Nation*

J.B.S. and M.F.K.

1*

New York, February 8, 1894

TO THE EDITOR OF THE NATION:

Although the German universities are not as yet formally open to women, nevertheless in several of them women are and have been for some time admitted to many of the courses of lectures. This is especially the case at Leipzig; but at Heidelberg, too, at Freiburg, and quite recently at Berlin, women have been permitted to pass the portals so long sacred to the male sex. The conditions under which the rule excluding women may be thus infringed—for it must be borne in mind that it is an infringement of rule—are restricted, even humiliating. The woman student is not recognized as such except by courtesy. She is not recognized at all officially. She is not permitted to take a degree; she is not allowed even to register her name on the university lists, or to claim in any way connection with it. She may even be ordered off its premises, if caught going into the lectures by any officer of the university or any member of its faculties who is hostile to the presence of women there—and in one case within the writer's knowledge this was actually done. She is usually allowed, however—though not always—to pay her fees; and when her money is accepted, the professor concerned will give her privately the regular examination that the male student is put through, and his personal certificate testifying to her proficiency. Indeed, the arrangement, in this particular at least, is not greatly different from the back-door method by which

* J.B.S., letter to the editor, "Women at the German Universities," *Nation*, February 15, 1894.

the students of Harvard Annex, or Radcliffe College, as it is now to be called, extract their certificates from unwilling Harvard.

In the German universities the whole matter is entirely optional with the individual professor as an individual teacher, and to him, not to the university that retains him, the would-be woman student applies. If he is not personally opposed to the higher education of women, sometimes even if he is, he will readily, often cordially and kindly, consent, for the German *Gelehrter* [scholar] is generally a most good-hearted man. There is, however, in this matter of admitting women to their lectures a considerable difference among professors, and it would seem to be even more a *Fach* [academic discipline] than an individual difference, though in this case the *Fach* may express the man no less than the man the *Fach*. For instance, the professors of art, political economy, history, the classics and philosophy properly so called, would seem to be favorable to women about in the order named, and admission to the lectures on these subjects may almost invariably be obtained, especially at Leipzig, the least difficult of any of the universities so far as admitting women is concerned. The medical lectures, on the other hand, are quite impossible for women, though there is a larger proportion of professors in favor of admitting them in this than in any other faculty. In this case, however, something more than the option of the individual teacher is necessary to set aside the rule. Law and theology are, of course, even more absolutely closed. Indeed, the lecturer on ethics in the theological faculty of one of these universities refused a woman who wished to hear him, on the ground that ethics was a subject quite out of woman's sphere. It is to be hoped that he would not maintain the same of the practical side of his subject, and hold that morals, too, are quite out of woman's sphere. It is only fair to add that the stand taken by this *Gelehrter Herr Professor* was exceptional, and is, perhaps, best explained by the remark of another professor in the same university, but not the same faculty, to whom the woman in question related the incident: "Das war ja nur zu erwarten, mein liebes Fräuline: der Kerl ist ja ein Theolog" [That was only to be expected, my dear young lady: the young man was a theologian].

The consent of the professor being the sine qua non of her admission, the woman student's first step is to obtain it, and she must do this in person. A proxy or even a letter is almost sure to be fatal to her hopes, whereas the application in person is almost sure to succeed. This indispensable performance is sometimes, particularly to the new hand, not a little of an ordeal, but it may have its amusing features too. Repairing to the professor's house at *Sprechstunde* [office hours] (the time he devotes to such business), the woman student will generally find a number of male students there—indeed, she is more likely than not to be ushered into a room full of them—whereat an astounded silence will fall as they realize the situation, a mental gasp as it were, then one or two, perhaps four or five, will recover sufficiently to spring up and offer chairs, and every pair of German eyes in the room, generally rendered formidable by glasses, will proceed to "size up" the *Emancipirte*, not rudely—the German student is seldom rude—but with the curious wonder one has for the strange beasts in a menagerie. By the time the Herr Professor's study-door is opened, however, and he is ready to receive the next visitor, the youth whose turn it is will invariably and most gallantly insist on yielding his place to the lady, and, if this be her first experience, she is most gratefully to accept.

Alone with the professor, the affair is simple enough. She states her errand in the German she can command, and if she have mother wit about her, as well as sufficient of his mother tongue—he seldom speaks hers—she may even add that she has crossed the sea for the sole purpose of hearing him, or some such phrase, which is very apt to make him look flattered and give his consent more ado. Not always, however, does this sort of diplomacy produce such a softening effect. There is one professor, a noted psychophysicist, who though he does admit qualified women to his courses, cannot be brought to anything like a cordial agreement to do so. "If you choose to attend my lectures, no one will interfere with you," is the non-committal sort of reply with which the applicant to him must be content.

After the professor come the lectures, and the first two or three are a test for the woman student and still more for the Germans whose customs, traditions, opinions, and prejudices she defies by intruding herself among them. They could have her ejected if they chose, but they do not. They simply stare, some aghast, some in wrath, some in ridicule. Then they observe her critically: if she takes notes, those who are near her look over her page. But by the third or fourth lecture they have made up their various minds about her, and she is generally left for the rest of the term unnoticed and in peace. If she happens to be pretty, the wonder lasts longer, for a German student cannot conceive why a pretty woman should want to be wise. *Blaue Strümpfe* and personal plainness are necessary corollaries to him, and it is a severe shock to preconceived ideas to find the "blue-stocking" less plain than prejudice painted her. An American girl who happened not to be plain, coming out of her lecture one day, was met by two students, one of whom had evidently brought the other there to see her. "She a student!" exclaimed the one as the other nudged him. "Impossible, she's *pretty*!" and his astonishment, voiced in tones so loud she could not but hear, betrayed how hard it was for him to reconcile the apparent contradiction.

As a general thing the German student does not thus obtrude his remarks or himself, and his manners, both in the lecture-room and out of it, are very good. He will often, indeed, show, by little acts of kindness, genuine good feeling for the *Fräulein Studentin.* She need never, unless she wish, meet her male comrades personally at all, but such acquaintances are exceedingly agreeable as well as useful to her, and it is a very good thing for the German student to be given such an opportunity of finding out for himself that a woman may pursue the same severe course of study that he does, and yet be a woman still—a view he does not commonly hold.

As a social being the woman student will generally receive from her professors, too, some, often a great deal of, attention. It is the proper thing for all students, male and female, to call socially at the beginning of a semester on their professors and their families; if the professor is not married, the student does not call. An invitation to dinner or supper—usually for a Sunday—will soon follow, as an acknowledgment of the call and assurance that further acquaintance is desired. On these occasions the wives and daughters of the professors will be met, and very ordinary women they are. There are, of course, exceptions, but as a rule the German *Gelehrter* is content to dwell at home in the dullest sort of domesticity with his ill-educated women. As his wife is, he lets his daughter grow up to be, whereas to his son he gives the liberal education he himself has had.

To return to the more serious side of the subject, the profit to any student of a course at a German university may be immense; and though the limitations at present imposed on the woman student undoubtedly diminish hers, she nevertheless may also derive a share. Perhaps in no other way is the lesson of thoroughness in things intellectual to be learned so well. The German *Gelehrter* exhausts his subject, and when you have heard him through on it, you may rest assured you have got all that there is to get in regard to it. Often, indeed, in their insistence on thoroughness, they sacrifice completeness. Instead of condensing their lectures to fit the length of the course, they plod laboriously and conscientiously on through all the details, and leave the lectures as a whole unfinished at the end. There was a certain course of the late Professor Zarncke of Leipzig University that never had been read through to the finish, having been originally written too long even for the longer semester. But this made no difference to the genial old man, who began again at the beginning with the beginning of the term, and read as far as the time permitted, leaving his students to find out the rest for themselves from the guides he gave them. These and other defects of the lectures the male student can make up by means of the *Seminar*—the real class-room of the German university—but from this the woman student's sex bars her out, and she must do all the special work of her course by herself, or with a tutor, who, however, may be a member of the *Seminar*, and thus enable her indirectly to share in its advantages. It is precisely this independent work that the woman student must do that benefits her most. Forced to rely herself and to get what she wants under difficulties and in spite of opposition, she applies herself as she otherwise might not, and consequently her acquirements generally represent more real work than do those of the male student.

For the American woman at least—and most of these pioneer women students are Americans—the advantages of such a course are quite as great as they are for the American man, and the initiated know what that means. For her, as for him, the fact of having studied in Germany enhances—often quite disproportionately—her intellectual value in the estimation of those who have not done so, while, by those who have, it is accepted for what their own experience has made its worth to them. If she means to teach, her chances, like the man's, for a good position are by so much the more increased.

It may be considered by the conservative unwarrantably bold in American women thus to push themselves abroad as they could not at home—for instance, at Johns Hopkins or Harvard—but it is not by passively waiting for them that such things come, especially to the individual; and it is undoubtedly due, in part at least, to these pioneer women that the agitation is so general now throughout Germany in favor of admitting women to the universities on the same terms as men.

J.B.S.

2**

TO THE EDITOR OF THE NATION:

SIR: The letter in your last number regarding "Women at the German Universities" will probably call forth others. Perhaps a few more words upon this subject may not come amiss.

** M.F.K., letter to the editor, "Women at the German Universities," *Nation*, February 22, 1894.

To my knowledge, a studious woman was admitted to lectures (on anatomy, I think) in Leipzig; and when male students made audible protest, the professor gave them a most unexpected lecture on manners, and unqualified praise of a brave woman's work in medicine, much to the gratification of a young American student present, who a little later, related the facts to us at supper.

University instructors in Germany have been so kind and helpful to lady students that few will forget it who have been recipients of such favors, by no means rare; and this kindness brought sometimes quite trying results. For instance, at Leipzig it became known that certain lectures were opened to ladies, not officially, but by permission of the instructor; to these quite a number of ladies came who had no such permit, who could not understand German, much less the subject treated, who came simply "to learn German," "to see what it was like," etc. These ladies sometimes talk in loud voices before the lecture begins, causing every one to turn around to look at them, whisper during the lectures, observe folks and things going on in the street, and otherwise disturb the delightful quiet of the place. Of course these ladies were suffered to remain; yet this abuse did close to women one lecture-room at Leipzig which had been opened to them before.

A young girl, pretty or not, going in and out of university halls and lecture-rooms which for centuries have been occupied by men alone, when she is very self-conscious, trying evidently "not to mind," *is* out of place; and the fact that many come unchaperoned, which they certainly would not do in such places at home, unless they had officially their place in such work, makes the matter worse. Nice American girls, even while they are attending university lectures, often feel this to the quick, as I more than once had occasion to when such girls responded to an older lady's kindly word with "Please do let me sit beside you, it is so hard to be here alone." When asked why they had come thus, the answer always was: "I thought I ought to come, and had no one to come with me."

Many instructors are not averse to having woman students, and are ready to help open doors to them, but do demand gravely and decidedly that such students come with at least the same preparatory knowledge which is expected of the men, and insist that quiet, thoughtful work is essential, as well as that reserve which every well-bred girl and woman has when among strangers. The manner with which the American woman accepts such permissions—enters such open doors—and her work while there, will open or close German university courses to women, at least from foreign lands, and may greatly hinder the needed admittance of German women, which sooner or later is sure to come.

M.F.K.
Northampton, Mass., February 16, 1894

3***

TO THE EDITOR OF THE NATION:

SIR: I am glad to hear through the letter of "M.F.K." in the *Nation* for February 22 that women *are* being admitted again to medical lectures at Leipzig. At the time I was a student in that University (89–'91), I was told by a prominent member of the medical faculty that women were not and could not be admitted to the medical lectures, and for the following reason: Some years ago—eight or ten, he said—women were admitted quite generally to the medical as they have continued to be to many of the other lectures, and a number of Russians took advantage of the opportunity to follow a course of study for which, as is well known, they have a special predilection. Among these women, however, came one who was not only extremely beautiful, but also extremely light-minded. She quite upset the sober German students, and that, too, with deliberate intent—as a woman myself, it is with regret I write it. Whenever she was present, the lecturer found his audience disturbed and distracted by the handsome and coquettish Slav. Moreover, from flirtation with the many she soon proceeded to more serious entanglements with a few, and at last drove one of her admirers to such a frenzy of jealousy that he shot and killed himself. The unfortunate affair made a fearful scandal, of course, and the result was that the medical lectures were closed to all women by order of the Cultusminister [minister of culture] at Dresden.

The professor who is my authority for this story is himself personally in favor of admitting women to the study of medicine, but he, nevertheless, would not admit me to his lectures at the time I mentioned, because, as he said, he could not, in face of the order from Dresden. He, however, repeated for me *privatissime* the same course he was holding in public, giving me freely of his precious time and special instruction. It is such deeds of kindness as this that one who has been the recipient of them never forgets, as your correspondent truly states.

*** J.B.S., letter to the editor, "Women at the German Universities," *Nation*, March 1, 1894.

I must differ from your correspondent, however, in regard to chaperones. It seems to me that the need of a chaperone is the very negation of co-education, and the girl or woman who feels it ought not to attempt to attend lectures with men. The presence of a chaperone under such circumstances is a confession no self-respecting woman should make, *i.e.*, that she is not capable of taking care of herself, or fears the men may think so. Her work should be, and always is when she is in earnest about it, an all-sufficient "chaperone."

J.B.S.
New York, February 23, 1894

CHAPTER 25

Decree on the Admission of Women to Universities*

A. Universities

125) Admission of Women as University Students

With the highest authority I promulgate on this day the following decree concerning the admission of women to universities. I sincerely request that you communicate these to the academic officials, as well as mandate what their declaration requires. I also note that as women enroll as university students, special consideration should be given to number 4.

The Minister of Ecclesiastical Affairs,

Holle

To university rectors [Kuratoren], to the president of the Lycee Hostanum in Braunsberg in Königsberg in Prussia, as well as to the rector and the senate of the Royal Friedrich Wilhelm University in Berlin.

Decree, concerning the admission of women to universities.

1. Women will also be admitted as university students beginning in the winter semester of 1908/09.

* From *Zentralblatt für die gesamte Unterrichtsverwaltung in Preussen*, no. 8 (Berlin, August 18, 1908).

2. The regulations for students at state universities from October 1, 1879/ January 6, 1905 apply to women, with the stipulation that female citizens of the Reich in the event of situations addressed in section 3, paragraph 1, and for foreign females in all cases, the approval of the minister is required.
3. Under extraordinary circumstances, women can be excluded from participation in individual lectures, provided the minister has given his approval.
4. It shall be understood that with matriculation women do not obtain, just as men do not, a claim to admission to a state or church exam, doctoral degree, or habilitation. For admission to these, the requisite regulations for exams, doctoral degrees, and the habilitation will be strictly enforced.

* Part 6 *

General Education

CHAPTER 26

General Education: Introduction

Despite their spirited disagreements about the ultimate ends and structure of the research university, American university presidents from Noah Porter and James McCosh to Daniel Coit Gilman and Charles Eliot all agreed that the new institution should not be confused with the college. The university advanced knowledge. The college formed students.

Until the end of the nineteenth century, American college curricula were organized around a common set of prescribed courses that emphasized training in Latin and Greek language, mathematics, and moral philosophy. The classical college curriculum was designed to foster mental discipline and develop moral character. Its purpose, as Princeton's president James McCosh put it in his inaugural address, was "to educate; that is, draw out and improve the faculties which God has given. Our Creator, no doubt, means all things to be perfect; he has left room for growth and progress; and it is a task laid on his intelligent creatures to be a fellow-workers with him in finishing that work which he has left incomplete."

The fixed curriculum was complemented by strict regulations that governed every aspect of college life, from requirements for daily chapel attendance to prohibitions against profanity or other "unmanly" activities. Together the curriculum and these codes of conduct lent the American college a unifying and coherent structure, which was grounded in an established Protestantism. Whatever their limitations, and there were many, these traditions provided colleges with a ready foundation on which they could build a coherent curriculum.

Then university presidents began to introduce electives and relax disciplinary codes as part of the effort to develop modern research universities. Critics in turn worried that these changes imperiled the traditional college curriculum and the very unity of a college education. The research university, claimed its critics, replaced the prescribed curriculum of the college with an incoherent mix of electives and concentrations. The new system encouraged either narrow specialists interested in one field or uninformed dilettantes content to spend four years "grazing" among introductory courses.[1]

Between 1870 and 1930, the same period that gave rise to the modern American research university, "general education" became the common term for what the newer curriculum of the university lacked. The very concept was an attempt on the part of higher education leaders to redress what they saw as the negative effects of the research university model on undergraduate education. As colleges and universities gradually drifted away from their curricular traditions, many struggled to recover the sense of wholeness and unity that the older, generally religious-based curricular orders had afforded.

From Columbia's and Chicago's core curricula to St. John's Great Books program, these curricular innovations were surrogates for what had been religious-based visions of the unity of knowledge, learning, and culture. General education was an attempt to address these concerns by supplementing departmental courses and giving a certain order to the increasingly dominant elective system, as initially proposed and implemented by Harvard president Charles Eliot in the late nineteenth century. General education was to supplement what the research university lacked.

But faculty and university leaders rarely agreed on what exactly was missing. Over the course of the twentieth century, "general education" was used to refer to a liberal as opposed to a professional education, a common or foundational knowledge, or an awareness and capacity to engage in broad public issues of the contemporary world.

Columbia University established one of the first general education programs shortly after the Armistice in 1919 and over the following two decades developed its renowned Contemporary Civilization and Humanities A and B series of courses. Columbia's president F. A. P. Barnard had endorsed Eliot's new elective system in 1872, but by the end of the century Columbia students, unlike their counterparts at Harvard or even Yale, could still choose only half of their courses; the other half was still under the control of the faculty. In 1900, Columbia College had only five hundred students, compared to the two thousand graduate and professional students enrolled in the university.

Contemporary Civilization was first taught in the fall of 1918, as "War Aims," by Frederick J. E. Woodbridge, a professor of philosophy and dean of the graduate faculties. Originally designed for members of the Student Army Training Corps, the course was, as Robert A. McCaughey writes, a course in "Allied apologetics with no pretense of objectivity or balance."[2] After the war ended, Columbia briefly considered implementing a follow-up course called "Peace Aims," but the post-Armistice course became Contemporary Civilization.

First offered in the fall of 1919, Contemporary Civilization was a yearlong course required of all freshman and directed by John J. Coss until his death in 1941. And, as its title suggests, it was focused almost exclusively on the contemporary world. The primary readings were textbooks written by course instructors. During the first decade of its existence, coverage never went back beyond 1871. It focused squarely on the present. The first syllabus read: "We are living in a world in which there are great and perplexing issues on which keen differences of opinion have arisen; and it is important now, no less than during war, that men should understand the forces which are at work in the society of their own day."

Columbia's Humanities A and B core courses emerged out of a course first proposed and taught by John Erskine, an English professor at and graduate of Columbia. Erskine first proposed a course on "great books." Erksine's intention was to introduce students to classic texts, not engage them in scholarly study of them. After the war broke out and with Erskine serving in France, the proposed course was tabled. But Erskine proposed another, similar course called "General Honors," which was taught as a seminar for the first time in 1920. Open only to upperclassmen, the course met Wednesday evenings for two hours to discuss the reading. Over the following two decades, Erskine's course gradually evolved into the "Colloquium on Important Books" taught by Jacques Barzun and Lionel Trilling. Humanities A (on literature) and B (on music and arts) were introduced in 1937 and required for all Columbia College students in 1947.

As Columbia was developing and refining its general education program, a group of faculty at the University of Chicago had begun to design what they referred to as the New Plan.[3] Led by Chauncey S. Boucher, a dean frustrated by the mediocre academic quality of Chicago's undergraduates, as well as by the university's general disregard of undergraduate education, a committee of faculty plotted a new curriculum organized around four yearlong survey courses covering the areas of the university's four divisions: biological sciences, physical sciences, humanities, social sciences. In the spring of 1931, Boucher oversaw the development of a general education curriculum that included a six-hour comprehensive final exam administered by an outside examiner. Students would be able to work through the four required courses at their own discretion. By 1935, Boucher could argue that the New Plan's intellectual rigor had produced results. Undergraduate students reported higher degrees of satisfaction with their education, time to degree decreased, and, as some liked to point out, Chicago's vaunted football program had collapsed.

But the New Plan had a powerful critic, Robert Maynard Hutchins, Chicago's new president. Appointed president at the age of twenty-nine, Hutchins left his position as dean of Yale Law School and arrived in Chicago just as Boucher was beginning discussions that would eventually result in the New Plan. Soon after his arrival, Hutchins began collaborating with a young and feisty philosopher named Mortimer Adler on a Great Books honors course modeled on Erskine's Columbia course (in which Adler had once taught). Chicago's Philosophy Department had refused Adler's appointment, so Hutchins secured him a position in the law school as a professor of the "philosophy of law."

Before his arrival at Chicago, Adler had been developing an underlying methodology and taxonomy for all sciences in a series of writings. Attracted to Adler's encyclopedic aspirations and academic ambitions, Hutchins enlisted him in a plan to remake the University of Chicago. Their Great Books course was their vehicle, and it represented a direct challenge to the New Plan.

Between 1934 and 1935, Hutchins, long since held up as the champion of Chicago's core, began a public assault on the New Plan, delivering a series of talks and speeches to faculty, alumni, and trustees in which he denounced the contemporary system of education as merely pouring "facts into the student with splendid disregard of the certainty that he will forget them." The university, he insisted, should be interested in ideas.

What followed was a public debate about the proper role of research and professional scholarship in undergraduate education and, perhaps more fundamentally, the possibility of a unified curriculum in the age of the modern research university. The debate took place in faculty meetings and memoranda and in the *Daily Maroon*, the undergraduate student newspaper. And, as John Boyer has recounted it, the debate soon pitted supporters of the New Plan, with its commitment to empirical sciences as well as humanistic learning, against the advocates of the Adler-Hutchins Great Books vision of general education. Hutchins made his case for a new undergraduate curriculum most publicly in *The Higher Learning in America*, which was published in 1936 as a series of essays on education.

One of the most trenchant responses to Hutchins's plans, and *The Higher*

Learning in America in particular, came from a young Chicago economist named Harry Gideonse, who had chaired the New Plan's yearlong social science course and had been a vocal critic of Hutchins's reform efforts. After Hutchins had denied the Economics Department's bid to grant Gideonse tenure in 1936 and 1937, Gideonse published a blistering review of Hutchins's book, accusing him of, among other things, attempting to impose an "absolutist system" on the undergraduate curriculum and eschewing modern science. Gideonse soon left Chicago. And in January 1942 the Chicago faculty voted to adopt a new, all-general-education undergraduate curriculum that was strengthened in another vote in 1947.

These early models and debates at Columbia and Chicago are still in many ways the basis for general education programs today. When faculty members debate revisions to their undergraduate curricula and consider the ends and appropriate structure for their institutions, they return to the same questions and invoke concerns similar to those of their early twentieth-century predecessors. They lament the specialization of undergraduate education; they worry about the incoherence of most students' curricular experiences; and they make arguments about what a real undergraduate education should do. And in these proposals, the echoes of their predecessors are easily discerned. In their attempts to address what they claimed was lacking in research universities, proponents of general education have offered a few basic supplements: the cultivation of liberal values as distinct from simply professional ones, the development of basic knowledge in preparation for more specialized study, the exposure to universal questions about what it is to be human, or the cultivation of an awareness of contemporary problems and concerns. And the "search" for a unified, cohesive curriculum, as the Harvard report *General Education in a Free Society* put it in 1945, continues.

CHAPTER 27

Editorial: A Focus for Freshmen

Charles Sears Baldwin

The freshman, apparently, must have his work cut out for him. True, the formula of the course commonly prescribed forty years ago, Greek + Latin + mathematics + English + French or German, has long been antiquated; but only less antiquated is the free election meantime practised locally for a few years. If the old formula $3G+3L+3M+3E+3F$ is wrong, have we corrected it by the mere substitution of history for Greek, or of chemistry for Latin, or even by offering more leeway of choice? Some college teachers who have looked long at actual freshman schedules have observed that the leeway of choice is illusory, since the conditions pressing up from the schools and down from the later college years often operate as restrictively as formal prescriptions. And these teachers have questioned the formula itself, not merely this item or that, but the system of addition. They ask, is $3H+3C+3M+3C+3F$ better fundamentally? It is more various; it opens more methods of study; but, whatever the items, should freshmen year be a sum, an aggregation? Should not the formula be $X\times Y\times Z$? Is not what we are seeking a product?

There is little difficulty in agreeing to this abstractly. Most concrete applications, however, are still in the stage of laboratory experiment. The oldest and commonest is the making of the single course in history or in English literature preparatory to all later studies in that department by making it a "survey." The idea is to scan the whole field of the subject and open vistas. The results are at worst to provide a chronological dictionary or a guide-book telling less of how to think than of what to think. More truly preparatory seem those freshman courses in physics or chemistry which teach laboratory method; but even these may move only within the walls of the single subject, as the history may be taught apart from the literature. What we seem most to lack is not a focus in the future, but a focus in freshman year itself. Without detailing other schemes, for example the Amherst teaching of economics as a general education for citizenship, we may fairly say that none has an established success. The question recurs, then, Can we focus while we deal with subjects singly, while we teach solely by departments? Apparently it is possible for freshmen to begin a number of well considered and separately well taught college studies without necessarily beginning a college education. We have abandoned uniformity; we are still seeking unity.

In the matter of unification something may be learned from the recent experience of the best freshman courses in English composition. Observation of "English A" is obviously worth while because this is the only course now prescribed universally. What is more to the point, it is the only course in which combination with other studies is a necessity. The day for making it a review of high-school exercises, or a detention hospital, or a proof-reading bureau, is past, though some few colleges are still unaware of the march of time. The best freshman courses in composition draw from the fact that rhetoric has no subject matter the practical conclusion that in college it is meant to serve all freshman studies while it provides training for the more advanced studies beyond. The best teachers of composition are aware from the long history of rhetoric that it is always perverted by being segregated. "English A" at its best, therefore, has been an effective freshman focus.

While we were at this stage of reflection and experiment, there burst upon us S. A. T. C. Here, at least was focus, not the focus we intended or proposed to maintain, but at any rate focus. The S. A. T. C. apparatus was hardly more than well set up before it began to be taken down. Our experience of it, therefore, can hardly be called an experiment. Nevertheless, some of its methods were tried long enough and generally enough to be suggestive. The course that was prescribed universally and for the whole period of training was the one dealing with the issues of the war. With whatever local variations, moreover, this course was uniform throughout the country at least to the extent of dealing with matters of vivid current interest, of meeting daily, and of demanding the cooperation of several, usually many, departments.

For "War Issues" demanded history, economics, philosophy, politics with the comparative study of governments, not to mention as much literature, law, physiography, and other topics as could be brought to bear. More than this, it had to combine not only instruction, but instructors. Including the whole student body, it had perforce to draft a large proportion of the faculty. There had to be—no small task—a syllabus to draw the subjects together intelligibly; but there had to be also frequent and regular conferences of the most various staff ever gathered into one college room. There was something essentially different from any "group" of studies printed together in a catalogue, but administered separately and singly in the classroom. This was really a group of studies, students, and instructors, but especially of studies. For though sections were in some colleges combined on certain days to hear lectures by the elder academic statesmen, the general procedure necessarily was to assign a single section to a single instructor, were he sociologist, historian, or critic, to be taught by him continuously. The studies were combined in his person.

It is significant, therefore, that in spite of obvious defects due to haste and pressure, "War Issues" stirred the corporate imagination. No sooner was it mustered out with the rest of S. A. T. C. than its teachers began to ask one another, Should we not introduce this method in our regular freshman program? They recognized, even in difficult conditions, a readier realization of certain educational values than they had hoped; and they were stimulated and guided by working more closely together than had seemed possible. The crossing of department boundaries, which before had been oftener suggested than tried, was found to be largely feasible. The doubling of class-hours per week, and the consequent halving of the total of courses taken simultaneously, was fairly familiar as a method of intensification from the experience of summer sessions. The combination of these advantages in a single system gave so much larger significance to the old word *group* that the associate instructors began to hope that they had found in fact a new formula.

To make the most obvious application of this idea, suppose a course of five or six hours a week, required of all freshmen, combining the typical first college course in history with elementary economics, politics, and philosophy, planned and administered by a stable cooperative body of instructors from all four departments, and taught in small sections of which each shall have a single instructor throughout. It is now evident from even so short experience that to make such a course go we must no longer hitch either the instructors or the subjects tandem. This is a four-in-hand. To arrange a succession of instructors may be merely to provide one more of the ill-starred series aptly styled in student slang vaudeville courses. To arrange a succession of subjects within a given boundary may be merely a change in bookkeeping, not a change in teaching. The new aim is to make each component subject help the interpretation of the others more immediately and to bring out their common bearings. But skeptics ask, "Why not include literature? And if literature, which was to be included in the grandiose scheme of 'War Issues,' why not any other subject open to a freshman? Having then appropriated most of his time, why not take it all? Why not make the whole freshman course a single prescribed group? And, if you do, what have you actually accomplished of substantial change, except to risk having some sections or some subjects taught by the wrong instructors?" If this series is intended as a *reductio ad absurdum*, the answer is that such a freshman year is not absurd abstractly and necessarily, but that, whether absurd or not, it is not the freshman year proposed. The proposal is to demand a third of every freshman's time for a single course combining those studies which most obviously gain by interaction. Each of the studies enumerated above gains by combination with the others in its initial stages, *i.e.*, for a freshman. Mathematics, on the contrary, would neither gain nor contribute directly at this stage, though later, of course, it serves both the statistics of economics and the metaphysics of philosophy.

French or Spanish, again, cannot bear directly at this stage, though later it will serve both literature and history. As for English composition, it is already in a position to become a helpful *organon* for any freshman scheme whatsoever. It would readily serve such a combination course; it would neither gain nor contribute the more by coalescing. But history, economics, politics, philosophy, as they can be made actually available to actual freshmen, can apparently constitute a substantive group. The real flaw in the idea as it was carried out in "War Issues" is quite different. The typical failure of the "War Issues" course was in being forced here and there by haste or by pressure of numbers to lay down the issues instead of making the students find them. The idea of the course was to interpret a world-wide movement of urgent concern by focusing the wisdom and the information of those who were specialists in its various elements. But in college studies, interpretation is not something ready-made, to be accepted and learned; it is a process. It demands the lively and progressive cooperation of the student. It must be reached, not accepted; and it must be reached by him. Unless he is interpreting—and therefore collating information and opinion, the interpretation tends to become after all only one more "survey." True, he needs guidance; but none the less—rather, all the more—he needs to handle the materials before he weighs conclusions. The typical danger of the "survey" is that, instead of being a guide in study, it should become a substitute for study. This danger of predigested intellectual food is greater in history and politics than in literature; and where the instructors were not numerous enough to guide reading and discussion, or the library not large enough to provide generally more than a few compends, "War Issues" tended to become an examination cram.

But this seems rather a failure in administration than a defect in the method. The practical difficulties of making books enough available and of making students use them critically are, indeed, great; but, to judge from certain large elementary courses in history and from the "case system" in law schools, they are not insuperable. At any rate, the combination course is likely to stand or fall on its capacity to provide not only interpretation, but interpreting, to focus not only the subjects, but the methods of study and the student himself. If it can do this, it is likely to win its way.

CHAPTER 28

The New Freshman Course in Columbia College

John J. Coss

In September Columbia College will give for the first time a course which combines the work usually offered in several departments. It is called "An Introduction to Contemporary Civilization," will be required of freshmen, and will meet five times a week through both semesters. The course is interesting chiefly for three reasons: its genesis, its administrative policy, and its content. The idea for the course was taken from the War Issues Course given during the S. A. T. C. under the leadership of the Dean of the Faculties of Political Science, Philosophy and Pure Science.[1] With the end of the war the faculty sensed the need for considering the issues of peace and felt that the students should be stimulated to reflection on present-day problems very early in their study. After much discussion and planning, the new course emerged as the solution.

In the administration of the course five departments are jointly interested. History and Philosophy have given up each a required course to combine in the new enterprise; and in addition the departments of Government, Economics, and Sociology have both contributed to the subject matter and will provide from their own staff instructors who will teach throughout the year. In its production and in its teaching the course is a cooperative enterprise. It has long been clear that each of the departments named considered the problems of the present; but for the first time it has seemed possible to unite their efforts to furnish students the facts, problems and proposed solutions of the issues of our time. Earlier attempts to accomplish a similar end have been made by having a series of lecturers, each one presenting some phase of the subject. In a course administered by this method it was impossible to preserve unity and continuity; and the difficulty of presenting piecemeal the contributions of different disciplines remained. In the new course each instructor will teach the entire subject matter. This itself presents a difficulty; for from the outline of the course, which is given below, it will be evident that no one man knows in detail all the subjects which will be treated. Each instructor will teach for a portion of the time in a field which is not his specialty. This means that the teaching staff will be educating itself as well as instructing the students. It is not unlikely that this will prove a benevolent requirement, since it will tend to break down those "idea-tight" compartments in which learning too often isolates itself. The students, as well as the instructors, will have an opportunity to cooperate in the course, since each class will be represented in the monthly conference of instructors and students by one member, standing for election four times a year.

The content of the course is planned to introduce the students to the insistent problems of to-day through acquainting them with the materials of their situation: nature's resources and human nature and its recent history. At the outset, through map studies and the preparation of statistical graphs, a survey is made of natural resources and the distribution of races. An attempt is then made to present those human traits which are of importance because men have to work together and get on with one another in an orderly fashion.

With this background the controlling ideas of the world today in the fields of intellectual, economic, and political endeavor are studied. The view of nature as subject to man's control through science, and of man as himself perfectible by natural means; the change in production methods from home to factory and the great social changes which have accompanied this economic revolution; the abandonment of monarchical forms of political control for democratic, nationalistic rule;—all are treated with many concrete illustrations.

In the second semester the more recent history of the great nations is reviewed in order that the social and political forces operating may be understood, that light may be thrown on the final section of the course for which all the rest exist, the perplexing issues which men face and for which no ready-made remedies exist. Among these problems are: how to produce many and cheap goods without sacrificing human nature; how to achieve political and legal forms which are at once flexible and stable; how to eliminate human and material waste of every kind; how to preserve national integrity and still enjoy the benefits of international organization; and finally how to provide an education which will advance personal and social interests, cultural and industrial. To state these issues is useful; to present the proposed solutions is clarifying; to solve the problems with words impossible. This fact is taken at its full face value by those who are sponsors for the course; but it is their belief that the first step towards solution is information.

The success of the course depends not so much upon its genesis, its administration, or its content, as upon the ability and the enthusiasm of the teaching staff. Men from the five departments named, History, Philosophy, Economics, Government, and Sociology, have worked together in the preparation of the course, and are convinced that it is an enterprise so important that any amount of effort will be worth while to realize the end in view, actually to acquaint college students with the world in which they live and to encourage reflective participation in the issues which they will all have to face.

CHAPTER 29

General Education

Robert Maynard Hutchins

My excuse for dedicating one chapter to general education in a series on the higher learning is the relation between the two. We can never get a university without general education. Unless students and professors (and particularly professors) have a common intellectual training, a university must remain a series of disparate schools and departments, united by nothing except the fact that they have the same president and board of trustees. Professors cannot talk to one another, not at least about anything important. They cannot hope to understand one another.

We take it for granted that we shall always have specialists; yet neither the world nor knowledge of it is arbitrarily divided up as universities are. Everybody cannot be a specialist in every field. He must therefore be cut off from every field but his own unless he has the same basic education that other specialists have. This means more than having the same language and the same general interest in advancing knowledge. It means having a common stock of fundamental ideas. This becomes more important as empirical science advances and accumulates more and more data. The specialist in a narrow field has all he can do to keep up with the latest discoveries in it. Other men, even in his own department, struggling to stay abreast of what is happening in their own segments of the subject, cannot hope to keep up with what is happening in his. They may now expect to have some general understanding of what he is doing because they all have something in common; they are in the same department. But the day will shortly be upon us when even this degree of comprehension will be impossible, because of the infinite splitting of subject matters and the progressive submergence of any ideas by our insistence on information as the content of education.

Efforts to correct this tendency by administrative devices are mere palliatives. Roving professorships at Harvard, the divisional organization at Chicago, the Institute of Human Relations at Yale, noble and praiseworthy as they are, serve to mitigate and not to remove the disunity, discord, and disorder that have overtaken our educational system. If professors and students had a common stock of fundamental ideas, it might be possible for those in physiology to communicate with those in physics, and even law and divinity might begin to find it worthwhile to associate with one another.

In this chapter I should like to talk about content, not about method. I concede the great difficulty of communicating the kind of education I favor to those who are unable or unwilling to get their education from books. I insist, however, that the education I shall outline is the kind that everybody should have, that the answer to it is not that some people should not have it, but that we should find out how to give it to those whom we do not know how to teach at present. You cannot say my content is wrong because you do not know the method of transmitting it. Let us agree upon content if we can and have faith that the technological genius of America will solve the problem of communication.

Economic conditions require us to provide some kind of education for the young, and for all the young, up to about their twentieth year. Probably one-third of them cannot learn from books. This is no reason why we should not try to work out a better course of study for the other two-thirds. At the same time we should continue our efforts and experiments to find out how to give a general education to the hand-minded and the functionally illiterate. Even these attempts may be somewhat simplified if we know what a general education is.

Please do not tell me that the general education I propose should not be adopted because the great majority of those who pass through it will not go on to the university. The scheme that I advance is based on the notion that general education is education for everybody, whether he goes on to the university or not. It will be useful to him in the university; it will be equally useful if he never goes there. I will admit that it will not be useful to him outside the university in the popular sense of utility. It may not assist him to make money or get ahead. It may not in any obvious fashion adjust him to his environment or fit him for the contemporary scene. It will, however, have a deeper, wider utility: it will cultivate the intellectual virtues.

The trouble with the popular notion of utility is that it confuses immediate and final ends. Material prosperity and adjustment to the environment are good more or less, but they are not good in themselves and there are other goods beyond them. The intellectual virtues, however, are good in themselves and good as means to happiness. By the intellectual virtues I mean good intellectual habits. The ancients distinguish five intellectual virtues: the three speculative virtues of intuitive knowledge, which is the habit of induction; of scientific knowledge, which is the habit of demonstration; and of philosophical wisdom, which is scientific knowledge, combined with intuitive reason, of things highest by nature, first principles and first causes. To these they add the two virtues of the practical intellect: art, the capacity to make according to a true course of reasoning, and prudence, which is right reason with respect to action.[1]

In short, the intellectual virtues are habits resulting from the training of the intellectual powers. An intellect properly disciplined, an intellect properly habituated, is an intellect able to operate well in all fields. An education that consists of the cultivation of the intellectual virtues, therefore, is the most useful education, whether the student is destined for a life of contemplation or a life of action. I would remind you of the words of Newman:

> If then the intellect is so excellent a portion of us, and its cultivation so excellent, it is not only beautiful, perfect, admirable, and noble in itself, but in a true and high sense it must be useful to the possessor and to all around him; not useful in any low, mechanical, mercantile sense, but as diffusing good, or as a blessing, or a gift, or power, or a treasure, first to the owner, then through him to the world.[2]

I shall not be attentive when you tell me that the plan of general education I am about to present is remote from real life, that real life is in constant flux and change, and that education must be in constant flux and change as well. I do not deny that all things are in change. They have a beginning, and a middle, and an end. Nor will I deny that the history of the race reveals tremendous technological advances and great increases in our scientific knowledge. But we are so impressed with scientific and technological progress that we assume similar progress in every field. We renounce our intellectual heritage, read only the most recent books, discuss only current events, try to keep the schools abreast or even ahead of the times, and write elaborate addresses on Education and Social Change.

[. . .]

Our erroneous notion of progress has thrown the classics and the liberal arts out of the curriculum, overemphasized the empirical sciences, and made education the servant of any contemporary movements in society, no matter how superficial. In recent years this attitude has been accentuated by the world-wide depression and the highly advertised political, social and economic changes resulting from it. We have been very much upset by all these things. We have felt that it was our duty to educate the young so that they would be prepared for further political, social, and economic changes. Some of us have thought we should try to figure out what the impending changes would be and frame a curriculum that embodied them. Others have even thought that we should decide what changes are desirable and then educate our students not merely to anticipate them, but also to take part in bringing them about.

One purpose of education is to draw out the elements of our common human nature. These elements are the same in any time or place. The notion of educating a man to live in any particular time or place, to adjust him to any particular environment, is therefore foreign to a true conception of education.

Education implies teaching. Teaching implies knowledge. Knowledge is truth. The truth is everywhere the same.[3] Hence education should be everywhere the same. I do not overlook the possibilities of differences in organization, in administration, in local habits and customs. These are details. I suggest that the heart of any course of study designed for the whole people will be, if education is rightly understood, the same at any time, in any place, under any political, social, or economic conditions. Even the administrative details are likely to be similar because all societies have generic similarity.

If education is rightly understood, it will be understood as the cultivation of the intellect. The cultivation of the intellect is the same good for all men in all societies. It is, moreover, the good for which all other goods are only means. Material prosperity, peace and civil order, justice and the moral virtues are means to the cultivation of the intellect. So Aristotle says in the *Politics*: "Now, in men reason and mind are the end towards which nature strives, so that the generation and moral discipline of the citizens ought to be ordered with a view to them." An education which served the means rather than their end would be misguided.

I agree, of course, that any plan of general education must be such as to educate the student for intelligent action. It must, therefore, start him on the road toward practical wisdom. But the question is what is the best way for education to start him and how far can it carry him. Prudence or practical wisdom selects the means toward the ends that we desire. It is acquired partly from intellectual operations and partly from experience. But the chief requirement for it is correctness in thinking. Since education cannot duplicate the experiences which the student will have when he graduates, it should devote itself to developing correctness in thinking as a means to practical wisdom, that is, to intelligent action.

[...]

A modern heresy is that all education is formal education and that formal education must assume the total responsibility for the full development of the individual. The Greek notion that the city educates the man has been forgotten. Everything that educated the man in the city has to be imported into our schools, colleges, and universities. We are beginning to behave as though the home, the church, the state, the newspaper, the radio, the movies, the neighborhood club, and the boy next door did not exist. All the experience that is daily and hourly acquired from these sources is overlooked, and we set out to supply imitations of it in educational institutions. The experience once provided by some of these agencies may be attenuated now; but it would be a bold man who would assert that the young person today lived a life less full of experience than the youth of yesterday. Today as yesterday we may leave experience to other institutions and influences and emphasize in education the contribution that it is supremely fitted to make, the intellectual training of the young. The life they lead when they are out of our hands will give them experience enough. We cannot try to give it to them and at the same time perform the task that is ours and ours alone.

Young people do not spend all their time in school. Their elders commonly spend none of it there. Yet their elders are, we hope, constantly growing in practical wisdom. They are, at least, having experience. If we can teach them while they are being educated how to reason, they may be able to comprehend and assimilate their experience. It is a good principle of educational administration that a college or university should do nothing that another agency can do as well. This is a good principle because a college or university has a vast and complicated job if it does what only it can do. In general education, therefore, we may wisely leave experience to life and set about our job of intellectual training.

If there are permanent studies which every person who wishes to call himself educated should master; if those studies constitute our intellectual inheritance, then those studies should be the center of a general education. They cannot be ignored because they are difficult, or unpleasant, or because they are almost totally missing from our curriculum today. The child-centered school may be attractive to the child, and no doubt is useful as a place in which the little ones may release their inhibitions and hence behave better at home. But educators cannot permit the students to dictate the course of study unless they are prepared to confess that they are nothing but chaperons, supervising an aimless, trial-and-error process which is chiefly valuable because it keeps young people from doing something worse. The free elective system as Mr. Eliot introduced it at Harvard and as Progressive education adapted it to lower age levels amounted to a denial that there was content to education. Since there was no content to education, we might as well let students follow their own bent. They would at least be interested and pleased and would be as well educated as if they had pursued a prescribed course of study. This overlooks the fact that the aim of education is to connect man with man, to connect the present with the past, and to advance the thinking of the race. If this is the aim of education, it cannot be left to the sporadic, spontaneous interests of children or even of undergraduates.[4]

[. . .]

The variations that should be encouraged fall not in the realm of content but in that of method. Allowances for individual differences should be provided for by abolishing all the requirements except the examinations and permitting the student to take them whenever in his opinion he is ready to do so. The cultivation of independent thought and study, now almost wholly missing from our program, may thus be somewhat advanced. And this may be done without sacrificing the content of education to the obsessions of the hour or the caprices of the young.

If we are educators we must have a subject matter, and a rational, defensible one. If that subject matter is education, we cannot alter it to suit the whims of parents, students, or the public. Whewell, Master of Trinity College, Cambridge, one hundred years ago, said:

> Young persons may be so employed and so treated, that their caprice, their self-will, their individual tastes and propensities, are educed and developed; but this is not Education. It is not the Education of a Man; for what is educed is not what belongs to man as man, and connects man with man. It is not the Education of a man's Humanity, but the Indulgence of Individuality.

In general education we are interested in drawing out the elements of our common human nature; we are interested in the attributes of the race, not the accidents of individuals.

If our course of study reflects today an interest in the accidents of individuals; if the permanent studies are conspicuous by their absence from it, I can only say that these are the reasons why our course of study is bad. We know that our course of study leads to the most unfortunate results in the organization of education, in the qualities and activities of professors and students, and in the cultivation of our people. It is surely not a criticism of the permanent studies that they have had no share in producing these results.

[. . .]

Let us avoid all questions of administration and method. Let us assume that we have an intelligible organization of education under which there is a four-year unit, beginning at about the junior year in high school and ending at about the end of the sophomore year in college. Let us assume that we are going to try to teach in that unit everybody who can learn from books. Let us assume further that the conclusion of their work in this unit will mark the end of formal instruction for most students. They will not go on to the university. Nevertheless we must have a curriculum which will, in the main, do as well for those who are going on as those who are not. What shall this curriculum be?

We have excluded body building and character building. We have excluded the social graces and the tricks of trades. We have suggested that the curriculum should be composed principally of the permanent studies. We propose the permanent studies because those studies draw out the elements of our common human nature, because they connect man with man, because they connect us with the best that man has thought, because they are basic to any further study and to any understanding of the world. What are the permanent studies?

They are in the first place those books which have through the centuries attained to the dimensions of classics. Many such books, I am afraid, are in the ancient and medieval period. But even these are contemporary. A classic is a book that is contemporary in every age. That is why it is a classic. The conversations of Socrates raise questions that are as urgent today as they were when Plato wrote. In fact they are more so, because the society in which Plato lived did not need to have them raised as much as we do. We have forgotten how important they are.

Such books are then a part, and a large part, of the permanent studies. They are so in the first place because they are the best books we know. How can we call a man educated who has never read any of the great books in the western world? Yet today it is entirely possible for a student to graduate from the finest American colleges without having read any of them, except possibly Shakespeare. Of course, the student may have heard of these books, or at least their authors. But this knowledge is general through textbooks, and textbooks have probably done as much to degrade the American intelligence as any single force. If the student should know about Cicero, Milton, Galileo, or Adam Smith, why should he not read what they wrote? Ordinarily what he knows about them he learns from texts which must be at best second-hand versions of their thought.

In the second place these books are an essential part of general education because it is impossible to understand any subject or to comprehend the contemporary world without them. If we read Newton's *Principia*, we see a great genius in action; we make the acquaintance of a work of unexampled simplicity and elegance. We understand, too, the basis of modern science. The false starts, the backing and filling, the wildness, the hysteria, the confusion of modern thought and the modern world result from the loss of what has been thought and done by earlier ages. The Industrial Revolution begins our study of history and the social sciences. Philosophy begins with Descartes and Locke and psychology with Wundt and William James. Natural science originates with the great experimenters of the nineteenth century. If anything prior is mentioned, it is only as a reminder that our recent great achievements in these fields must, of course, have had some primitive beginnings in the dark earlier centuries. The classics, if presented at all, are offered in excerpts out of context, and for the most part for the sake of showing the student how far we have progressed beyond our primitive beginnings.

[. . .]

You will observe that the great books of the western world cover every department of knowledge. The *Republic* of Plato is basic to an understanding of the law; it is equally important as education for what is known as citizenship. The *Physics* of Aristotle, which deals with change and motion in nature, is fundamental to the natural sciences and medicine, and is equally important to all those who confront change and motion in nature, that is, to everybody. Four years spent partly in reading, discussing and digesting books of such importance would, therefore, contribute equally to preparation for specialized study and to general education of a terminal variety. Certainly four years is none too long for this experience. It is an experience which will, as I have said, serve as preparation for advanced study and as general education designed to help the student understand the world. It will also develop habits of reading and standards of taste and criticism that will enable the adult, after his formal education is over, to think and act intelligently about the thought and movements of contemporary life. It will help him to share in the intellectual activity of his time.

In order to read books one must know how to do it. The degeneracy of instruction in English grammar should not blind us to the fact that only through grammatical study can written works be understood. Grammar is the scientific analysis of language through which we understand the meaning and force of what is written. Grammar disciplines the mind and develops the logical faculty. It is good in itself and as an aid to reading the classics. It has a place in general education in connection with the classics and independently of them. For those who are going to learn from books learning the art of reading would seem to be indispensable.

I do not suggest that learning the languages or the grammar in which the ancient classics were written is necessary to general education. Excellent translations of almost all of them now exist. Unless it can be shown that the study of Greek and Latin grammar is essential to the study of English grammar or that the mastery of the Greek and Latin languages is essential to mastery of our own, I see no reason for insisting on these languages as part of general education. The modern languages, of course, are no necessary part of it. Time should be allowed for students to acquire them; but the examinations reflecting general education should not contain them. They are an extracurriculum accomplishment or a tool for advanced work rather than a fundamental portion of general education.

I add to grammar, or the rules of reading, rhetoric or logic, or the rules of writing, speaking, and reasoning. The classics provide models of excellence; grammar, rhetoric, and logic are means of determining how excellence is achieved. We have forgotten that there are rules for speaking. And English composition, as it is commonly taught, is a feeble and debased imitation of the classical rules of writing, placing emphasis either on the most trivial details or on what is called self-expression. Self-expression as here understood is, of course, the exact reverse of the discipline which rhetoric in all ages up to the present was used to give. Logic is a statement in technical form of the conditions under which reasoning is rigorously demonstrative. If the object of general education is train to train the mind for intelligent action, logic cannot be missing from it.

Logic is a critical branch of the study of reasoning. It remains only to add a study which exemplifies reasoning in its clearest and most precise form. That study is, of course, mathematics, and of the mathematical studies chiefly those that use the type of exposition that Euclid employed. In such studies the pure operation of reason is made manifest. The subject matter depends on the universal and necessary processes of human thought. It is not affected by differences in taste, disposition, or prejudice. It refutes the common answer of students who, conformable to the temper of the times, wish to accept the principles and deny the conclusions. Correctness in thinking may be more directly and impressively taught through mathematics than in any other way.[5] It is depressing that in high schools and junior colleges mathematics is not often taught in such a way as to achieve these ends. Arithmetic and geometry are there usually presented to the student as having great practical value, as of course they have.[6] But I have had students in the freshman year in college who had never heard that they had any other value, and were quite unwilling to consider mathematical questions until their practical possibilities had been explained. To this pass has our notion of utility brought us.

We have then for a general education a course of study consisting of the greatest books of the western world and the arts of reading, writing, thinking, and speaking, together with mathematics, the best exemplar of the processes of human reason. If our hope has been to frame a curriculum which educes the elements of our common human nature, this program should realize our hope. If we wish to prepare the young for intelligent action, this course of study should assist us; for they will have learned what has been done in the past, and what the greatest men have thought. They will have learned how to think themselves. If we wish to lay a basis for advanced study, that basis is provided. If we wish to secure true universities, we may look forward to them, because students and professors may acquire through this course of study a common stock of ideas and common methods of dealing with them. All the needs of general education in America seem to be satisfied by this curriculum.

CHAPTER 30

The Higher Learning in a Democracy

Harry D. Gideonse

In the destruction of political, economic and intellectual freedom in the totalitarian countries of Europe, the universities were early victims of the forces that contrasted the "confusion" and the "chaos" of freedom with the "order" of the dictatorships. Similarly, in the defense of a free society in America, education has become a battleground for those who think of the school as an instrument of public policy and for those who regard it as an institution for the development of the potentialities of our youth and for the unfettered pursuit of knowledge.

Vested interests of diverse descriptions have sought to impose upon our educational institutions their own particular pedagogic nostrums. Some professional educators have deserted the traditional search for objectivity in which they claim to see a mask for the perpetuation of the *status quo*. They have quite deliberately sought harmony and order by the choice either of a collectivist frame of reference or of a set of metaphysical principles within which experience would be systematically ordered. Upsetting questions about the postulates, implied in the choice of the framework have been conveniently overlooked by both groups.[1]

To this controversy Abraham Flexner and Robert M. Hutchins have contributed a special note by their emphasis on the university and its functions. Mr. Flexner's book, published in 1930, can be summarized in one of its sentences: "No sound or consistent philosophy, thesis, or principle lies beneath the American university of today."[2]

American education is, for a fact, critically in need of a searching scrutiny of its ends as well as its means. No one should resent informed and constructive criticism of institutions that have developed with amazing speed in a hit-or-miss fashion to meet a large variety of needs and pressures. Unfortunately, however, these recent criticisms have tended to confuse rather than to clarify the essential issues.

It is possible to agree with a great many of the specific criticisms of Flexner and Hutchins and still be thoroughly dissatisfied with their proposed solutions. They failed to recognize the forces that led to present conditions, and to supply specific evidence of the direction in which reorientation should take place. In the writings of both these critics the question that presses is the question that is begged: How find a metaphysics, if there be one, which will remedy rather than intensify prevailing "confusion"? It may be true that no consistent philosophy or metaphysics "lies beneath the American university of today." It would be more significant to inquire how much more consistency a country's educational institutions can have than the society in which they exist. It would be an even greater contribution to suggest—if only for discussion—the specific character of the metaphysical principles which would bring "rational order" out of our free "chaos." The plea that the entire structure of higher education should be recast to accord with some set of metaphysical principles turns upon the nature and acceptability of those principles. To write volumes in support of the thesis that there should be a unifying philosophy, without specific indication of the type of unity or of philosophy, is to miss the essential problem underlying the modern dilemma.

If the higher learning is to be unified, is the unity to be voluntary or mandatory? If the unity is to be voluntary, must it not be developed within the community of scholars and based upon the multiplicity of contemporary data and methods of attaining insight? If the unity is to spring from *agreement*, will it be the fruit of "the single-minded pursuit of the intellectual virtues"? or will it be derived from a new stress on human values? And if the unity is to be mandatory, rather than voluntary, who will choose the philosophy that is to be imposed from above? Is there not acute danger that the "clarity" of the unifying metaphysical principles will be achieved by sacrificing a multitude of contemporary methods of acquiring knowledge and insight?

American scholars and scientists are not unaware of these intellectual problems. Our best educational institutions are today experimenting with a wide variety of departures from traditional objectives and procedures. There is little or no mention of this vigorous self-criticism in *The Higher Learning in America.* Hutchins' own criticism of the confusion that has arisen as a result of the freedom of selection, which President Eliot's generation used as the most effective weapon against the rigidity of the traditional college curriculum, is a college administrator's reflection of a broad movement that has been visible in our leading colleges since the war. With the abandonment of the classical kernel of the academic curriculum, we have witnessed a variety of efforts to devise a curriculum based upon a defensible discipline. The new plan in the college at the University of Chicago is one such attempt to substitute a twentieth-century *cosmos* for the *chaos* that has arisen as the unplanned result of our rebellion against the traditional curriculum.

Mr. Hutchins' administrative office at the University of Chicago might easily lead—and has led—into a confusion of his personal views on this subject with the actual program now pursued at the University of Chicago. To correct such misapprehensions, this contribution to the discussion of the issue particularly stresses the comparison of the current program at the University of Chicago with the proposals its president has submitted for discussions in his two volumes. The following pages will deal first with the general intellectual orientation of Mr. Hutchins' criticism, then with the college and general education on the one hand and the university, research, and professional training on the other hand, while a concluding section will once again return to the fundamental principles involved in the entire discussion.

THE INTELLECTUAL BASIS OF MR. HUTCHINS' CRITICISM

The heart of Mr. Hutchins' indictment of the higher learning in America lies in the charge of "confusion," "chaos," or "disorder." The essence of his proposal for change is a plea for a return to a rationally ordered unity to be achieved by restoring the primacy of "metaphysics" in the curriculum.

No doubt is permissible as to the negative side of the proposed curriculum. With the exception of mathematics (as taught by Euclid) and of a few classics such as Aristotle's *Physics* and Newton's *Principia*, science is conspicuously absent in the college and subordinated to metaphysics in the university. In the university program the natural sciences, the social sciences, and even the professions are to get their first principles from metaphysics[,] recent "observations" being introduced to "illustrate, exemplify, or to confirm these principles" (HL, 108).[3] Education is to be called back to the Great Tradition, to the "fundamental principles of rational thought." It is explicitly held that "the false starts, the backing and filling, the wildness, the hysteria, the confusion of modern thought and the modern world result from the loss of what has been thought and done by earlier ages" (HL, 79). The sores of modern education, and through it the sores of the modern world, are to be healed by contact with the science of first principles, metaphysics.

But what metaphysics? Here again only the negative side of Mr. Hutchins' argument is clear. He explicitly repudiates the Cartesian tradition. He completely neglects modern logic and modern philosophy. His only suggestion of a positive answer is in the form of constant reference to the writings of Plato, Aristotle, and Aquinas. It is true that he often refers favorably to Euclid, Galen, Galileo, and Newton, but in general he approves of the sciences only in so far as they carry on an ancient heritage: "Contemporary physical and biological research inherited the analytical procedures which, combined with observation, constitute a science; and to a great extent the heritage has been fruitful." By a process of elimination many readers and most reviewers have come to the conclusion that the heritage in question is the Platonic-Aristotelian-Thomistic tradition. This is precisely the tradition from which modern science progressively freed itself. Is this the metaphysics which is to be used as the core of the higher education and the norm for the contemporary world?

It may be that Mr. Hutchins' objectives are compatible with a variety of methods, but it is highly questionable whether for the modern world a reversion to the older metaphysics is either feasible, desirable, or necessary. In the course of the last few centuries the scientific approach has been gaining acceptance as the guiding principle for the intellectual activities of Western man. While it may be argued on various grounds that science is not an unmixed blessing, it can hardly be blamed for all our ills, and we cannot repudiate science without repudiating in the same breath our confidence in knowledge and in human reason. Nor is science without its own techniques of rational analysis; indeed, it had to develop its own techniques precisely because of the inadequacies of the inherited metaphysics. Science stresses generalization, logical analysis, and systematization, but it insists that every analysis, every generalization, every systematization be held subject to revision whenever new data seem to warrant it. Thus scientific principles are necessarily formed in the presence of empirical data and, however much they are developed by logical analysis, they are never removed from the control of new data. The Great Tradition in metaphysics, to which Mr. Hutchins seeks to recall the modern university, seemed to hold that after confrontation with a certain amount of data it could reach first principles which were absolute and subject to no further modification. And so, under the emotional seduction of having achieved absolute truth, an early and in itself noble stage of thought came to be considered the final stage of thought.

The claim to have isolated immutable ideas and indubitable first principles has not fared well in the history of thought. Absolutism—as Santayana[4] said in the concluding sentence of *The Genteel Tradition at Bay*—"Smells of fustiness as well as faggots." The endless disputes between metaphysicians and the vagueness of the terms "metaphysics" and "firs[t] principles" do not produce confidence in such claims. Scientists have tried to rescue the eager and flexible mind of Aristotle from the dogmatic immobilization of that mind by the Aristotelians. Galileo's words are notable in this connection:

> Do you question whether Aristotle, had he but seen the new discoveries in heaven, would not have changed his opinions, amended his books, and embraced the more sensible doctrine, rejecting those silly gulls who go about so timidly to defend whatever he has said? Do those defenders consider that, if Aristotle were such a one as they fancy him to themselves, he would be a man of an untractable wit, an obstinate mind, a barbarous soul, a stubborn will, who, accounting all other men as silly sheep, would have his oracles preferred before the senses, before experience, and before Nature herself? It is the spectators of Aristotle that have given him this authority and not he who has usurped or taken it upon himself.[5]

Newton's words in the *Optics* came to represent the judgment of science upon the traditional metaphysics of form and matter:

> [Substantial forms and] . . . occult qualities put a stop to the improvement of natural philosophy, and therefore of late years have been rejected. To tell us that every species of things is endowed with an occult specific quality by which it acts and produces manifest effects, is to tell us nothing.[6]

The traditional logic, which became intertwined with metaphysical "first" principles, proved to "be inadequate to the demands of science for a logic of relations; it was found to harbor contradictions fatal to the development of mathematics; the whole logic of probability" and induction which science needed had to be erected—and in its development it was found that scientific method did not even have to assume the uniformity of nature which the metaphysician had laid down as a first principle. At present the traditional logic has become only a special case of a much vaster domain of logic. An increasing demand for rigor showed the logical gaps in Euclid, and the development of the non-Euclidean geometries finally removed all justification for the claim that Euclidean geometry had any privileged relation to existence. By the time of Newton, in fact, mathematics was no longer regarded as a special method of obtaining knowledge of nature; instead of being a rival to the method of obtaining knowledge by generalization from observations it had passed to the status of being an instrument used by science in knowing the observed world.

Parallel to these developments, the principles of Aristotelian physics had in the hands of Galileo proved to be inadequate, the Ptolemaic astronomy had as the result of the work of Copernicus outlived its usefulness, the anatomy and physiology of Galen had been vanquished by Vesalius and Harvey, alchemy and astrology had gone with the Aristotelian cosmology upon which they had been based, the four-elements, and four-humour theories of the Greeks had been discarded as bases for chemistry and medicine, and the advance of biology had shown the development and mutability of the very species which had led the metaphysicians to extol the immutability of forms and ideas. Thus modern science, on the basis of new data and new tools of intelligence, has replaced the old doctrines by new systems of greater generality—and so the process continues. In modern science confidence in methods has taken the place of confidence in the results obtained at any particular time by the use of any particular methods. The same Whitehead who formulated the scientific temper in the motto, "Seek simplicity—but distrust it" has also warned us that the ultimate anti-intellectualism is the enthronement as final of any particular stage of rational inquiry.

In the light of this intellectual history, Mr. Hutchins seems to many persons to have selected out of man's rich intellectual heritage one metaphysical tradition as the standard, and to have designed his program for higher education so as to inculcate this system of metaphysics. Those who do not accept this simplification of intellectual history may feel that all the major defects of Mr. Hutchins' proposals stem from his apparent selection of certain stages of human thinking as final, for the general description of his proposed college and university curriculum is determined by this selection.

We shall return to this fundamental question of the orientation of Mr. Hutchins' criticism in a general fashion in the concluding part of this discussion, but this brief introductory treatment seemed desirable because the orientation of the program is alien to the dominant tradition of American educational philosophy, and because most of the concepts involved in the specific criticism; and proposals derive their meaning from the philosophical framework in which they are set. Mr. Hutchins may disavow any intent to propound such a philosophic framework, but it is difficult to see how so many readers and reviewers have so uniformly misinterpreted his terse and pointed style. Mr. Hutchins has in fact in recent articles denied that his proposal imposes an absolutistic system of metaphysics, and that his emphasis neglects science.[7] He has not, however, stated how far he regards himself as misunderstood, nor developed explicitly the change of emphasis which these denials seem to involve. Certainly he cannot then believe that the reading of a few classical scientific books is adequate college training in science. Nor can he continue to stress the importance of past results to the neglect of present day methods as well as results. [. . .]

The dominant emphasis, the detailed criticisms, and the educational suggestions which Mr. Hutchins' books present originate from and make sense only within the framework of the traditional metaphysics of rational absolutism. It may well be that their author is changing his emphasis and perhaps to some degree his philosophical position. But until this is explicitly stated and the implications for specific problems are drawn, discussion must center around the larger published presentations of his views. No one would be more delighted than its author if Mr. Hutchins, recognizing in this essay the substance of his views, allays the apprehensions which his own pages have raised. But the fact remains that the misapprehensions—if misapprehensions they be—are responsible for the idea that the higher education in America is to forsake the path of science and humanistic concern for a democratic society and to return to the Ivory Tower of absolutistic metaphysics. There are even rumors—incredible as it may appear—that the faculty of the University of Chicago, nourished by Scholasticism, is to take the lead in charting this new course for the higher learning. This essay is contributed to the discussion with the purpose of correcting these misapprehensions and rumors.

In Mr. Hutchins' proposals the function assigned to the college is to provide "general education," which—as he informs us without further argument—"should be given between the junior year in high school and the end of the sophomore year in college" (HL, 9).[8]

We have as Mr. Hutchins' specific indication of the general education to be provided during these four years "a course of study consisting of the greatest books of the western world and the arts of reading, writing, thinking and speaking [elsewhere described as 'grammar,' 'rhetoric,' and 'logic'] together with mathematics." It is stated that "all the needs of general education in America seem to be satisfied by this curriculum" (HL, 85) which specifically *excludes* "body building and character building" (HL, 77) as well as modern science and foreign languages (HL, 82).

It is possible to share Mr. Hutchins' criticisms of athleticism, and still to cherish the classical maxim *mens sana in corpore sano.* It is possible to agree with Mr. Hutchins in his distrust of the loose talk current in some circles as to character building, and still to feel that it is not the objective that has been at fault but rather the means chosen to attain the end. It is also possible to deprecate with Mr. Hutchins the enormous waste involved in our current methods of language training, and yet to feel that the command of at least one language beside the native tongue is essential to a liberal education. Finally it is possible to share Mr. Hutchins' enthusiasm for the classics, and still to feel it pertinent to remark that modern readers who have never closely examined any of the "excellent translations" (HL, 82) of which Mr. Hutchins speaks so hopefully, might easily fail to realize the difficulty of preserving the fine intellectual edge in translation.

These are matters of varying importance. But the main issue lies elsewhere. The underlying principle of Mr. Hutchins' proposed curriculum is the rationally ordered unity without which all is "confusion," and with which all achieves clarity through pure intellectuality. Perhaps the significance of Mr. Hutchins' proposal is best illustrated by a comparison with the point of view of the College Faculty at the University of Chicago as reflected in some essential paragraphs from a resolution on *The Educational Objectives of the College in the University of Chicago*, adopted on April 21, 1934, after the present reorganization of the curriculum had been in effect for almost three years.

It will be noted that this program stresses the education of the "whole person," and that it eschews the isolated and exclusive cultivation of the intellect as such. It stresses the understanding and enrichment of "twentieth century life in all its phases," including therefore proper emphasis on the sciences and their dramatic significance to our culture.

The University of Chicago has been characterized by its devotion to research and its sense of responsibility to the community. It has remained far enough from the community to maintain perspective, but near enough to have a sense of the moral and social significance of its work. Its attitude has been at once scientific and humanistic.

The result has been that the University, and especially that part of it which constitutes the College, has sought to deal educationally with the whole person—with men and women as knowers and doers and appreciators. This concern with the true, the good, and the beautiful points to the University's basic objective: to produce well-rounded men and women, equipped with accurate knowledge and sound methods of investigation and reflection, appreciative of the best that has been produced in the various fields of human endeavor, and concerned with the understanding and enrichment of twentieth century human life in all its phases. This threefold expansion of a single aim, to be accomplished by whatever educational means may prove effective, clearly must encourage the initiative, the resourcefulness, and the responsibility of students.

In our judgment, devotion to ideas is incompatible with the cult of Ideas. As Whitehead has written, "A self-satisfied rationalism is in effect a form of anti-rationalism. It means an arbitrary halt at a particular set of abstractions." The ideal of a community of scholars and students recognizable as the University of Chicago is not compatible with that intolerance of liberal, scientific, and democratic attitudes which is characteristic of the anti-intellectual atmosphere of rationalistic absolutism.

For over forty years the University has led a distinguished existence without being officially committed to any single system of metaphysics, psychology, logic, religion, politics, economics, art or scientific method. To follow the reactionary course of accepting one particular system of ancient or medieval metaphysics and dialectic, and to force our whole educational program to conform thereto, would spell disaster. We cannot commit ourselves to such a course.

We are proceeding in the confident belief that a sound general education, consisting in part of intensive training, will in itself be an excellent preparation for more specialized work. To this end, the four General Courses (in the physical sciences, the biological sciences, the social sciences and the humanities) are designed to introduce the student to the main fields of knowledge. In a summary and perspective fashion they indicate the types of material, the problems and the methods of approach involved in the study of the physical universe, of the world of living organisms, including man, of human society, and of ideas and ideals and their expression in literature and the arts. To all of this the course in English Composition relates itself closely. A large part of the more intensive training which we regard as an essential part of a general education is provided by the several departmental or divisional sequences available to College students. The College Faculty believes that the program should be continued along its present general lines at least until the results of the program can be evaluated.

A project for the future development of the present program has recently been approved by the faculty. Its most interesting innovation provides for an experimental philosophy course to be staffed by faculty members drawn from the four general fields as well as from the philosophy department. Such an enterprise should grow out of the four general courses, and it will use the concepts and materials that are there presented to the students. Instead of imposing a set of metaphysical principles upon the subject matter, the materials of such a course should grow out of the basic courses and would ultimately react to the advantage of the general courses in so far as any significant synthesis of methods and values emerged from the joint enterprise.

If the general education in the college is to acquaint the individual with the best that men have thought in the various realms of knowledge and to give him an appreciation and understanding of the good, the true, and the beautiful as envisaged by man in all times including our own, it can obviously do so only by selecting from the total store of knowledge certain representative items which of necessity must include much of the thought of our own times. No one could possibly, even in several times four years, assimilate more than a fraction of the history, the art, the science, and the other products of human civilization. Nor could such a general education mean very much to those exposed to it if it confined itself exclusively to the most general ideas. As Kant put it, perception without conception is blind, but conception without perception is empty. The emptiness of the most general ideas and the bewildering accumulation of specific factual knowledge are equally incompatible with a general education. The four years to be spent in general education in the college must therefore aim at the mediation of these two extremes. Other things being equal, the test for deciding the inclusion or exclusion of a given subject matter in the curriculum must be its significance for living the life of our society. Nothing, however, should be included in such a curriculum merely because it has the prestige that comes with antiquity or because it is called a classic.

Apart from esthetic values—which are clearly not the main value to Mr. Hutchins—it is hard to see any justification for the central position assigned to the classics in his scheme. In the present College program the student is given an opportunity through two full years to acquaint himself with a large number of literary, scientific, and philosophical masterpieces. In general, the material chosen must be based upon the fullest and most fruitful collection of data. In the natural and social sciences this must—in the very nature of the case—generally be material resulting from modern work. Hence there are obvious limitations that govern the use of the classics in college instruction.

The test to be applied to what Mr. Hutchins proposes as general education is therefore not merely the test of the universality and permanent validity of the ideas to be taught but of their significance and relevance. If there is any meaning, as he seems to think, in the statement that the good and the true and the beautiful are the same in all places and in all times, it is still evident that the aspects significant for education vary in time and place.

The present program in the college at the University of Chicago was chosen for comparison simply because of this author's familiarity with its content and its history. It is certainly not perfect and its experimental traits could be matched in other institutions. It is in constant revision in the light of accumulating experience, and the devotion of its faculty to the task guarantees a continued self-criticism. This program is based upon a rejection of the same excesses of elective freedom which Mr. Hutchins criticizes so sharply. In other words, the existence of such critical efforts at reconstruction illustrates the inadequacy of Mr. Hutchins' picture of the higher learning in America because it entirely overlooks such major efforts within the American system to overcome the difficulties that have arisen. We believe that Mr. Hutchins is under obligation to deal with such programs and to deal with them in specific detail.[9] This he has not done thus far in his writings, at least with reference to the specific content of the curriculum now offered, except to state that the reading and discussion of a number of books mostly consisting of the so-called classics is a method of acquiring a general education superior to the reading and analysis of modern work. Assuming that average students could profitably read the writings Mr. Hutchins suggests, assuming furthermore that they could acquire enough knowledge about the times and circumstances under which these writings were produced to comprehend their meaning, it is still his obligation to show that these materials have a prior claim on the students' time in comparison with other subject matter. He must still demonstrate that more time should be spent upon them than is now being spent in the present college program. Examination of the content of the courses in the college will reveal how widely inclusive of significant contributions to man's thought the present materials are.

Our modern conception of education is not separate and distinct from knowledge of any particulars. General knowledge is valid only in so far as we have valid particular knowledge upon which to base it, and vice versa. General ideas are constantly being changed by the discovery of particular notions, in the light of which they have to be modified, and while there are certain rules for discovering and testing truths which have a broad or even universal validity, reasoning calls for assessment of ideas in the face of data and experience, and its conclusions must constantly be tested in the light of results.

[. . .]

ACKNOWLEDGMENTS

We provide bibliographic information for the German originals in the individual sections. All of the English-language texts have been previously published, and we acknowledge those here. Texts are listed in the order of their appearance in the volume.

The Letters of George Ticknor. In *The Papers of Thomas Jefferson: Retirement Series (1815–1816)*. Vol. 9. Princeton, NJ: Princeton University Press, 2004.

The Letters of George Bancroft. *The Life and Letters of George Bancroft.* Edited by Mark Antony De Wolfe Howe and Henry Strippel. New York: Charles Scribner's Sons, 1908.

Richard T. Ely. "American Colleges and German Universities." *Harper's New Monthly Magazine* 61, no. 362 (July 1880): 253–60.

Henry P. Tappan. "Bonn and Its University." In *A Step from the New World to the Old, and Back Again: With Thoughts on the Good and Evil in Both.* Vol. 2. New York: D. Appleton, 1852.

Henry P. Tappan. "The Development of Educational Systems and Institutions." *Biblical Repository and Classical Review* 4, no. 3 (July 1850): 509–45.

James M. Hart. *German Universities: A Narrative of Personal Experience.* New York: Putnan, 1874.

Daniel Coit Gilman. "The Utility of Universities." In *University Problems in the United States.* New York: Century, 1898.

G. Stanley Hall. "Opening Exercises." In *Builders of American Universities*, ed. David Andrew Weaver, 1:363–87. Alton, IL: Shurtleff College Press, 1950.

Andrew D. White. "The Relations of the National and State Governments to Advanced Education." In *Advanced Education.* Boston: Office of Old and New, 1874.

William Rainey Harper. "The University and Democracy." In *The Trend in Higher Education.* Chicago: University of Chicago Press, 1905.

Charles W. Eliot. "The New Education." *Atlantic Monthly* 23, no.136 (February 1869): 203–16.

Noah Porter. "Inaugural Address." In *Addresses at the Inauguration of Professor Noah Porter.* New York: Charles Scribner, 1871.

Charles William Eliot. "Liberty in Education." In *Educational Reform: Essays and Addresses.* New York: Century Co., 1898.

James McCosh. *The New Departure in College Education, Being a Reply to President Eliot's Defence of It.* New York: Charles Scribner's Sons, 1885.

Charles Sears Baldwin. "Editorial: A Focus for Freshmen." *Columbia University Quarterly* 21, no. 1 (January 1919): 74–84.

John J. Coss. "The New Freshman Course in Columbia College." *Columbia University Quarterly* 21, no. 3 (July 1919): 247–250.

Robert Maynard Hutchins. "General Education." In *The Higher Learning in America.* New Haven, CT: Yale University Press, 1936.

Harry D. Gideonse. "The Higher Learning in a Democracy." *The Higher Learning in a Democracy: A Reply to President Hutchins' Critique of the American University.* New York and Toronto: Farrar & Rinehart, 1937.

NOTES

Notes by the original authors are supplemented with additional notes furnished by the editors. The latter are distinguished by the inclusion of "—Ed." at the end of the note.

CHAPTER ONE

1. Johann Stephan Pütter (1725–1807), a professor of law at Göttigen from 1744 to 1807, wrote a history of the university, *Versuch einer academischen Gelehrten-Geschichte von der Georg-Augustus-Universität zu Göttingen*, as well as the influential legal history *Historische Entwickelung der heutigen Staatsverfassung des Deutschen Reichs*.—Ed.

2. Johann Heinrich Christian von Selchow (1732–95) was a scholar of law and an administrator at Göttingen and later Marburg.—Ed.

3. Ernst Gottfried Baldinger (1738–1804) was a physician who served during the Seven Years War and later held positions at Göttingen and Marburg.—Ed.

4. Georg Ludwig Böhmer (1715–97) was a scholar of law and privy justice councilor at Göttingen. Johann David Michaelis (1717–91) was an orientalist and theologian at Göttingen. He served as director of the *Akademie der Wissenschaften zu Göttingen*. In addition to his academic and theological works, he published *Raisonnement über die protestantischen Universitäten in Deutschland*, also excerpted in this volume.—Ed.

5. Johann Gottfried Eichhorn (1752–1827) was an orientalist, historian, and privy justice councilor in Göttingen. In addition to many works on history, he also wrote introductions to the Old and New Testaments, his *Historisch-kritischen Einleitung in das Alte Testament* and his *Einleitung in das Neue Testament*.—Ed.

6. Christian Gottlob Heyne (1729–1812) was a classicist at Göttingen, where he also served as director of the university library. During his time as director, he expanded the collections of the library substantially and aligned them more directly with faculty research interests—a novelty.—Ed.

7. Johann Lorenz von Mosheim (1693–1755) was a German theologian and one of the founders of modern church history. In 1747, he was appointed Göttingen's first chancellor.—Ed.

8. Christian Wilhelm Büttner (1716–1801) served as chair of chemistry and natural history at Göttingen. He was known for his remarkable library and natural history collection, the latter of which Christian Gottlob Heyne acquired in 1773 for the University of Göttingen.—Ed.

CHAPTER TWO

1. Philipp Jacob Spener (1635–1705), a Lutheran theologian and active promoter of the pietist movement, published a work pleading for reform of the Lutheran Church, *Pia desideria oder herzliches Verlangen nach gottgefälliger Besserung der wahren evangelischen Kirche*, in 1675, and was later involved in the founding of the university at Halle.—Ed.

CHAPTER FIVE

1. It may perhaps not be superfluous to add here that such assignments—meant to ascertain that a student's self-directed activity using what he understands—are possible not only in the theoretical domains of knowledge but also in entirely empirical fields. It is well known that philology, theology, and so on offer an almost unlimited scope for one's powers of combination and conjectural textual criticism, in which, assuming for the moment that the results are insignificant in themselves, the self-directed activity of the mind can nonetheless be practiced and documented. But even the professor of World History can, it seems to me, make up some event that did not really happen and assign his students the task of showing what its most probable consequences would have been in this or that context they have studied; or the professor of Roman Law can invent a case and ask the class to supply a law that applies to that case, one which follows logically from and fits organically into the Roman legal system as a whole. The student's attempt to solve this problem will doubtless clearly reveal, first of all, whether he truly knows his history or his Roman law, and secondly, whether and to what extent this knowledge has penetrated into his spirit, or, on the contrary, been merely mechanically memorized.

2. Fichte is referring here to Johann Heinrich Pestalozzi (1746–1827), a Swiss pedagogy reformer who was highly influential throughout Germany.—Ed.

3. Since one often unexpectedly encounters misunderstandings of this most important principle of all our lives and efforts, it may perhaps not be superfluous to add a few words about it here.

Blind fate has guided the human condition—bearably, and, though slowly, at least to certain improvements of the whole—for as long as the good and evil principles in humanity have been conjoined and intertwined, shrouded in darkness. This state of things has now changed, and thanks to this change a new age has dawned, one which people often struggle not to recognize. Entirely new tasks have arisen in this new age. The evil principle has been released from its intermingling with the light; it has completely declared itself and it strides forward free, deliberate, and utterly without fear or shame. Clarity always defeats obscurity, so the evil principle will doubtless remain victorious until the good, too, reaches clarity and the level of deliberate art.

In all human relations, but especially in education, the old and traditional are dark and obscure regions one neglects to penetrate with clear concepts and handle with deliberate art, and from which one awaits God's blessing without any action of one's own. In this belief system, it is entirely inconsistent to try to add human direction and supervision to this divine dispensation. After all, what is old is known to everyone, and it exists to be obeyed; no plans need to be drawn up; success comes from above, and no human intelligence can accomplish anything; there is nothing to guide, and supervision is entirely superfluous. Only where assertions of free and deliberate art such as ours make themselves heard and try to have an influence is there a role for supervision to play: namely, opposing renewal with all its might and clinging fast to the old, traditional darkness.

No one speaks of supervision when the safety and security of this old and well-trodden path is praised, when the insecurity and risk of any renewal is feared. But if we remain with the old, we will meet with little success, that much is certain—for, since the world is the way it is, nothing but evil will come of darkness. Is the hope that we will be able to tell ourselves that at least we did nothing to actively bring on evil, that it arose on its own, and that it would have been fine with us if everything had happened to turn out well? It is the easily consoled indeed who would be satisfied with this. And why should it be such a daring deed to pursue a clear and firm idea? It is daring only if one is not master of one's idea, or if one has not decided in advance to throw everything one has into carrying it out. But nothing is forcing us into either of these two positions.

Least of all would we accept the following basic idea about the university. Some say that the university is not an institution for raising our young, whose unerring success we must therefore do as much as possible to ensure; rather, it is a fundamentally superfluous cultural institution, like, say, the Werckmeister Museum, a freely given gift that anyone can use however he wants, should he find himself in a position to do so, or not use. If these cultural institutions exist at all, they exist only for wise men and successful citizens already reconciled with the state in terms of their personal destiny and a fixed career, not for young men still seeking a career. Furthermore, the state—this too is an old and traditional practice, and we will no doubt have to leave it at that—the state has up to now seen universities as a necessary, hitherto irreplaceable institution for rearing a class of people of great importance to it. We can easily predict what would happen if, for just three straight years, it pleased all the students in their freedom to not use the university in the right way. Or should we assume that in the middle of our educated state there are still groups of people born to the privilege of immunity from anyone's claim on their power and education, who must be left free to choose whether they will do something or nothing because they have their own lives to live, aside from all such considerations? Should we invest in this or that cultural institution, leaving it free and subject to no calculations, simply so that these privileged people can, if they want, spend their idle future lives as amusingly as possible? Even granting all that, this privileged class should then pay for the satisfaction of its desires on its own; the state should in no way be burdened with the costs of such institutions.

CHAPTER SIX

1. Georg Christoph Lichtenberg (1742–99) was a mathematician and physicist at Göttingen. He was known for his exceptional teaching style and aphoristic wit: "A book is like a mirror: If an ass stares into it, one should not expect a prophet to look out."—Ed.

CHAPTER SEVEN

1. Over the course of the nineteenth century, the habilitation emerged as a second academic qualification required in addition to the doctorate to lecture at German universities. Initially, it was only an exam that required a lecture, but the process later developed to include a written text, the so-called *Habilitationsschrift*.—Ed.

CHAPTER EIGHT

1. Karl Maria Ehrenbert Freiherr von Moll (1760–1838) served as statesman and privy councilor in Salzburg and Bavaria. He was also a natural scientist and became a member of the Academie der Wissenschaften in Munich. He was an avid collector of plants, minerals, and books on natural history.—Ed.

2. Pierre Samuel du Pont de Nemours (1739–1817) was a French economist and author of *Physiocratie, ou constitution naturelle du gouvernement le plus avantageux au genre humaine* (1768), a foundational text of physiocracy. He later immigrated to the United States, where he was active in diplomacy, playing an influential role in the Louisiana Purchase.—Ed.

3. Andrzej Tadeusz Bonawentura Kościuszko (1746–1817) was a Polish general who fought against Russia and Prussia for the Polish-Lithuanian Commonwealth and supported the revolutionaries during the American Revolutionary War.—Ed.

4. Presumably Jean-Baptiste Say (1767–1832), a French businessman and economist.—Ed.

5. Like his friends Ticknor and Bancroft, Edward Everett studied classics intensively at Harvard and went to Göttingen to gain advanced education in that area. He was the first American to be awarded a doctorate at a German university.—Ed.

6. Georg Ludolf Dissen (1784–1837) was a classical philologist in Marburg and Göttingen.—Ed.

7. Friedrich Gottlieb Welcker (1784–1868) was a classical philologist and archaeologist who held academic positions in Gießen, Göttingen, and Bonn.—Ed.

8. Georg Friedrich Benecke (1762–1844) was a philologist specializing in German literature of the Middle Ages at Göttingen.—Ed.

9. Gottlieb Jakob Planck (1751–1833) was a Protestant theologian, church historian, and rector at Göttingen.—Ed.

10. David Julius Pott (1760–1838) was a Protestant theologian and prorector at Göttingen.—Ed.

11. Freifrau Dorothea von Rodde-Schlözer (1770–1825) studied at Göttingen and was the first woman to receive a doctorate from that university.—Ed.

12. Presumably August Ludwig von Schlozer (1735–1809) .—Ed.

13. John Thornton Kirkland, president of Harvard University from 1810 to 1828.—Ed.

14. August Böckh (1785–1867) was a classical philologist at Heidelberg. He went on to establish the philology seminar at the new Berlin University (later the Humboldt University), where he taught for almost four decades.—Ed.

15. Friedrich August Christian Wilhelm Wolf (1759–1824) was perhaps the foremost classical philologist of the eighteenth century. He taught in Halle and later became a member of the Prussian Akademie der Wissenschaften in Berlin.—Ed.

16. Philipp Karl Buttmann (1764–1829) was an educator and author of a widely used Greek grammar, *Griechische Grammatik* (1792). He later became a member of the Prussian Akademie der Wissenschaften.—Ed.

17. Karl Ludwig Harding (1765–1834) was an astronomer who discovered the planet Juno. He was also a professor at Göttingen and author of the *Atlas novus coelestis*.—Ed.

18. Karl Friedrich Stäudlin (1761–1826) was a professor of theology at Göttingen.—Ed.

19. Arnold Hermann Ludwig Heeren (1760–1842) was a historian and later administrator at Göttingen.—Ed.

20. On Pestalozzi, see n. 2, chap. 5 above.—Ed.

CHAPTER NINE

1. Albert Schwegler (1819–57) was a theologian and philosopher at Tübingen.—Ed.

2. The writer does not consider the theological schools, because that is a matter which each Church must take care of for itself, so long as state and church are entirely separate. Where there are so many sects as in the United States it may be well that the schools of divinity should be by themselves.

CHAPTER TEN

1. Friedrich Ludwig Georg von Raumer (1781–1873) was a historian at Breslau and Berlin.—Ed.

2. August Johann Wilhelm Neander (1785–1850) was a theologian and professor of church history at Heidelberg and Berlin.—Ed.

3. Thomas Arnold (1795–1842) was an English historian and educator. He also served as headmaster of Rugby School.—Ed.

CHAPTER ELEVEN

1. Medicine seems to form an exception; the universities do teach the practice of medicine very thoroughly. Yet the exception, which is apparent rather than real, only serves to illustrate the general principle. It is precisely because medicine is so much a matter of empiricism, so little a matter of pure science, that the German universities teach it as they do. Were it possible to establish a science of medicine, as distinguished from the mere tentative treatment of disease, we should find the practice thrown into the background of the university course, as is the case in law and theology. Even as it is, the study of medicine is made as theoretical as it well can be.

CHAPTER THIRTEEN

1. G. Stanley Hall.

2. Presumably William Stubbs (1825–1901), Anglican bishop and historian at Oxford.—Ed.

3. Henry James Sumner Maine (1822–88) was a British historian and jurist at Oxford and Cambridge and author of *Ancient Law* (1861) .—Ed.

4. Edward Augustus Freeman (1823–92) was a politician and historian at Oxford.—Ed.

5. Presumably Sir John Robert Seeley (1834–95), historian at University College London and at Cambridge.—Ed.

6. Johann Kaspar Bluntschli (1808–81) was a Swiss politician and professor of law at Munich and Heidelberg.—Ed.

7. Wilhelm Georg Friedrich Roscher (1817–94) was a historian and economist at Göttingen and Leipzig, author of *Grundriss zu Vorlesungen über die Staatswirtschaft nach geschichtlicher Methode* (1843), and a founder of the historical school of political economy.—Ed.

8. Richard Claverhouse Jebb (1841–1905) was a classicist at Glasgow and Cambridge. He published his *Life of Bentley*, a biography of the English classicist Richard Bentley, in 1882.—Ed.

9. Presumably John Worsley (1696–1767), English educator and classicist.—Ed.

10. Presumably Samuel Butcher (1850–1910), politician and classicist at Edinburgh.—Ed.

11. Arthur Cayley (1821–95) was a British mathematician at Cambridge. —Ed.

12. James Whitbread Lee Glaisher (1848–1928) was a mathematician and astronomer at Cambridge.—Ed.

13. William Whewell (1794–1866) was an Anglican priest, scientist, philosopher, and administrator at Cambridge. He published his *History of Inductive Sciences* in 1837.—Ed.

14. Henry Smith (1826–83) was a mathematician and administrator at Oxford.—Ed.

15. William Thomson, 1st Baron Kelvin (Lord Kelvin) (1824–1907), was a mathematical physicist and engineer at Glasgow and is known for his work in thermodynamics.—Ed.

16. Michael Faraday (1791–1867) was an informally educated English scientist known for his work in the fields of electromagnetism and electrochemistry.—Ed.

17. Presumably Sir Benjamin Thompson, Count Rumford (1753–1814), an American-born physicist who lived in England and Bavaria.—Ed.

18. John Dalton (1766–1844) was a chemist, meteorologist, and physicist who developed Dalton's Law of Partial Pressures in 1801.—Ed.

19. Justus Freiherr von Liebig (1803–73) was a chemist at Gießen and Bonn and is considered a founder of organic chemistry.—Ed.

CHAPTER FIFTEEN

1. Tony Judt, *The Memory Chalet* (New York: Penguin, 2010), 162.—Ed.

2. Édouard René Lefèbvre de Laboulaye (1811–83) was a French politician, and jurist and administrator at the Collège de France.—Ed.

3. Charles Kingsley (1819–75) was a clergyman, novelist, and professor of modern history at Cambridge.—Ed.

CHAPTER SEVENTEEN

1. "In the course of the winter of 1846–47 arrangements were made by the government of the University for the organization of an advanced school of science and literature. It is intended that Instruction shall be given in this school to graduates and others in the various branches of exact and physical science, and in classical learning."—*Annual Catalogue of Harvard College, for 1847–48*.

In the spring of 1848 this further statement was added: "It has been deemed advisable by the Corporation, for the present, to limit the operations of the school to the Department of Physical and Exact Science."—*Harvard College Catalogue.*

"It has long been felt at Yale College to be important to furnish resident graduates and others with the opportunity of devoting themselves to special branches of study, either not provided for at present, or not pursued as far as individual students may desire. . . . With the hope of accomplishing this object more fully and satisfactorily, the Corporation. . . . in August, 1847, established a new department called the Department of Philosophy and the Arts. . . . The branches intended to be embraced in this department are such as in general are not included under theology, law, and medicine; or, more particularly, mathematical science, physical science, and its application to the arts, metaphysics, philology, literature, and history."—*Annual Catalogue of Yale College*, 1847–48.

The actual addition to the facilities of the College consisted in a laboratory of applied chemistry.

2. ". . . Although this [Latin] is not yet required as a condition for admission, it will probably be so at an early day."—*Catalogue* of 1864–65.

". . . And, after the examination of 1868, some proficiency in Latin will be included among the requisites for admission."—*Catalogue* of 1867–68.

3. While this article is in press the Harvard College Catalogue for 1868–69 has appeared. There are changes for the better in the Scientific School; but they are not of a fundamental character.

4. Colonel and Brevet Brigadier General Sylvanus Thayer (1785–1872) was superintendent of the Military Academy at West Point, which became the first college of engineering in the United States.—Ed.

5. "The object of the (Columbia) School of Mines is to furnish to the students the means of acquiring a thorough scientific and practical knowledge of those branches of science which relate to mining and the working up of the mineral resources of this country, and to supply to those engaged in mining and metallurgical operations persons competent to take charge of new or old works, and conduct them on thoroughly scientific principles."—*Annual Catalogue*, 1864–65.

6. ". . . Those who have been already recommended to the trustees for graduation, and those who will be so before the approaching Commencement, may be safely pronounced to be accomplished professional men, capable of undertaking the management of important works in engineering or metallurgy, and wanting only a few years of experience to place them with certainty in commanding positions." —*Annual Report of the President of Columbia College*, June 1, 1868.

7. "Persons desiring to secure the service of mining engineers, metallurgists, or chemists to take charge of mines or manufacturing establishments are requested to apply at the school in person or by letter."—*Circular of May* 15, 1868.

8.

1860,	number of students,	437.
1861,	" " "	390.
1862,	" " "	352.
1863,	" " "	285.
1864,	" " "	295.
1866,	" " "	223.
1867,	" " "	199.

9. The term "learned profession" is getting to have a sarcastic flavor. Only a very small proportion of lawyers, doctors, and ministers, the country over, are Bachelors of Arts. The degrees of L.L. B. and M.D. stand, on the average, for decidedly less culture than the degree of A.B., and it is found quite possible to prepare young men of scanty education to be successful pulpit exhorters in a year or eighteen months. A really learned minister is almost as rare as a logical sermon.

On the catalogue of the University of Michigan for 1867–68 there stand the names of three hundred and eighty-seven law students, not one of whom appears to have possessed at that stage of his education any degree whatever. There are four teachers. To enter the school, a young man must be eighteen years of age, and he must present a certificate of good moral character. Nothing else is required. To obtain a degree he must follow certain courses of lectures through two terms of six months each. Nothing else is required. It is possible that the degrees really possessed by law students have been omitted; but degrees are printed against the names of their possessors in other departments of the University on the same catalogue. Among one hundred and forty-six persons who received the degree of L.L. B., in that year, seventeen had other degrees—a very small proportion.

On the same catalogue there are enrolled four hundred and eleven medical students, of whom nineteen already possess a Bachelor's degree. There are eleven teachers. The school is established in the small town of Ann Arbor, quite remote from large hospitals. Poor humanity shudders at the spectacle of so large a crop of such doctors.

Such professional schools may, indeed, be the best which the hastily organized, fast-growing American communities will support; but the word "learned" can only be conventionally applied to professions for which the preliminary training exacted is so short and so loose.

CHAPTER EIGHTEEN

1. Presumably Carl Ritter (1779–1859), geographer at the University of Berlin and a founder of modern geography.—Ed.

2. Karl Immanuel Nitzsch (1787–1868) was a theologian in the tradition of Schleiermacher and a university rector and preacher in Berlin.—Ed.

3. August Detlev Christian Twesten (1789–1876) was a theologian deeply indebted to Schleiermacher and held positions at Kiel and Berlin.—Ed.

4. Christian August Brandis (1790–1867) was a German philosopher and professor at Berlin and Bonn.—Ed.

5. Carl Joseph Anton Mittermaier (1787–1867) was a jurist and politician. He held academic positions at Landshut, Bonn, and Heidelberg.—Ed.

6. John Wesley (1703–91) was an Anglican minister and theologian and one of the founders of Methodism.—Ed.

7. George Whitefield (1714–70) was an Anglican minister and founder of Methodism. He traveled to the American colonies, where his preaching gave rise to revivals known as the "Great Awakening."—Ed.

8. Edward Bouverie Pusey (1800–82) was a professor of Hebrew at Oxford and a leader of the Oxford Movement.—Ed.

9. John Henry Newman (1801–90) was an academic at Oxford and a leader of the Oxford Movement, which he later left to join the Catholic Church. He was created a cardinal in 1879 and went on to help found the Catholic University of Ireland, which became University College Dublin.—Ed.

10. Matthew Arnold (1822–88) was an English poet, cultural critic, and inspector of schools.—Ed.

11. Richard Whately (1787–1863) was an economist, a theologian, and archbishop of Dublin. He advocated a nonsectarian educational system in Ireland.—Ed.

CHAPTER TWENTY

1. The Nineteenth Century Club meant to make the debate three-cornered, but somehow one of the sides of the triangle fell out, and instead of a triangle we have two sides facing each other.

2. Professor Hoffmann, as Rector of Berlin University, says that it is the opinion of the University that "all efforts to find a substitute for the classical languages, whether in mathematics, in the modern languages or in the natural sciences have been hitherto unsuccessful." In Princeton College Dr. Young and the scientific professors unanimously are, if possible, more strongly in favor of Latin and Greek than even the classical professors.

3. In Princeton we have nearly all the branches taught in Harvard, but we do not subdivide and scatter them as they do; we put them under compacted heads. In his address to the Johns Hopkins University, Dr. Eliot refers to the supposed deficiency in teaching history in Princeton. In reply I have to state that we have a small examination on the subject for entrance; that in the Sophomore year we use one of Freeman's text-books to give an elementary view of universal history; that in the Junior and Senior the Professor of the Philosophy of History gives a historical and critical survey of the science and methods of history. More particularly each Professor is expected to give a history of his own branch, and so we have histories of Politics, of Philosophy, of Greece, of Rome, of the literature of Germany and of France, etc. I do not agree with Mr. J. S. Mill that history cannot be taught in a college (it would take forty years and more to go over all history); but I think the numerous narrative histories of epochs is just a let-off to easy-going students from the studies which require thought.

4. In the debate we were told that this is deep study; then the Degree of Master of Music (M.M.) should be given to it, but not M.A.

5. The Germans have, besides, their admirable gymansien, where all is prescribed, and which give instruction equivalent to that of the Freshman and Sophomore years in American colleges.

6. President Eliot would not have students enter college till they are eighteen years of age. If this be carried out it is evident that we shall have fewer young men taking a college education. A large number cannot afford to continue till twenty-five before they earn any money; not entering college till eighteen, continuing three or four years and spending another three years in learning a profession. In many cases many young men might he ready to enter college at sixteen, graduate at twenty, and then learn their professions. This would suit the great body of students. But one in ten, or one in five who have acquired a taste for more should be encouraged to remain in college, to take post-graduate courses, and devote themselves to special studies. We encourage this in

Princeton by seven or eight endowed Fellowships and have always 30, 40, or 50 post-graduate students. In this way we hope to rear scholars.

7. At the New York meeting I distributed the *Plan of Study in Princeton College*, showing how we carry into practical operation the principles laid down in this paper and combine the general with the special.

8. William Robert Grove (1811–96) was a Welsh judge and physical scientist. He published his *On the Correlation of Physical Forces* in 1846, which anticipated later works on the theory of the conservation of energy.—Ed.

9. George John Douglas Campbell, 8th Duke of Argyll (1823–1900), was a politician and author of works on science, politics, and religion, including *The Unity of Nature*, published in 1884.—Ed.

10. Thomas Henry Huxley (1825–95) was a biologist, educator, and advocate of Darwin's theory of evolution. He promoted the teaching of biology in universities, was an active member of the London school board, and, despite his own agnostic convictions, was in favor of the Bible being read in schools for moral purposes.—Ed.

11. Herbert Spencer (1820–1903) was an English philosopher, biologist, and sociologist. He was a developer of evolutionary theory and author of *Principles of Biology* (1864), in which he coined the phrase "survival of the fittest."—Ed.

12. I am waiting to hear whether this challenge is accepted.

CHAPTER TWENTY-ONE

1. The lecture had a long history in German universities. As its etymology from the Latin *legere*, "to read," suggests, it traditionally referred to a "reading or dictation from an authoritative text." And the German term, *Vorlesung*, comes from *vorlesen*, "to read before." Reading and lecturing were deeply related, each grounded in the authority of the particular canonical text that was read. The professor transmitted and safeguarded cultural information and traditions. The medieval and the early modern lecture, then, was an occasion for students to take extensive notes, a crucial resource for a book poor culture. Around 1800, this form of the lecture practice came under sharp critic by figures such as Schleiermacher, Fichte and Humboldt, who criticized professors who merely read directly from a printed text. They advocated instead for a more performative lecture in which the professor instantiated the very act of thinking. Lectures, that is, had to be creative and productive. With this new ideology, the lecture survived and even flourished as a mixed practice of reading, dictation, and note taking.—Ed.

2. One of the fabled traits of German universities, one celebrated by countless Americans who studied at German universities in the nineteenth century, was *Lehrfreiheit* and *Lernfreiheit*.—Ed.

3. Nietzsche is playing off of Kant's "What is Enlightenment?" essay, where Kant exhorts the human beings to maturity and enlightenment by freeing themselves from the "drawing strings" (*Gängelbande*) of others.—Ed.

4. Hegel in the *Philosophy of Right* writes: "What is rational is actual [wirklich]; what is actual is rational" (Section 7).—Ed.

5. In his notes for *We Philologists*, Nietzsche writes: "Big public lies. The ancients remain to an even higher degree our true masters and teachers—but not for young boys. Our gymnasium

teachers (our best ones) have different aims. They train scholars, which is what they have been doing, except now all they do is train students to be philologists. If we were honest, we would convert the gymnasium into a philological-historical academy, in the service of specialized scholarship." (7:381).—Ed.

CHAPTER TWENTY-TWO

1. With the Prussian Abitur Edict of 1834, the Abitur (final secondary school exams) became required for admission to the university in Prussia. The requirement remained in effect after unification.—Ed.

2. Friedrich Paulsen, *German Universities and University Study*, trans. Frank Tilly and William Elwang (New York: Scribner's & Sons, 1906), 115.—Ed.

CHAPTER TWENTY-THREE

1. Position Paper of the Berlin Association for Higher Schools for Women, p. 4.

2. In August of 1873, the Minister of Culture, Dr. Falk, convened a conference on the education of girls in Berlin. Many of the same people who participated in the Weimar conference attended the Berlin event. Of twenty participants, only five were women. The conference concluded, writes Lange, with an implicit endorsement of the Weimar position paper.—Ed.

3. Luise Büchner (1821–77) was a German writer and activist for women's rights. In 1873 she was the first woman asked to participate in a conference held by the Prussian Ministry of Culture on women's education.—Ed.

4. Ilsabetha (Betty) Gleim (1781–1827) was an educator, writer, and founder of a school for girls, the Lehranstalt für Mädchen, in Bremen in 1806. Many of her educational ideas were influenced by Pestalozzi.—Ed.

CHAPTER TWENTY-SIX

1. Laurence R. Veysey, *The Emergence of the American University* (Chicago: University of Chicago, 1965), 21–56; Julie A. Reuben, *The Making of the Modern University: Intellectual Transformation and the Marginalization of Morality* (Chicago: University of Chicago Press, 1996), 61–87.—Ed.

2. Robert A. McCaughey, *Stand, Columbia: A History of Columbia University in the City of New York, 1754–2004* (New York: Columbia University Press, 2003), 290.—Ed.

3. The following paragraphs on the history of the Chicago core draw directly on John W. Boyer, "A Twentieth-Century Cosmos: The New Plan and the Origins of General Education at Chicago," *Occasional Papers on Higher Education XVI* (College of the University of Chicago, 2007).—Ed.

CHAPTER TWENTY-EIGHT

1. Such a course is broached editorially in *Quarterly*, 21, 74 (January, 1919). The idea is considered abstractly in "A word about the New Wisdom and its obligations" by Professor Keyser in *Quarterly*, 21, 118 (April, 1919).

CHAPTER TWENTY-NINE

1. Cf. *Summa Theologica*, Part II, Q. 57, Art. 2–4.

2. Cf. Aristotle, *Politics*, VIII, 3: "to be always seeking after the useful does not become free and exalted souls."

3. "It is therefore evident that, as regards the general principles whether of speculative or practical reasons, truth or rectitude is the same for all, and is equally known by all," *Summa Theologica,* Part II, Q. 94, Art. 4.

4. Plato, *Republic*, Book IX: " 'And it is plain,' I said, 'that this is the purpose of the law, which is the ally of all classes in the state, and this is the aim of our control of children, our not leaving them free before we have established, so to speak, a constitutional government within them and, by fostering the best element in them with the aid of the like in our selves, have set up in its place a similar guardian and ruler in the child, and then, and then only we leave it free.' "

5. " 'You see, then, my friend,' said I, 'that this branch of study really seems to be indispensible for us, since it plainly compels the soul to employ pure thought with a view to truth itself.' " Plato, *Republic*, Book VII.

6. Plato on geometers: "Their language is most ludicrous, though they cannot help it, for they speak as if they were doing something and as if all their words were directed toward action. For all their talk is of squaring and applying and adding and the like, whereas the real object of the entire study is pure thought." Ibid., Book VII. See also Aristotle, *Ethics,* 1098a.

CHAPTER THIRTY

1. For the search for harmony and order through the adoption of a collectivist "frame of reference," see *A Charter for the Social Sciences in the Schools* by Charles A. Beard, Part I of the Report of the Commission on the Social Studies of the American Historical Association, and the subsequent volumes of this report.

For the search for harmony and order through the selection of a "metaphysics," see Robert M. Hutchins, *No Friendly Voice* (Chicago: University of Chicago Press, 1936) and *The Higher Learning in America* (New Haven, CT: Yale University Press, 1936). For a critical discussion see T. V. Smith, "The Chicago School," *International Journal of Ethics*, XLVI (April 1936), 378–87; James Weber Linn, "Notes on a Textbook," *University of Chicago Magazine* XXVIII (December 1936), 18–19; Charles E. Clark, "The Higher Learning in a Democracy," and Charner Perry, "Education: Ideas or Knowledge," both in *International Journal of Ethics*, XLVII (April 1937), 317–35 and 346–59 respectively.

2. Abraham Flexner, *Universities: American, English, German* (New York: Oxford University Press, 1930), p. 213.

3. Throughout the manuscript HL refers to *The Higher Learning in America*; NFV, to *No Friendly Voice*.

4. Jorge Agustín Nicolás Ruiz de Santayana y Borrás, known as George Santayana (1863–1952) was a Spanish-born philosopher who was educated in the United States at Harvard (where he also taught) and in England at Cambridge.—Ed.

5. *Dialogue on the Great World Systems*, in the Salisbury translation, rev., annotated and

with an introduction by Giorgio de Santillana (Chicago: University of Chicago Press, 1953), 123–24.

6. Reprinted from the 4th ed. (London: G. Bell & Sons, 1931), p. 401. Spelling is modernized.

7. Even in *The Higher Learning in America*, Mr. Hutchins disclaims the criticism that he is "arguing for any specific theological or metaphysical system" (HL, 105), but the remark is offset by evidence throughout the volume—and cited in this essay—that the Great Tradition is definitely envisaged. See also the qualification in Mr. Hutchins' position in his article "A Reply to Professor Whitehead," *Atlantic Monthly*, CLVIII (November 1936), 582–88 and in the series in the *Social Frontier*, III (1937), beginning with John Dewey's review "President Hutchins' Proposals to Remake Higher Education" in the January issue (pp. 103–4), continued with Mr. Hutchins' reply "Grammar, Rhetoric, and Mr. Dewey" in the February number (pp. 137–39), and concluded with John Dewey's rejoinder "'The Higher Learning in America' [Was President Hutchins Serious?]" in the March issue (pp. 167–69). In a later article, "What Is the Job of Our Colleges?" *New York Times Magazine*, March 7, 1937, pp. 1–2, 25, the earlier position is, however substantially maintained.

8. After Mr. Hutchins' sharp and deserved criticism of the tendency of education to yield to every current fad and fashion, it is puzzling to read that "under present economic conditions" our education must be recast to provide for the young "up to approximately their twentieth year" (HL, 15, 61). Does the proposed plan follow the fluctuations of the business cycle under the guise of a vision of eternity?

9. It is certainly not true of the University of Chicago program—and it is probably not true of the program of any reputable American university or college—that its "study of history and the social sciences" begins with "the industrial revolution," or that its study of philosophy "begins with Descartes and Locke," or of psychology "with Wundt and William James." Mr. Hutchins makes this unsupported assertion in *The Higher Learning in America*, p. 79.

BIBLIOGRAPHY

Albisetti, James C. *Schooling German Girls and Women*. Princeton, NJ: Princeton University Press, 1988.

———. *Secondary School Reform in Imperial Germany*. Princeton, NJ: Princeton University Press, 1983.

Alt, Peter-André. *Friedrich Schiller*. Munich: C. H. Beck, 2004.

Ash, Mitchell G., ed. *Mythos Humboldt*. Vienna: Bohlau, 1999.

Bender, Thomas, ed. *The University and the City: From Medieval Origins to the Present*. Oxford: Oxford University Press, 1988.

Bledstein, Burton. *The Culture of Professionalism: The Middle Class and the Development of Higher Education in America*. New York: W. W. Norton, 1976.

Bishop, Morris. *A History of Cornell*. Ithaca, NY: Cornell University Press, 1963.

Bok, Derek. *Higher Education in America*. Princeton, NJ: Princeton University Press, 2013.

Bowen, William G. *Higher Education in the Digital Age*. Princeton, NJ: Princeton University Press, 2013.

Boyer, Ernest L., and Arthur Levine. *A Quest for Common Learning: The Aims of General Education*. Princeton, NJ: Carnegie Foundation for the Advancement of Teaching, 1981.

Boyer, John W. "A Twentieth-Century Cosmos: The New Plan and the Origins of General Education at Chicago." *University of Chicago Record*, January 18, 2007, 4–24.

———. *The University of Chicago: A History*. Chicago: University of Chicago Press, 2015.

Buchler, Justus. "Reconstruction in the Liberal Arts." In *A History of Columbia College on Morningside*, edited by Dwight C. Miner, 48–135. New York: Columbia University Press, 1954.

Carnochan, W. B. *The Battleground of the Curriculum: Liberal Education and American Experience*. Stanford, CA: Stanford University Press, 1993.

Clark, William. *Academic Charisma and the Origins of the Research University*. Chicago: University of Chicago Press, 2006.

Conrad, Johannes, *Das Universitätsstudium in Deutschland während der letzten 50 Jahre*. Jena: Duncker, 1884.

Cross, Timothy P. "The Core Curriculum: Introduction." 1995. http://www.college.columbia.edu/core/oasis/history0.php. 1995.

Delbanco, Andrew. *College: What It Was, Is, and Should Be*. Princeton, NJ: Princeton University Press, 2012.

de Ridder-Symoens, Hilde, and Water Rüegg, eds. *A History of the University in Europe*. 4 vols. Cambridge: Cambridge University Press, 1992–2011.

Diehl, Carl. *Americans and German Scholarship, 1770–1870*. New Haven, CT: Yale University Press, 1978.

Emden, Christian. *Friedrich Nietzsche and the Politics of History*. Cambridge: Cambridge University Press, 2008.

French, John C. *A History of the University Founded by Johns Hopkins*. Baltimore, MD: Johns Hopkins University Press, 1946.

Geiger, Roger. *The History of American Higher Education: Learning and Culture from the Founding to World War II*. Princeton, NJ: Princeton University Press, 2015.

Haarlow, William N. *Great Books, Honors Programs, and Hidden Origins: The Virginia Plan and the University of Virginia in the Liberal Arts Movement*. New York: Routledge-Falmer, 2003.

Hammerstein, Notker. "Die Universitätsgründungen im Zeichen der Aufklärung." In *Beiträge zu Problemen deutscher Universitätsgründungen der frühen Neuzeit*, edited by Peter Baumgart, 263–98. Nendeln: KTO Press, 1978.

Hawkins, Hugh. *Between Harvard and America: The Educational Leadership of Charles W. Eliot*. New York: Oxford University Press, 1972.

Herbst, Jürgen. *The German Historical School in American Scholarship: A Study in the Transfer of Culture*. Ithaca, NY: Cornell University Press, 1965.

Hofstadter, Richard, and Walter Metzger. *The Development of Academic Freedom in the United States*. New York: Columbia University Press, 1955.

Hofstadter, Richard, and Wilson Smith. *American Higher Education: A Documentary History*. Vol. 1. Chicago: Chicago University Press, 1961.

Howard, Thomas Albert. *Protestant Theology and the Making of the Modern German University*. Oxford: Oxford University Press, 2009.

James, Henry. *Charles W. Eliot: President of Harvard University, 1869–1909*. Boston: Houghton Mifflin, 1930.

Jarausch, Konrad. *Students, Society, and Politics in Imperial Germany: The Rise of Academic Illiberalism*. Princeton, NJ: Princeton University Press, 1982.

Jeismann, Karl-Ernst. *Das preußische Gymnasium in Staat und Gesellschaft*. Vol. 2. Stuttgart: Klett-Cotta, 1996.

Kaufmann, Georg. *Geschichte der deutschen Universitäten*. 2 vols. Graz: Akademische Druck-U. Verlagsanstalt, 1958.

Keller, Morton, and Phyllis Keller. *Making Harvard Modern: The Rise of America's University*. 2nd ed. New York: Oxford University Press, 2004.

Keller, Phyllis. *Getting at the Core: Curriculum Reform at Harvard*. Cambridge, MA: Harvard University Press, 1982.

Kerr, Clark. *The Uses of the University*. Cambridge, MA: Harvard University Press, 1963.

Lange, Helene. *Kampfzeiten: Aufsätze und Reden aus vier Jahrzehten*. Vol. 1. Berlin: F. A. Herbig, 1928.

Levine, Arthur. *Handbook on Undergraduate Curriculum*. San Francisco: Jossey-Bass, 1978.

Marsden, George. *The Soul of the American University: From Protestant Establishment to Established Nonbelief*. Oxford and New York: Oxford University Press, 1996.

Mazón, Patricia M. *Gender and the Modern Research University: The Admission of Women to German Higher Education, 1865–1914*. Stanford, CA: Stanford University Press, 2003.

McCaughey, Robert A. *Stand, Columbia: A History of Columbia University in the City of New York, 1754–2004*. New York: Columbia University Press, 2003.

McClellan, James E. *Science Reorganized: Scientific Societies in the Eighteenth Century*. New York: Columbia University Press, 1985.

McClelland, Charles E. *The German Experience of Professionalization: Modern Learned Professions and Their Organizations from the Early Nineteenth Century to the Hitler Era*. Cambridge: Cambridge University Press, 1991.

———. *State, Society and University in Germany: 1700–1914*. Cambridge: Cambridge University Press, 1980.

Menand, Louis. "The Limits of Academic Freedom." In *The Future of Academic Freedom*, edited by Louis Menand, 3–20. Chicago: University of Chicago Press, 1996.

———. *The Marketplace of Ideas*. New York: W. W. Norton, 2010.

Müller, Ernst, ed. *Gelegentliche Gedanken über Universitäten*. Leipzig: Reclam, 1990.

Paulsen, Friedrich. *The German Universities and University Study*. Translated by Frank Thilly. New York: Scribner and Sons, 1906.

———. *Geschichte des Gelehrten Unterrichts auf den deutschen Schulen und Universitäten vom Ausgang des Mittelalters bis zur Gegenwart*. 2 vols. 3rd ed. Leipzig: Veit, 1919–21.

Plotkin, Howard. *Henry Tappan, Franz Brünnow, and the Founding of the Ann Arbor School of Astronomers, 1852–1863*. New York: Taylor & Francis, 1980.

Porter, James I. *Nietzsche and the Philology of the Future*. Stanford, CA: Stanford University Press, 2000.

Rosenthal, Michael. *Nicholas Miraculous: The Amazing Career of the Redoubtable Dr. Nicholas Murray Butler*. New York: Farrar, Straus & Giroux, 2006.

Reuben, Julia A. *The Making of the Modern University: Intellectual Transformation and the Marginalization of Morality*. Chicago: University of Chicago Press, 1996.

Roberts, John H., and James Turner. *The Sacred and the Secular University*. Princeton, NJ: Princeton University Press, 2000.

Shaw, William Byron. *The University of Michigan*. New York: Harcourt, Brace & Howe, 1920.

Schelsky, Helmut. *Einsamkeit und Freiheit: Zur sozialen Idee der deutschen Universität*. Düsseldorf: Bertelsmann-Universitäts-Verlag, 1960.

Schwartz, Paul. *Die Gelehrtenschulen Preussens unter dem Oberschulkollegium (1787–1806) und das Abiturientenexamen*. 3 vols. Berlin: Weidmann, 1910–12.

Spranger, Eduard. *Fichte, Schleiermacher, Steffens über das Wesen der deutschen Universität*. Leipzig: Dürr, 1910.

———. *Wilhelm von Humboldt und die Humanitätsidee*. Berlin: Reuther & Reichard, 1909; Tübingen: Max Niemeyer Verlag Tübingen, 1965.

———. *Wilhelm von Humboldt und die Reform des Bildungswesens*. 3rd ed. Tübingen: Max Niemeyer Verlag, 1965.

Stichweh, Rudolf. *Die Ausdifferenzierung der Wissenschaft: Eine Analyse am deutschen Beispiel*. Grünwald: Kleine Verlag, 1981.

———. *Der frühmoderne Staat und die europäische Universität: zur Interaktion von Politik und Erziehungssystem im Prozess ihrer Ausdifferenzierung (16.-18. Jahrdundert)*. Frankfurt am Main: Suhrkamp, 1991.

———. *Zur Entstehung des modernen Systems wissenschaftlicher Disziplinen in Deutschlands 1740–1890*. Frankfurt am Main: Suhrkamp, 1984.

Storr, Richard. *Harper's University*. Chicago: University of Chicago Press, 1966.

Sweet, Paul. *Wilhelm von Humboldt: A Biography*. 2 vols. Columbus: Ohio State University Press, 1978.

Tenorth, Heinz-Elmar, ed. *Geschichte der Universität unter den Linden: Genese der Disziplinen*. Vol. 4. Berlin: Akademie Verlag, 2010.

Thelin, John. *A History of American Higher Education*. Baltimore, MD: Johns Hopkins University Press, 2004.

Turner, James. *The Liberal Education of Charles Eliot Norton*. Baltimore, MD: Johns Hopkins University Press, 1999.

Turner, R. Steven. "The *Bildungsbürgertum* and the Learned Professions in Prussia, 1770–1830: The Origins of a Class." *Histoire Sociale/Social History* 13 (May 1980): 108–35.

———. "Humboldt in North America? Reflections on the Research University and Its Historians." In *Humboldt International: Der Export des deutschen Universitätsmodells im 19. Und 20. Jahrhundert*, edited by Rainer Christoph Schwings, 289–312. Basel: Schwabe, 2001.

———. "Prussian Universities and the Concept of Research." *Internationales Archiv für Sozialgeschichte der deutschen Literatur* 5 (1980): 68–93.

———. "University Reformers and Professional Scholarship in Germany, 1760–1806." In *Europe, Scotland, and the United States from the 16th to the 20th Century*, vol. 2 of *University in Society*, edited by Lawrence Stone, 495–531. Princeton, NJ: Princeton University Press, 1974.

Tyack, David. *George Ticknor and the Boston Brahmins*. Cambridge, MA: Harvard University Press, 1967.

Veblen, Thorstein. *The Higher Learning in America: The Annotated Edition*. Baltimore, MD: Johns Hopkins University Press, 2015.

Veysey, Laurence. *The Emergence of the American University*. Chicago: University of Chicago Press, 1965.

vom Bruch, Rüdiger. "Die Gründung der Berliner Universität im Kontext der deutschen Universitätslandschaft um 1800." In *Die Universität Jena: Tradition und Innovation um 1800*, edited by Gerhard Müller, Klaus Ties, and Paul Ziche, 63–73. Stuttgart: Franz Steiner Verlag, 2001.

Wellmon, Chad. *Organizing Enlightenment: Information Overload and the Invention of the Modern Research University*. Baltimore, MD: Johns Hopkins University Press, 2015.

White, Andrew Dickson, *The Autobiography of Andrew Dickson White*. Vol. 1. New York: Century, 1905.

Zwicker, Lisa Fetheringill. *Dueling Students: Conflict, Masculinity, and Politics in German Universities, 1890–1914*. Ann Arbor: University of Michigan Press, 2011.

INDEX